Pursuing What is Best for the World

**150 Years of Teaching, Research, and Extension —
Stories of the College of Agriculture and Natural Resources**

Kenneth VerBurg and
Raymond D. Vlasin

MICHIGAN STATE
UNIVERSITY

COLLEGE OF
AGRICULTURE
AND NATURAL
RESOURCES

Copyright @ 2006, Michigan State University
ISBN No: 1-56525-021-4

Copies of *Pursuing What is Best for the World* are available
from the MSU Bulletin Office, 117 Central Services Building,
Michigan State University, East Lansing, MI 48824-1001
(phone 517-353-6740), or on the Web at **www.emdc.msue.msu.edu**
Refer to CANR 400.

Table of Contents

Foreword

When I reflect on the stirring history of Michigan State University, I marvel at our founders' faith in their vision as they embarked on an uncertain future. Our land-grant mission has continued to guide this university in creating research-based knowledge and using that knowledge to make a difference in the lives of people. Today, we embody that vision and mission in four powerful words: "Advancing Knowledge. Transforming Lives."

In each successive generation, bold, perspicacious leaders have enabled this great institution to embrace an ever expanding role within Michigan, the nation and the world. Their stories, of course, are not the stories of individuals, but rather a collective history of the work of innumerable others whose contributions continue to affect our lives.

The delightful narrative accounts and photographs in *Pursuing What is Best for the World* trace the history of our early development, the prodigious difficulties our predecessors overcame and the establishment of the founding college of what is today Michigan State University. This book shares the stories of those individuals, both celebrated and obscure, who have made important contributions to the formation and advancement of the College of Agriculture and Natural Resources through more than 150 years of learning, discovery and engagement.

We continue to embrace the vision so captivatingly depicted in these pages. Today, however, we are expanding its breadth and scale as we aspire to become the land-grant university for the world. By bringing the remarkable talents of our community to bear upon complex societal challenges around the globe, MSU will, in effect, write the sequel to *Pursuing What is Best for the World*—a sequel that will chronicle powerful, transformative accomplishments we have only begun to envision.

Lou Anna K. Simon
President
Michigan State University

In *Pursuing What is Best for the World: 150 Years of Teaching, Research and Extension—Stories of the College of Agriculture and Natural Resources*, Professors emeriti Ken VerBurg and Ray Vlasin have painstakingly provided an invaluable and entertaining chronicle that will grace living rooms, studies, and offices for years to come.

The acorn and the oak tree are fitting metaphors for what begins as a story about the impetus to create the State Agricultural College and the unique historical context that made it possible even to conceive of such an undertaking. Little did the early educational pioneers know that their vision would transform higher education and, in the process, profoundly enhance economic development and the quality of life for Michigan and the world.

Some key themes emerge from the delightful collage of vignettes that inform each chapter of this attractive and lively book. The first is the inexorable journey from institutional uncertainty and challenge to stability and growth to national and international leadership.

Another central theme is one of the strong, resilient leadership of its presidents. To illustrate, T.C. Abbot worked to ensure survival; John Hannah was dedicated to growth and expansion, and Lou Anna Simon is committed to transforming the land-grant mission through the quality, inclusiveness, and connectivity of a fully engaged, global university.

Most importantly, perhaps, this history is ultimately a story about the devoted work of countless people—from faculty and staff members to students, alumni, and donors to the myriad of public/private partners—the people, past, and present, who have shaped the College of Agriculture and Natural Resources, MSU Extension, the Michigan Agricultural Experiment Station and our great university.

Jeffrey D. Armstrong
Dean
College of Agriculture and
  Natural Resources

Preface

The invitation to prepare this book presented an exciting opportunity. Little did we realize the complexity of the assignment.

We begin this story with the setting that gave rise to the formation of Michigan Agricultural College. The economy of Michigan, relying on its fur trading industry, grew rapidly after 1812 but then fell flat by 1830. Meanwhile, with the completion of the Erie Canal in 1825, residents of the New England states were eager to leave the rocky soils in search of better farming soils. Many of these settlers exited the canal at Detroit and made their way to the lands available in southern Michigan. To give readers a sense of the population settlement of the state, the first five chapters include a map showing the counties that met population standards qualifying them for formal organization. Each chapter also includes a chart of population data.

As the farm population expanded during the 1840s, the demands for an agricultural college likewise expanded. The editor of the *Michigan Farmer* played a critical role in communicating the wishes of the Michigan State Agricultural Society and disseminating the farmers' demands. The first state fair in Detroit in 1849 was also an essential event as it led to a revision of the state constitution and an instruction to the state legislature to provide for an agricultural college.

The legislature passed the law on February 12, 1855, the formal date of the founding of the college. Two years would pass before the college would open and accept its first class. At that opening, President J.R. Williams stated, "The acorn we bury today, will not branch into a majestic oak tomorrow." Throughout the chapters, we have placed acorns to highlight some of the many innovations that followed.

The first 50 years were times of struggle and uncertainty, but the leaders of the institution, the students and alumni, and the supporters from around the state remained confident and loyal. Their continued support enabled the college to endure those difficult years and, indeed, to develop into the great institution it has become.

As authors we would like to call the reader's attention to a few characteristics of the book's format. First, readers will note that much of the text is presented through the words of those who experienced life at the college. Our goal with this style is to enable the readers to experience the development of the college and gain an appreciation for the struggles and achievements the college endured and attained from its early days to the current time.

Second, the book is the story of the College of Agriculture and Natural Resources (CANR). As such we begin with the story of the founding of the Michigan Agricultural College and carry a broad account of the development of the institution through the early 1900s including adoption of congressional acts that initiated federal funding for the Agricultural Experiment Station (MAES) and the Extension Service (MSUE), respectively. Thereafter, as the institution matures and broadens, the focus of the story is directed to the activities of the CANR and its elements rather than the entire university.

Third, the CANR has linkages throughout the university. Twelve units of the college are formally linked to other colleges of the university, largely through the MAES and MSUE. The linkages are mainly to the College of Natural Science and Engineering, Human Medicine, Osteopathic Medicine, Veterinary Medicine, Social Sciences, and International Studies. We would like our readers to know that we appreciate the contributions of these units even though they may not be mentioned in many of the stories.

Finally, one of our goals is to have those who come after us learn about the efforts, trials, and accomplishments of those who came before them. We trust that the stories will generate a strong sense of their responsibilities to carry the torch for the college and the university forward and hold it high so those working and studying at the time of the MSU Bicentennial will appreciate the efforts invested in this institution.

We genuinely thank all those who have had a role in providing assistance in developing this book. We thank those who contributed their stories for the book. The staff members of the University Archives and Historical Collection were very instrumental in making this book possible, as were personnel of the MSU Museum, and Elizabeth A. Shirer, a student assistant. Staff members of ANR Communications — Kenneth Fettig, Alicia Burnell, Margaret Weaver, Leslie Johnson, and Director Kirk Heinze — were very helpful with the production, design, editing and proofing of the book. Thanks to offices that gave us access to the various records and photographs as well as to others who shared such resources with us. We also owe thanks to Gale L. Arent, director of stakeholder relations, and Jeffrey D. Armstrong, dean of the College of Agriculture and Natural Resources, to directors and staff members of the MAES and MSUE, and others in departments, schools, centers, and institutes, and to the many cooperating friends of the institution.

We close with apologies to those whose good works and contributions did not receive a mention. One of the most difficult tasks in putting together a book of this nature is deciding what to include from the immense wealth of possibilities. We trust the readers will understand that this book is but a small sampling of the lives, events, actions, and achievements, big and small, that made the college, the MAES, MSUE, and the allied units great.

We hope the book will enrich its readers' appreciation for the college and their dedication to the continuing success of its future.

Kenneth VerBurg
Raymond D. Vlasin

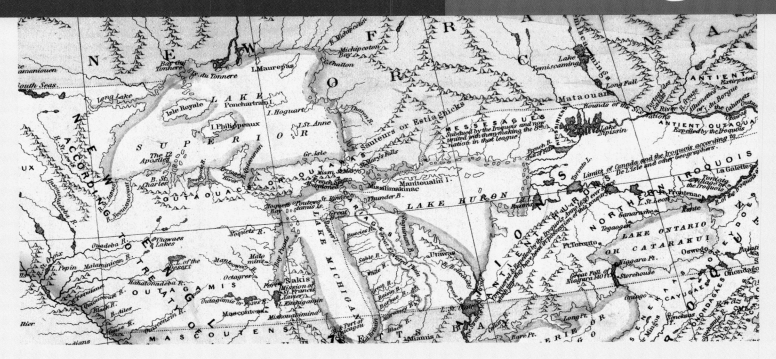

Founding of the Pioneering Agricultural College

"The Legislature of our State has adjourned. One [act it has passed] is so important that we give it a prominent place in this number. It is the act to establish the State Agricultural School."

Michigan Farmer, March 1855

Early Michigan

Northwest Territory Roots

Michigan's legal origin can be traced to the Northwest Ordinance of 1787 and an intermediate action in 1805 when Congress established the Territory of Michigan and its territorial government. Michiganians would wait 32 more years for statehood — to have their constitution (drafted in 1835) recognized.

People Prize Education

Gradually the population of the state expanded as people came from the Northeast to develop a new way of life. Michiganians placed a strong emphasis on education for their youth — the state constitution provided funding for local public schools and for a state university. In addition, several religious communities established private colleges.

Classical vs. Practical Education

These institutions tended to concentrate on classical rather than practical teaching, overlooking the desire of agricultural communities for the opportunity to develop and learn the sciences of agriculture. This led to a continuing demand for an agricultural school and experimental farm. The drive for such an institution gathered strength in the late 1840s and reached a plateau as the 1850 constitutional convention included in the constitution a directive to the legislature to address these desires and needs.

Legislators Pressured

Five more years of lobbying and pressure would be necessary, however, before the legislature would enact a law establishing a state agricultural college. The legislature passed the law on February 12, 1855, and the governor signed it the following day.

Thank the Activists

The many advocates for a state agricultural college included many state residents, ranging from the editors/owners of the *Michigan Farmer* newspaper to readers, farmers, and other leaders. Credit them for the institution that 150 years later would continue to be seen as a leader in agricultural and natural resources, science, instruction, and service.

Northwest Territory

In 1787, Congress enacted the Northwest Ordinance, a law establishing provisions for settling and organizing the area lying east of Pennsylvania and bounded on the south by the Ohio River, on the west by the Mississippi River, and on the north by the U.S.-Canadian border. Eventually the territory would be divided into five states: Ohio, Michigan, Indiana, Illinois, and Wisconsin.

Organization Process

The ordinance established provisions for organizing the state and local governments

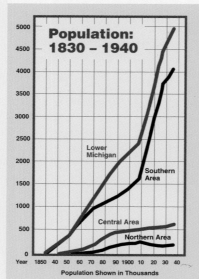

Michigan State Archives

as the population reached specified levels. In the meantime, territorial councils governed the prospective state areas. Counties and townships were permitted to organize when they reached the minimum population level.

Settling the Territory

For the Territory of Michigan, the 1832 map reflects the current boundaries of counties of Wayne, Macomb, and Monroe. The map of organized counties by 1836 reflects more directly the pattern of mobility made available by the opening of the Erie Canal in 1825. Settlers traveled through the canal to the Michigan border and began settling the Michigan territory. As is reflected by the maps of organized counties, the new settlers tended to purchase lands first in the lower three tiers of counties and then gradually in counties farther north.[1]

Population growth, 1830-1940

From 1830 to 1940, the population of Michigan grew from 5,000 to 5 million. By 1860, Michigan had become a democratic community of farmers, artisans, and lumbermen. The population was derived mainly from New England, New York, Pennsylvania, and Ohio, with some immigrants from Canada, Great Britain, Ireland, Germany, Holland, and Scandinavia.

Population: 1830 – 1940

Lower Michigan

Southern Area

Central Area

Northern Area

Year 1850 40 50 60 70 80 90 1900 10 20 30 40

Population Shown in Thousands

Organized Counties of Michigan, 1832.

CHIPPEWA

BROWN

MICHILIMACKINAC

OAKLAND

Richard W. Welch

What is the Vision?

Michigan Emphasizes Education Early

America Has No Model for Ag College

Most Enlightened

"Of all the articles in the Michigan Constitution, the one on education was probably the most enlightened and farsighted. It stipulated that the legislature should encourage 'the promotion of intellectual, scientific, and agricultural improvement.'"[2]

Primary Schools

The legislature moved immediately in 1837 to enact a law to establish a primary school district in each township. It also directed the proceeds from the sale of section 16 lands in each township to be distributed by the superintendent of public instruction to primary schools on a per student basis.

A State University

Another act establishing a state university defined the purpose as providing "inhabitants of the State with the means of acquiring a thorough knowledge of the various branches of literature, science, and the arts." The board of regents would supervise the institution, which would be placed in Ann Arbor on a gifted 40-acre parcel.

The state university opened in 1841. The location of the site created some controversy because many had expected that the university would have several branches that would teach agriculture and mechanical arts as well as serve as teacher training centers. In addition, farmers were especially angered because they wanted the state to provide for and operate a demonstration farm.

Teacher Training

Another early statute required each teacher to have a "regular course of training," and in 1849 the legislature established Michigan Normal School and placed it under the supervision of the state board of public instruction. This institution later became Eastern Michigan University.

The question that remained:

How best to serve the educational needs of farmers?

Because no models for an agricultural college existed in the United States, the advocates turned to Europe for examples. Henry Colman, a member of the Royal Agricultural Society of England and national societies of France and the United States, shared his views regarding such an institution in lectures around the country. Below are excerpts from his plan.

Need for Agricultural Education

"First, then, in every system of agricultural education should be an institution for the thorough indoctrination of the pupils in natural science, and in mechanical philosophy, so far as it can be made to bear upon agriculture."

A Model Farm

"Secondly, there should be a model farm, which should be accessible to the pupils, and where they might see an example of the best management, and the best practices in husbandry. To [this] should be added an experiential farm."

An Experimental Garden

"Connected with the whole should be most extensive gardens, first, for purposes of botanical instruction, giving the pupils an opportunity of becoming acquainted with all the principal plants, grasses, forest trees, fruit-trees, and weeds, which enter into their cultivation; and next, for making them thoroughly acquainted...with the cultivation of all the varieties of vegetables and fruits which may be required for use, profit, or luxury."

Managers and Faculty

"One or two instructors should be employed to manage the agricultural department, and to give the necessary practical instruction. Beyond this, no resident instructors would be required, but regular and full courses of lectures and experiments in geology, mineralogy, botany, comparative anatomy, the veterinary art, and chemistry, by competent professors of these sciences, who might be employed for these objects annually, without the necessity and expense of constant resi-

dence, as is now frequently done at our medical schools. In this way, the best talents in the community might be commanded, and at a reasonable expense."

Student Labor and Lodging

"I would require, in the next place, that the pupils should be placed in a condition of perfect equality, and that a certain amount of labor should be made compulsory on all, at such a rate of wages as should be deemed just....

"Their board and lodging should be settled for by themselves, without any interference on the part of the directors of the institution, beyond keeping the charges within a stipulated price; and the keepers of the boarding-houses should be required to purchase, at reasonable rates,

(continued on page 12)

Population, 1830	
	Number
Ingham County	n/a
Michigan	32,000
USA	12,866,020

Awaken Spirit of Inquiry

Benefits of Learning

Knowledge of agricultural science is needed and can be easily obtained —
so says this writer from Oakland County.

"Mr. Editor:

"I flatter myself that I can contribute a mite toward the great objects of your valuable paper. I cannot call myself a farmer; but I ... have made some observations and made some inquiries of men who can be relied upon. The point which I wish to present ... is this: That the farmers in our state generally, very much need more knowledge of the science of agriculture; and that this knowledge they may easily obtain."

Applying Labor and Expense Intelligently

"Our State possesses superior advantages for agricultural pursuits, and a population distinguished for industry, enterprise and general intelligence. Yet they do not reap one-third part of the profits that they might, from their farms if [their] labor and expense were only intelligently applied. Knowledge is power....

"The great mass of farmers do not seem even to know that agriculture is a science capable of indefinite improvement."

Others are Getting It Done

"Need our citizens be informed, that the State of New York has ... witnessed an agricultural revolution? There are farmers in that state who have increased the productions of their farms to more than three fold, and that too with little increase in labor and expense.

"I suppose our sandy and loamy soils are well adapted to turnips, bagas, beets, &c. Incredible quantities of these may be raised on a given space, with deep and repeated ploughings and good manuring. I raised a great crop of the white and yellow bagas, and round turnips, on a piece of inferior sandy soil, with one deep ploughing and a little stable manure...."

Awakening a Spirit of Inquiry

"But knowledge of the cultivation of soil is only a part of what is needed. There are a thousand and one points besides, on which we need information, and which we may obtain from agricultural writers.

"It would at least be very likely to awaken a spirit of inquiry and prompt men to avail themselves of means of information.

"Yours,
Philanthropist, Oakland County"[3]

Study Practical Arts

The editor of *Michigan Farmer* drew on Henry Colman's arguments supporting the need for agricultural colleges in America.

"COLLEGE EDUCATION: We have long been of the opinion that reform was nowhere more needed than in the course of studies pursued at our colleges. The necessity for this reform is well set forth in the following paragraph which we take from one of Mr. Colman's agricultural addresses."

Classical vs. Practical Learning

"Classical learning, so-called, which occupies now a large portion of the best years of those who pursue it, excepting as a matter of mere taste, pastime, or embellishment, is of little substantial use to anyone.

"It is a notorious fact, and in my opinion sufficiently disgraceful to the boasted wisdom of the age, that at least two-thirds of the young persons who enjoy the best advantages of a liberal and classical education, and come out adorned with the highest honors of our colleges and universities, are even then incapable of keeping themselves from starvation, and have then to begin to learn the practical arts of life: and the remaining third are able to do it, not from anything they have learned at those places of education, but from what they were compelled, perhaps by a stern necessity, to learn elsewhere."[4]

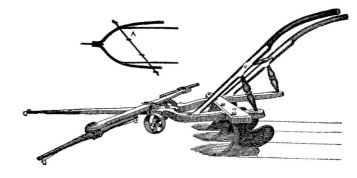

Wiard's Gang Plow. Designed more especially for the second and third plowing of summer fallows. It turns three or four furrows at once.[5]

Pressure Continues

Classical Education Is Not Sufficient

"Mr. Isham:

"Sir: You are the constituted champion of the farmer and laboring men of Michigan. Well, what of it?...We farmers support the University: for whom is the system of education and the facilities for obtaining knowledge therein, designed? Not for the farmer or mechanic, for no one can participate who shall not have acquired a certain degree of Latin and Greek."

Youth Need Practical Education

"I had a son whom I wished to educate as a mechanic. It was my desire that he should know German, some French, and have the advantage afforded by the lecture on scientific subjects, and on moral and political philosophy. In short, I wished him to have a practical education. I wished to participate in the benefits of an institution that should be adapted to the wants of the chief occupations of our people....

"Science and literature, as you know, are more practicably useful to the mechanic and farmer than to the lawyer and doctor. The clergyman should know everything, if Cicero's notions of an orator are correct.

"Well, our University — what does it do to educate the farmer's son, for a farmer? — what to make scientific mechanics? — what to form business men?"

"Yours,
"J.S. Scott, ADRIAN, 29th, Jan. '51"

EDITOR'S RESPONSE: "While we would not abate one iota from the completeness and thoroughness of a college course, as carried out in our best institutions, there can be no doubt that such a modification of it will enable all to avail themselves of its advantages, to qualify themselves for their various pursuits, without going through the entire routine, is highly desirable, and an improvement which the exigency of the times demands. -Ed."[6]

Need for Ag Education, but Not College?

"From this document it appears that the indefatigable officer at the head of the Department of Public Instruction has, within the past year, visited and held educational meetings in every organized county in the state, except four. In most of the counties visited, educational societies were formed, whose especial object is the improvement of Common Schools. Nearly 60,000 have been taught in these 'People's Colleges' the past year. The whole number in the state between the ages of four and eighteen is 97,658.

"We are glad to notice in the list of books recommended for use in Primary Schools, that Johnston's 'Agricultural Chemistry and Geology' holds the first place among the text-books on chemistry. We presume the Catechism of Ag. Chemistry and Geology is intended. This excellent little work brings the science of which it treats down to the comprehension of the schoolboy, and presents it in such a manner as to interest while it instructs. In our judgment, the time for its study, which need not exceed three months, could not be better spent by any youth who intends to become a tiller of the soil. The price of the book is 20 cents."[8]

Should Michigan Farmers Take a Hint?

"We read of several eastern institutions, in which Agriculture has been introduced as a department of study. Cortland Academy, N.Y., is about to introduce a regular course of Agricultural Chemistry and Geology. An effort is to be made this winter, to induce the Legislature of New York, to establish near the city an Agricultural College, and Experimental Farm. In Scotland, the study of Agriculture has been introduced into about 90 Parish schools.

"Shall we take a hint?

"H. Hurlbut, Editor and Proprietor"[7]

Organized Counties of Michigan, 1840

Richard W. Welch

A Key Step

State Fair Stimulates Action

In September 1849, the Michigan State Agricultural Society (MSAS) held its first Michigan fair in Detroit. The *Detroit News* reported that some 15,000 people attended. Though Lewis F. Allen, president of the New York State Agricultural Society, was a key speaker, E. H. Lathrop of Schoolcraft was remembered in the months following for the speech inspiring his listeners to keep on pressing for the establishment of an agricultural college.

A Resolution for Action

Bela Hubbard, a member of the MSAS Executive Committee from Oakland County, drafted the following statement:

"Resolved, That our legislature be requested to take such legislation as shall appear necessary or expedient, for the establishment of a State Central Agricultural Office, with which shall be connected a Museum of Agricultural Products and Implements, and an Agricultural Library, and as soon as practicable, an Agricultural College and Model Farm."

Unanimous Vote

The committee adopted the resolution unanimously and directed Mr. Hubbard to forward it to the state legislature.[9]

The Population of Michigan Continues to Grow

1840

	Number	Percent change, 1830-1840
Ingham County	2,498	-
Michigan	212,267	563.3
USA	17,069,458	32.7

1850 Michigan Constitution, Article 13, Section 11

Section 11. The legislature shall encourage the formation of intellectual, scientific and agricultural improvement; and shall, as soon as practicable, provide for the establishment of an agricultural school. The legislature may appropriate the twenty-two sections of the salt spring lands now unappropriated, or the money arising from the sale of the same where such land has already been sold, and any land that may hereafter be granted or appropriated for such purpose, the support and maintenance for such school, and may make the same a branch of the University, for the instruction of agriculture, and the natural sciences connected therewith and place the same under the supervision of the regents of the University.

Constitutional Revision Convention

Revise Basic Law

The state held its second constitutional convention in 1850. The purpose was to revise the basic law adopted in 1837. The convention provided the opportunity that advocates of an agricultural college needed to advance their cause.

Agricultural College Authorized

The revised Section 11 was key. It directed the legislature to address the wishes of the agricultural community for an agricultural college. The new language did not specify many details, such as the makeup and location of the college, and left open the door for the state university or the Michigan Normal College to take on the responsibility.

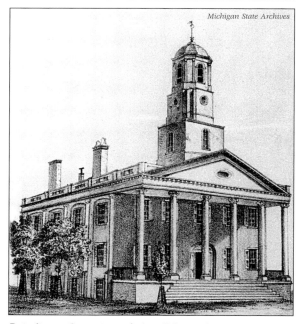

Michigan State Archives

Detroit was the state capital until December 1847.

The Constitutional Mandate

Indecision Dominates

"Despite the directive in the newly revised constitution, the legislature took little action. However, it did adopt a resolution requesting the establishment and endowment of an agricultural college and a board of education in Washington. It also asked Michigan's delegation in Congress to "secure a grant of lands from Congress for an agricultural college."[10]

During the prior month, the legislature passed a law giving the board of education, in connection with the Michigan Normal School, the "duty, from time to time, as the means at their disposal may warrant, to provide suitable grounds and buildings, implements of husbandry and mechanical tools," etc., for instruction "in the mechanic arts and in the arts of husbandry and agricultural chemistry."[11]

A NEW GRUB PULLER.

PATENTED BY JOSEPH FREY

SIMPLE, CHEAP AND DURABLE,

And will pull all ordinary sized GRUBS with ONE TEAM as fast as you can hitch them. Territory and Machines for sale. Address

BURNHAM & CO., AGENTS.

FARMERS' WAREHOUSE,   BATTLE CREEK, MICH.

An Earnest Plea! Do Something!

Exercise your Power!

"Mr. Editor: In the midst of my perplexity and discouragement, it is quite natural for the weak to ask the protection and advice of the strong. Will you bring the power you possess, (or at least, are supposed by your subscribers, to possess,) to bear upon this subject? I will state my case and would fain believe that I am not alone in this predicament."

Common School is not Enough!

"Circumstances, as well as inclination, make me a farmer in name if not in deed — having received what is called a common school education, [I] can read, write and cipher. I am not satisfied with that, although some of the oldest and best farmers, who raise as much 'corn and wheat as their neighbors,' say it is not enough."

The Classics Won't Do the Job

"The extracts that have from time to time appeared in yours and other agricultural publications, upon the sciences of Geology, Botany, &c., have awakened in my mind an earnest desire to make their acquaintance. But where shall I go? I do not wish to read four of the best years of my life in the dirty pages of what are called the classics. This may [be the] answer for D.D.'s and Dr's of Law or Medicine."

Farmers Pay Taxes, Too!

"In all of our institutions of Learning, there is not a single course of study calculated for farmers. Do not we toil enough? Have we not been taxed enough to build and sustain Institutions to educate the other classes? Can we not have a portion, say another of those wings that the state has built at Ann Arbor, for our express accommodation, Professor, Library &c.?"

Wake the Legislators

"Mr. Editor, you may think me too fast, but sir, I feel my own ignorance about the everyday matters of life, and I ask, earnestly ask, cannot something be done for the better? Do thunder in the ears of our legislators until they will wake up to this matter.

"Respectfully yours, &c.
Alex F. Corning
Glass Creek, Barry Co.
July 2, 1851"[12]

Organized Counties of Michigan, 1852

MACKINAC

Richard R. Welch

Why Have an Agricultural College?

Excerpts from Letter to Editor:

"MR. EDITOR: I was very much pleased to see in the June number of your excellent periodical a suggestion for an agricultural college in this state. This is a question on which I have thought much for the local papers."

Constitutional Amendment not Enough

"When the convention for revising the constitution was in session, I had the temporary charge of a paper, and urged the propriety of making some provision for raising a fund for the establishment of such an institution. Something was done by the convention, but it was not what the importance of the subject demanded."

Farming, Art, or Science?

"Still, however, every change is looked upon with a good degree of suspicion by the farming community and a great prejudice exists against what is called 'book farming.' There are two sources for this prejudice, to wit: The false supposition that farming is simply an art and not science applied to art, and that some 'book farmers' have failed. It is well known to men of observation, that scientific principles are not ascertained and settled without experiment, and that before the experiment is sufficiently settled to determine the principle, many failures must occur."

Leading Scientific Profession

"I think that it requires but a little observation to be satisfied that this is the most scientific profession…. Is there any science in agriculture? I think that it requires but a little observation to be satisfied that this is the most scientific profession to which our attention can be directed. I have claimed, and still claim, that it should not only be placed among the learned professions, but at the head of them.

"How many farmers can give a satisfactory reason why they plow at all?… Much of the practical farming depends on a solution of this question. Science reveals the why of it. I am very glad to find people's attention being drawn towards the subject of suitable training of our young men for this noble calling…."

Benefits to be Gained

"The question is asked, what are the advantages to arise from an agricultural college? I can but glance at the answer at this time. One very important advantage is that it would at once elevate the occupation and remove one source of discontent from our youth…. The young man going out from the college, conducted on a proper plan, uniting in beautiful harmony the theoretical and the practical, would be better prepared than the most industrious could be even after many years' toil. There are two leading designs in every well-devised system of instruction, to wit: To furnish information and to instruct the mind how to think.

"Yours, X."[13]

Can Others Address Needs?

Michigan Normal College Action

"While in accordance with this provision [the 1850 legislative act to direct the Michigan Normal School to provide education and mechanical arts education programs] some attempt was made to introduce agriculture as a study in the Normal School, to which fact Mr. Sherman, Superintendent of Public Instruction, called the attention of the State Agricultural Society in September, 1852."

State University Responds

"The university went still further, and instituted a two months course of daily lectures, in the spring of 1853 for the agricultural community. In 1854, the Rev. Charles Fox, A.M., editor of the *Michigan Farmer*, was appointed Lecturer on Theoretical and Practical Agriculture. He died shortly thereafter and was never replaced."

State Agricultural Society Inquiry

"A committee of the MSAS made visits to both the University and the Normal School … they were unanimously of the opinion that an institution was needed especially for the education of the farmer."[14]

What is the Best Course of Action?

Bird in the Hand?

From the policy perspective at the time, the issue of how to address the educational needs of the agricultural community was not clear. For a time it appeared that the farmer community wanted its own agricultural college.

Or, Bird in the Bush?

But with the delay by the state legislature, it appears that some began to wonder whether it might not take the "bird in the hand" rather than wait for the "bird in the bush." The above stories provide some insight into the nature of the ongoing debate.

A Coming Together?

Not Everyone Agrees

A Resident of Scio Speaks Out

"Editor of the Farmer:
I notice that the propriety of establishing State Agricultural Colleges has of late been considerably discussed in several of the Eastern States, and has also excited some interest in our own. Altho' the majority of the farming community seems to become readily prepossessed in their favor, yet weighty objections may be urged against their establishment. Some of these, I propose to enumerate.

"They are UNNECESSARY.

"The theory and practice of agriculture can be well learned without the teachings of a State Institute.... Individuals become eminent as chemists, geologists, astronomers, and mathematicians, without receiving their education at public expense.

"Such an institution would be EXPENSIVE

... at first and would become more and more so. In order to make it worthy of the State, it must have several hundred acres of land; numerous ... buildings;

choice stock; valuable implements, and a large library ... [and] at least half a dozen professors with liberal salaries....

"It would be UNDER CONTROL OF A POLITICAL PARTY.

"It would be filled by persons conspicuous for party services, rather than by men well qualified....

"It would be INEFFICIENT in accomplishing the object intended.

"I do not say that it would not be good; for I think it could not fail to be productive of benefits to some extent. What better chance for an education can be asked for, than that held out by the University of Michigan? Yet, [the] population of more than 400,000 send less than forty students to it....

"The ... proposed institution [would be] EXCLUSIVE AND ARISTOCRATIC.

"It opens peculiar and exclusive privileges to one class of the community, at an expense which all must contribute to pay.

"The Legislature's granting a request of one class only, would be UNJUST to others.

"Should [the legislature] comply with the wishes of each class in succession, we would have upon us all the evils of class legislation; each division of the community at war with the rest....

"The State ought, indeed, to provide for the welfare of the blind, the insane, the deaf and dumb, and the helpless; because they cannot take care of themselves; but State institutions for the advancement of the business interests of a particular part of community, stand on a basis entirely different....

"Scio, April 17, 1852
"*T.F.*"[15]

"The Board of Regents would respectfully announce to the agriculturalists of the State, that there will be given free a course of lectures in the University of Michigan, upon Agricultural Science, commencing the 27th day of April, and closing the 28th day of June. During this time there will be from three to four lectures daily. (Saturdays excepted.)

"These lectures will embrace the following topics.

"**FIRST.** Lectures by the Rev. Charles Fox, principal editor of the Farmer's Companion, on Theoretical and Practical Agriculture....It is designed that this course will be eminently practical in its character, and from the well known reputation of the Lecturer as a Practical Agriculturalist, long a resident in the West, his knowledge of English, French, and German Agriculture, acquired from actual observation, as well as his extensive literary and scientific acquirements, it is confidently believed, that it will prove greatly advantageous to the agricultural interests of the State.

"**SECOND.** Lectures by Prof. S.M. Douglass, on the Elements of Chemistry applied to the Arts, Meteorology, and Climate. In the delivery of this course, the extensive Chemical and Philosophical Apparatus of the Institutes will be brought into requisition, affording a series of experimental illustrations....

"**THIRD.** Lectures by Prof. A. Sagar, upon the general and comparative organization of plants, from which the principles of their classification will be deduced and illustrated; and vegetable physiology, comprising the source and mode of nutrition of plants, and their various modes of development....."

Parallel Course

"A parallel course on the general and comparative anatomy and physiology of animals, their classification, habits and relations to the human interests, will be given during the term."

Lectures on Geology and Mineralogy

"In addition to the above courses, occasional lectures will be given upon Geology and Mineralogy, by Prof. Douglass, in which will be embraced the useful applications of the science of mining, drainage, construction of public works, &c."

Goal: Useful to All Classes of Community

"In making the first announcement of an Agricultural Course of Lectures in the University of Michigan, the Board of Regents hope and trust, that they will be sustained in their efforts to make the institution useful to all classes of community. "

Lodging Available

"As the lectures are necessarily dependent upon each other, students are requested to be prompt in their attendance upon the first lectures, and thus have the advantage of the entire courses. Good board and lodging can be obtained at from $1.50 to $2.00 per week."

JAMES KINGSLEY,
Chairman of Ex. Com. Board Regents.
UNIVERSITY OF MICHIGAN
March 14, 1853[16]

Course Still Unclear

UNIVERSITY OF MICHIGAN AGRICULTURAL DEPARTMENT

THIS Department will be opened for the present University year on Monday December 1st. The following Lectures will be delivered:

1. CHEMISTRY, with application to Agriculture, Geology, and Meteorology, four days in a week, by Prof. DOUGLASS.

2. PRACTICAL AGRICULTURE AND VETERINARY SURGERY, every day, by Rev. C. Fox.

In addition to the above, the students will have an opportunity of attending the class in Political Economy, or any other class of the Scientific Course they may select.

The Scientific Course is now fully opened, and a number of students have already been admitted to it.

Students for this Course are examined in English Grammar, Geography, Arithmetic, and Algebra through Equations of the First Degree.

The whole Course comprises four years; and all who satisfactorily complete it, are graduated as Bachelors of Sciences, and become, like Bachelors of Arts, candidates for the higher degree of Master of Arts.

Students who are prepared are admitted to an advanced standing in this Course, according to the usual practice of the Classical Course.

There is also a Partial Course for those who do not wish to become candidates for a Degree.

The Agricultural students will have access to the books in Agriculture which may be found in the University Library. A valuable addition has been made to this department of the Library by recent purchases both in Europe and in this country.

HENRY P. TAPPAN, Chancellor.
Ann Arbor, Oct. 12, 1853[17]

The item above appeared in the November 1853 issue of the "*Michigan Farmer*" in the Advertisements and Announcements section.

MSAS Suggests University Branch

The MSAS Executive Committee, meeting in Detroit on December 14, 1852, adopted a resolution urging the legislature to act on the provision of Article 13, Section 11 of the state constitution. The committee offered a compromise embracing the following action.

"A resolution was offered by the Hon. Titus Dort for the appointment of a committee, to memorialize the legislature on the subject of establishing an agricultural school as a branch of the university, to be erected on some section of university lands, at a distance from that institution...; passed and committee appointed, consisting of Messrs. Dort, Shoemaker, and Moore...." [18]

Don't Pay Three Profits

If you are going to pay for a carriage why not pay the least you can for the best vehicle? Get all you can in material and workmanship—pay as little as you can for handling and "extras."

You save the jobber's commission and the retailer's profit when you buy direct from the factory. You pay the cost of making with one moderate profit added. We are not agents, but manufacturers of buggies, carriages, surreys, phaetons, wagons, harness and horse accessories. Everything guaranteed. With our illustrated catalogue you can order easily and safely. If what you order does not suit, send it back and we will pay the freight both ways. First, get the catalogue. You are welcome to a copy.

No. 3034 Buggy. Price $37.25 With Leather Quarter Top.

THE COLUMBUS CARRIAGE & HARNESS COMPANY, COLUMBUS, O.

Michigan Farmer

Organized Counties of Michigan, 1856

Richard W. Welch

Can You Believe It?

MSAS Leadership Charts the Course

New Resolution

In its December 1854 meeting, the MSAS Executive Committee revisited its earlier decision and adopted the following resolution:

"Resolved, that it is the sense of the committee that an Agricultural School should be entirely separate from any other institution."

The committee again petitioned the legislature and presented to the committee of the legislature a bill for its establishment and organization, which, with a few amendments, became law.[19]

Michigan Farmer Announces VICTORY!

"The Legislature of our State has adjourned, and among the acts passed by it, are several which relate to the interests of agriculture, and which we shall publish as soon as we can make room for them. One, however, is so important that we give it a prominent place in this number. It is the act to establish the State Agricultural School!"[20]

Public Act 130, 1855

An Act to Establish a State Agricultural School

Section 1. *The People of the State of Michigan enact; That the President and Executive Committee of the Michigan State Agricultural Society be and are hereby authorized to select, subject to the approval of the State Board of Education, a location and site for a State Agricultural School; within ten miles of Lansing and subject to such approval, contract for and purchase for the State of Michigan such lands not less than five hundred acres, nor more than one thousand acres, in one body for the purpose of an experimental farm and site for such Agricultural School: Provided, That the amount to be paid for such farm and site shall not exceed fifteen dollars per acre, and that the conveyance or conveyances be made to the State of Michigan....*

Section 5. *The course of instruction in said college shall include the following branches of education, viz: An English and Scientific course, natural philosophy, chemistry, botany, animal and vegetable anatomy and physiology, geology, mineralogy, and political economy, with bookkeeping and the mechanic arts which are directly connected with agriculture, and such other as the Board of Education may from time to time see fit to prescribe, having reference to the objects specified in the previous section....*

Section 6. *There shall be two Scholastic terms in each year — the first term commencing on the first Wednesday in April and ending on the last Wednesday in October; the second term commencing on the first Wednesday in December and ending on the last Wednesday in February; and no pupil shall be received for less than one term, unless by special permission from the Board of Instruction.*

Approved February 12, 1855

*Kinsley J. Bingham
Rec. and Filed
February 13, 1855*

Michigan State Archives

Governor Kinsley S. Bingham (1855-1858)

Gov. Bingham had an extensive political career. As a Democrat he served four terms in the Michigan House of Representatives (some as Speaker) and two terms in the U.S. House. Earlier he had been a justice of the peace and probate judge. On July 6, 1854, while heading a coalition of Whigs and Free Soilers, Bingham became the nominee of the brand new Republican party that was formed "under the oaks" in Jackson, Mich.[21]

Michigan Farmer

Michigan subsoil plough, designed more especially for the second and third plowing of summer.

America has no Model... *(continued from page 3)*

from the farm whatever supplies they might require, which the farm would yield."

Tuition

"A tax should be levied upon the student for the payment of all instructors and lecturers, and the use of the library, and the chemical and philosophical apparatus; and likewise to meet any extraordinary expenditure made upon the farm."

Discipline

"... I would advise, in every case, that the residence should be absolute, the rules exact and stringent, and the annual or occasional examinations as severe as at the military school at West Point, so that an equal proficiency might be secure.

"Such, in my opinion, is a plan for agricultural education which demands no great

advance, and involves no risk. I throw out these hints to my countrymen ... but to show that an institution for a practical and scientific education in agriculture may, without any hazardous expenditure, or any large investment, be made almost immediately attainable."[22]

The Population of Michigan Continues to Grow		
1850		
	Number	Percent change, 1830-1850
Ingham County	8,631	245.5
Michigan	397,654	87.3
USA	23,191,876	35.9

Period in Review

Education a Common Goal

The settlers coming to Michigan from foreign countries as well as from New England and down the Erie Canal evidenced a strong interest in education. Those early residents gave testimony to that interest not only by including a state university in its first constitution but by establishing several other colleges that continue in the 21st century as private colleges.

Primary Education Support

Further evidence of the strong interest in education was the assignment of one section of land in each township that was to be sold and the proceeds used by the state to fund primary schools.

Trained Teachers

The residents of the state realized that these institutions would have to be supported, not only financially but by trained personnel as well.

To attain this goal, the state established the Michigan Normal College in Ypsilanti, later to become Eastern Michigan University, as an institution specializing in the education of teachers for the primary school system.

Agricultural Education Goal

The preceding stories of the Prologue reveal the struggles that the advocates of an agricultural education endured to bring about the formation of an unprecedented agricultural college in America.

Lessons to be Learned

Some of the lessons to be learned from their stories are as follows:

• Provide a forum for discussion.
• Bring the common interests together.
• Consider the alternatives.
• Never give up!

"*Established on no precedent, it is like a pioneer in the march of men and the march of mind.*

"*The acorn we bury today, will not branch into a majestic oak tomorrow.*

"*The orchard we plant this year will not afford a harvest of fruit the next.*"

President J.R. Williams, 1857

"*It may take years to put this institution upon a firm basis, but the time will come when the 'Agricultural College' will be the pride and boast of the State.*"

Governor Moses Wisner, 1861

The Beginning Steps

Chapter Overview

Selecting a Campus Site

The first duty of the new college was to locate a site. The conditions the legislature established for the committee limited the number of sites from which the committee could choose. In addition, the site would have to be accessible, and with the limited roadways, options were limited.

Options were Limited

The committee selected a site equal to a square mile located approximately 3 miles from Lansing. Because the site was not well-drained and was a virtually natural area, the site required a good deal of conditioning before it could be occupied.

Site Preparation was Challenging

Preparing the site for occupancy was another of the challenges. The Lansing area was lightly populated, and experienced construction workers were scarce. Thus, significant structural problems had to be corrected before the buildings could be occupied.

Facing the Expectations

Another challenge was organizing a curriculum. This college had no models — it was a pioneering effort. Supporters for founding the college had ambitious expectations about how an agricultural college would affect their lives. Many expected results now!

Policy and Administrative Differences

The lack of immediate fulfillment of the expectations led to other difficulties. Quarrels between the board and administrators led to the resignation of the first president, indecision regarding a successor, and even a major revision in the academic calendar. Members of the faculty were so distressed that they resigned in protest. Later, the resignations were ignored.

Reorganized Structure

Under the leadership of the MSAS, the legislature established the Board of Agriculture, which assumed jurisdiction of the college from the Board of Public Instruction. The new board restored public support for the college and appointed T.C. Abbot as president.

The First Decade — a Trying Time

The first decade of the college was a trying time. Yet, the college leaders persevered and prepared the institution for the next decade.

Search for A Campus Site

Authority to Search for Site

Public Act 130, 1855, authorized the MSAS to search for a site for the college. The legislature established four conditions:

1. The site must be within 10 miles of the state capital.
2. The land may not cost more than $15 per acre.
3. The size of the site must be 500 to 1,000 acres.
4. The State Board of Education must approve the choice.

Select One of Nine Sites

The MSAS Executive Committee met on June 12, 1855, and visited nine sites in the area over the next three days. The committee recommended a 676-acre site about 3 miles east of the capital city along the Detroit, Howell, and Lansing plank roads. The Board of Education approved the recommendation.

Salt Spring Sections Finance Purchase

The proceeds from the sale of the 22 sections of land granted by the legislature were used to acquire the property at a cost of $10,150. The amount remaining was about $7,000.[1]

Word of the College Reaches East Coast

The *Rural Intelligencer* of Augusta, Maine, offered the following comment on April 14, 1855, after learning about the new Michigan college. "At length we are to have a real, live College, especially devoted to the business of educating young men to be farmers, in the U.S. The Michigan Legislature has appropriated money for the purchase of an ... Agricultural College and Experimental Farm. The tuition is to be forever free to pupils from Michigan. We wish we had more hope for specific education than we have."

MSU Museum

THE LANSING REPUBLICAN.

BY H. BARNS.   LANSING, INGHAM CO., MICH. 1855.   VOL. I.—NO. I.

Tour the College Grounds with Editor, June 1856

Stand in the City and Look East

"If you have taken the trouble to read what I have already written, you must now be pretty well acquainted with Lansing ... but come with me and ascend to the second story of the brick building on Capitol Square ... Stand here and look out at this east window; the road which you see stretching away to the east, is the Middle Town Plank Road. It is straight, and beautifully undulating.

"Now take this spy-glass, and by its aid you will discover ... at a distance of about three miles, a tall pine tree. That tree stands upon a high bank of the Cedar River, and is the property of the State, for it stands upon the grounds of the State Agricultural College....

"As we cross this river ... further up the hill we cross the state road to Jackson; this white house on the left, about a half a mile from the river, belongs to Col. W. Jones, and is occupied by the ladies of the Female College, as their residence."

Pine Tree Landmark

"A few steps forward and we cross the west line of the college grounds; step a little to the right, and from a height of thirty-five feet we look down upon the Cedar River, and at this point stands the old pine tree; it, as well as old Okemos, who still resides hereabout.

"We will pass down this road to the left, and come out on the Lansing and Detroit Plank Road. On the road the farm has a front of about one mile; its west and east lines are near the three and four mile stakes; the width of the farm being between the two stakes.

"The greater portion of the farm lies south of the Cedar River, but the improvements now being made are between the Cedar River and the plank road.

"Many hands are now employed upon the work, and it is progressing rapidly, handsomely, and substantially, and thus far [it] is highly creditable to the contractors, and to S.M. Bartlett, Esq, who is acting as agent of the Board, in superintending its work...."

Already a Destination Site

"Already the Agricultural College Farm has become a fashionable resort for the people of Lansing and its vicinity."[2]

Lansing Republican masthead courtesy of *Lansing State Journal* history department.

The Campus Site

1855-1899

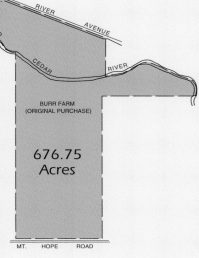

BURR FARM (ORIGINAL PURCHASE)

676.75 Acres

MT.   HOPE   ROAD

Promising for Students and College

The original site was bound on the north by what is now Grand River Avenue, on the south by the present Mt. Hope Road, and on the east by the present Bogue Street. The western boundary did not extend to the present Harrison Road.

Richard Reynolds

"That tree stands upon a high bank of the Cedar River ... upon the grounds of the State Agricultural College."

Preparing to Educate

The Guidance of John C. Holmes

Key Organizer

John C. Holmes, a Detroit resident, merchant, and school board member, made significant contributions to the founding of the agricultural college. He was a key organizer of the MSAS, its secretary from the founding, and a month-long monitor of the legislature during its consideration of Public Act 130 in 1855.

Campus Planning

His service was critical. But equally essential was his assistance in selecting the campus site.

Course Planner

The Board of Education had been speculating about the structures needed for a college whose central mission was teaching science and agriculture. They had no precedents or models.

As 1855 was coming to a close, the board contacted Holmes and invited him to offer a design. When he asked about the course of study, the board could only ask him to prepare a plan of courses, too.

Fisk and Goadby Assist

Holmes consulted with Lewis R. Fisk, then of the Michigan Normal School, and Dr. Henry Goadby of Detroit. Together they outlined the course plan and the required facilities.

The board accepted Holmes' building plan recommendations and invited bids for the construction.[3]

The First Building

Brick Construction

The college was under the control of the State Board of Education, and the board "procured the erection of a Boarding Hall of brick; eighty-two by forty-three feet, three stories and basement; a College Building of three stories and a basement; a stable; 300 feet of shed; and four dwelling houses for professors; all being of brick. They spared no expense on the Chemical Laboratory. Philosophical apparatus, mathematical instruments, and other means of illustration were purchased."[4]

Flawed Construction

"As the buildings neared completion, they revealed major flaws which delayed the opening of the College. Some doors would not open, others would not close, and a few would not lock. It found flooring of soft pine, flooring that was grossly uneven [and] so shrunken that it did not reach the walls. Baseboards were loose, basement cisterns leaked, and the kitchen range was a 'smoky concern' described as 'entirely useless.'"

Leaking Roofs

"Because the roofs leaked, every rain moistened the plaster until it weakened and fell; not until the roofs were rebuilt was the plaster reasonably secure. The foundations were beginning to settle and in the opening month of classes piers were placed under the sagging partition of College Hall.... A financial settlement adjusted the visible defects."

State of Michigan Archives

College Hall

The 50- by 100-foot three-story structure was located where Beaumont Tower now stands. The first floor held a large lecture room and laboratories. The two upper floors provided four classrooms, the library, and an agricultural museum. Years later, college officials learned that the building rested on plank footings and that one corner of the wall enclosed a large stump.[5]

Long-term Effects

"Because the contractor had been careless if not dishonest and because the Board had neglected to supervise the construction adequately, the College would be plagued in its critical early years by inconveniences and expenses of defective building."[6]

Courtesy UAHC

College residence hall affectionately called "Saints' Rest."

STATE AGRICULTURAL COLLEGE APPLICATION ANNOUNCEMENT

The Agricultural College of the State of Michigan is located three miles east of the village of Lansing, upon a farm of nearly seven hundred acres. The west wing of the College's Buildings and a Boarding House have been erected and arrangements will be made for opening the Institution the first Wednesday of April next [1857].

Limited Accommodations; Limited Acceptances

As but a limited number of students can be accommodated, owing to the want of the necessary buildings, and as applications from the various counties of the State are entitled to preference in the order of time in which they are made, it becomes important that the persons desirous of securing situations, make their applications for admission at an early day. These may be made to the Secretary of the State Board of Education, by letter, at Lansing, any time before the fifteenth day of January.

Age and Scholarship of Applicants

Applicants for admission as pupils must have attained the age of fourteen years and must have acquired a good primary school education.

Tuition and Board

Tuition will be free to pupils from this State. Arrangements will be made to accommodate students with board at reasonable rates in the boarding house on the premises.

Manual Labor Required

Every student will be required to devote a portion of each day to manual labor for which he will be entitled to receive an equitable remuneration.

Course of Study

The course of study has been arranged with direct reference to the wants and interests of the agricultural class in our State. It will embrace a wide range of instruction in English Literature, Mathematics, and Natural Science. Special attention will be given to the Theory and Practice of Agriculture in all its departments and minutiae.

Term Time And Attendance

The first term of the Institution will commence on the first Wednesday in April [1857], and will end on the last Wednesday in October. The second term will commence the first Wednesday in February. Students will not be received for less time than one term, unless for special reasons satisfactory to the Board of Instruction. Persons desirous of admission, should present themselves for examination at the College the Monday previous to its opening.[7]

By order of the State Board of Education
IRA MAYHEW, Secretary

1st President Announced

Joseph R. Williams is Choice

"We perceive that the Board of Education has tendered the presidency of the Agricultural College at Lansing, to Joseph R. Williams, Esq. All the friends of the institution consider this a very judicious choice. Mr. Williams was formerly a resident of Constantine, St. Joseph Co., where for some twenty years he was connected with agricultural interests of that portion of southern Michigan."

Well Prepared and Ready

"He will bring to the institution an active mind, well stored with varied and extensive reading, much practical experience as to the educational wants of the students who may resort to the College, and that administrative tact, and the suggestive faculty so useful in the planning and arrangement of a new enterprise of this kind. All the appointments of professorships have not yet been filled, but probably will be before the end of the session of the Legislature."[8]

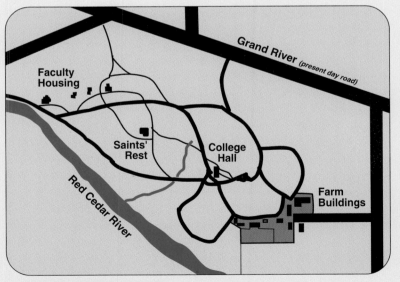

Buildings at college opening.

The College Opens

DEDICATION PROGRAM

The Michigan State Agricultural College will be opened, with appropriate dedicatory exercises, on Wednesday, the 13th of May. These exercises, upon which the public is invited to attend, will commence at 9 o'clock, A.M., and will consist, in part, as follows.

HON H.L. Miller, President of the Board, will make the opening address on behalf of the State Board of Education, on the delivery of the College and Farm to the care of the President and Faculty of the Institution.

HON. Joseph R. Williams, President of the College, and Director of the Farm, will respond on the part of the Faculty, in an address indicating the design, objects, and policy, of the institution.

His Excellency Kinsley S. Bingham, Governor of the State, will follow with an address on behalf of the Commonwealth of Michigan.

The Faculty of the Institution — which will be filled at an early day — consists, at present, of the following gentlemen:

HON. JOSEPH R. WILLIAMS
President and Director of the Farm

ROBERT D. WEEKS
Professor of English Literature and Farm Economy

REV. L. R. FISK
Professor of Chemistry

J.C. HOLMES
Professor of Horticulture

D. P. MAYHEW
Professor of Natural Sciences

C. TRACY
Professor of Mathematics

Students desiring admission to the Institution should present themselves at the College for examination by the Faculty, on Monday, the 11th of May, at 9 o'clock, A.M.[9]

By order of the State Board of Education,
IRA MAYHEW, Secretary

College and Farm Delivered to President

"On Wednesday morning the 13th [1857], the Board of Education of the State of Michigan, comprising the Hon. H.L. Miller [Board of Education President] of Saginaw, Hon. John R. Kellogg, of Allegan, the Rev. Mr. Willard, of Battle Creek, and the Hon. Ira Mayhew, the Superintendent of Public Instruction, delivered the State College buildings and farm into the charge of the President and Faculty of the College....

"[All this took place] in the presence of a large concourse of citizens from the various parts of the State, many of whom had brought their sons for the purpose of enjoying the benefits of the institution. About 10 o'clock A.M., Mr. Miller [made] some brief remarks."

Proverbs 3, Prayer, Song

"The Rev. Mr. Willard then read the third chapter of the Book of Proverbs, and the Rev. Mr. Mahon offered a prayer.

"Next a choir sang the Song of Labor, by Frances S. Osgood, which had been set to music by M.H. Ingersoll, of Lansing.

Perfecting Michigan Youth

"The President [then] said he was happy to announce that the Board ... had made the choice of the Hon. Joseph R. Williams as the President of the Faculty, and that John R. Kellogg would deliver to them and to the Faculty of the College and farm, a brief address including the following remark:

'To you, Mr. President of the College, in the name and representing my colleagues on the Board of Education, is now committed the charge of this important institution. To you, sir, and carrying out this great work to a perfection

(continued on page 21)

Joseph R. Williams

Harvard Law Graduate

Joseph R. Williams, a graduate of Harvard University, began practicing law in New Bedford, Mass. His practice involved assisting purchasers of lands in Michigan. This led to his relocation to Constantine, Michigan, and a variety of career changes. He became a gentleman farmer, author of articles on agriculture, a merchant, and editor of the Toledo Blade in 1854.

Courtesy UAHC

Public Policy Activist

As a Whig, he twice sought appointment to the U.S. Senate, competing against Lewis Cass. (Later on, he was instrumental in the formation of the Republican Party in Ohio.) His involvement with the formation of the agricultural college began with his service as president of MSAS. He played a key role in the adoption of the Michigan Constitution change that provided the directive to form the college.

Acorn Planting Begins Tradition

Excerpts from President Williams' Remarks

No Precedent

"New York and Pennsylvania are maturing, and two or three other States are taking the initiatory steps toward establishing Agricultural Colleges. Here on the very margin of the cultivated portions of our country, where the 'forests primeval' are just vanishing before the encroachments of civilization, the youthful and vigorous State of Michigan, first among her sister States, dedicates this Institution to the instruction of men who are devoted exclusively to the cultivation of the earth. Established on no precedent, it is alike a pioneer in the march of men and the march of mind.

"The elements of the Institution around us are rough and crude, but even in the embryo, we recognize an enlightened forecast, that would do honor to those venerable commonwealths which have stamped their indelible impress on the history of mankind."

Just an Experiment?

"I will at the outset, deal with some of the objections to this Institution. Men will brand it as an experiment. They will demand results before they are willing to afford aid or sympathy.... The charge that an enterprise is an experiment has no terrors for me ... the great [Erie Canal] was denounced as the insane vision of a theorist, and his surveys were branded as imposture."

Is It Too Costly?

"The next objection ... will be its cost, and the alleged taxation necessary to its support. The Institution has been initiated, and thus far matured, exclusively from the $56,000 derived from the Salt Spring Lands donated to the Territory of Michigan by the general government, and not a dollar of the additional $40,000 appropriated by the Legislature, for use during the next two years, is yet consumed."

Teachable Skills?

"The next objection is embraced in a question triumphantly asked, 'How can you teach a man to plow or hoe?' That is, 'How can his practical skill be improved?' I contend that even in this narrow view, the mere application of labor, there is much to be learned.... The exhaustion and deterioration of the soil ... is a great national practical error and sin. Has the farmer nothing practically to learn?"

Patience, Wisdom...

"We have no guides, no precedents. We have to mark out the Course of Studies, and the whole discipline and policy to be followed in the administration of the institution. Friends and enemies will demand too much, and that too early.

"The acorn we bury today, will not branch into a majestic oak to-morrow. The orchard we plant this year will not afford a harvest of fruit the next. The Institution itself, like the seeds, the plants, and the trees, the breeds, the very implements which come under its ordeal, requires patience, wisdom, time, for trial and development."[10]

First Students Came From Southern Counties

"The Agricultural College commenced its second term on the 8th day of December [1857]; with ninety-six students, of which only about one half continue from the previous term. Some of those who were present at the summer term have left for the purpose of teaching school during the winter, to obtain the means to enable them to prosecute their studies for the future."

Southern Counties Well Represented

"New arrangements of the buildings now permit nearly one hundred pupils to be accommodated; and it will be said that twenty-two counties in the state are now represented."[11]

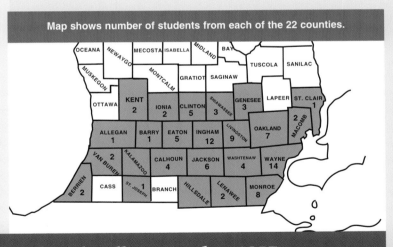

Map shows number of students from each of the 22 counties.

State Agricultural College Faculty, 1857

Joseph R. Williams, President
John C. Holmes, Horticulture and Secretary of the College
Robert D. Weeks, English and Farm Economy (Massachusetts)
Lewis R. Fisk, Chemistry (Michigan Normal School)
Calvin Tracy, Mathematics (Ohio)
D.P. Mayhew, Natural Science (Michigan Normal School)
Henry Goadby, Entomology, Physiology, and Comparative Anatomy (Detroit)[12]

Student Life

Schedule of Courses

Freshman Class

First Half: Algebra, History, Analysis of Language

Second Half: Algebra, Geometry, Philosophy, Physical Geography, Meteorology, Rhetoric

Sophomore Class

First Half: Solid Geometry, Trigonometry, General Chemistry, Botany

Second Half: Mensuration & Farming, Leveling, Plotting and Drainage, Analytical Chemistry, Logic, and Bookkeeping

Junior Class

First Half: Mechanics and Farming, Chemistry applied to Agriculture, Arts, and Rhetoric

Second Half: Roads & Rivers, Canals, Ditching & Draining, Vegetable Physiology, Anatomy & Animal Physiology, Topographic Surveying & Drawing, Geometric Drawing

Electives: Literature and English Language

Senior Class

First Half: Astronomy, Entomology, Veterinary Art, Mental Philosophy

Second Half: Mental Philosophy, Moral Science, Geology, Mineralogy, Political Economy, Constitutional Law[13]

Courtesy UAHC

Courtesy UAHC

Student Work Schedule

5:15 Awake and get up.

5:30 Attend chapel for morning service.

5:50 Breakfast

6:15 1st Working Division: Report to the Farm Director at the Barn and be in the field with teams or implements at half-past six.

9:15 2nd Division: Perform field assignments.

12.30 Students quit work and bring in their teams and implements.

1:00 Lunch

2:45 3rd Division: Reports for work and works from three to six in the afternoon.

On Saturdays, students do not have recitations and so they work only in the morning. The third division joins divisions one and two.

Examples of Field Work

Monday	Cultivating amongst trees in the garden
Tuesday	Harrowing for corn
Wednesday	Spading up marsh
Thursday	Planting corn
Friday	Harrowing in orchard
Saturday	Spade up marsh

The compensation rate for this work is at least 5 cents per hour and as much as 8 cents for the most experienced and skilled students.[14]

College Gets High Grades

THE LANSING REPUBLICAN.

BY H. BARNS.   LANSING, INGHAM CO., MICH. 1855.   VOL. I.—NO. I.

Report on State Agricultural College

A Negative Lead

"The Board [of Public Instruction] entered upon their duties with a great deal of distrust in regard to the success of the instruction, and opened the College the present year with many misgivings as to the result."

Lingering Doubts Dispelled

"But the promptness with which students flocked to it from all parts of the State, and the prosperous condition in which they found it at their last meeting, dispelled all lingering doubts of its success which they entertained. The institution has nearly or quite overcome the financial embarrassments which have hitherto crippled it, and the end of its permanent wastefulness has begun."

Farm and Gardens Taking Shape

"The farm proper, as our readers are aware, contains some six hundred acres. Two hundred and twenty acres have been in crops, and some forty acres more have been cleared. The thrifty appearance of the crops, and the air of neatness pervading the farm indicated that this department is placed in the hands of a thorough farmer."

Recitation, Farm Labor, Homework

"The students devote three hours to recitation, three hours to labor on farm, and the balance of the time to study, recreation, &c. The labor they perform is highly conducive to their health, and we attribute to that the remarkable clearness of mind and vigor they bring to their recitation to this cause. We noticed this particularly during a recitation in trigonometry, under charge of Prof. Abbot."

Faculty Challenged, Too

"There are no drones about the institution, and each one seems to know just what is required of him, so that everything moves on like clock work. The labors of the Professors are quite onerous, owing to the limited number appointed.... This is especially true of Prof. Fisk, who teaches History, Mental Philosophy, and Political Economy, outside of his professorship."

Specimens and Diagram

"A Museum of Natural History was commenced in November last under the direction of Prof. Miles, who is industriously engaged in preparing and arranging specimens, and has already made an attractive feature of the College.... The Laboratory, one of the most complete in the West, affords ample facilities for illustrations in General, Analytical and Agricultural Chemistry, and is placed in competent hands."

Specimens in Hand

"A Herbarium, the property of Prof. Thurber, is another very valuable addition to the institution. It comprises an extensive collection of botanical specimens throughout the world, but especially the United States."

The Library Collection

"The Library contains some 1,300 volumes, and in the commodious Reading Room may be found most of the papers of the State, and nearly all the Agricultural periodicals of the country."[15]

Courtesy UAHC

The Opening Ceremonies... *(continued from page 18)*

which shall elicit the thanks of coming generations ... to the gentlemen associated with you as the professors, and your aides in perfecting a large portion of this youth of Michigan, in a knowledge of the capabilities of the soil, is given the glory....'"

Williams and Bingham Speak

President Williams then delivered his remarks. After the choir sang "the beautiful ode composed by I. M Cravath, Esq., of Lansing expressly for the occasion," Governor Bingham "in an eloquent and appropriate address reviewed the history of the educational system of the state."

Concluding Song and Benediction

"The ceremonies concluded with the singing of the Hymn of Labor, by J. G. Whittier, to the music of Old Hundred, and the pronunciation of a benediction by the Rev. Mr. Moore."[16]

Lansing Republican masthead courtesy of *Lansing State Journal* history department.

Land-Grant Campaign: Act One

Act One Ends In Veto

Working Congress

In an effort to achieve financial security for the college, President Williams, in 1858, began pressing for a Congressional land-grant act. He was one of many in Washington the day Congressman Justin S. Morrill introduced the bill. Williams successfully encouraged the support for the bill of U.S. Rep. D.S. Waldridge and U.S. Senator C.E. Stuart, both of Kalamazoo.

Courtesy UAHC

Justin S. Morrill

Information Campaign

Williams, drawing on his political skill, printed and mailed some 5,000 copies of a 60-page booklet telling the story of the Agricultural College of the State of Michigan. He also mailed circulars supporting the legislation. Many farmer-oriented newspapers extended the message around the country.

Rescuing the Land-grant Bill

Waldridge's minority address in the House of Representatives rescued the bill, which the House adopted at the close of the 1858 session. In early

1859, the Senate passed it after Sen. Stuart obtained an amendment giving the newer western states a fairer share of the land grants.

Michigan's Influence

One Virginia editor reported that Williams "is an able and zealous advocate in the cause of agricultural education, and no man has done more, or as much, to promote the passage" of the Morrill bill.[17]

Land Grant Vetoed

Now the bad news: President James Buchanan vetoed the legislation. Enactment of the bill would have to await a new president.

Congress Ambivalent

"... We had little hope, from the evident complexion of the party vote, that [the bill] would ... become a law. Hence, the return of the bill by the President, without his signature, was no surprise...."

Buchanan's Objections

Buchanan had six objections to the bill:

"1. The low condition of the public treasury does not warrant such a disposal of a large portion of the public lands....

"2. It would be impolitic to admit such a precedent, as it would have the effect of inducing the States to rely on the general government for aid ... in other matters.

"3. The new States would be greatly injured by the facilities which would be afforded by means of the sale of land script at low prices to speculators to obtain large portions of the lands.

"4. It is doubtful whether the bill would have the effect of promoting education of the kind designated.

"5. The bill would be likely to interfere with existing colleges in the several States, and have an injurious effect.

"6. Congress does not possess the power to grant lands because it does not possess the power to appropriate money raised by taxes, for the purposes of educating the people of the United States."

Buchanan's Reasoning not Endorsed

"Each of these objections is sustained ... by a series of reasoning, that in no one of them is fully satisfactory ... every proposition is susceptible of being ... not in accordance with either the practices or the theory of the government." [18]

The Emerging Financial Crisis!

Public Delusion

In the words of the *Michigan Farmer*, "There seems to be much delusion in the public mind, in consequence of persistent and continuous misrepresentations, in regard to the cost of the Agricultural College."

The Appropriations

The editor reported that as the third school year was about to begin, the college had received over the prior two years a total of $133,820; $56,320 of that came from lands sold by the state. In February 1857, the college received $40,000, and in

February 1859, an additional $37,000. The latter appropriation was to fund the college until January 1861.

The Take-back

The financial crisis surfaced when the Department of Public Instruction deducted

(continued on page 23)

...and Organizational Crisis!

President Williams Resigns

"Hon. Joseph R. Williams has tendered his resignation of the Presidency of the Agricultural College. This step, made necessary by private interests, cannot but be regretted by the State. The high personal character of President Williams, his earnestness in the cause of agricultural education, and his scholastic endowments, made him for that position one man among a thousand.

"His whole-souled devotion to the general subject of reform in respect to the union of manual labor with educational advancement, and especially his efficient agency in the passage of the Agricultural Land Bill, made him well known to every friend of this cause throughout the Union.

"The efforts of Mr. Williams have been unsparingly given to the advancement of the efforts of the best interests of our State Institution since his appointment and if they have been less successful than he could wish, that result is plainly attributable to combined agencies, within and without, at work against him."[19]

Will College Survive?

Delayed Appointment Stirs Worry

The resignation of President Williams and the failure of the board to appoint a replacement contributed to a good deal of uncertainty among the loyal supporters of the college. The commentary in the *Michigan Farmer* illustrates the concern.

Supporters are Concerned

"During the past month, we have received many letters from various quarters asking for information as to the time of the commencement of the next terms of the agricultural college, and also whether there would be any new students received."

Will College Reopen?

"Some letters even asked whether the College was to be opened during the term. To enable us to answer these inquiries, and at once do away with all uncertainty on the subject, we addressed a letter to one of the members at the Board of Education, and his reply is that the College will be opened at the time fixed for the commencement of the term, namely, Wednesday, the 6th of April, and that is when courses of instruction will be continued."

Admit New Students?

"Whether there will be new students received, will depend, we suppose, on the number of the old ones who may present themselves to take their places. There have always been a few at the end of each term heretofore."[20]

Vacancies in Faculty Ranks

"The vacancies left in the faculty by the resignation of President Williams and of Professor J. C. Holmes, will undoubtedly be filled either provisionally or permanently, at an early day; and we hope to have the Institution moving to a career of usefulness, creditable to the State, without fear on the part of its friends that it will be other than an establishment in the highest degree honorable to Michigan."[22]

Road to the campus — Michigan Avenue.

The Emerging Financial... (continued from page 22)

$13,472.73, the amount the college had overspent during the first two years. (This reflected, in part, the costs of correcting building construction gaffes.) With the deduction, the funds available to the college from 1859 to 1861 were about $24,000.

Deepening Crisis

Two other factors contributed fiscal stress. First, the enabling legislation for the college stated that Michigan residents were to be admitted free. The second was the understanding that the college would make a profit from its products.

Farm Not Ready for Profits

Those closest to the situation, however, maintained that such production was not yet possible because the lands required still more tree clearing, stump removal, drains, and land preparation.[21]

Storm Clouds Persist

Is Enrollment Dwindling?

The question of the college enrollment persisted. In late November 1858, the *Lansing Republican* published the following notice that caught the attention of the superintendent of public instruction.

Challenging Inquiry

"There has been a marked falling off in members during the academical term just now closing, which may have an influence in guiding the Superintendent to his conclusion; but whether so or not, we are unable to state. If not misinformed, the summer term had in all more than one hundred students, and closed with about fifty, a significant fact, not unlikely to have had its effect upon the mind of the Superintendent, and the action of the Board of Education."

The College Response

"Professor Fisk, the interim 'president' of the college responded in part as follows: 'I infer from [the] editorial that you are laboring under some misapprehensions in regard to the College. The facts are these:'"

Fact One

"The term commenced with eighty students, about the same number as in the winter, but twenty less than at the opening of the summer term the year before, and closed with sixty, a number equal to that which was in attendance at the end of the year...."

Fact Two

"The falling off was, therefore, 20 per cent, less than the year previous. Moreover, at the commencement of the summer term of '58, there were nearly twenty young men that were examined but not admitted because the College was full ...."

Why Students Leave

"Fisk offered three reasons for the 'dismission' of students from the college:

"1. Some young men come to the Institution thinking that their labor will cover all the expenses including board, books, clothing, etc. Thus, some are compelled by poverty to leave early.

"2. Sickness at times thinned the ranks.

"3. Some parents have brought their sons whom they could not control at home, hoping that by the labor and discipline of the Institution they might be reformed."

Irritated by Media?

He went on to maintain "that many more young men have applied for admission into the College at the opening of the next term, than there are vacancies now."

Fisk closed his response to the *Lansing Republican* with the following: "I trust you will concede the justice of publishing the above statement of facts."[23]

Just a Two-year College?

Criticisms Frequent

In the waning years of the 1850s, the State Board of Public Instruction had to deal with several criticisms about the level of enrollment and finances as well as whether the curriculum was meeting farmers' expectations.

One report suggested "the young farmer should be permitted to study agriculture alone without being compelled to do ... the extraneous and irrelevant studies in order to graduate."

Two-year Curriculum

In December 1859, the board adopted a major reorganization plan for the college. The plan cut the program from four to two years and established five departments of instruction: Agricultural Chemistry, Botany and Vegetable Physiology, Zoology-Animal Physiology, Civil and Rural Engineering, and Theory and Practice of Agriculture. The goal of these changes was a curriculum focusing on scientific and practical agriculture.

The Faculty Resign

The faculty members objected and resigned their positions. Most, however, were reappointed.

Emphasize Agriculture!

Not everyone disagreed with the plan. The *Michigan Farmer* editorialized some dissatisfaction that "instead of being a professional college of Agriculture and Horticulture, it has been in reality a manual labor school of high grade, at which numbers of young men could gain excellent education in all that relates to English Literature, and in several sciences which have a general relation and bearing on Agriculture...."

Create Board of Agriculture?

The Board of Education also expressed its frustration by moving to ask the legislature to create a Board of Agriculture and give it the responsibility for overseeing the college.[24]

More Sun Than Clouds

MSAS Meeting

Near the end of 1860, the MSAS Executive Committee met to discuss the management of the institution. A report said "the discussion did not assume the form of a debate, but rather that of a conversational consultation as to the best methods of attaining certain results." The following is a summary of this discussion.

What Do We Have After Four Years?

"The Agricultural College has now been in operation for four years, at a cost to the State of about $128,000 [including the buildings] .... This institution was designed to turn out young men educated ... in the practice of agriculture, [and] capable of bringing ... to that practice the results of scientific inquiry."

The College Would Cost Little

"In so doing, it was believed, the State would benefit from the diffusion of knowledge amongst its agricultural popu-lation that was ... necessary to promote full development of the agricultural resources but [to] pay back the outlay [to the people]."

A Sound Plan Was Absent

Because of the "difficulties incident to the establishment of an experimental institution ... the plan of organization ... was not based on any settled or well considered plan of operations, and today, after four years of trial, not a single finished scholar has issued from its walls, to which the people can refer as getting something for their expenditure."

A New Board of Control

"But then how shall we go to work to attain this result? Alter the organization of the Institution, and place it in the hands of the Board of Control, who shall be responsible for its management only, is the advice of the executive committee."

(continued on page 28)

On December 11, 1860, the MSAS Executive Committee adopted these resolutions:

- That the Legislature establish an independent board to govern the ag college.
- That the board consist of five to seven persons appointed by the governor, a majority of whom shall be members of the Executive Committee of MSAS.
- That three designated members "memorialize" the legislature and request passage of the bill.
- That the committee members do what they can "to redeem the State Agricultural College from the difficulties surrounding it, and to make it what it should be — an institution beneficial and creditable to the State, which every citizen shall regard with pride and satisfaction."

The action was consistent with a recommendation of the Board of Education, in part in response to an earlier report by a committee of the MSAS chaired by James Bayley, the farm superintendent whose son had been a student at the college.[25]

Legislature Approves New Plan!

Williams' Product

The Michigan Legislature took the bill up in February 1861. The *Michigan Farmer* stated, "The Institution seems to be the sport of fate and the politician, and a brief resume' of its position will probably add little interest to the report ... which was submitted to the Senate by Hon. Ira H. Butterfield, chairman of the Committee on Agriculture, but which bears the unmistakable marks of Senator [former College President] J.R. Williams."

Six Gubernatorial Appointees

The proposed new board would have eight members including the "Governor and the College President; the other six members would be gubernatorial appointees chosen from a list of recommendations by the county agricultural associations."

Theoretical and Practical

Among numerous other provisions, the bill proposed that the institution is to "supply a high seminary of learning, in which the graduate of the common school can pursue and finish a course of study terminating in thorough theoretic and practical instructions in those sciences and arts which bear directly upon agriculture and kindred industrial pursuits."

Tuition Permissible

The new law would permit the board, in its discretion, to charge tuition and require at least 2.5 but not more than 4 hours of labor per day.

Final Consideration

The legislation was late in coming and thus delayed opening of the 1861 term. The appropriations were $16,500 for 1861 and 1862 and $18,000 for each of the following two years.[26]

Governors Endorse Plan!

Governor Wisner Affirms Plan

Suggestions Right

In his farewell address on January 1, 1861, retiring Governor Moses Wisner dedicated a significant part of his remarks to the agricultural college. As the editor of the *Michigan Farmer* put it, "His message, which though long, is unquestionably an able and well considered State paper ... and we quote his suggestions because we know from previous knowledge that what he suggests is right."

Gov. Moses Wisner

Will Be "Boast" of the State

"There is no institution in our State that more strongly commends itself to the good wishes of the people than the agricultural college, and it should be the especial duty of the Legislature to cherish and watch over its infancy.... It may take years to put this institution upon a firm basis, but the time will come when the 'Agricultural College' will be the pride and boast of the State."

Expect Expenses

"Suppose it should continue to be a bill of expense to the State? I ask, what institution of learning have we that has not been and is not now a bill of expense to the State?"[27]

Gov. Austin Blair

New Governor Agrees

Incoming Governor Austin Blair's comments were a bit unsettling because his remarks, as seen below, were conditioned on the phrase "if [the college] is to go on."

Endorses Board Change

However, his comments continued, "In accordance with the opinion of the Board of Education, I recommend you to commit the future care of this College to the State Board of Agriculture, to be appreciated as may seem to your judgment best."

Supports Funding But...

"The Board asked for an appropriation of $25,000 – $15,000 to pay salaries for two years, and the remainder for buildings, tools, and the like. Most of it seems indispensable, if the institution is to go on, and therefore I recommend that the appropriation be made, or as much of it as you think essential."[28]

Lincoln's Call to Arms

On April 15, 1861, President Abraham Lincoln issued a proclamation calling forth "the militia of the several States of the Union to the aggregate number of 75,000, in order to suppress said combinations, and to cause the laws to be duly executed .... The senators and representatives are, therefore, summoned to assemble at their respective chambers at twelve o'clock, noon, on Thursday, the fourth of July next, then and there to consider and determine such measures as, in their wisdom, the public safety interest may seem to demand."

Plow-Boy Guards in Parade

On that national Independence Day, botany professor George Thurber marched his "Plow-Boy Guards" in the Lansing parade. They were students in the college's military training program. That evening, in the words of Madison Kuhn, some 5,000 people came to the campus to celebrate the day of patriotism.

Students Join Michigan Regiment

That summer, a few students responded to the call and enlisted in the Michigan Regiment. After a visit from an army captain looking for surveyors, all but one of the class members who were to graduate in 60 days volunteered to serve under General Fremont in Missouri. With reluctance, the faculty excused them and made them members of the college's first class to graduate even though all were absent.[29]

The Civil War made an immediate impact on the campus. Members of the first class to graduate, shown above, left before finishing the term and were absent from what would have been the first graduation ceremony.

The Population of Michigan Continues to Grow

1860

	Number	Percent change, 1850-1860
Ingham County	17,435	102.0
Michigan	749,113	88.4
USA	31,443,321	35.6

New Plan Underway

First Meeting of New Board

While the War Between the States continued, prospects at the college campus nonetheless were improving. The February semester opened on the 26th and students were coming in rapidly.

Governor Blair Participates

The newly constituted Board of Agriculture met for three days the previous week with "Governor Austin Blair, ex officio chairman of the board present. He took an active part in the business before them .... During this time, they have been busily engaged in the discussion and formation of the plans for the future operation, and are determined to make the college all its friends could reasonably ask. A series of experiments in farm culture and the care of the stock are to be inaugurated at once."

Motions and Actions

"J.C. Crippen of Coldwater was appointed to fill a vacancy in the Board, occasioned by the resignation of B.A. Yerkes of Ionia, who is now in [Civil War] service as Lieutenant of the Thirteenth Regiment.

"A resolution was adopted to build a farm barn the present season 46 by 60 feet."

An Encouraging Word

"We understand that Gov. Blair, and other members of the Board expressed their satisfaction with the present condition of affairs in the institution, and their faith in its ultimate and complete success."[30]

New Board Names New President

Theophilus C. Abbot
President, 1862-1885

Period of Turmoil

The period following President Williams' resignation was chaotic. After the Board of Public Instruction changed the college program to a two-year schedule, the faculty had dropped to two professors — Lewis R. Fisk and Theophilus C. Abbot. Abbot reported that the number of students had fallen to 19, then subsequently risen to 49 following a compromise between the two- and four-year programs.

Faculty Elects Fisk

During this time of crisis when the board chose not to fill the position of president, the faculty elected Fisk president pro tem. Meanwhile, Abbot served as secretary.

T.C. Abbot Promoted to Presidency

Following adoption of the establishment of the Board of Agriculture, the tension began to subside. In February 1862, the board appointed T. C. Abbot to the position of president.

Abbot had joined the faculty in 1858 as an instructor in grammar and rhetoric. He had bachelor's and master's degrees from Colby College in Maine. He had also studied theology at Bangor Theological Seminary. At the age of 29, he moved to Berrien Springs to become a teacher, and a year later principal of Ann Arbor Union School.

A Thorough Scholar

The board appointed Abbot professor of English literature, but as Madison Kuhn noted, his teaching assignments ran well beyond English to include grammar, rhetoric, argumentation, ancient history, logic, Anglo-Saxon history, and botany. "A thorough scholar, Abbot made meticulous preparation for his classes and expected the same from his students."[31]

Act Two: Lincoln Signs Morrill Bill

During this difficult period of the youthful college, advocates for the land-grant legislation renewed their effort with Congress. Congress responded by enacting the new law. President Lincoln signed it July 2, 1862.

Named After Sponsor

The law became known as the Morrill Act, after Sen. Justin S. Morrill, the bill's principal sponsor. It provided each state with a grant of federally owned lands to be sold with the proceeds to be used to endow colleges for the "benefit of Agriculture and Mechanical Arts."

State Shares

Each state was to receive an appropriation of land based on the number of members in its Congressional delega-

(continued on page 28)

State Ag Society... (continued from page 25)

Farmers Should Have Influence

Placing the board of education in charge of the agricultural college was seen as the most economical and conservative plan that could be adopted. But, the organization was a hindrance. The reason for this is simple:

"When the Legislature undertook to build up a college for the agricultural community it passed a law that said to farmers of the State, we are about to establish an institution at which young men can get a thorough knowledge of your business and for the benefit of your sons, but you must have nothing to do with it."

Change It or Close It

"We are willing to place it in the hands of lawyers, ministers, and teachers, but the agricultural interest is to be ignored .... The time has come, when either this condition of the college must be changed, or else it must cease.

"It is principally representing these views that the MSAS Executive Committee proposed a change in the organization of the institution, with the design of popularizing it ... and benefiting from the experience of men connected with agricultural affairs."[32]

Act Two: Lincoln... (continued from page 27)

tion. Michigan, under the act, was to receive approximately 240,000 acres.

Which Lands to Select?

The lands to be selected were to be of the highest potential market value, and for Michigan, that term generated some debate. Some wanted the Michigan Legislature to select forested lands still under federal control in the northern parts of the state because of their value and potential for a quick sale. Others argued that such lands were too risky because they feared the forested lands would burn and then be worthless and so promoted the selection of farmland instead.

The Lands Chosen

The legislature forged a compromise and selected some of both types. The lands selected were located primarily in northern Michigan counties from Alpena and Bay counties on the east to Emmet and Oceana counties on the west. The accompanying figure shows the counties in which the first 150,000 acres were selected.

Security Evasive

Though officials at the college were pleased to be recipients of the federal land grants, the Morrill Act did not bring immediate peace and security to the institution. Land sales did not take place immediately, and many of the transactions were payable over time, therefore not bringing in cash quickly.

Relocate College?

The third reason was that a joint legislative committee had issued a majority report proposing the state close the Agricultural College campus to make it part of the state reform school with the Morrill land grant being assigned to the State University.

The editor of the *Ann Arbor Argus*, for example, wrote, "We have long regarded the [agricultural] institution as a fifth wheel to a wagon, an entirely unnecessary addition to the educational institutions of the State."[33]

Period in Review

Difficult Decade

The first decade of the State Agricultural College was a difficult period for the college. The college site was ready for use as neither a college campus nor an experimental farm. Nor was it readily accessible to the population center that would have enabled it to accommodate students more readily.

Unfilled Expectations

The beginning of the college was turbulent also because of unfulfilled expectations. Some support groups expected the college to establish immediately a highly successful demonstration farm from which everyone could learn. Others, including some state legislators, thought the college would become self-supporting almost immediately without the need for state appropriations.

Board Uncertain

The Board of Public Instruction seemed entangled in competitive interests involving development of a public school system and building an institution to train teachers. The board's inability to deal with the active leadership style of President Williams and its refusal to appoint a successor, plus the outbreak of the Civil War, placed the college in a very difficult and threatened position.

Confident in Stress

Yet, the college survived these stresses and emerged with a new sense of direction and leadership under President T.C. Abbot. It was not that the college would no longer experience stressful times. Rather, there was confidence that the college had survived difficult times before and could do so again.

Land-grant selections in Michigan counties.

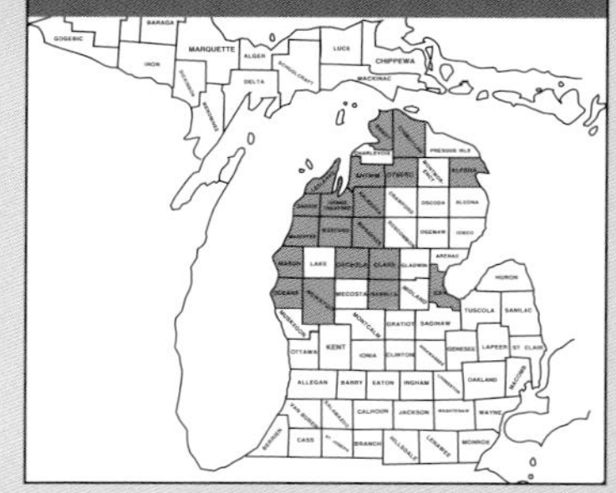

Early Selections in Michigan Counties

Remainder to be selected, 90,000 acres

Source:
Samuels Lacey
Agent for Land Grant Board
in Report to Governor Austin Blair

"When tillage begins, other arts follow. The farmers, therefore, are the founders of human civilization."

Daniel Webster, lawyer and statesman, Boston, 1840
(Posted in Greenfield Village, Dearborn, Michigan)

"If the alumni are faithful to their duty, they shall prove the institution a power and blessing to the world."

George A. Farr, Class of 1870

"Thus the College, chartered in 1855, came into being through a legislature made up largely of farmers. It was their desire to aid Michigan agriculture and individual farmers in their struggle to overcome the handicaps and hardships of pioneer conditions."

R.J. Baldwin,
History of Cooperative Extension
Michigan State College of Agriculture and Applied Science, 1941

College Future not Guaranteed

Chapter Overview

Period Threatening

The college's transition to the second decade did not generate a sense of security. Indeed, even though the Morrill Act was assuring, it also gave rise to threats that the State Agricultural College's responsibility to fill farmers' educational needs would be reassigned to the State University.

Expectations Unmet

The progress of the college did not meet farmers' expectations. Journalists were critical of the college's progress and did little to attribute responsibility to the legislature, which was caught up in an internal battle over funds for a much needed dormitory and laboratory.

Signs of Security

A good deal of the uncertainty related to the board of instruction's multiple responsibilities for the ag college, Michigan Normal College, and public schools. Thus the establishment of the State Board of Agriculture and its jurisdiction over the college

was a modest turning point. The key, however, was the legislative decision to fund a new dormitory. The facility would enable the college to admit more students, and it symbolized the state's commitment to the fledgling college.

Campus Life Challenging

Student and faculty life on the campus was difficult. The absence of a model for an agricultural college and the general absence of agricultural science meant that the faculty and students together would have to generate the knowledge. Gradually the number of graduates increased and began to meet the needs of other agricultural colleges around the nation.

Support Gathers

The college began to gain respect from newspapers as well as agricultural support groups. It established a benchmark by admitting women as students, even though the number was limited by the lack of housing.

A Case of Bad PR?

Sources of Insecurity

The college insecurity did not end with the adoption of the land-grant act and the state legislature's assigning it to the college. "In the legislative sessions of 1865, 1867, and 1869, bills to transfer the college [to the university] enjoyed substantial support.

"Even though [these bills] failed, their support was numerous enough to defeat all proposed building appropriations. By the late 1860s the one boarding hall was so crowded that ... as many as half of [those] who applied for admission [were rejected].

Yet opponents argued logically that if the college was abandoned, further construction at its present site would be folly."

Campus Inaccessible

"Unfortunately for its defense, the college lacked the enthusiastic patronage of some rural legislators. Because Lansing was remote from the best-developed agricultural areas and accessible only by stagecoach for many years, few farmers visited [the college except] during the biennial legislative sessions."

Bad Timing, Too

"Legislators and their followers came to the capital in January when the school was least able to create a favorable impression. College Hall was closed. There were neither classes nor students and scarcely a professor because the latter were studying at some other institution, visiting relatives, or buying livestock and laboratory equipment. The dormitory was vacant save for the steward and his family. Little wonder that legislators found it difficult to remember that the college was more than a farm."[1]

Student Memories

Continuing threats and a developing sense of security marked the second decade of the college. S.M. Milland, a member of the class of 1864 and a lawyer in 1898, described for his fellow alums his memories of the difficult circumstances that characterized the early period on the campus.

Crude Beginnings

"Crude were our beginnings; rough and unkempt was the raw material from which to construct the temple of learning."

Civil War, Diphtheria

"Dark days were they in the '60s when Class No. 2 enlisted in a body and went into the army. Dark days were they

when for weeks all classes were in doubt whether the powers that were would wreck the college in the interest of other institutions of learning. Dark days were they when the epidemic of diphtheria spread through and thinned our ranks within a few days and absolutely closing the doors of the college."

(continued on page 42)

Many Needs Unmet

Highest Student Enrollment

"The past year has been, in many respects, a pleasant and successful one in the history of the college. The number of students has been greater than during any previous year, there being 108 on the roll.

"Not all these have been in attendance at once, for the dormitories, when crowded to their utmost capacity, will accommodate but 82 students. When a student has for any cause been obliged to leave the institution, others have stood ready to take his place.... More than thirty applicants have been denied admission...."

Dorm Rooms Overcrowded

"Of the twenty-one rooms for the use of students, nineteen have been occupied by four students each.... The necessity that four students should occupy a room has been an evil to the college since its first opening."

More and Better Dorms are Prime Need

"The greatest need of the college at present is ... enlarged arrangements for boarding. If the college had accommodations for one hundred fifty students, it could have that number in attendance the coming year, and the number of applications will soon be much greater than that."[2]

Crowding Requires Drastic Action

"Because of the overcrowding of dormitory rooms, the president, with the advice of the State Board of Agriculture, decided to discontinue the practice of a preparatory class, a practice established in the late 1850s.

"The college gave notice to this effect through public papers before opening the term. Experiences have shown the injudiciousness of crowding the room with students to the degree that had previously been done. It was resolved to change the course in this respect."[3]

Capital Funds Difficult to Obtain

"How long this obstacle [lack of funds for new facilities] for the Institution will be allowed to exist, we cannot tell. The college is making every practical exertion, with the means at its disposal, to provide accommodations that are evidently required."

No Aid for Capital Improvements

"But the appropriations lately made by the legislature, have been sufficient only to defray current expenses, leaving no funds for [new] buildings or for other improvements, except what may have been derived from the sale of swamp lands. Although something has been realized from this source, it has chiefly been applied to relieving the more pressing wants of the institution, in regard to the shelter of livestock, providing a greenhouse, the repairs of buildings, &c."[4]

Courtesy UAHC

New Lab Is Essential

Abundant Light and Ventilation Required

"The need of a new laboratory must be apparent to any one who considers the necessity of abundant light and free ventilation in a laboratory devoted especially to chemical analysis. Chemical analysis often depends entirely on good light, as the evidence of the presence or absence of a given substance is found often in delicate shades of color, or in the existence of precipitates, which can be seen only in a good light. The present laboratory, 27 x 50, is lighted by two windows, and the tables are so arranged as to intercept a large part of the light."

Makeshift Adjustments Fall Short

"Some improvements have been [made] ... thus securing a third window, but even now the supply of light is entirely inadequate in the best weather, and on cloudy and stormy days the students must frequently suspend their analysis.

"There are no means of securing sky light or vertical light, which is very important. The facilities for ventilation are equally unsatisfactory."[5]

Public Sentiment Divided

Courtesy UAHC

Public Attitude Equivocal

Misrepresentations Remain

Grads Find Ag Careers?

"I do not see why the Agricultural College may not well be proud of its graduates ... all of them are esteemed and upright, honorable, industrious intelligent citizens.

"The graduates of 1870 consisted of 12 gentlemen from nine different counties.... The whole number of graduates is 56.

"Of the forty-one living graduates of the classes previous to the ones just graduated, sixteen ... are farmers. Five others are superintendents of gardens and orchards in state institutions, thus showing more than one half are farmers or horticulturists."

An Error Once Stated...

"Yet the statement is not infrequent in the papers that our graduates do not go upon farms. An error once stated keeps it place in the public prejudice. The very last report of the Department of Agriculture contains the statement, that not one in four goes to farming.

"A later Shiawassee paper says the same, and assigns a reason that educated persons will not do manual labor....

"One Washtenaw paper, in stating that two out of the 43 to graduate from the University in 1869 intended becoming farmers, adds, 'A better showing than the Agricultural College can make.'"[6]

As president of the MSAS, W.C. Beckwith, in January 1867, expressed his confidence in the future of the college. But he was aware of the equivocal feelings the public expressed about the college. Excerpts from his remarks follow.

Generating Interest?

"We have a State Agricultural College, an institution for the success of which our entire population should feel a deep and abiding interest. But whether the facts in the case would warrant my saying that such an interest is really felt, I leave to the practical men of Michigan to determine.

"As for myself, I do not hesitate to say that much may be done to stimulate that institution, to bring the college up to the point where the masses will regard it, and speak of it with pride, rather than in that equivocal manner when reference is made to it."

High Goals Sought

"They should be convinced that it is an institution for the thorough education of our young men, in all the branches of practical agriculture. We should be able to look up to its graduates as men well qualified to manage our farms ... acknowledged at once as scientific and practical, which shall be adapted to our various soils, climate, local circumstances and surroundings."

Discussion Needed

"As a means to secure this end, I would suggest that you recommend ... that a committee be appointed by [the legislature] to meet a like committee appointed by you; that the committees thus formed, meet with a

committee of the board having control of the college, for the purpose of conferring together upon subjects connected with the management and prosperity of the institution."

College Constraints

"Those having charge of the college have succeeded as well as could be expected of them.... They doubtless labor under many embarrassments which proper legislation might remove. As the MSAS is designed to foster our agricultural and mechanical interests, it is reasonable to suppose that those controlling its efforts should look to the college as a powerful auxiliary, whose interests are identical, whose success or failure depends upon public favor."[7]

The Population of Michigan Continues to Grow		
1870		
	Number	Percent change, 1860-1870
Ingham County	25,268	69.0
Michigan	1,184,059	67.3
USA	38,558,371	81.5

New Board Provides Leadership

College Property Tax?

In his 1870 report, the secretary ... mentioned a new way to fund the college. "The ... College has an excellent reputation throughout the nation, with those who interest themselves in scientific and agricultural education.... If sustained, it should be made to do honor to the state."

Half of One-tenth Mill

"I know the smallness of a tax is no proof that the tax can be afforded, yet it is nevertheless true that if the institution is doing good, and succeeding in the work of educating farmers, a work which many say is impossible to be done, then the state can afford it all it asks, which amounts to one-half of a tenth of a mill on a dollar, for each of the two years 1871 and 1872, taking Governor Baldwin's estimate of the aggregate assessed valuation ... of the state. The tax is $1 on $1,000 [of property value]."

Maintain Ranking

"Shall [the college] not be permitted to keep its present high rank ... and be enabled to improve from year to year?"[8]

Cooperation Grows

"The committee to whom was referred that part of the president's address relating to the State Agricultural College, and the subject of the agricultural museum, in connection with the State Normal School, at Ypsilanti, would respectfully report."

Location Issue Settled

"... they heartily endorse the remarks and suggestions of the president in relation to the Agricultural College. Whatever differences of opinion may have existed with regard to the location of the institution, there has been no question as to its importance and usefulness, and the duty of this society, as representing the agricultural interests of the state, to render it all the encouragement and assistance in its power, to meet the wants, the wishes and the reasonable expectations of the agriculturalists of the state.

"... No good would result from any further discussion as to the propriety or impropriety of its location, as many of the objections heretofore urged are gradually losing somewhat of their force by reason of the rapid growth and development of that section of the state and the opening of new lines of railroad connection, and we may regard the question of location as settled.

"Your committee, therefore, believe[s] it the duty of this society to unite most cordially and heartily with the State Board of Agriculture in endeavoring to dispel popular prejudice — to arouse popular interest, and in winning to it support from all the agriculturalists of the state.

"Your committee [has] been gratified to notice the position taken by the executive of the state in relation to the Agricultural College, and other institutions of learning, and also the cordial sympathy that exists between the president of the Michigan University and all these institutions, and they are satisfied that if these subjects can be properly presented to the legislature, that there will be on their part no lack of sympathy and support, and the adoption of the following resolutions, embracing the substance of the foregoing recommendations, is commended to your consideration."[9]

Ag Board Sets New Tone

"*Resolved:* That the Agricultural College ... is now giving substantial evidence of its progress ... what was contemplated in its original creation under ... our constitution, and that we regard it as one of the instrumentalities that is placing the science of practical agriculture in the same honorable position that our University is conferring upon law and medicine, and our Normal School on teaching."

"*Resolved:* That we again recommend to the authorities of the college a course of lectures on agricultural and kindred subjects during the winter months, satisfied, as we are that they would be largely attended by a class of farmers' sons who are partially released from ... the farm at that season."

Governor Thanked: Higher Ed Unified

"*Resolved:* That the special thanks of the Society and of the producing classes of the State are due to Gov. Crapo for his able presentation of the agricultural and manufacturing interests of Michigan in his message to the Legislature...."

"Resolved: That we commend the generous sympathy manifested by President Haven, of the Michigan University, in his address delivered before the members of the legislature, commending their fostering care and patronage, to the Agricultural College and State Normal School, as well as the University of Michigan and kindred institutions, all necessary and desirable, with no rival interests, but all essential agents in promoting the great educational interests of the state."[10]

External Factors Improving

Attacks Subside

A New Relationship

Peace and friendship followed. In June 1871, the university conferred an L.L.D. upon President Abbot.

The following November, President James B. Angell delivered the commencement address at the college.

"You have enjoyed the facilities for the study of scientific agriculture," he told the class of 12, "superior to those offered by any other similar institution in the land, for I can safely say that the Agricultural College stands unrivaled. This lays upon you a heavy responsibility."

Detroit Tribune Chastises Critics

"Relations between the College and the University continued harmoniously throughout Abbot's presidency and beyond, but it did not follow that legislative sessions were uniformly uncritical. Much of the friction between the two schools had been generated by men who were critical of one or the other or both.

"Such men were not silenced when the merger failed. In the 1871 legislative session they repeated the old arguments until the *Detroit Tribune's* correspondent refused to report them, referring readers to his articles of 1867 and 1869. 'Certain sections of the State,' he explained, 'send men up here, who feel that to maintain their standing at home they must do all they can to cripple this institution.'"

Some Farmers Critical

"The college had also encountered 'the steadfast hostility of a certain class of farmers, namely, those who do not believe in scientific farming.... The skepticism of these gentlemen in regard to all modern implements in agriculture is invincible.' By meager appropriations, he suggested, they retarded the growth of the institution so they could return each biennium to criticize the lack of progress."[11]

M.A.C. Moves into Favor

Supportive Editorial

"While *The Detroit Free Press* and *Post* and the *Adrian Times*, had been bitterly hostile, it was pleasing to find this editorial in the *Detroit Tribune* in 1874 ... 'The Michigan Agricultural College has steadily worked its way into general favor.'"

Wise Management

"The careful and judicious management of the State Board of Agriculture, the excellent, practical qualifications of the members of the faculty for their duties, all together have given the college a worthy name and record the world over.

"We are happy in knowing that in our Agricultural College there are no *stand stills.*"[12]

Editor's New Perspective

Visitor Views Work and Study

After visiting the campus, the *Genesee Farmer* editor wrote: "During the morning the students attend to their various studies. President Abbot took me into the rooms where they were reading, and a finer set of young men I never saw together.... In the afternoon they work for three hours on the farm, in the garden, or tool-house.

"Some were cultivating corn; others pulling out stumps with a machine; others were helping the sheep-shearers, tying up the fleeces, weighing those of different breeds and grades, and entering the weights in a book, with appropriate remarks in regard to the length of the staple, fineness, &c.

"One was pushing a hand-cultivator through the best crop of onions I ever saw growing ... others were in the hay-field, where a new mower and hay-tender were about to be started."

Farm Skills in the Making

"You need not tell me that a young man will not learn much at such an institution. Leaving science out, what he sees of good cultivation, will go far towards making him a good farmer.

"Success to the Agricultural Colleges, and may one day soon come when trained minds and skilled hands shall banish drudgery from American farms.... I believe in work, but I want work to tell."[13]

Artist's rendering of college buildings (L-R) Saints' Rest, Williams Hall, College Hall.

New Era Dawns

Factors Favoring M.A.C.

An Enduring College

Even though threats remained, conditions were gradually generating an enduring college. Numerous factors came into play during the later 1860s.

Visitors Increase

"Visitors came in greater numbers and they found the farm, under Manly Miles, both more efficient and more scientific than during the early years of the college. Graduates ... were beginning to assume leadership in rural communities.

"More important than the support provided by ... friends was the growing suspicion aroused by the partisan source of opposition arguments. Because petitions for removal came chiefly from southeast Michigan, men from the north and west began to fear that this campaign might be followed by one to relocate the capital from Lansing to Detroit."

University to Teach Practical Farming?

"Finally, university officers sided with the college when they began to realize that the addition of an agricultural department supported by the Morrill income, would subject them to pressure from a group of rural leaders who were at the moment attempting to oust Abbot and Miles and replace them with practical farmers."

New Residence Hall is Breakthrough!

Perhaps the most important event, symbolically, was the legislature's decision to appropriate funds for a new residence hall. "In March, 1869, the opposition crumbled and the legislature approved not only the annual appropriation and $30,000 for a new dormitory.

"The new hall, later named for President Williams, was a four-story structure, surmounted by a mansard roof and tower that rose one hundred feet above the grade. Not only did it promise room for students previously denied admission, it also symbolized the independence of the college. 'Thus ends, trust forever, a ten years' fight,' wrote the editor of the *Lansing Republican*. 'This is the fifth battle for the college that we have had a hand in, and though ready to enlist for life, the paper rejoiced in victory.'"[14]

Grange Forms New Support

The Michigan Grange

The Burnside Grange, formed in 1872 in Lapeer County, was the first local Grange in Michigan. Soon thereafter some 20 additional local chapters organized. The Michigan State Grange organized in April 1873. Together they built strong relations with the college, both providing support and defining local service requests.

The National Grange

Preceding the formation of the state and local Granges was the organization of the National Grange or, more precisely, The Order of Patrons of Husbandry. It organized on December 4, 1867. The organizational meeting occurred in Washington, D.C., where the superintendent of propagating gardens in the Department of Agriculture had his office. There, seven men planned and organized what has become the Grange.

Improve Lives of Farm Families

The organization was formed after the American Civil War to unite private citizens in improving the economic and social position of the nation's farm population. The National Grange was one of the first formal groups to admit women to membership on an equal basis with men.

The Grange is an agriculturalist organization with grassroots units in some 3,600 communities in 37 states.[15]

Newspapers Endorse Practical Education

The *Free Press* editor wrote: "On the subject of education the [governor's inaugural] message exhibits a commendable desire on the part of the governor to foster our educational institutions, and to increase their usefulness. We trust that his recommendations for adding to the facilities now possessed by the University and the Agricultural College for giving practical technical instruction will be favorably received. We have long been of the impression that very much more might be done in this regard than is now done, especially at the Agricultural College."

The *Detroit Tribune*, reported: "The message warmly urges a liberal policy towards our state institutions, and we heartily endorse its strong and emphatic utterances. Michigan's educational, reformatory, and eleemosynary [charitable] institutions are the jewels that combine to crown her with a rare diadem, and they cannot be guarded or cherished too carefully.

"We do not favor extravagance in this matter, but in all outlays in this direction generosity is an attribute of true economy. Mr. Bagley's recommendations of the addition of a School of Technology to the Agricultural College strikes us favorably, and its feasibility deserves careful investigation."[16]

Sun Shining on M.A.C.

New Williams Hall

Significant Structure

The new residence hall, completed in 1870, was a key addition to the campus facilities. It enabled the college to accept more of the many applicants.

The L-shaped frontage of the structure was 101 feet; the other wing was 109 feet.... The four-story structure with its 100-foot tower was steam heated and outfitted with water service.

Facilities Permit Growth

"Anticipating further growth and the need perhaps, for a new building for ladies and gentlemen, the dining hall, kitchen, washing and ironing rooms, &c. have been large enough for perhaps double the number of students that can now be received.

"The cost of the structure ... was $43,075. The college financed the structure from a legislative appropriation of $30,000 and $7,000 from the sale of swamp lands, thus leaving the institution with a debt of about $6,000."[17]

Courtesy UAHC

More Campus Improvements

Big Marsh Drained

The college was able to devote some funds to draining the "Big Marsh." Great improvements in the grounds were the result.

Sale Funds Greenhouse

The college was also able to sell some lots and generate resources to build a long-wanted greenhouse and stock it with plants, to erect a barn for the Horticultural Department, and to make various improvements in the cattle and horse barns.

New Road, Pasture Fencing

The college also built a new road through a portion of the farm and installed fencing to enclose land for pasture.[18]

A Spike in Enrollment		
	1869	**1871**
Seniors	11	12
Juniors	13	9
Sophomores	27	26
Freshmen	28	81*
Special Course		8
Ladies		4
Chem & Physio.		1
Total	**79**	**141**

*The unusual size of the freshman class was probably owing to the existence of a large preparatory class the previous year.

Report to the State Board of Agriculture, 1870-72

Courtesy UAHC

New Chemical Lab

The legislature of 1870-71 appropriated $10,000 for a new chemical laboratory.

Dr. Kedzie Plans Facility

"The very important and difficult work of drawing out plans for a building that would afford all the modern conveniences for manipulating in the various branches of chemical analysis pursued at the present day, and meet the requirements for lecture-room, study, private laboratory, and analytical rooms, devolved upon Dr. R.C. Kedzie, Professor of Chemistry.

"That all the plans were well drawn, thoroughly considered, and carefully followed in the execution of the work, it is attested by the fact that almost nothing remains to be desired; the possible exception being to have the rooms a little larger."

Possibilities Well Researched

Dr. Kedzie and President Abbot in the fall of 1869 "visited the principal laboratories in the United States and Canada, with a view to examining all the modern improvements connected with such institutions. The new laboratory is the result of these investigations. It combines the conveniences of all, with the addition of 'Bonn Self-Ventilating Evaporation Hoods,' and possesses the defects of none."[19]

Campus Improvements Underway

Legislature Appropriates More or Less Willingly

"While T.C. Abbot was president, expenses were kept small and estimates sent to the legislature were low.

"Note President Abbot's words concerning estimates for 1872: 'The estimates are submitted to the good sense of the legislature. They are put as low as it was known to make them. Certainly there was no thought of putting in a margin to be cut off.'

"The legislature has not cut down the appropriation for current expenses below what the Board of Agriculture has asked since 1863 when the reduction was $1,000."

Only Absolute Necessities Requested

"Nothing not absolutely necessary has been asked but put off to the time when the endowment fund [Morrill Endowment interest earnings] can be used for them.

"Year after year the demand for appropriations grew and the legislature responded more or less willingly."[20]

Courtesy UAHC

Seven Willows Bridge

"In 1874, two rustic bridges, so long a familiar sight at the college, were made of oak logs, peeled to make them more durable. One was a footbridge over the open ditch by the seven willows in the path from the professors' houses to the college buildings. The other was a wagon bridge, 16 feet wide, with five piers, over the brook and hollow just to the west of the chemical laboratory. These bridges were much admired by almost everybody."[21]

More Farm Buildings!

The year 1871 was a good year for campus improvements.

New Horse Barn

A 100- by 35-foot horse barn was begun and partly finished. The building would contain an office for the farm superintendent, a harness room, a tool room, stalls for horses, six box stalls, a shed for hitching teams, and a large loft for hay.

New Piggery

Under the supervision of Dr. Miles, the students put up a piggery. "The building is of wood, thirty-four feet by eighty, with a projecting room in front twelve by sixteen feet, for boiler, well, and scalding-tank.

"Passing through this projecting room we come into a feeding-alley eight feet wide, extending the whole length of the building. The pens are ten in number, twenty-six feet deep .... In the front of the troughs are doors, so arranged that food can be put into the troughs without interference on the part of the pigs."

Marsh Land Sale Generates Funds

The college, in 1871, spent $3,239.45 on these and other buildings. The funds came from the "sale of part of the large marsh, for which the sum of $3,730 was realized."[22]

Short Courses for Farmers — The Idea

A Germinal Idea

In 1867, the idea for one of the most important of all the developments of the college appeared — that of short courses for practical farmers. The development of the idea, though, did not come until years later. The suggestion came through the MSAS as a result of a meeting of committees of the society and the legislature. These committees adopted the following resolution.

"*Resolved:* That we are satisfied that the industrial interests of Michigan will be subserved and promoted by liberal appropriations on the part of the legislature for the support of the college, including items for a winter course of lectures."[23]

The Bubble—First Student Publication

Seven Issues Only

The first student publication, *The Bubble*, was published during the summer of 1868. It was short-lived, having been issued only seven times. In the words of Madison Kuhn, "... it consisted of a not too subtle mixture of humor, irony, and satire overlying its serious substance: observations on books, study, lectures, and the evils of tobacco."

Used to Poke Fun

"It took greatest joy in offering insults to neighboring communities. It praised the people of Okemos for preserving their town 'from the appearance of having been visited by the disturbing spirit of modern civilization' and described Lansing as a sparsely inhabited oak opening, surrounded by swamp, and 'noted for beautiful women, ugly men' and that 'oasis in the desert, the Female College.'"

Bubble Graduated

The Stoical Pen Yankers' Society published the periodical; the editor, Frank S. Burton, wrote under the pen name of Hezekiah Z. Solemnstyle. The publication ended when Burton graduated.[24]

Courtesy UAHC

The Bubble, Published and Burst in 1868

The header on the issue read "Issued on Saturday, June 16th; again on Saturday, July 18th, and at intervals of three weeks thereafter, until all seven numbers have been published.... Subscription price for the last numbers, 25 cents."

Coeds Admitted in 1870

Although the college did not establish a "women's course" until 1896, it did enroll 10 women in 1870. The college was among the American pioneers in coeducation.*

Dorm Space, Distance Limit the Numbers

The greatest impediment to coeducation was insufficient dormitory facilities. Of those admitted in 1870, four lived at home. The others lived in rooms in Williams Hall.

Enhanced Civility

"In the presence of those young ladies, student life became more civilized, although apparently not with the speed that President Abbot desired. His chapel talks in the spring of 1870, as noted in his diary, turned frequently to the qualities of a gentleman."

One morning he reminded the boys "to take off hats on going to class, or in parlor or in dining-room" and on another day, do not "throw water from windows."

Courses and Labor

In that first year the coeds enrolled in regular freshman courses — algebra, geometry, trigonometry, surveying, history, geology, and book-keeping — and omitted only the lectures in practical agriculture.

In their three hours of afternoon work, the women were assigned to the horticultural department, where they cut seed potatoes, set tomato plants, picked potato bugs, hoed, pruned shrubbery, gathered small fruit, and helped in the greenhouse.[25]

*The university in Ann Arbor also enrolled its first women students in 1870.

Campus Bell Calls Students to Duties

"I do not know when the bell first came to the college, but ... it has given tongue to the duties of the hour. Its home at first was under the shade of an old oak tree, south of the walk and about midway between College Hall and Williams Hall, resting on a crude frame about ten feet above the ground."

Dousing the Bell Boy

"The life of the bell has not been entirely uneventful. When it dwelt under the oak, on its frail shelf, somebody would occasionally turn the mouth of the bell upward, filling it with water and leaving it so insecurely braced that when the bell boy came at five o'clock in the morning to ring the rousing bell, 'he received a baptism from on high' that did not seem to improve his religious nature."

The Stolen Voice

"In 1862 somebody stole the clapper, and the voice of the bell was no longer heard. After a two-day hilarious hunt, a lucky student found the clapper. This was restored to its normal position, and 'all went merry as a marriage bell.' In 1863 the clapper was again stolen, found, and returned."

The Clapper is Secured

"Frank Gully and Robert Kedzie unscrewed the nut that fastened the clapper in the bell, swabbed the inside of the nut and thread of the bold with solution of salammoniac, screwed the nut firmly in place, where it would rust tight, riveted the bolt upon the nut, and the clapper has never left the bell since that time.

"A new one took its place. The old original cracked bell is hung in the belfry of the village school where it answers a very good purpose saying, 'Come to school and prepare for college.'"[26]

Organized Counties of Michigan, 1872.

Richard W. Welch

Moving Beyond Textbooks

Both Science and Teaching Primitive

"It was a primitive college, and the teaching of the sciences was primitive. We may smile now at the kind of instruction ... of that day but it must not be forgotten that science teaching was new in all colleges at the time.

"It was a pioneer in science teaching, and its primitive methods were due to the fact that nowhere were better methods known or practiced.

"It was emphatically the period of the textbook. Some of the professors gave lectures, but in every subject the student always had his textbook as the basis of his study...."

- **Geology:** "This was a textbook-only subject. There was no thought of the use of specimens or rocks or fossils by the class.... Yet there were in the museum ... many such specimens. The idea of their use by the students had not yet taken hold of teachers in American colleges."

- **Entomology:** "Even this was mainly a textbook study. We memorized so many pages and repeated them as nearly as possible verbatim. Here we looked at specimens brought to class [and made] some desultory collection of specimens.... Now and then a student was seen frantically pawing the air with a 'bug-net,' in his efforts to capture some beetle, bug, or butterfly."

- **Physics:** "In contrast, the presentation of physics was a wholly textbook study. We used Olmstead's Natural Philosophy reciting and demonstrating (on the blackboard) from its pages...."

- **Botany:** "My own science was then mainly confined to daily recitations from a textbook, accompanied later by dissections and analyses of plants in the classroom...."

- **Chemistry:** "We had one lecture or recitation a day ... in addition to daily laboratory work. In the lecture, the professor accompanied his presentation ... by demonstration experiments, greatly to our edification...."

- **Surveying:** "This was made a living subject for us by the addition to a stiff textbook, of a considerable amount of field-work, with compass, transit, and level, and accurate plotting of results."

- **Zoology:** "We used a textbook, but its use was small indeed. Professor Miles loved to talk to us, and he led us in his talks far deeper into the subject than did any textbook...."

Women Students!

The following provides insight into the status of women suffrage in the 1870 era. "The long uphill battle for women suffrage in Michigan had been in progress long before ... with little success.

"The state's first Equal Suffrage Association was organized in 1870, and four years later a suffrage amendment to the existing constitution was decisively defeated at the polls —135,957 to 40,077. This discouraged members of the group and they disbanded.

"New hope was gained, however, in 1881 when the legislature extended school suffrage to women ... three years later a new association for equal suffrage was founded...."[27]

Old Memories and New Visions

A Student's Recollections

Few Trips to Lansing

"The most convenient method to get to Lansing was to walk, hence the students did not visit the city very often. There was no reason we should go, as nearly all our needs were supplied by the steward or some department of the college."

Social Duties Limited

"Our social duties were neither extensive nor expensive, consisting of an occasional reception by some of the faculty or possibly once a year to visit the female seminary in North Lansing, then called 'Lower Town.' There was but one dancing party on the grounds during my college course, and not another until many years later. During the latter part of my time President and Mrs. Abbot held receptions on Saturday nights, which the students much appreciated."

Getting the Mail

"It was the duty of one student to walk to Lansing each afternoon and carry all the mail going to and from the college. For nearly half my course this position was filled by a one-armed veteran of the civil war."

"We had both class and college debating societies that flourished more or less."

Farm Labor

"The labor system was a very important part of the institution. We worked regularly three hours each week-day. All the early spring was devoted to cutting wood used on the grounds, where buildings and rooms were heated by wood stoves. During the growing season about all of the work on the farm and garden, except teaming, was done by students."

The Winter Break

"In the winter vacations a large number of the students taught district school, to earn money to help on college expenses, and often at the same time, acted as solicitors for more students from among their pupils."

Manly Miles' Methods

"Until 1865, though the College was designed to teach agriculture, there was no professor of agriculture; the principles had not been formulated so that they could be taught. But, in 1865, Dr. Manly Miles ... professor of zoology since 1861 became Professor of Practical Agriculture and Superintendent of the Farm. He was the first man in this country to attempt such teaching or to outline such a course in an agricultural college."[28]

Courtesy UAHC

Recipients of bachelor of science degrees, November 11, 1874.

New Governor Defines the Mission

John J. Bagley, governor of Michigan, 1873-1876.

In his inaugural speech in January 1873, newly elected Governor, John J. Bagley articulated the mission of the college.

"The Agricultural College, in its sphere, and with a much smaller number of students [than the State University with 1,200], is a co-worker with the University, and has a proportionate demand upon your considerate attention. Its trustees and faculty are laboring with earnestness and zeal to increase its usefulness, and enlarge its power for good.

"By its system of labor and study combined, it offers to all, without expense, a liberal, practical collegiate education. The attendance is not so large as its merits ... deserve."

Practical Technical Program Needed

"There is an education that our schools, university, or agricultural colleges do not yet offer, which we need and should have; and that is a practical technical education, that will fit men and women to grapple with life as they find it — earnest, laborious, and real."

Learned Professions are Essential to State

"No state in the Union needs, more than ours, educated farmers, mechanics, manufacturers, architects, engineers, chemists, etc. Our forests and fields, our mines and railroads, our manufacturing and agricultural interests, all require the services of educated skill ... and offer to all as remunerative employment, honorable career, and ultimate success, as ... the 'learned professions.'

"Might not the Agricultural College, ... be enabled to furnish this much needed education, combining the study of agriculture with that of mechanics, engineering and manufacturing, chemistry and mining, architecture and designing, and eventually give to the state a band of practical, scientific workers, fitted and ready to take hold the world's work...."[29]

Ag Practices Under Study

The *Lansing Republican* reported the address of George A. Farr, class of '70. Excerpts follow.

What a Man Can Do

"The Alumni have come together, after three years that were fuller, richer, and riper in interest than any the world has known. They met ... to sorrow for the loss of one whom the wing of the death-angel had touched; to rejoice for the blessings of the past, the comforts of the present, and the hopes of the future.

"This is a practical age that cares not for what a man knows of Virgil or Homer, but an age that asks '*what a man can do.*'

"There is a cry against the college because its graduates do not appear as a solid phalanx of farmers. This is unjust and unreasonable."

Farmer's Duties

"The present is a time for the wise counsel; grave duties devolve upon the educated farmer. His is the work of educating the popular mind to the principle of equal rights. His duty is to purify and regenerate the condition of the masses, and to preserve inviolate the right of every class of humanity.

"If the Alumni are faithful to their duty, they shall prove the institution a power and blessing to the world."[30]

Testing Crops, Farm Practices, and Breeds

"Professor Manly Miles carried out several experiments during the year. One involved Indian corn first to ascertain the relative advantages of hills and drills and second to determine variation in the natural productiveness of soil, without manure. He is in the process of experimentation to show the relative value of different breeds."

Soil Experiments

"Professor Kedzie has been conducting experiments in reference to the value of muck, variously combined with unleached and leached wood ashes, with lime, and with salt in reference to the volatile constituents of animal excrements, to show under what circumstances ammonia may be saved or lost, as manure."

Potato Variety Tests

"In the Horticultural Department, Professor Prentiss was testing the earliness, productiveness, and other qualities of thirty-six varieties of potatoes. His exhibitions at the MSAS in Detroit and at the Central Michigan Society at Lansing attracted much attention."

Instruction is Key

The superintendent of the farm remarked, "In its management, its use as a means of instruction has been kept prominently in view. Although the strictest economy has been practiced ... the direct pecuniary profit to be derived from the system pursued, has been a matter of secondary consideration.

"The leading object of the farm being thus incompatible with the idea of direct pecuniary results, they should not be regarded as the exclusive standard by which the success of its management is to be measured."[31]

Students in horticulture gardens.

Courtesy UAHC

Advances in Horticulture

Improvements Forge Ahead

"In the Horticulture Department, a fair degree of success has attended most operations. Though the dry weather reduced the quantity of produce, it was favorable to the employment of labor....

"In the vegetable garden the benefits of a plan by which horse labor has been substituted for manual labor, have been strikingly advantageous...."

Fruit, Shelter Trees

"The trees in the pear orchard have ... made a good growth, and a few of them fruited. The apple orchard is in good condition; the trees are most handsome and thrifty, though growing too fast to bear much fruit.

"A nursery of evergreen trees has been started — the trees ... to shelter a portion of the grounds from cold winds, to which they are much exposed."

Small Fruits and Vegetables Abundant

"Most of the smaller fruits, and vegetables of all kinds ... have been produced in abundance; [and] the floral and ornamental grounds ... have presented an attractive appearance.

"For the year 1867, expenditures for the Horticultural Department totaled $1,517.12; receipts, $1,067.12."[32]

41

Decade Firms College Foundation

Land Improvements

Stumps Being Cleared

"In the improvement of the farm, considerable advance has been made. The powerful stump machine belonging to the college has been much used.

"Several large fields are now cleared from stumps, given free course to the plough, and permitting the ground to be brought into a condition, not only more agreeable to the sight, but also better adapted to the production of crops, and much better fitted for the use of labor saving implements screening them."

Fields Drained, Seeded

"A portion of the ground thus prepared, was sown to wheat the past autumn. Under-draining has been extended, including a deep drain required to take the water from the ground near the cat-tle barn and the cellar of the farm house, and several drains in other places.

"New lines of fences have been built, the lane which was intended to divide the cleared portion of the farm into east and west divisions, has been extended, so that with little additional labor, it will lead from the highway on the north line of the farm, to the woods on the south."

Gated Entrance

"A self-acting gate has been set up at what is hereafter to be the entrance to the college grounds from the highway, and from that point a board fence has been substituted for the former rail fence along the road, and will be extended to the north-east corner of the farm as soon as the state of the ground will admit of it, the coming season."[33]

Courtesy UAHC

Professor Manly Miles

Miles Rallies U.S., Canadian Colleagues

A circular entitled "TO THE FRIENDS OF AGRICULTURAL EDUCATION" was mailed to agricultural, mechanical, and industrial colleges in the U.S. and Canada inviting people interested in agricultural experiments to come to the Prairie Farmer Building in Chicago in August 1871 to attend a conference and form a national association.

Dr. Manly Miles, along with a colleague from Illinois Industrial College, played a key role in planning and organizing the convention. Sixteen colleges participated – from Massachusetts to Missouri and from Wisconsin to Mississippi. Miles was chosen first vice-president of the Agricultural Experiments Association.[35]

Period in Review

Second Decade — A Settling Time

Purposes Clarified

Conditions at the college were still basic as the second decade closed. Yet, this decade can be considered to be a settling period. The decade began with a farmer interest group that had a different view of what "their" college should be — a place to *train* their young men and return all of them to a career in farming. Others saw the college and especially its farm as a *demonstration farm* — a place to visit to learn the best techniques in raising crops and caring for animals.

College Survives Challenges, Threats

Many of the part-time, politically sensitive legislators were confused by these demands and the way the college was responding to them. Moreover, journalists and interest groups pressured legislators as they proposed transferring the Morrill land-grant proceeds to the state university in Ann Arbor and to have that institution teach agriculture. That pattern, after all, was one that several other states had followed.

College and Board Persevered

Despite these challenges and threats, the college and the Board of Agriculture persevered. Perhaps the turning point was the legislative decision to fund a new dormitory hall that enabled the college to enroll and house more students. These actions, the development of new relations between the college and the university, and the support of numerous groups led to the settlement of the debate over whether the college would become a permanent element in the state's educational framework.

Student Memories (continued from page 30)

Few Now Understand

"We have many times wondered how our gallant band of determined men in classes two and three stood by the college, and fought out the days and years of trials and tribulations. Few men ... understand the heroism of our pioneer students. And we are glad it is so."

No College Yell

"We never had a 'college yell' but of memory, pleasant thoughts and sweet recollections of the men we knew as classmates, and whom we learned to love."[34]

Courtesy UAHC

"...He told the young farmers that the education was given to them by the State, not for their own personal and selfish ends, but as a trust to be used for the good of the community in which one dwelt, and of the State at large."

Michigan Governor John J. Bagley, 1875

"I do not present the agricultural college as a piece of perfection. But I present it to you as growing. It has come out of the forest, out of a surrounding of stumps and swamps, and puts on in the summer ... a face of beauty."

President T.C. Abbot, 1875

The Acorn is Surviving...

Sparse Budgets, Setbacks, Pains, Gains

The third decade of the college (1875-1884) was a period of sparse budgets, some setbacks, growing pains, and significant gains. M.A.C. added to its initial base of agricultural research. The college gained increased national stature for its findings. It initiated an outreach program — the Farmers Institutes — that extended new knowledge to practitioners.

The college continued its commitment to involve all students in educational work experience. The college evidenced some growth in enrollment despite constrained legislative support, faculty departures, and faculty shortages.

Setting the Example

The accounts of the period offer evidence of M.A.C.'s development into an institution more beneficial for students and Michigan farmers. Although the college was trying to define its mission and its plan to achieve it, the college was of benefit to society at large. By its preparation of students, it was also a significant benefit to other land-grant institutions where M.A.C. graduates administered and taught.

Farmer Education in State and Out

The appointments of many M.A.C. graduates to presidencies and professorships around the nation were evidence of increased recognition of the college among the broader scientific, educational, and agricultural communities.

The accounts from the decade also show that the case for farmer education must continue to be made, and that legislative support remained an elusive goal.

Knowledge is Power

At the 1875 session of the Michigan Legislature, President Abbot delivered an address to the House of Representatives.[1] The speech was lengthy — an estimated 16,500 words. Excerpts provide insights into his view of the value of education for farmers.

"The world was for many ages coming up to this opinion of the ancient Roman historial, Sallust, until at last Lord Bacon supplied these later ages with its watchword in the short sentence, 'Knowledge is power.'"

Right to Knowledge

"Have the farmers, as a class, shared as largely as others in this course of improvement? Are they equally with others using mind in the operations of their calling, and so keeping abreast of the age in its advance? No class of men is of more importance to the state; no interest is so large as theirs."

Half of People Farming

"The statistics of Michigan for 1870 give the occupation of 379,764 persons, of whom 187,211, or almost one-half, are agriculturalists. The same proportion holds true of the country at large. On agriculture the wealth of nations must in the main depend, with all their commercial and manufacturing interests.

"...The business of a farmer is highly complicated as compared with that of a carpenter, a miller, a manufacturer.... When a farmer understands breeding and care of his cattle and the raising of his crops, there is other knowledge needful still. His business has wide relations to the affairs of other men. These he needs to understand. He should be acquainted with the laws of transportation, of trade, and of money."

Program for Women

"I am strongly in favor of adding a department for women, and can see no reason why such a one should not be useful and successful. Our limited experience has been in favor of the plan.... Could we accommodate the ladies who apply for admission? They might receive technological training in the application of chemistry to common household arts...."

Wide Range of Study

"Shall the course of study be purely professional? Such courses exist in any school. Take a medical course of study; its chemistry belongs to manufacturers as well as medicine; its anatomy and physiology are not part of medicine.... The wider range of study is in accordance with general desire and the law. The inaugural address of President Williams, the law organizing the college, the law of re-organization, the various addresses and reports of similar institutions in the country; all agree in recommending this wide range of study."

Morrill Act Objective

"The [Morrill Act] provides that the interest of the fund 'shall be inviolably appropriated to the endowment, support, and maintenance of at least one college, where the leading object shall be without excluding other scientific and classical studies, and including military tactics, to teach such branches of learning as are related to agriculture and the mechanic arts ... in order to promote the liberal and practical education of the industrial classes in the several pursuits and professions of life.'"[2]

Courtesy Michigan State Archives

President Abbot delivered his speech in the first Capitol in Lansing, constructed in 1847.

...But Thriving Remains Evasive

College Responds to Industrial Change

Programs in Mechanic Arts

Michigan's College of Agriculture was not alone in its pursuit of courses and programs in the mechanic arts. As Lowell Eklund noted in his dissertation on the influence of the Morrill Act and land-grant colleges, "The beginning years of the Land-Grant Colleges paralleled the start of the so-called Industrial Revolution."

Industry Coming Into Its Own

"With an unlimited supply of raw materials, the extension of more rapid transportation, and the increase in market possibilities, industry came into its own. The total value of manufactured products in 1869 was approximately $1.9 billion. By 1884 it had risen to $9.5 billion. Products manufactured from iron and steel were valued at $36.5 million in 1860 and $479 million in 1890. The period witnessed a tremendous development in production...."

College-level Mechanic Arts Demanded

"There was no doubt that some form of 'mechanic arts' at the college level was needed and even demanded. Its teaching would be less sensational than that of agriculture, chiefly because other institutions had pioneered in the field. There was no suspicion of engineering 'book-learning' as there was of 'book-farming.'"

Industry Needed Now!

The changing environment was noted by Andrew D. White, the first president of Cornell University, during the 1870s: "What is the want of our great Western States at this moment? Greater agricultural production? No. What they want is the development of great and varied industries, so near them that it shall no longer take two-thirds of a bushel of corn to carry the other third from producer to customer."[3]

Growing Interest in Applied Engineering

The growing interest in engineering was reflected in R.C. Carpenter's annual report to the president and the Board of Agriculture. He stated, "The course in the text book was supplemented by lectures on the strength of materials, principles of framing, strength of frame, strength of bridge, and the principles of road-making."[4]

Bagley Challenges Grads

Education is Trust

On November 10, 1875, the college conferred degrees on 15 students. *The Flint Globe* reported,

"Perhaps the most notable feature of the occasion was the address of Governor John J. Bagley, in which he told the young farmers that their education was given them by the state, not for their own personal and selfish ends, but as a trust to be used for the good of the community in which each one dwelt, and of the state at large.

"The added ability, capacity, usefulness, and manhood resulting to every young man going forth from college halls, is simply an investment made by the state — capital loaned — and it was due to the state ... that the interest should come back in the shape of better manhood, better private life, and better public service."

Educating Youth Pays

"In speaking to the audience, he said that 'we, as a people, have got beyond grumbling over taxation for educational purposes. We have demonstrated that it pays to educate our children and our youths.'"[5]

Fire at "Saints' Rest"

It was December 9, 1876. The term had ended. The "Saints' Rest" dormitory was undergoing repair at the hands of carpenters and masons. That evening the building was aflame. The Lansing hook and ladder company hastened to help the college. The firefighting through half the bitterly cold night was to little avail. The building was destroyed. The Lansing firefighters received no compensation, although the college paid their necessary expenses. Admission of new freshmen was postponed from February to September.[6]

Courtesy UAHC

Red Cedar River

The College Reaches Out With Farmer Institutes

Faculty Supports Institute Proposal

In response to numerous requests to extend information to Michigan farmers, the faculty adopted, on May 7, 1875, two resolutions presented by Professor R.C. Kedzie.

Develop Institutes Plan

"*Resolved,* That a committee of three be appointed by the President to draw up a scheme for a series of Farmers' Institutes to be held in different parts of the state during the next winter; including in the exercises of such Institutes lectures and essays by members of the Faculty; that the several members of the State Board of Agriculture and leading farmers residing in the vicinity of the place of holding Institutes, be respectfully and earnestly requested to participate in the exercises by lectures, essays, and discussions."

Discuss Plan and Execute

"*Resolved,* That said committee be instructed to confer with the board, at its next meeting, to make all necessary arrangements for inaugurating and carrying out such series of Farmers' Institute."

Committee Acts

President Abbot appointed professors Kedzie, Beal, and Carpenter to the committee. On June 1, 1875, the committee forwarded a letter to the Board of Agriculture requesting its endorsement of the proposed institutes.

Board Lends Support

The board responded by appointing its own committee, and at its August meeting the board received statements from the Armada Agricultural Society and the Rochester Grange indicating their willingness to host institutes.

In September, several newspapers published information about the organization and format of the institutes.

Communities are Eager Hosts

More than 16 communities applied to host institutes, but the committee had decided earlier that it should limit the number to six and chose the following: Armada (Macomb County), Rochester (Oakland), Allegan (Allegan), Decatur (Van Buren), Adrian (Lenawee) and Coldwater (Branch).[7]

Editor's Note: On September 21, 1875, the *Lansing Republican* reported on the Farmers' Institutes for 1876. The following is an abbreviated version of the newspaper article.

Want to Know More About Institutes?

INTRODUCTION

At a meeting of the State Board of Agriculture held last June, the board determined to hold a series of Farmers' Institutes during January 1876. These institutes are the first of a series to be held winter after winter if the interest of the agricultural public shall warrant.

LENGTH OF MEETINGS

The design is that the institute shall not ... wear out the patience and endurance of the community. Short, spicy, wide-awake meetings are desired.

WHEN TO BE HELD

They will begin with the week commencing January 10, and two institutes will be held each week.

WHERE WILL THEY BE HELD

Application has been made for one institute by the Armada Farmers Club, and another by the Detroit and Bay City District Council of Patrons of Husbandry. These invitations have been accepted and the first institute will be held in Armada and the second at Rochester. Four more institutes are yet to be located.

TO WHOM TO APPLY

The committee having charge of these institutes consists of [three] members.... A local committee should be appointed at each place where an institute is to be held, to assist the committee of the board in perfecting the details of the meeting.

EXPENSES

The community where the institute is held will be expected to furnish the hall, and provide for warming and lighting the same. All other expenses will be paid by the board.

WHO IS INVITED

Everyone who tills the soil or is interested in agriculture. Farmers and their wives and families are especially invited; also all who honor or would benefit from the noblest of all industries.

ORDER OF BUSINESS

The order of business will be determined by each institute for itself.... The institute is to close with an evening meeting with an essay or lecture, and discussion. The meeting will be held so short that every farmer and his wife can afford to attend the whole meeting.

OBJECTIVES

• It is the design ... to meet and talk over ... matters of vital interest to the farmer.

• To be secured is to bring the farmers, the board, and the faculty of the college in closer relations to each other.

• To gather up and preserve in permanent form the results of agricultural experience and the view of leading farmers in different parts of the state.

• To give broader scope to the instruction of the college and to make it more fully than ever before the exponent of the most progressive and advanced agriculture of our state.[8]

College Research Praised

National Journal Exhorts College

Don't Abandon Research

In 1873, the budget difficulties gave the administration cause to consider complete discontinuance of the experimental program that the college was carrying on. The editor of the *American Agriculturalist*, however, exhorted the college "by all means" to continue its program to avoid a "serious loss to agriculture."

Experimentation Planned and Patient

"[The college] has made some most important experiments. They have been evidently planned with great thought and after patient investigation. They were made with a definite object [and] ... bear the marks of scrupulous accuracy.

"Nothing is covered up; nothing omitted ... not pen and ink experiments. No one doubts their entire trustworthiness. They are not common experiments, such as any of us can make, and ought to make on our own farms. They are scientific experiments."

M.A.C. Research

Quite objectively, he pointed out that when he was a professor at Cornell University, he had visited M.A.C. to examine "their methods of conducting experiments."

Until then, his experience with such programs had demonstrated that results were of "little interest or value ... and settled nothing. Unless a better system is adopted," he wrote, "they never will give us the information we so much need." But at the M.A.C. he found "a bright exception to this dark picture."[9]

Organized Counties of Michigan, 1876.

Richard W. Welch

Practical Research at the College

Cook's Bird Study

The college professors regularly conducted research and reported their findings in the *Annual Report to the State Board of Agriculture*. The publication had wide distribution throughout the state. The following report by A.J. Cook, entomology professor, may illustrate the research to which the editor of the *American Agriculturalist* was referring.

Bird Stomachs Examined

"I have made a thorough and persistent examination of these birds [robins and blackbirds], not by closely observing them, but by repeated examination of the contents of their stomachs, and have arrived at the following facts.

"First, these birds are excessive insect eaters throughout the entire summer. Second, it is very rare to find beneficial insects in their stomachs. Third, a principal part of their food consists of cutworms and white grubs.

"Hence, the advantage of fall plowing to destroy the cutworms, and the exceeding ravages of the white grub in those sections where fruit is a specialty, and where the birds are destroyed to save the fruit."[10]

Discovering Behaviors of the Codling Moth

Professors at the college did not have sophisticated equipment or methods to conduct their research. Yet, their observations and reports added substantially to the farmers' knowledge of pests encountered in their daily lives. Below is his report on the codling moth.

A.J. Cook

Codling Moth Findings

- The larvae seldom ever drop from the tree. This was determined by setting tubs partly filled with water under the apple trees.

- These larvae do not leave one fruit to complete their growth in another apple. This was maintained by putting affected apples in a box with sound ones, by examining affected apples and finding that the size of the opening and of the larvae always corresponded, and by repeated examination of wind falls.

- A confirmation of the previously asserted truth; fully one-half of the larvae never descend to the ground.

- Larvae rarely pupate after September 1st.

- The first brood of moths continue to come forth till about the 8th of July.

- Fine wire gauze placed in the windows of otherwise tight apple cellars will entrap very many moths that would otherwise escape and work mischief.

- Sweets will not attract the moths in the least. The last point I have tested fully. I have placed differently scented sweets all about the apple trees, and while I have caught hundreds of other moths, I never secured a single one of these [codling moths.]"[11]

President Abbot Critiques Lawmakers

How should a college president deal with a state legislature that regularly fails to address the needs of the college? President Abbot dealt patiently with legislatures. However, his following remarks exhibited his frustration while recognizing the state legislature's challenges of the past but concluding that funding, nevertheless, was inadequate.

Funding in Past Insufficient

"The institution has, no doubt, been costly, and the state [generous], and considering the unsettled questions of location and usefulness, very [generous]. But if you leave out these considerations, and the reluctance to invest largely in a novel experiment, the appropriations have not been so large as they should have been.

"The sum expended looks exceedingly large in the aggregate, as did the long years of ticking and swinging backward and forward to the discontented pendulum seen in one view."[12]

Growth Goes Unfunded

The enrollment was gradually increasing, but the legislature was doing little to fund additional faculty positions. When enrollments were smaller, many of the junior and senior classes were combined, but President Abbot reported that was no longer possible. Similar problems with the larger freshmen classes meant that these had to be divided into two sections....

"Before the growth of the college rendered it inadmissible, the professor of agriculture gave instruction in civil engineering or physiology, and the professor of horticulture in several branches outside of his especial field."[13]

Governor Supports Funding

In addressing the legislature in 1879, Governor Charles M. Croswell said:

"The Agricultural College grows in favor. It ... stands on a better footing than ever before. The whole number of students in attendance ... last year was 239, and the graduates, 33.

"The managers ask an appropriation for current expenses of $6,271.80 each for 1879 and 1880, and a special appropriation of $15,998.32 each year for buildings, improvements, and extraordinary expenses; a full statement of which will be found in their report. They further solicit an appropriation of $13,000 for the construction of a new hall, *with a view to the admission of females and the co-education of sexes at the college, the reasons for which will be found duly assigned.*"[14]

Faculty Salaries Cut

These unfunded needs, along with the failure to fund appropriation requests for faculty salaries, compelled the board to reduce salaries from $2,000 to $1,800 per year.

Women's Hall Unfunded

It also voted funds for "the Botanical Laboratory, the new dwelling, the gardener's rooms in the green-house, and the propagating pits which are on their way to completion." But as the board secretary said, "The bill for the erection of a hall for ladies failed to pass."[16]

Building Insurance Needed*

President Abbot said, "No insurance is kept upon the buildings or other property of the college." He noted that the board had requested such funds for 1876 and 1877, but the legislative committees cut them.

The legislature adopted a joint resolution stating money should not be expended for insurance. As it turned out, during the following year, fire destroyed the "Old Hall."[17]

Legislature Unpersuaded

As is evidenced in the board secretary's report, the governor's message was not entirely persuasive.

"A statement of estimates, far exceeding in its detail those of any other institution, was placed before the legislature, and printed in the journal of March 23, 1879. From these [requests] the legislature struck off that for the enlargement of the chemical laboratory, very much crippling the growth of that department, and making necessary the rejection of several applicants for admission to the college.

"They also struck off $1,000 for a house with a furnace, and a barn for the professor of agriculture, leaving $3,000 including $1,500 for improvements and $900 for various departments."[15]

Lesson Learned — Insurance Approved

Interestingly, the legislature did include in its appropriations an amount of $600 for insurance. Another lesson learned led to approval to purchase 12 Babcock fire extinguishers to defend against the next fire.[18]

* The college had requested funds for fire insurance, but the legislature removed the item. The burned building had a book value of $15,000, which would not have been adequate to fund a replacement. With the absence of insurance the legislature decided to fund the new structure — a three-story brick structure with accommodations for 130 students, more than twice that of "Saints' Rest."

College Marked by Changes

Academic Calendar Revamped

Three Terms

In 1875 the board approved a change in the academic college year. "Under the new schedule, the first term begins with the last Tuesday of February and continues for thirteen weeks. After a week-long recess the second term of twelve weeks begins, and the third term of twelve weeks begins after another week's vacation."

Fairchild Justifies Change

Professor Fairchild chaired a faculty committee that planned the change. In reporting to the board he stated, "The new plan better suits the time devoted to many of the studies; gives a natural division for settlements with students; puts Junior Exhibition with its interruption of the usual routine of duty at the close of the term; brings the first examination of the freshmen, which is a sifting of the idle and incompetent nearer the time of their entrance; gives students more frequent periods of absence for any duties away from college, and equalizes somewhat the burden of studies of different terms."[19]

Further Change Following Year

In his 1877 report, President Abbot stated that the schedule was to be changed again in 1878. At that time the new school year would begin in the autumn.

Faculty: Losses and Shortages

M.A.C. Alums Sought

M.A.C. professors continue to be attracted to other institutions. In its 1879 report, the board reported that Professor George T. Fairchild left to go to the Kansas Agricultural College to become its president. Fairchild graduated from M.A.C. and was at the institution for 15 years as professor of rhetoric and English literature librarian.

Professor Charles L. Ingersoll accepted an academic appointment to Purdue University. Ingersoll, too, was graduated from the college in 1874. According to the board, he was comparatively under-compensated by $400 to $500 per year.[20]

Too Few Professors

In one of his most aggressive appeals for additional state funding, President Abbot noted, that "In 1870 we had one instructor to each eighteen students, the junior and senior classes were small enough to be united for instruction in some branches, and the freshman and sophomore classes could each recite without division."

Classes too Large

"Now we have 30 students to each professor, the upper classes are too large to unite and the freshman and sophomore classes have to be heard in two sections in most of their studies."

Faculty Spread Thinly

"The professor of botany and horticulture has been burdened with practical duties, and the professor of agriculture had, besides the duties of his responsible department, to give instruction in various branches of study lying completely apart from agriculture."

Student-teacher Ratios Elsewhere

To put the college's student-teacher ratio in perspective Abbot noted that the agricultural colleges in Iowa, New York, Illinois, Massachusetts, Texas, and Kansas had ratios ranging from 10 to 14 students per professor.[21]

Student Dorm Governance Under Way

Managing the Residence Halls

"Perhaps it was in 1878, a report came that at Iowa Agricultural College there was in vogue a system of self-government among the students that was very successful. It was tried at M.A.C.; as numerous other devices have been tried from time to time. The prime object was to maintain order in the dormitories, and secure the general comfort of students."

District Officers

Usually 10 rooms were assigned to a "district," each to elect one captain and one lieutenant; all elections were to be subject to the approval of the college president.

"The duties of the officers of the students' government were to arrange all trials and act as judges. Captains and lieutenants were to make it their first duty to prevent any disturbance within their districts."

Plan too Complicated

"Rules were also made concerning testimony, verdicts, penalties, records, appeals, and pardons. The plan was too complicated and was soon modified, though, when well looked after, it was a partial success."[22]

Courtesy UAHC

Wells Hall replaces Saints' Rest.

Legislature's "Short Leash"

Comprehensive Reporting

The legislature, in 1881, adopted changes in the reports that state agencies, including educational institutions, were required to follow. For educational agencies, the reports were to include:

- "The condition of the educational interests of the institution.

- "The number and names of the various professors, tutors, and instructors.

- "The number of students or pupils in the several departments, and in the different classes.

- "The courses of study pursued, and the books of instruction used.

- "Such other information and suggestions as said Board may deem important, or the Superintendent of Public Instruction may request, to embody in his annual report."

Comprehensive Inventory

Other items included a "full and accurate inventory" including acres and value of land, number and type of buildings, types and value of personal property, as well as a "regular account of all moneys received and disbursed."[23]

Library Resources

President Highlights Problem

The president's 1880 report included the following remarks:

Linton Hall today; in 1882 it was the college library and museum.

"The Library of the college contains about 4,000 bound volumes, and 700 pamphlets. It is open to students two hours a day, and each one may have out one volume at a time. Two hundred students will have out two hundred books. Whenever reference is made to certain books by the professors in their lectures, the books will be removed from the library by the first to come for them, and their use lost to other students until perhaps the interest in the subject has given place in some other."

Appoint a Librarian

"As soon as the college can afford it, the good of the students requires that a librarian should be appointed who should keep the library open the whole day and evening."

Develop Index System

"There are, besides, many periodicals in the library and many books, whose use to a large extent is lost to both officers and students, for lack of an index of their contents.... All libraries of any note now index the contents of each magazine that is to be bound, and of each volume of miscellaneous matter as soon as it comes into the library. *It is almost as essential that books be indexed, as that they be possessed.*"

Legislature Recognizes Need

As it turned out the following year (1881), the legislature, on the recommendation of incoming Governor David H. Jerome, appropriated $25,000 for a new library and museum and $3,000 for library operations.[24]

Departments Approved, Denied

Veterinary Medicine

"A half term's lectures in veterinary hygiene will be given each year provided competent instruction can be secured for that time."

Vet Department Dream

"A veterinary department, which is often called for by those who desire to see the usefulness of the college increased, would involve a distinct course of study for from two to three years, a distinct faculty of from three to six professors, a veterinary hospital, a special museum, and ... residence[s] for one or more officers. If the state is ready to incur the expense of its establishment and maintenance, it is well."

Vet Science Benefits All

"But meanwhile the college, which already gives some of the instruction given in veterinary colleges ... might enlarge this instruction for all its students by lectures on veterinary hygiene [and by] giving such information as every farmer ought to know about the hygiene treatment of stock, the simpler operations of surgery, and uses of medicine. No attempt would be made to graduate veterinary surgeons, but only to give to farmers knowledge of practical value to them."[25]

History, Economy, Political Science

The board approved a new Department of History, Economy, and Political Science in 1881.

Board Eliminates It Two Years Later

The department was short-lived. Two years later President Abbot wrote, "I regret to say that the board has found it necessary to give up this professorship. I regret to say that the funds of the college did not seem to the board to warrant the retaining of the professorship. I certainly hope the time will soon come when this important field will be given a larger place...."[26]

College is National Model

As many of those interested in the development of the college have noticed, it had no model. Instead, as President Abbot noted, the college became a model for agricultural colleges.

Visitors Attracted to Study Model

Abbot observed that the first three presidents of Massachusetts Agricultural College visited the agricultural college grounds in Lansing. Ezra Cornell, founder of the New York college and its president, A.D. White, visited Lansing twice. Similarly, officials of Maryland, West Virginia, Indiana, Ohio, Arkansas, and Minnesota came to learn from the institution.

Scottish Visitor — "Oldest and Best"

And James McDonal, "who was sent out by the Edinburgh *Scotsman* to report on cattle raising in the United States, wrote a prize essay on the agricultural colleges of the country. He selects ours as the one to describe at length, as being one of the oldest and the best."

Michiganians — Recognize Success

"Since we in the state live so near the institution as to see whatever imperfections it has, it seems to me not unbecoming to suggest that it has a relative standing; and to show that in its success, the reputation of the people of Michigan for her educational institutions is not endangered, but is enlarged."

Fitting Resort for Information Seekers

"We should all be glad to see the college so supplied with competent instructors in all branches of agricultural science in the largest extent of the term ... as to make it the fitting resort of those who seek information on anything related to agriculture and kindred branches."[27]

The Population of Michigan Continues to Grow		
1880		
	Number	Percent change, 1870-1880
Ingham County	33,676	33.3
Michigan	1,636,937	38.3
USA	50,189,209	30.2

Beal: Knowledge Sharing Is Key

Visitors Seek His Wisdom

W.J. Beal, in his 1880 report, said that visitors to the campus "have appeared in large numbers, and during July and August many of them were teachers or professors in other institutions." His willingness to share his knowledge and time with numerous visitors was a key element in the building of relations across the state.

"I have a number of times spent three hours in one day showing visitors about the horticultural department, and then did not get all through it. At one time, the party included four professors of agriculture from other colleges. None of these spent less than four days at our college."

Multistate Cooperation Emerges

"During their visit, these professors expressed themselves very much interested in some experiments which I am making. Seeing the advantage in concert of action, five of us, in as many different states, agreed to begin and continue for at least two years, a specified experiment with Indian corn. Each agreed to furnish the others with his report for publication."

Sharing Knowledge Beyond Farmers

Beal went on to report the kinds of "community involvement" in which he had been engaged. They included lecturing and being a delegate at various Grange meetings, attending the state teachers association, attending a meeting of the American Pomological Association in Rochester, N.Y., and delivering a paper there, helping to start a county horticultural society in Ingham County, attending and reading a paper with Dr. Kedzie at a meeting of the American Association for the Advancement of Science, and other participation.[28]

Profs Help Form New Association

President Abbot's 1880 annual report noted, "It may not be out of the way to mention that a new society was formed in Boston the present year, by persons in attendance upon the sessions of the American Association for the Advancement of Science — a society for the advancement of agriculture. It is made up of a few earnest workers in agricultural chemistry and vegetable physiology."

Beal Chosen President

"Professors Kedzie, Beal, and Cook ... are among those who have organized it, and Dr. Beal was made its President. The society holds its next meeting in Cincinnati, August 17th, 1881. Persons become members only by invitation."[29]

Some years earlier, Dr. Miles played a key role in bringing those interested in agricultural, mechanical, and industrial education to Chicago for a convention. The event led to the forming of a new association of these interests.[30]

Walking tour on the campus.

Courtesy UAHC

Abbot's Guests Visit

In June 1879, President Abbot invited two key support groups to visit the campus. The MSAS committee and the Grange officers came to see firsthand what the college was doing and how it was serving Michigan's agricultural communities.

The following are excerpts from President Abbot's report on the visit. We leave to the reader's imagination the experience of walking through the various facilities of the campus.

Chemistry Lab

"The guests were invited to visit the laboratory where ... we were met at the lecture room of the laboratory by Dr. Kedzie. Here he had his own special analytical work going on, amongst which ... was the examination of the waters, sent from about thirty wells, to find out which was the least liable to incrust the boilers of locomotives [so] that the Grand Rapids and Indiana Railroad Company might learn which were the most available points for sinking their wells and erecting their tanks for a supply of water on the line north to Petoskey."

Boarding House

"Leaving the laboratory and its busy students and the hard-working professor, we crossed over the grounds to the new and neat but rather quaint looking boarding hall. Here we found one of the young men in the armory, which was furnished with muskets in the racks of the wall...."

Greenhouse

"Very few of the party cared about ascending to the third story of this building; hence we crossed along its front to the green-houses of Mr. Cassidy. Here, outside, everything was suffering from drought...."

Barns

"Dinner [lunch] being over, Professor Ingersoll took the party ... to the barns and the office of the farm department. In the barn the teams and some of the students were occupied in drawing in hay and illustrating how steam was used for running the machinery in cutting and grinding feed...."

Cattle Yard

"Our next visit was to the cattle yard, where there were some good piles of manure, but we missed the great piles of compost which are the favorite works of Mr. Gulley, and which he regarded as a necessity for the farm on the north side of the Cedar River."

Crops Area

"While the cows and heifers were being driven up, the haying teams were pressed into service to take the party down across the bridge over the Cedar River, and to that part of the farm devoted to crops. We came across a meadow ... where the classes ... were laying down tile drains under the charge of Professor Carpenter."

Thank you, M.A.C.

"Most ... of the group were due at the depot at half past five, P.M. But they took time to offer the following resolution:

"*Resolved*, That the Executive Committee of the SAS have great pleasure in testifying to their high appreciation of the value of the efforts thus far made by the college in its instruction and management in promoting the interests of agriculture in all its departments; and we most heartily endorse the institution, and see in its future a most powerful influence for good to the state, fully compensating for all expenses incurred; and we most heartily commend it to the farmers of the state, as worthy of their confidence and support."[31]

Grange Resolution

"*Resolved*, That to the list of standing committees another committee be added, to be known as the Agricultural College Committee, whose duty it shall be to consider the relations and workings of said college to the people of the state; its ability to advance our agriculture, to elevate our social surroundings, and to set forth to the Order the special advantages to be derived from this state institution by our sons and daughters; that the committee be composed of three or more members selected from the executive committee and the State Grange officers, and required to report annually.

"We advise such committee be made up from these officers, as they only hold over from year to year, and therefore are the only ones from whom a report could be assured."[32]

MSAS—College Ties

"During the past year a step worthy of record here has been taken towards a closer union of the college and the society, - a step due to the suggestion of Mr. W. L. Webber, president of the society.... He now proposed that the executive committee should meet from time to time at the college on the invitation of the State Board of Agriculture...."

State Board Arranges Meetings at M.A.C.

Cordially responding to the action of the executive committee of the society, the state board invited the committee to meet them at the college on June 25. The board also invited the president and secretary, and the executive committee of the State Grange to meet with them.

The day was spent examining the workings in several departments and the farm and horticultural plots.

Closing Resolutions

The executive committee and the officers of the Grange adopted resolutions including the following statements:

- **Interests are Similar**
  "*Resolved*, That in the opinion of the SAS, the end and aims of this Society, of the College, and the State Grange are the same, that of educating and elevating the farmer class."

- **College is to be Commended**
  "*Resolved*, That the members of the SAS commend the work done by the College, and that they believe it to be exerting a great and good influence in behalf of agriculture."

- **Half the Grads are Farmers**
  "*Resolved*, That we learn with pleasure that more than 50 percent of the graduates are farmers, and that we believe the influence exerted by these graduates is a hopeful promise for the College and for the elevation of the farmer."

- **Legislative Restrictions Regretted**
  "*Resolved*, That the MSAS express a feeling of regret that the last Legislature denied the College the appropriation asked for by the Board."[33]

The Grange and the College

"The Grange and the agricultural college both tend to the same object, that of educating the farmer. But it seems that these sister educators have as yet to learn their relations, which, if learned, would greatly benefit both."

Where are the Young Men of the Grange?

"At every session of the State Grange a great deal of interest in the agricultural college is manifested ... but this interest and enthusiasm apparently ceases when the session is closed ... since only one-seventh of all students are grangers, and not more than one-fourth of them are grangers' sons."

Grangers Want Experiment Station

"The grangers, eager to gain knowledge, but not ambitious enough to make the necessary experiment themselves, have argued long for an experimental station at the college. This we think would be a good thing, yet it is not without its objections. On account of so great variety of soil and climate ... many experiments might prove valueless. At present a great deal of experimenting, valuable to the farmer and horticulturalist, is being done by the professors ... but reports of the experiments do not reach as many farmers as they should...."

Press Legislature for Women's Needs

"The experimental station can be secured only by continually applying to the legislature, and by proving to that body their necessity and by explaining the benefits that could be derived from them.

"The Grange [has a need] that differs from a great many organizations, and in which the agricultural college differs from every other college in the state. The Grange owes its success to a vast extent to the admission of women within its order. In view of this fact the grangers cannot help but think that the condition of the college and of their daughters could be greatly improved if some provision could be made for the accommodation of ladies at the college."

Call for Cooperation

"Now since the interests of the Grange and the agricultural college are so nearly alike, why do not these near realties become better acquainted, and each work for the interests of the other, and patiently wait for wise legislation to provide for their respective needs?"[34]

New Student Newspaper

Alumni Reunion

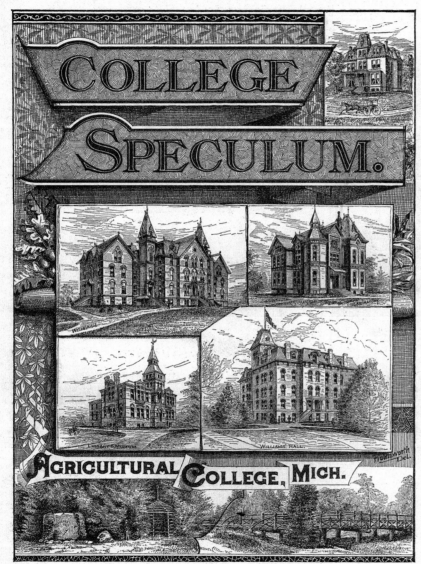

VOL. V; NO. 1.—WHOLE NO. 17.

COLLEGE SPECULUM.

AGRICULTURAL COLLEGE, MICH.

W. S. GEORGE & CO., PRINTERS & BINDERS, LANSING, MICH.

Courtesy UAHC

The Bubble Was First

The Bubble was the first student newspaper at the college. It was published in 1868 — but for only seven editions.

College Speculum Follows

The next student newspaper, the *College Speculum*, surfaced on August 1, 1881. The introductory comments in the paper were as follows:

"It is with a feeling of assurance that the *Speculum* makes its bow to the public; an assurance that it will meet with a hearty reception at the homes of students and alumni of the college, and of all who are interested in college topics. It is the determination of the students and editors to make a paper of general interest; it will contain such college news and personals of former students as to at once draw into a nearer relation the alumni and their alma mater; it will give to the public at large such scientific and general reading as may be interesting or useful, and the general conduct and contents of the paper will be indices of student work and character."

A Student Newspaper

"But the *Speculum* is not an advertisement of the agricultural college. It is a student paper, organized and entirely controlled by them. The frequently expressed desire among the students for a college paper took form early in June, when at a general meeting it was decided to organize as soon as possible a periodical to which all might freely contribute, and through which they might learn of the alumni, and keep fresh the memories of classmates and alma mater when they were no longer residents...."[35]

Good Participation

The college alumni held a second triennial reunion at the college in August 1879. A total of 79 members participated and several made special contributions. Professor W.W. Daniels (1864) of Wisconsin University and Professor R.C. Carpenter (1873) addressed those attending. Frank Hodgman (1862), former glee club director, revived memories of that time as he directed music provided by the graduates of the college.

Meeting with Board

In the afternoon, the alumni and faculty held a joint meeting with the board of agriculture. No details regarding the conversation were reported except to say, "There was a free interchange of thought regarding the interests of the institution."

Alumni Careers in Industrial Arts

The alumni at this point number 186, and 108 "are found to be directly employed in business related to the industrial arts."[36]

...In Class and on Farm

The twilight shadows softly fall
  Along the College green,
And faintly glimmering through the trees
  The summer moon is seen.
Along the level green I walk,
  Tho' thick the dew and damp,
Tho' o'er the river bed the mist
  Hangs like a sleeping camp.

With halting step I pace tonight
  Along the dampened grass;
By each remembered rock and tree
  With saddened heart I pass;
The sound of some old college song
  Comes throbbing soft and low,
And tender memories fill my heart—
  Sad thoughts of long ago.

The simple, foolish words and tune,
  How dear they seem tonight-
How oft with boyish heart I sang.
  While all the world seemed bright!
The weary years of toil and care
  Roll back before that strain.
The burden of my life seems gone.
  I'm but a boy again!

It seems but yesterday since I
  Viewed trouble from afar,
When in the twilight's deepening gloom
  We sang "The Last Cigar."

And yet that sweet song rouses still
  Old memories long untold.
But now a weary man I come,
  With heart grown stern and cold,

I've seen the hopes and joys of years
  Fade in the distance dim;
I've watched beside a blighted heart
  Where once proud hope had been.
I've seen the friends of years agone
  Pass from my sight away;
I've stood beside a grave that held
  The dearest of earth's clay.

It all comes back to me, as slowly
  I pace the college green;
Down through the vista of the years
  My hard life's work is seen.
What dreams lie buried in the past-
  What hopes lie cold and dead-
What noble deeds might have been done—
  What tender words been said!

But on the air the study hour
  By evening bell is borne,
And all the sweet song dies away,
  And all my dreams are gone.
But dearest of all memories
  We meet life's path along.
Are those so softly called to life
  By that old college song. [37]

Courses Studied

Freshman Class

Autumn Term
Algebra
Ancient History
Rhetoric
Moral Philosophy

Spring Term
Geometry
Drawing
Agriculture

Summer Term
Geometry
Botany
Rhetoric

Sophomore Class

Autumn Term
Geometry
Elementary Chemistry
Botany
Landscape Gardening

Spring Term
Trigonometry
Surveying
Organic Chemistry
English Language

Summer Term
Mechanics
Analytical Geometry

Junior Class

Autumn Term
Mechanics
Anatomy
Horticulture
Agricultural Chemistry

Spring Term
Human and Comparative
  Physiology
Chemical Physics
Rhetoric

Summer Term
Entomology
Meteorology
English Literature

Senior Class

Autumn Term
Logic
Civil Engineering
Zoology
Geology

Spring Term
Psychology
Botany
Moral Philosophy
Veterinary Medicine

Summer Term
Agriculture
Constitution of U.S.
Political Economy
Philosophy of History
Astronomy[38]

Student Labor: A Dilemma

Tweaking Insufficient

The college made some minor changes in student labor practices. Initially, two-thirds of the students were assigned to the farm. The change resulted in having the sophomore students begin their year of work on the farm and juniors begin their year in the horticultural department.

Issue: Making Student Labor Educational

The concern was how to make the labor more educational and yet worthy of the wages paid. Dr. Beal's approach took "...the juniors out in sections almost every afternoon to work for an hour under his immediate instruction...."

A Farm Internship

Some discussion took place with respect to the approach used at Cornell University. There "... after the four years' course of study is completed, the student can receive his agricultural degree, if he was brought up on a farm. If he has not had this home experience, he is sent to spend a season from early spring until winter with some farmer."[39]

Tender Memories

President Abbot Bids Farewell

In 1884, T.C. Abbot made his last report as president and in review wrote as follows:

Morrill Act Provided Hope

"The college passed, owing to a faith in the general plan of it on the part of people of the state, through the dark days of the rebellion. In 1860, it had no income except legislative appropriations, and had less than fifty students in all. The congressional grant of 1862 gave the college the strong defense of hope, but it was not until 1870 that the institution, realized an income from the sale of lands."

College not a Political Pet

"By scrupulous impartiality of treatment of political parties the college has passed from being called the expensive pet of one party, to being, I believe, one of the institutions of the state whose interests all the people gladly combine to further, and in whose prosperity they all delight."

Opponents into Warm Friends

"I early laid down as a rule that no opposition to the college should be held to be a ground of ill feeling against any person, and now I have the pleasure of seeing former opponents of the college among its warm friends and the general agricultural organizations among its best supporters."

Patience Pays

"The State Agricultural Society, State Horticultural Society, and State Grange all endeavor to make known and recommend the college. Personally, I have cause to be very grateful for the patient encouragement that these organizations, and the several farmers, stockmen, and horticulturalists have extended to me, as an individual, as well as to the college over which I presided."

Second to None

"At home I look upon grounds which are models of beauty, upon good buildings for nearly every department, upon stock and other equipments of an agricultural college, second to those of no institution of a like character of the land."

My Wish — Enlarged Success

"Surely, I can but carry out of the presidency grateful memories of members of the board and of previous boards, of the officers of the college, its long succession of students, and of the citizens of the state whose encouragement and friendship I have so constantly enjoyed. I can but wish for the college, under some new president, enlarged prosperity and success."[42]

Brief Notes

Admission By Diploma

The board resolved to admit pupils from approved high schools to the freshman class of the college without examination. This was referred to as "by a certificate."[40]

Experiment Stations

Funding for agricultural experiment stations would have to wait. In 1884 Congress considered a bill to "grant means for conducting experiments. The bill, however, was not adopted."[41]

Period in Review

Abbot Presidency Closes

With the close of the third decade came the close of T.C. Abbot's presidency. His was the third presidency (Williams, 1857-59, and Fisk, 1859-1862). One could argue that Abbot's presidency was the most crucial for the survival of the college.

Legislative Relations

By all accounts Abbot had a very hands-on approach in working with the faculty and students, despite frequent physical discomforts. His was also a time requiring nearly endless patience in dealing with the penurious legislature of the time. His strategy was to request only minimal appropriations and never exaggerate budget requests in the hope that legislators would not reduce funding to the minimum required. Midway in his administration (1875), Abbot delivered a lengthy speech to legislators in making the case for educating farmers.

Advancing Public Understanding

Abbot and his colleagues were effective in reaching out to the public through the Farmers Institutes, building loyalties with various agricultural groups, and convincing various newspaper editors not only of the need to educate farmers but to gain an understanding of its benefits to the broader society and state economy.

Keeping the Oak Alive

Although the "acorn" planted by President Williams in 1857 had not yet grown into a "giant oak," the Abbot administration was successful in keeping the oak alive during arid periods and enabling it to develop deep roots and emerge as a growing tree, albeit slowly.

Courtesy UAHC.

"The theoretical man who develops the principles of a science is not to be ignored, but it is the man who can apply the principles evolved by the man of theory that commands the situation."

President Edwin Willits, 1885-1889

"What a grand and noble work this is, the lifting up of the agricultural masses through the medium of our young men. It is a worthy ambition to be a professor of agriculture."

Professor of agriculture P. M. Harwood, 1892

Chapter Overview

Under New Leadership

The fourth decade ended with new leadership. Dr. Abbot retired at the end of 1884 but stayed on until his successor, Edwin Willits, could assume the duties.

Public Uncertainty Wanes

Abbot guided the college through a difficult period marked by Congress' adoption of the Morrill Act. Still, the state legislature was tentative during much of the period as the public remained largely uncertain about the need for a college education in the practical lives of people.

Confidence Grows

Some quarters of the state continued to question the value of an agricultural college, but state policy-makers gradually were persuaded that the college had growing public support and also that it could have a strong practical effect on many Michigan residents.

Becoming a Reliable Source

The challenge for the college in its fourth decade, then, was to devise ways to generate scientific and technical knowledge and give it practical application. At the same time, the college had the ongoing duty to provide an environment in which some of Michigan's youth could share in the application of such science and technology.

Slowly but Steadily

As with most fundamental change, it came slowly, building on what had come before. As residents began to see the evolving industrial revolution, few could know how that would develop, but many saw the college as guiding and assisting their entry into the evolving new world.

Change in Presidents

From Abbot to Willits

T.C. Abbot remained in office until Edwin Willits assumed the duties July 1, 1885. He had been the principal at the State Normal School in Ypsilanti.

Washington Convention

Just seven days after taking office, Willits went to Washington, D.C., to attend a convention of agricultural colleges from 31 states and territories. They reported the discussions were of great interest and mutual benefit. Willits presented a paper on industrial education.

Institutional Cooperation

The convention was "an effort to bring all the agricultural colleges and experiment stations into harmonious co-operation through the U.S. Department of Agriculture, so as to assign and develop the experiments devised and to secure a consolidated report of the results."

Experiments and Reporting

"It was found that in nearly all cases the colleges were crippled for means necessary to conduct and report their experiments. The convention appointed a committee to present the matter to the next Congress."

Michigan Involved

"The committee consisted of Presidents Atherton of Pennsylvania, Lee of Mississippi Agricultural College, and Willits who were to visit Washington during the next December or January."[1]

Willits' Biography

New York to Michigan

Born in Otto, New York, Edwin Willits migrated with his parents to Washtenaw County, where he received his primary and college education. He studied law and was admitted to the state bar in 1857.

Lawyer, Administrator

He practiced law for a time but went into teaching and school management in Adrian and Monroe. His interest in education also led to his 12 years of service on the State Board of Education and later as principal of Michigan Normal School.

Public Officeholder

He held several other governmental positions. In 1860, at 30, he served as Monroe County prosecutor. Thereafter, he was postmaster in Monroe city, a delegate to the 1973 state constitutional convention, and editor of the *Monroe Commercial* newspaper. Subsequently, he was a representative in Congress for three terms.

His term as college president was short-lived. In 1889, Willits became assistant secretary of agriculture. A change in presidents led to his resignation of that position in 1894.

Admired by Students

A student, H.B. Cannon, said of Willits, "The student body almost at once recognized him a master hand in administration. There was an atmosphere of hope about him.... The venerable look of the man, his fatherly ways, his eagle's eye — all impressed us and moved us...."[2]

Courtesy UAHC

President Edwin Willits, 1885-1889.

...and Expanding Mission

Willits Wants Mechanic Arts

Need for New Department

President Willits made the case for establishing a department of mechanic arts in his inaugural speech. "The time is now propitious for the new department.

"[However,] it was hardly practicable to establish it sooner. There was no great demand for it. The grant [Morrill Act] in fact was in advance of the general public sentiment, but the leading spirits who advocated the land-grant saw that ... industrial education, in all its phases, would be a leading factor in our educational system.... It is so today."

Capability to Advance

"Our purpose and wish is to take the young man who has an aptitude and taste for mechanical industry from the shop, and give him a thorough course in drawing and design, thorough instruction in all those general principles which he cannot obtain elsewhere ... give him daily practical work in the shop, and then return him to the shop, with a skill competent to take his place as a journeyman, and an intelligence fitting him for foremanship...."

Applied Science Institution

"The second general purpose of this college is to make it an institution of applied science. The sciences deal with the *non ego*, more directly with the great world outside of the personality of the individual, first with the facts and then the laws of the material universe...."[3]

Liberty Hyde Bailey, Jr., reared in the South Haven area and a member of the 1882 class, was named professor and superintendent two years after graduating. He served until August 1888. A long-time professor at Cornell University, Bailey became known as the "Father of Horticulture."

New Vet and Mechanic Labs

Courtesy UAHC

Veterinary Laboratory.

The legislature appropriated funds for four new buildings in 1885. Among them were veterinary ($5,400) and mechanical ($7,800) laboratories. These structures were essential for these areas to operate as "independent" departments. The college also constructed an assembly room for military drill and general lecture purposes.

Advanced Vet Lab

The veterinary laboratory provided an operating room, a lecture hall, and a dissecting and model room. In the model room they placed skeletons of principal domestic animals, sets of veterinary instruments and medicines, and a life-sized model of the horse "so arranged that it can be completely dismembered and exhibit the internal organism, etc."

New-level Lab

"The mechanical laboratory also helped to bring this area of study to a new level. Included in the building was a blacksmith shop and brass foundry, an iron workshop furnished with an engine, seven engine lathes, a planer, a shaper, a power drill, emery wheels, benches, vises, and other tools and machinery."[4]

College Serves Public, Too

Not for Students Only

In 1885, President Willits reported, "It may be proper to note that the Agricultural College does not exist for students alone.... The fact that it has not had this full attendance should not make us oblivious to the fact that the college occupies a field of great public utility aside from its instruction of students."

Inquiries Numerous

"If the general public were aware of the correspondence of some of the professors, notably those of agriculture, chemistry, botany, entomology, horticulture, and veterinary, always ... with citizens of the state [who make] inquiries about seeds, and soils, and [other agricultural matters] and the thousand and one matters that fill the fertile brain of our active inquiring people ... much of the criticism heretofore indulged in would fall to the ground."

Responsive Faculty

"I am happy to state that the professors ... are prompt in their response, working early and ... fully alive in the respective spheres to the importance of bringing whatever of practical information they may have to the ... public."[5]

Students at Mechanic Arts Lab.

Courtesy UAHC

Getting to Know Farmers

Willits was relatively new to farmers and so participated in some of the institutes. His comments remain helpful in coming to know him.

Leadership of College

In one speech, for example, he told the audience, "In my first visit, Professor Beal asked me what kind of cattle I liked best. I said, I didn't know." [Remember that Willits was a lawyer by training.] "Said Beal, 'isn't it a little funny for a president of an agricultural college to know nothing about cattle?'

"I said I should not pretend to know nothing about which I did not know, but that I did not believe it was essential that I should know all these details in order to be a capable head of the institution. My work is to be a captain to these lieutenants and see that they have opportunities to work, and I shall make it my business to see that the legislature is not left in the dark as to the character of the work that is being done...."[6]

Farmers' Institutes a Success

Ten Years Running

At the midpoint of the 1880s, farmers in Michigan had experienced 10 years of Farmers' Institutes. For 1885, institutes were scheduled in Plymouth (Wayne County), Flushing (Genesee), Albion (Calhoun), Paw Paw (Van Buren), Manchester (Washtenaw), and Monroe (Monroe).

Overcoming Education Myths

G.A. Starkweather's comments in Plymouth provide some insight into these events.

"The time is recent, Mr. Chairman, when Farmers' Institutes had not been heard of. We need not go far back in our recollections to reach the time when education was thought unnecessary for practical farming — in fact, incompatible with it.

"The farmer boy who graduated from college was expected to enter one of the learned professions; and for him to take his education and culture back to the farm was thought an evidence of mental weakness.

"Agriculture was the great absorbent of ignorance — an occupation where illiteracy exalted and education debased its followers."

Improved Methods Quest

"For this, farmers were largely responsible.... They stolidly held to the old ways, and maintained the pursuit of knowledge to be a waste of labor.... The logic of events forced the more intelligent farmers to ask for improved methods of agriculture. **But from the sad lack of knowledge no satisfactory response could at the time be given.**"

Pride in Our College

"We of Michigan are justly proud that ours was one of the first of the states of this nation to establish an agricultural college. ...it has overcome difficulties, conquered prejudices, silenced criticisms, and stands today as one of the fixed institutions of the state."[7]

Willits Relates to Audience

The Right Pieces

About veterinary science, said President Willits, "The legislature gave us money to set us up and we take a horse to pieces as they take a man to pieces at Ann Arbor. I want to talk a little about this subject of veterinary [science]."

Horse Doctor More Valuable

"Dr. McCosh, President of Princeton, laughingly said of President White of Cornell, that he had imported from Europe a philosopher and a horse doctor. President White retorted that he had secured the two professional gentlemen referred to, but of the two, the so-called horse doctor was the more valuable."

Vet Science Independent?

"I made it one of the conditions of my acceptance of the presidency of the Agricultural College that the state should place veterinary science on an independent basis at the college."[8]

...and Tending College Issues

Significant Enrollment Growth

The years 1886 and 1887 were years of significant enrollment growth. In 1887, students numbered 295. The number was predicted to rise to 350 in 1888 if accommodations permitted.

Suggested Higher Standards Resisted

These increases led some to push for higher admission standards. Willits' response was, "I am clearly of the opinion there should be no change in the requirements for admission. The standard is practically the same as that at the Military Academy at West Point and the Naval Academy at Annapolis."

Students Come Direct from Local Schools

"The present requirements have the merit of taking the young men right from the well-appointed school district, with a habit for work well-formed, and their taste for manual labor unimpaired. This is a very important consideration in an industrial institution like ours. Two years' additional study away from home before entering college tends to lead the young man away from industries and into the so-called professions."

Grammar Not a Student Strength

"While I adhere to the present standard for admission ... many of the applicants that come to us are not so strong as they should be in some of the primary studies — notably grammar."[9]

Defining "Department"

What Is It?

Over the years, reports made references to "departments." The meaning, though, was not well-defined or uniformly applied.

Four are Established

President Willits defined the concept in 1887. He noted,

" ... in the last four years there have been placed on an independent basis the Veterinary, Mechanical, Military, and Horticultural departments, all with their laboratories, shops, and drill hall. [This] completes the round of development necessary to equip all departments required by the Land Grant Act of 1862."[10]

Overuse Leads to Water Crises

Malarial Fever

President Willits reported that the college had been experiencing "a malarial fever that showed some typhoid characteristics." He wanted "to place on the record the fact that in no degree can it be charged to the want of the ordinary sanitary precautions for which the college authorities may be held responsible."

Well in Constant Use

Willits explained the campus had been the site of many parties and visitors kept the remaining well in constant use. "The result was that when night came the water was low and turbid, the students went thirty rods with their pitchers to a well which had always been pure. This well was found unhealthy, and was dismantled."

Artesian Well Drilled

Subsequently, officials requested funding to drill an artesian well. The legislature appropriated $3,000 for the well and an extended water system.[11]

Courtesy UAHC

Troubled Bridge Over Streaming Waters

Entire Bridge Unsafe

Professor Samuel Johnson, reporting on farm operations, said, "A stone abutment has been completed at the south end of the bridge crossing the Cedar River. At its last meeting the board authorized the building of one at the north end. The old bridge is much dilapidated and not safe. We are running great risks in using it longer...."[12]

"Never Stand Still, Experiment!"

The Hatch Act: Support for Experimentation

Experiment, or Cease to Grow!

Establishment

Section 1. "In order to aid in acquiring and diffusion among the people of the United States useful and practical information on subjects connected with agriculture, and to promote scientific investigation and experiment respecting the principles and applications of agricultural science, there shall be established ... in each state ... an agricultural experiment station."

Purpose

Section 2. "...[T]he object and duty of experiment stations [shall be] to conduct original researches or verify the experiments on the physiology of plants and animals ... and such other researches or experiments bearing directly on the agricultural industry of the United States...."

Reporting

Section 3. "...[I]n order to secure ... uniformity of methods and results to the work of said stations ... the U.S. commissioner of agriculture [shall] furnish forms ... for the tabulation of results of investigations or experiments...."

Bulletin Publication

Section 4. "...[B]ulletins or reports of progress shall be published at said stations at least once each three months, one copy of which shall be sent to each newspaper in the State in which they are ... located, and to such individuals actually engaged in farming as may request the same...."

Funding

Section 5. "For the purpose of paying the necessary expenses of conducting investigations and experiments, and printing and distributing the results as hereinbefore prescribed, the sum of $15,000 is hereby appropriated to each State to be specifically provided for by Congress from year to year...."

Unexpended Funds

Section 6. "Whenever it shall appear in the annual [financial report] of any said station, that a portion of the preceding appropriation remains unexpended, such amount shall be deducted from the next succeeding appropriation to such station...."

Legal Relationship

Section 7. "Nothing in this act shall be construed to impair or modify the legal relationship between any of the colleges and the government of the United States."

Existing Stations

Section 8. "States having colleges entitled ... to the benefits of this act, and having also authorized experiment stations established by law separate from said colleges ... shall be authorized to apply such benefits to ... stations so established by such states."

State Consent

Section 9. "The grants of moneys authorized by this act are made subject to the legislative assent...."[13]

Willits' Account of Act's Passage

Grow or Decay!

"Institutions should never stand still; like individuals, when they cease to grow, elements of decay soon appear. With added years come new demands and to keep abreast of the age every college must be alive to demands [and] ... new wants.

"When first founded agricultural colleges were essentially educational. The land-grant of 1862 was primarily for educational purposes."

Historically Sporadic

"The importance of experimental work was but incidentally recognized. As years passed the importance of experimental work became more apparent and efforts in that line were made, but being subject to the leading purpose of the college — education — the efforts were sporadic and unsatisfactory.

"It was found, moreover, that experiments were costly, and the funds could not be spared from the current expenses of the college already stocked for educational work."

Appeal to Congress

"Recognizing these facts, it was determined to appeal to Congress to supplement the endowment of 1862 ... by an annual appropriation of $15,000 for each college which should be exclusively devoted to experiments in agriculture and cognate sciences."

Ag College Convention

"On July 8, 1885, a convention of all the agricultural colleges in the United States was held in Washington and a united effort was initiated to present the matter to the Forty-ninth Congress, to assemble the following December."

Effort Pays Off

"But by dint of hard work, it passed the Senate in a mutilated form and went to the House of Representatives, where, near the close of the session, under suspension of the rules, and therefore without chance for amendment, it passed by an overwhelming vote and went to the President, who signed it March 2, 1887."[14]

Message Received

Early Actions in Forestry

Tour Model Sites

The Hatch Act imposed new challenges on the college. In early 1888, the board delegated a board member and Samuel Johnson, farm superintendent, to visit experiment stations around the country to learn about their activities and plans.

Station visits included Wisconsin, Iowa, Guelph, Cornell, and Amherst. Upon their return, they said, "If we are doing good work in our several departments, as shown by similar work in other institutions, it will be a source of encouragement, and the man must be dull indeed who does not get many valuable suggestions from such visits."

Puzzling Questions

"So, too, as members of the board, a careful inspection of methods, work performed, and results secured in similar institutions could not fail to be wonderfully suggestive and helpful in deciding many of the puzzling questions that boards ... are called upon to determine."[15]

Beal's Concern

Professor Beal began exhibiting his concern for trees and forests as early as 1875 when he began planting tree species on the campus. He emphasized his concern for the forests by changing his position title from professor of botany and horticulture to professor of botany and forestry.

Concern Takes Root

His concern for the forests in the state, as well as others, began to take root. In 1887, the legislature adopted a law assigning the board the role of functioning as an Independent Forestry Commission (IFC).

IFC: Assess and Report

The act directed the IFC to conduct an inquiry into the effect of current practices — wasteful cutting, fires, clearing for tillage or pasturage, etc. — on the forests, ponds, rivers, and water power, and in disturbing and deteriorating the natural conditions of the climate.

College Forests: Demo Sites

The board adopted the following resolution in 1894: "... to place the forest area of the college farm in such a condition as to illustrate, as far as possible, the most advanced methods of properly handling woodlands for continuous and lasting profits...."

Department Established in 1902

This board action did not create a department of forestry at the college. That took place in 1902.[16]

Courtesy UAHC

W.J. Beal (left) and colleagues in office discussion.

Beal Critiques Forest Practices

Forest Areas Diminishing

"After traveling extensively in all the southern counties during the last 18 years, I feel confident in saying that the area of land in the forest is constantly diminishing. I know of no pieces of land of much extent where timber has been planted or where trees once cut are allowed to sprout and grow."

Quality Dropping

"In places where the area remains undiminished, the quality in nearly all cases is deteriorating [by] removing many of the most valuable trees. It is a custom well-nigh universal among farmers, to pasture the wood-lot. By turning in the cattle, sheep, horses, and swine, the seedlings are all destroyed [and] the young trees are often killed...."

Manage for Profit

"It needs no deep deliberation of a philosopher to see that the days of all wood-lots thus treated are numbered. Some may say that it is not worthwhile to try to retain any forest in the older portion of our state. That we can buy timber cheaper than we can raise it; still we feel sure that nearly every farm is managed with greater profit to the owner where more or less of it is kept in forest."[17]

Good Year for Building Funds

Improvements Made

Legislative appropriations in 1887 enabled the college to add and improve several facilities. Willits stated that $5,000 received for a horticultural laboratory "will enable us to construct one of the finest and best appointed in the U.S." The college received $3,000 for the extension of the shops and $1,500 for two new boilers.

New Dorms — Higher Enrollment

The college received $10,000 for new dormitory space and an apartment building for assistant professors, some of whom had been living in dormitory rooms. The new structure was expected to increase the capacity to 400 students.[18]

Courtesy UAHC.

Entomology Laboratory, built in 1889, was the first agricultural laboratory.

Collection Donated

Senator James McMillan of Detroit donated a collection of butterflies and beetles to the entomology laboratory. It included 8,000 butterfly species and 12,000 specimens, and 8,000 beetle species and 40,000 specimens.

A Forerunner?

The reporter wrote, "It is hoped that this kindly act ... is to be a forerunner of many other gifts from patriotic sons and daughters of Michigan, who would like to see her state agricultural school thoroughly equipped in every respect."

Valued Start

"Our college has now a valuable beginning in a museum, cabinets, and library. And yet those who use these most [professors and special students] find them by no means complete."[19]

English Alum Donates Flagstaff

Englander's Appreciation

"A few years [have passed] since a young man came to us from England and spent some two years at our college. It was a source of constant amazement to him to find here such wonderful facilities for scientific study free of charge, and he always expressed a desire to show his appreciation of the benefits in some way."

100-foot Flagstaff

Willits said, "I am in the receipt of a certificate of deposit, which with accumulated interest will amount to about $150. It will be used, with his approval, in the erection of a one-hundred-foot flagstaff in front of the Armory. At his request his name is withheld from the public."[20]

Courtesy UAHC.

New Botanical Laboratory.

Courtesy UAHC.

The Horticulture Building (now Eustace-Cole) was designed under the direction of Liberty H. Bailey. The first college greenhouses and work room are to the right.

...Challenged as Well

Enrollment Problem Not Yet Solved!

Student Influx Anticipated

The college was expecting to enroll 97 new students in September 1885 and in the following spring "a large influx of new students, who are able to pass the fall studies. So if that experience is verified this year," said President Willits, "we shall have ... at least 150 new students."

More Crowded Dorms

"If so, we shall be obliged to put three students in a room.... We can accommodate with reasonable comfort in the halls and on the grounds 230 to 250 students, and no more, according to the number who can find private quarters."

Plant Justifies More

"This brings us face to face with a more serious question. We have a plant here that has cost nearly $400,000, and it justifies and demands at least 500 students. At the last commencement, in an address the Governor said that the institution fell short of its duty if it had less than 500 students...."

More Dorms Are Key

"But it is manifest that without additional accommodations we cannot meet their just demands. We are three miles from Lansing and too far to secure quarters for the surplus attendance, unless some easy and cheap means of transportation is provided...."

Choices: Street Car or More Dorms

Two ways were suggested for the extra 250 students: one was to build a street railway to Lansing, and the other was to build more dormitories.[21]

Who Should Run the College?

Willits Brings Change

Professor A.J. Cook, in commenting on the Willits administration, said, "With President Willits came a change in the management of the college. I think it was a sad mistake, not to say a disastrous one."

Faculty not Consulted

"Before this, changes in internal management were suggested and all new appointments to the faculty were nominated by the president, but only after the fullest conference with and approval of the faculty. The board only confirmed. **No college board ought ever to do more.**"

College Suffers Setback

"Selections thus made from time to time in the opinion of the writer [W. J. Beal] have been the cause of setting the college back in its progress fully fifteen years. 'The lamentable change' referred to [by Cook] came during the latter part of the administration of President Abbot, while the Hon. Henry Chamberlain was chairman of the committee on employees...."[22]

Talent Drain Ongoing

Faculty Turnover Costly

"[Professor E. Davenport] had shown unusual tact and skill in the work during the brief period of two years, but alas! He resigned to accept the presidency of the first agricultural school in South America, just as he had fairly got underway in plans for teaching students and breeding cattle for making experiments. This move may have been a good thing for South America, but agriculture at M.A.C. dropped again to the foot of the ladder, where it would take a successor another two years to get fairly on his feet."

Faculty Changes Handicap College

"These frequent changes of professors and instructors have been the severest handicaps which the college has had to meet. During 1890 changes in professors and instructors were frequent."[23]

Courtesy UAHC

College Faculty 1888

First row: E. Willits (president), W.J. Beal (botany and forestry), R.C. Kedzie (chemistry), E.J. MacEwan (English), H.G. Reynolds (secretary); second row: W.L. Simpson (military science), R.C. Carpenter (mathematics and English), S. Johnson (agriculture), W.F. Durand (mechanical engineering); third row: L.R. Taft (horticulture), A.J. Cook (zoology and entomology), E.A.A. Grange (veterinary science).

Oscar Clute Assumes Presidency

Departure Surprising

Upon the unexpected departure of Edwin Willits in April 1889, the board selected Oscar Clute to fill the vacancy. Clute, a graduate of the 1862 senior class, had been employed as a professor.

School Administrator

Prior to coming to the college, Clute, at age 17, was principal of Binghampton schools in Shiawassee County. He served two years in that position and then as principal of Ionia schools.

Theologian Before

His years in education, it seems, did not satisfy his career desires. He left the college in 1868 for Meadville, Pennsylvania, where he studied theology. Upon graduation from the Theological Academy, Clute became a church pastor at Vineland. He served as a pastor in several other churches, and in May 1889 he had just completed one year of such service in Pomona, California, when the board asked him to become president.

Service — 1889-93

Clute's term as president ended in August 1893. He complained of ill health but then assumed the presidency at Florida Agricultural College. He served there for four years and then returned to the church in Pomona.[24]

Courtesy UAHC

President Oscar Clute.

Steps Forward in Serving the State

Summer School

President Clute reported on ways the college could use facilities during off-periods. "The valuable apparatus, laboratories, and library of the college, its able professors, and its healthy and beautiful location make it a desirable place for a 'summer school' for the benefit of students who desire to give themselves better training in special studies."

Summer Lab Offerings

"A number of graduates of other colleges, and teachers in the grammar schools and high schools of the state summered with us this year. Their faithful devotion to their specialties kept them employed not less than ten hours a day at the laboratory."

Drill Hall Camp-out

"There is difficulty in providing rooms for these students. Next summer we shall probably advise them to bring with them such bedding as will enable them to 'camp out' in the Drill Hall, which is a light, well-ventilated, airy building, very pleasantly located. It will give good accommodations to a large number of gentlemen."[25]

Veterinary Degree Plan

"At the state fair, a large and attractive exhibit made by a number of departments drew great crowds. The exhibit revealed a plan to expand the Veterinary Department into a school awarding the degree of V.S. [Veterinary Surgeon]."[26]

The Population of Michigan Continues to Grow		
1890		
	Number	Percent change, 1880-1890
Ingham County	37,666	11.8
Michigan	2,093,890	27.9
USA	62,979,766	25.5

Like to Make a Gift?

Courtesy UAHC

Librarian Mary Merrill, 1885.

Library Resources

The college library had steadily been expanding its collections. Many of the items had been donated rather than purchased.

But President Clute said, "Perhaps the most pressing need is for books for the library, in history, biography, travel, literature, and philosophy. We need books in all these departments." He suggested library gifts.

"Are there not wealthy men in Michigan who have made their wealth from the farms, the merchandise, the land, the lumber, the mines, or the salt of the state who will be glad to supply this need, as an expression of their appreciation of the state that has dealt so well by them?"[27]

...but Productivity Continues

Substations at Work

From Bulletin to Action

Bulletin 55 "on small fruits obtained from MSAS President T. T. Lyon was so well received that the Board of Agriculture voted to establish a permanent sub-station on the Lake Shore [in South Haven]." The interest of growers, researchers, and others was high. A 5-acre donation evidenced the interest. "By this arrangement, we secured the use of five acres belonging to President Lyon, which were planted three years ago with an experimental collection of fruits, and which furnish us immediate results."

Fruit Plants Selection

"In the spring, the collection of small fruits was largely added by purchase and by donation ... and quite a number of varieties of large fruits were also obtained. At present we have 112 varieties of apple trees, 50 varieties of pears, 74 of plums, 102 of peaches, 43 of cherries, 126 of grapes, 20 of currants, 14 of gooseberries, 62 of raspberries, 13 of nuts, 27 of blackberries, 49 of strawberries, 7 of quinces, 7 of apricots, 6 of mulberries in addition to asparagus, rhubarb, and others."

Grayling Station

A second substation was located in Grayling. Of interest there were the growing population in northern Michigan and identifying plant varieties that would grow at that latitude.[28]

Construction Experiment

Hort Handicapped

"For a number of years the work of this [horticulture] department has been handicapped by want of proper forcing houses in which to start the plants required for experimental and other purposes.

"To remedy this, the board ... in 1889, authorized the erection of two houses, each 50 by 20 feet, together with suitable workrooms, furnace rooms, etc...."

Sheltered Location

"The site selected was just within the limits of the vegetable garden, and about one hundred feet southeast from the Horticultural Laboratory; a spot centrally located for our work ... where the force of the wind was broken by buildings and large evergreens."

Commercial Model

"Our primary objective was to construct houses adapted to our wants, but we also endeavored to so arrange them that, with slight modifications, they could be used as a model by anyone who proposed to put up a commercial greenhouse."

Knowledge for Public

Employing these various construction and design techniques prepared horticulture personnel to provide advice on the benefits and shortcomings of the several approaches.[29]

"Sheep Paths"

Stone Walks Installed

The college received a $3,500 appropriation enabling the college "to put down nearly two miles of artificial stone walks...."

"Every important building can now be reached in a fairly direct manner from nearly all points upon the grounds, without leaving the walk. It is hoped that there will be fewer 'sheep paths' across the lawns now that we have the stone walks."

Appropriations Short

"The appropriation was not sufficient for constructing all that are needed ... although a considerable amount was obtained by the work of the department men and teams drawing gravel, grading, etc., and it is hoped that the system can be, in the near future, completed."

Other Improvements

"Among the other improvements ... are grading, sodding, planting and laying out of walks and drives to the new buildings, the rebuilding of the dam ... to provide a sufficient supply of water for fire purposes, and a quiet pond from which a supply of ice could be obtained."[30]

Courtesy UAHC

M.A.C.'s 1890 freshman class.

Courtesy UAHC

Botany Laboratory Burns

Started Near Chimney

Late on a March Sunday evening, "the Botany Laboratory ... took fire in the upper story ... of the building, near the large chimney.... The night was still and pleasant, and the fire seemed to take slow progress. Many of us believed that the hose from the water-works was going to throw water and extinguish the fire, but it failed to do much good, and the building burned down."

Many Items Saved

"Several of the faculty and assistants, and many students did good service in removing nearly everything from the office and other rooms on the main floor of the building, including the college and local herbarium of mounted plants — about 19,000 sheets — the microscopes, other apparatus, reports, nearly all of the books, a few small tools, part of a barrel of alcohol from the cellar, quite a number of forestry pictures on the walls of the second floor, and some valuable fragments — possibly one-tenth part in value of the museum."

Loss of Specimens

"The greatest loss, to some extent irreparable, was that of the museum specimens....

"A fire sooner or later was to be expected in such a building, and is another warning to the colleges: never trust valuable museums and libraries in a tinder box."[31]

Abbot Remembered

At the passing of Dr. T. C. Abbot on November 7, 1892, President Clute introduced his lengthy memoriam of Abbot with the following words:

"A pure, strong, brave spirit has gone from among us. These halls where for so many years his work was done will know him no more. Not again will he pass under these beautiful oaks; his daily tasks will lead him not again over these green lawns.

"This great school, which he did so much to establish, will remain and grow, but for it his personal work has ceased.

"In the lives of many students, whom he quickened and strengthened, his influence will grow from year to year, but his voice will no more be heard to counsel and to inspire."[32]

Land Grant Interest Earnings, 1869-1886

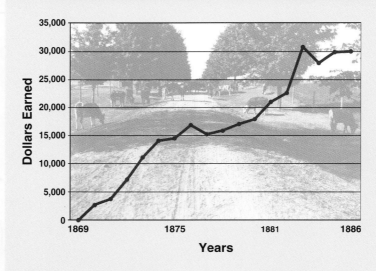

Progress on Morrill Lands

President Clute said the "...land granted by the 1862 Morrill bill [now 30 years later], was not immediately rushed into the market and sacrificed for a few dimes per acre. [Rather] the land located in Michigan had a minimum price of $2.50 per acre ... advanced to $5.00 per acre."

Pricing Rewarded

"By thus putting a fair price on the land, it became necessary for Michigan to appropriate money for current expenses of the college for several years longer, for the land did not sell rapidly at the prices fixed.

"But by this careful and economical method, the sum realized from the land thus far sold now amounts to $453,719.44, and the college has still 115,216 acres of land for sale."

Pioneering Applauded

"Surely Michigan deserves honor for its early devotion to the cause of agriculture, for its zeal in beginning the pioneer college in agriculture at a time when the State's great resources were but slightly developed."[33]

Teaching On and Off Campus

Challenge: Teaching Ag

P. M. Harwood, professor of agriculture, posed the question, "What shall the professor of agriculture teach?"

Ag Needs Expertise

"The professor of agriculture has a unique and difficult position to fill. Not only is he generally called upon to perform the three-fold duties of [teaching, managing the farm, and work of the experiment station] but the ground he has to cover in teaching is so large and of such diversified nature that it can be treated only superficially at best, and is more properly the work of several men, *each an expert in his own department.*

"My answer in one word is agriculture; in two words, practical agriculture...."

Assign Experts

"The ideal instruction, towards which we are all working, I believe, will be given only when there has been a perfect division of labor and each and every branch of agriculture is taught by experts."

Sequence of the Possible

"The logical place to begin in the teaching of agriculture is with the soil itself and from that point, build.

"Passing to the sophomore year we give instruction in soils, fertilizers, drainage, crops, and how to cultivate them.

"In the junior year we give instruction in the breeding and feeding of live stock, and the relation of the stock to the crops of the farm.

"In the senior year specialties in farming are taught."[34]

Plan for Extension Classes

The Society for Extension of University Teaching had been promoting college courses away from campuses. Professor N.D. Corbin (history and political economy) took on the task of developing a plan for the college.

Organization and Management

"The best way to proceed in organizing classes is to secure the support of some local society or club, whose aims are literary, scientific, or philanthropic.... One or two influential men in a community can do wonders in starting a thing of this kind.... Newspaper agitation and public meetings might, in turn, play their part."

Course Offerings

"These should be such as appear upon our regular curriculum. The college has a particular field to occupy and should keep within it.

"Yet should the demands come for courses in literature, history, and moral science, it seems only proper for the college to supply teachers in those subjects, when we have them...."

Student-Teacher Relationship

"The teacher would be in each case a college officer and ... would be the means of direct control over the labors of the class. Upon completion of each course, students who pass should receive a certificate to that effect and credit given toward a degree." [Residency requirements would be at least one year.]

Financing Program

"The local expense for class room... and for incidentals of various kinds should be borne by the class.... In the east, the charge is about $10.00 per lecture."

Recommendations

"That it be the duty of the above committee to prepare a careful report ... in a coming decision upon whether college extension shall become a part of the policy of the Institution."[35]

Tweaking Institutes

President Clute told of an experiment for the institutes. "Usually the institutes have continued not more than four or five sessions, beginning in the afternoon or the evening of one day and closing the evening of the next day."

Three-day Institutes

"As at these short institutes the interest continually increased until the closing session, it was suggested to have the institutes for ten sessions beginning on the evening of the first day and continuing for three full days. This would lead to much greater enthusiasm...."

Idea Well Received

"The experiment was tried, and proved eminently successful. We shall try more of them during the present winter, and if they are again successful it is possible that 'long institutes' will make up a large part of the institute work."[36]

Courtesy UAHC

Cattle grazing on the campus farm.

Decade's Third Presidential Change

Gorton Replaces Clute

Courtesy UAHC

President Lewis Gorton, 1893-1895.

Oscar Clute retired as president in 1893. To take his place, the board appointed Lewis G. Gorton, a man just 33 years of age.

College Experience Lacking

Gorton graduated from Chelsea High School and the State Normal School. His career had been associated with teaching and administration in schools. W.J. Beal stated Gorton "had had no experience in college work; no knowledge of agricultural education, and soon found his task a heavy one."

As had been fairly common at the college, Gorton faced significant instability in the faculty on his arrival — five of the 13 professors left that year.

Resignation Requested

The Gorton administration was short-lived — the board requested his resignation in December 1895. Board Chairman C.J. Monroe reported, "We have carefully weighed and added together the numerous things which have come to us ... and believe their sum forms ample grounds to warrant our action in asking for his resignation." Gorton refused to resign. The board placed him on permanent leave of absence.[37]

Misplaced Judgment?

The *Grange Visitor* editor weighed in on Gorton's dismissal. "The difficulty regarding President Gorton at the Agricultural College seems to have been one of misplaced judgment [and] in our opinion he was not at all fitted for the position of president.... The chief blame that can be attached to the action of the Board of Agriculture consists 1st, in ever having chosen President Gorton; 2nd, in not dismissing him a year and a half ago when they must have known he was not the man they needed...."[38]

Extension Classes — A Year Later

After the year's experience, Professor Corbin reported on the extension classes held in Lansing and Charlotte. The Capitol Grange co-sponsored the Lansing class; an individual promoted the Charlotte class. Attendance in Lansing varied from 40 to 70; in Charlotte, 31 attended.

Lectures Preferred

"At both places," Corbin said, "the class membership dwindled considerably. Those who simply came to hear the lectures kept coming, but many of those who undertook to study the book and to prepare on topics, found it more convenient to stay away.... In each place there were a few who worked well and with creditable results clear through. Ten lectures were given at Lansing and six at Charlotte."

Needs More Trial

"As a final and general conclusion let me say that college extension work, properly managed, has a positive value, a desirable influence, and reasonable effectiveness. Yet it cannot at all compete with collegiate residence as a means to an education.... I recommend further trial."[39]

Analysis Improves Quality

Institutes' Draw

Farmers' Institutes provided an outlet for information that the faculty generated. Often the reports delivered at the institutes were published as part of the annual reports. In 1885, in part at the urging of farmer groups, the legislature appropriated funds to publish and distribute two bulletins annually.

Kedzie Requests Commercial Samples

The issuance of one of these bulletins had an interesting outcome. Dr. Kedzie had urged the legislature to pass a law requiring fertilizer manufacturers to submit a sample of each fertilizer product along with a $20 fee. Kedzie then analyzed the nitrogen, phosphorus, and potash content and published the information. The information became even more widespread as newspapers reported his findings.

Tests Undercut Ruse

One product, manufactured in Ohio, was found to consist of "furnace slag and salt worth $.34 per ton."

Company representatives came to Lansing to protest the dissemination of the information. They asked, "Do you realize that before you published your statement about the fertilizer we were selling it rapidly in the state for $20 a ton wholesale; that after your statement appeared in the papers the sales fell flat.... We now have 1,800 tons of this fertilizer which we cannot sell, inflicting on us a pecuniary loss of $36,000." The company threatened a lawsuit.

Product Improves

The consequence of this quality control was that "...fertilizers sold in 1895 were not only more accurately labeled but were much higher in chemical content.... Dr. Kedzie was acclaimed as the defender of both the people and of the honest manufacturers."[40]

Advancing Industries and Careers

Sugar Industry Roots

Professor R.C. Kedzie, the director of the experiment station, reported on the development of the sugar beet industry in Michigan.

Visit to Grand Island

"By permission of the Board in November 1890, I visited Grand Island, Nebraska, to ... gain information on the subject of sugar beets and the manufacture of sugar from beets as an industry for our state. Glowing reports of the success of the Oxnards [owners] in Grand Island published in newspapers made many people eager to begin the work in Michigan."

Needs Study

"The results in Nebraska, as well in other states, convinced me that it was risky business for the farmer to contract to raise sugar beets, unless they know that the climate and soil are adapted to raising these beets and the beets [would be] rich enough in sugar to pay for working. Many farmers in Nebraska ... found sugar beets a losing crop and had been obliged to sell their farm stock to make good the loss on sugar beets...."

Seed Trials

"It was determined, therefore, to raise some preliminary crops in different parts of [Michigan] to test the fitness of our soil and climate to raise sugar beets. For this purpose the board directed the purchase of about 1,700 pounds of the best French and German sugar beet seed for such trial."

College-Farmer Trials

"Four kinds of seed were [distributed to Michigan farmers] who applied for the same and promised to raise the seed as directed, and to report the results, with specimens of the beets for analysis. Between 300 and 400 persons received the seed in this way, free of cost."

Release of Information

"The results of this investigation will be given to the public next winter in the Farmers' Institutes."[41]

Dairy Course Popular

Six-week Course

As part of the special courses program, the college in 1892 offered a six-week winter dairy course. Faculty members conducted the course in the basement of the agricultural laboratory. The course was in high demand. Many persons applied, but space allowed for only 27.

Babcock Testers and Separators

Using the Babcock tester was the first exercise. Participants then turned to the separators. "These costly machines were studied and handled until they understood every detail of their construction and management, and until [a student] could be safely entrusted with one in actual operation in a creamery." Next, the students studied various creamers to learn their operation and the details of setting and skimming milk.

Ripening Cream

"Then came a careful study of the conditions requisite to the development of the right flavor in ripening cream. Cleanliness, right temperature, and right set of bacteria were described as necessary...."

Now Essential Student Course

"After the close of the course, opportunity has been afforded the regular college students to take dairy work. Hereafter, this work will be required of all agricultural students and will form an essential part of their course."[42]

Advancing Technology

Equipping Department

Charles L. Weil, professor of mechanic arts, told of the department's developments and how it was being equipped. Among the advances, he said, "The blacksmith shop and foundry (except placing the crane in later) have been completed and the wood shop altered according to plans at that time....

"The blacksmith shop now contains twenty forges, and the system, proposed in [his] report for 1893, in use for furnishing blast and removing smoke and gases gives the utmost satisfaction. The Case engine purchased for use with the foregoing system performs its work excellently."

Foundry in Operation

"The foundry has been in practical operation during the spring and summer terms.... The foundry has been found to be a valuable addition to our laboratory, as it both increases the scope of instruction and cheapens the former cost of finished material."[43]

Courtesy UAHC

Short course dairy students.

College Studies Change Lives

Courtesy UAHC

College cadet band circa 1884. The first Wells Hall is in the background.

Applied Instruction in Horticulture

Juniors Practice Gardening

"Throughout the college year, members of the junior class are assigned duties to give them practice in gardening operations.

"During the first half of the spring term, before regular out-door work of the year begins, they are given such practical work as both root and top grafting by the various methods; cuttings of all kinds; pricking out, potting and repotting plants; sowing vegetable and flower seeds; and making hot beds.

"They also study the construction of greenhouses of various kinds, drawing plans and esti-mating the amount and cost of the material required; preparing insecticides and fungicides from the various approved formulae; and prun-ing grapes and the various orchard and small fruits."

Practice is Broad

"During the remainder of the year practice is afforded in various other operations such as planting trees, setting out small fruits, sowing the seeds of the various vegetable crops and caring for and transplant-ing those ... started under glass....

"Considerable attention is also given to nursery work, beginning with the planting of the grafts that were made in the spring and ending with digging and heeling in the trees that are large enough for orchard planting."[44]

Organized Counties of Michigan, 1885.

Richard W. Welch

Courtesy UAHC

"On this industrial foundation will grow habits of thrift, the love of work, economy, and ownership in property, and a bank account. Out of it in future generations will grow classical education, professional education, positions of public responsibility."

Booker T. Washington
1900 Commencement Address,
Michigan Agricultural College

"More is expected of the woman of today than ever before. Her education must give her high ideals and practical habits which will enable her to fill any position which the coming century may bring."

Pearl Kedzie,
1898 Commencement Address

Signs of Advancing Maturity

The fifth decade of the college had its challenges and struggles, but it was also a period of accomplishments and successes. The time was difficult economically, especially for the agricultural communities. Low prices on farm goods made it difficult for farmers to send their sons and daughters to college.

Enrollment Frustration

Low enrollment remained a continuing problem at the outset of the period. However, the establishment of a three-member faculty committee to study the matter provided new directions. One recommendation led to the forming of a women's program. A second led to a shift in the college schedule. Changing the "long" vacation from winter to summer enabled more farm youth to attend college. The active communication carried on by President Snyder was also instrumental in increasing enrollment.

Funding Change

The legislature's action to fund M.A.C. with an annual property tax levy was an important breakthrough for the college. A request by the college for an increase of 1/15th of a mill was raised to 1/10th of a mill and approved, albeit with a $100,000 annual limit.

This state funding together with land-grant earnings and federal funding gave the college new confidence in planning for the future.

Leadership Change

These changes, together with a change in leadership with the appointment of Jonathon L. Snyder, put the college on a sound footing for a progressive decade. Changes in electrical service, neighborhood development, transportation, and other emerging signs of modernity had a significant impact on campus life.

Organized Counties of Michigan, 1895.

Richard W. Welch

The 40th anniversary of the State Agricultural College's founding was celebrated in 1895. Numerous speakers shared their views of the impact of the college on the lives of Michiganians, their thoughts on how practical education affected Americans, and their memories of their life at the college. (We report excerpts of the comments.)*

President of MSAS

William Ball commented, "The great work of educating the farmer, the citizen, and the student, has been transferred to this grand institution where it properly belongs. No grander monument need be erected to the wisdom and foresight of the State Agricultural Society than is here located, in this beautiful spot adorned by nature...."

Master of State Grange

George B. Horton said, "The nearly 20,000 men and women comprising the membership of these farmers' clubs are loyal to education — [dedicated] to the 'full and high development of ... the faculties and powers of our being' ... opportunities for research...."

Farmers' Clubs President

"These few things that I have mentioned," said J.T. Daniels, "...underneath these more practical and necessary things, we know that our college has also taught us the value of beautiful home surroundings ... in which the sacredness of family ties, the responsibilities of citizenship, and the obligation to be true and faithful to ourselves have all been emphasized."

James Satterlee

A member of the class of 1869 praised the college by saying, "The [M.A.C.] has been a prime factor in diffusing and popularizing agricultural education; first because it has been a pioneer in this field of education; second because of the wholesome trend of her course of study toward agricultural pursuits."

Purdue Professor

W.C. Latta (class of 1877) observed, "First to take up the work and foremost in rank, M.A.C. has not only led the movement, but has, in large degree, set the pace in agricultural education. Owing to her contributions of men to other institutions, M.A.C. may properly be styled the Mother of Agricultural Colleges.

"Her graduates are identified with industrial institutions as professors of chemistry, botany, zoology, physics, entomology, agriculture, horticulture and veterinary science in probably three-fourths of the states and territories. Thus, her influence has gone out to almost all parts of this great nation. Nor is this all. She has left her impress upon agriculture of Japan and Australia."[1]

---

*George Willard was a member of the board of education when the legislature established the college in 1855. His comments were presented in connection with the opening of the college in 1857.

Emerging Community

Lanterns to Generator

Madison Kuhn wrote, "Until 1892 there was only the moon to betray mischief-makers who might be abroad at night. President Clute then placed kerosene lanterns atop posts at strategic points, but these served more as beacons by which a traveler might steer a course.

"Electricity had been used to light the chemistry laboratory since 1884 when Dr. Kedzie installed an Olds engine to turn a dynamo. Durand lighted the shops in 1889 and library in 1890, but not until P.B. Woodworth secured a dynamo was electricity general on the campus. His system carried 160 lamps distributed through the buildings and hung from trees."[2]

Campus Power Plant

"President Snyder in 1896 reported, however, that an electric light plant was put in for lighting the grounds, library, corridors of dormitories, barns, and some laboratories.

"'This work,' he wrote, 'was done almost entirely by the students.'"[3]

Private Company Provider

"Two years later, President Snyder expressed his gratitude for an appropriation of $5,000 to improve the electrical system.... Mr. Piatt [of Lansing] installed a power line to the campus to provide power continuously, 'if desired.'"[4]

1895 Enrollment

	Agric. (men)	Mech. (men)	Women	Total
Freshmen	52	36	5	93
Sophomores	53	32	1	86
Juniors	28	30	3	61
Seniors	30	15	-	45
Graduates	29	3	5	37
Subtotal	**192**	**116**	**14**	**322**
Special students	33	8	13	54
Dairy students	29	-	1	30
Total	**254**	**124**	**28**	**406**

The enrollment was a new high for the college. It was becoming a state college as students came from 51 of the state's 83 counties. With students from 14 states and six nations, the college's national and international reputation was growing. Eleven students came from other countries.[5]

Readers of M.A.C. history recall that the college was born in a "wildland." During the first decades, the college was its own community, providing housing for faculty members and dormitories for male students. The neighborhood emerged slowly.

East Lansing Begins

Interestingly, as busy as Professor Beal was with all of his college, family, and outreach activities, he managed to help form the neighborhood. In 1887, he and R.C. Carpenter, professor of mathematics and engineering, organized the first subdivision and neighborhood.

Collegeville Plat

They filed the Plat of Collegeville, a 69-lot subdivision bounded by Cedar Street on the south (now Michigan Avenue), West Street (Harrison Road), Forrest on the north (Oak Street), and East Street (Beal Street). The site did not attract faculty members because the quarter-mile walk was too far from the campus. Numerous others, however, settled in Collegeville.[6]

Courtesy UAHC

Street car service from Lansing went as far east as what is now known as the Beal entrance.

The development was slow at first, but the pace quickened in the mid-1890s. Beal expanded Collegeville in 1895 by 13 lots just north of the first plat.

Michigan Avenue Extended

At about the same time, a triangular parcel was separated from the college by the extension of Michigan Avenue east to the Lansing-Howell Road. Beal had used this site for many of his experiments. The land was sold and subdivided as "College Delta." It later became part of the business center of the new neighborhood.[7]

Streetcar Arrives

Another important development occurred about this time — extension of the electric streetcar line. The line was first extended to the western edge of the campus, a little east of Harrison Road.

A New School

By 1900, the college was part of Lansing and Meridian townships. The two townships jointly established a school in 1900 to serve the college and neighborhood. It was first housed in the YWCA room of Williams Hall.[8]

Courtesy UAHC

Committee Advice

The committee to study the enrollment situation delivered its report, including the following recommendations.

Advertise

"Establish a continuous campaign of advertising and education and present a clear and authoritative definition of our courses."

Technical Courses

"Emphasize agriculture and practical farm operations earlier in the program."

Summer Vacation

"Farmers cannot spare their sons in the summer season. Change the college calendar."

Teach Ag in Schools

"Teach agriculture early. Give it new meaning and interest so the life of the farmer becomes the 'goal of youthful ambition.'"

Begin Ladies' Course

"Offer a course in domestic economy for women and provide a place for them at the college. 'This is the day of coeducation. It is no longer an experimental but a well recognized and thoroughly approved feature of modern education.'"

Prep Course

Establish a preparatory course because many are not properly educated for college. "The establishment of such a course would be merely to openly confess a condition that actually exists."

Lower Entry Fee

"The matriculation fee [should] be reduced to one dollar or entirely abolished.... Organize a boarding hall under private management, with the single requirement that the board shall not be over two dollars per week."

Commuter College

"Eliminate dormitories by encouraging more street-car facilities and a new way of board and room for students in close proximity to the college."

Advertise Extensively

"Let us carry the school to the people, tell them where we are, what our equipment is, and what we can do for the farmer and mechanic."[10]

Committee: Why Not More Students?

In 1895, the college established a committee to determine why the college is "not getting our annual supply of students...."

They wrote letters, interviewed prominent people and former students, reviewed newspaper reports, and inquired what other colleges were doing.

Opinions Gathered

The feedback from the committee interviews generated the following observations.

"'You are not turning out practical farmers. You are not teaching farmers' sons how to make a business success of farming' — such is the almost uniform opinion expressed in farmers' clubs."

Diverting Men

Some respondents alleged a tendency at the college to divert young men from the farm. "This opinion has been expressed again and again and appeared so often ... that quotations are not needed."

Depressed agriculture was another explanation. "Whenever the question has been put to the farmer, 'Why do you not send your son to the college? ... one part of the answer is well nigh universal: 'Times are too hard.'"

College Unknown

"It is a noteworthy fact that in all parts of the State the farmers are grossly ignorant of the work done at the college.... The reason for this ignorance lies in our omission to advertise largely."

Lack "Feeders"

"High schools are manned by University alumni and they loyally direct [students] to the University. District schools are controlled by Normal graduates and they use their influence [to promote] the Normal [School]. Thus the college is left without definite feeders...."

"Another ... cause for stationary attendance ... has been the antagonism of some influential papers of the State...."

Initial Fee Too High

"Too much cash [is] required at entrance. The necessary burdens of expense should be distributed as evenly as possible during the course.... At Albion [College] for instance, the advanced payment is $12.00."[9]

Road Map to Boost Enrollment

State Board Supports Roadmap

Board of Visitors on Campus

Following the receipt of the faculty committee report, the Board of Visitors (BoV) established by the legislature visited the campus to make an intensive inquiry.*

Visitors Welcome

"In the performance of our duties we spent three days at the institution familiarizing ourselves with [the college]. We were further greatly aided by the full and valuable report of the Committee ... which we take as the basis of our recommendations."

M.A.C. Not Fully Appreciated

"In ... our opinion, M.A.C. has superior equipment for the work of its several departments, and a faculty composed of enthusiastic and capable gentlemen.

"The facilities which the college can afford for obtaining an education ... have not, we believe, been fully appreciated by the people of our state...."

Recommendations

"Taking up the recommendations of the Committee ... we would suggest:

- "A school for technical and professional training in farming and engineering is good.

- "Our observation has been too limited to endorse a course more technical in order that students may sooner enter ... scientific phases of agriculture.

- "The change of vacation is heartily endorsed [although] a revised schedule might interfere with the farmers' institutes.

- "The shift of vacation would bring the college into touch with those who cannot be spared from field and home during summer.

- "The study of elementary science in the district schools to stimulate a desire for the knowledge to be obtained at the college is wise, if practicable.

- "We do not approve of a preparatory course.... Cheaply bought is lightly appreciated...."

- "Keeping boarding fee to $2.00 or less per week, and other economies, meets our approval. Economy should not be had at the expense of wholesome food, properly prepared and served.

- "The dormitory system should be abolished, but only as fast as other adequate and wholesome facilities are provided."

The Board of Visitors report ended with: "We are pleased to learn that most of the suggestions made by the Committee ... have already been adopted by the Board...."[11]

*The board's comments are paraphrased for space considerations.

Courtesy UAHC

One Student's Decision to Attend M.A.C.

The following vignette, of course, is not typical of all decisions of the era about whether to go to college. However, the story does provide insight regarding both the individual struggles and the college's struggle with enrollment.*

Shall I Go to College?

"One harvest day in 1897 my father and I were in the wheat field. While the horses rested and we oiled the reapers he was talking, I believe, about the care of the machinery. I was hardly listening. I was deciding whether this was the time to ask him about college, and, if so, how to go about it."

Paternal Guidance

"I put the question to my father when we were about to start work again. He was halfway up the reaper.... Finally he dropped to the ground and came over to me. After an interminable silence and endless scrutiny, he said, yes, that I could go to college to study a profession, but if I wanted to be a farmer, to stay on the farm. No more than other farmers of his day did he fancy 'scientific' farming."

Lasting Impression

"In 1898 I enrolled at M.A.C., which was then out in the country three miles east of Lansing.... Within a month I fell ill and went home to convalesce. But I had attended classes with agricultural students and mixed with them at meals in the boarding club. I liked what I had heard about scientific farming."[12]

Clark L. Brody, some years after graduating.

*The decision to attend was a life-altering decision: in later years, Brody was influential in organizing the Michigan Farm Bureau, was a member of the MSU Board of Trustees, and is the person after whom the residence hall complex west of Harrison Road is named.

New Approach

Sixth M.A.C. President

Jonathan LeMoyne Snyder became the sixth president of M.A.C. The State Board of Agriculture named him to the position in February 1896.

He grew up in Pennsylvania, one of 11 siblings. His parents were highly committed to educating their children — 10 became college graduates.

Professional Educator

Courtesy UAHC

President Jonathan L. Snyder

After graduating, Snyder entered teaching and superintending. He introduced free kindergarten, manual training, and home economics in his school.

He received a doctoral degree from Westminster College in psychology and philosophy. The University of Michigan in 1908 conferred on him the degree of doctor of laws. He served as president of M.A.C. for nearly 20 years.*

*At the time of his appointment, his Ph.D. was the only one on the faculty, other than W.J. Beal's honorary degree from the University (Kuhn, p. 197).

Survey: What Persuaded New Students?

First Evaluation

"Soon after the present school year opened, a circular of inquiry as to influences which persuaded each student to enter this college was sent to all new students. One hundred seventy-nine replies were received. These are conflicting in many respects and perhaps do not signify anything very definitely."

Persuasive Factors?

The survey, with the number of students answering each question in the affirmative, is given at the right.

Four Key Questions

One: Please designate which of the following influences *affected your decision* to attend M.A.C. (Column One.)

Two: Which of the following, directly or indirectly, *first started* you to think of attending this college? (Column Two.)

Three: Which of the following were most influential in keeping you or your parents *interested in* the college? (Column Three.)

Four: Which of the following finally *decided* you, or were most influential, in *deciding* you to enter? (Column Four.)

Summary of Survey Responses

		One	Two	Three	Four
1.	Any graduate of M.A.C.	62	32	17	13
2.	Any former student but not a graduate	52	32	18	16
3.	Any farmer not in the above two classes	12	6	3	1
4.	a. Any school teacher of yours	34	-	-	-
	b. Was he a graduate or former student of this college?	18	10	6	6
5.	Any college circulars you read	26	10	8	4
6.	A catalogue of this college	101	50	37	43
7.	An advertisement in a newspaper	7	3	2	2
8.	"The M.A.C. Record"	44	14	27	10
9.	Any visit to the college by you or friends	62	19	16	22
10.	Anything said or done in any Grange or Farmers' Club	6	3	2	-
11.	Attending Farmers' Institute	18	6	6	2
12.	Interview with M.A.C. professors	21	5	7	8
13.	Letters from the President or other official of the College	57	12	12	21

Reaching Out to Youth and Parents

Promotional Campaign

The printed page was the most available form of advertising. College officials were enthused about its use. Snyder's 1898 report stated, "With the very able assistance of the College Field Agent, Mr. K.L. Butterfield, a systematic course in advertising has been carried out."

Many Copies Distributed

"During the year there have been carefully distributed 5,000 copies of college calendars, 18,000 envelope catalogues, and 10,000 copies of the college year book, or perhaps more properly called the farmer's almanac. Nearly 5,000 copies of the regular college catalogue have been distributed, principally upon request."

Snyder Sends Letters

"A very large correspondence has been carried on by the president with young people anxious to secure a higher education. Every request for a catalogue has been honored and in addition a personal letter sent out to the inquirer."

Direct Messages

"In the letters and publications the true purposes of the college have been emphasized. No bid has been made for students who expect to enter one of the learned professions, except, of course, the profession of mechanical engineering."[13]

The Key Influences

The college catalogue, former graduates and students of M.A.C., visits to the college and letters from college officials were the most influential factors. This survey was pathbreaking and informative for future actions.[14]

More Changes at M.A.C.

Reaching Out, Bringing Them In

Excursions to College

The end of the century was still a time of limited mobility for most Michigan residents. How then were people around the state to visit THEIR college? Officials arranged to have various railroads provide low-cost excursions to the campus.

Three such excursions were held in August 1897. One brought more than 300 visitors from Battle Creek to the campus. A day later some 1,300 came from Holland and Grand Rapids. About 1,400 came from Greenville and Plymouth on the third day.

Visitors Pleased

"Nearly all of the visitors to the college with these excursions were good substantial farmers, who while interested in the college, had never been on the campus before.... They were very happily surprised at the beauty of the campus and the number and character of the buildings. Many very favorable comments were made."

Future Schedules

"Four similar excursions were scheduled for August 1898.[15] On a day in 1899, some 23 coaches were gathered at the Trowbridge Road train-stop to transport some 3,000 people who had come to the campus for a one-day tour.... The one-day tours brought as many as 8,000 people to the campus in what had become "excursion week."

"A part of the credit for the influx [of students] must go to President Snyder who campaigned for new students in a fashion unimagined by his predecessors.[16] Often Snyder would converse with the visitors, respond to questions, and instill interest and excitement about M.A.C."[17]

Women's Program — Supportive Schedule

President Snyder, in introducing the idea of the women's course, made the following comments:

Home Can Benefit

"It has been believed by many that what science has done for the farm and shop it can do for the home. With this in mind, a course for young women, governing four years of work, has been outlined and adopted."

Courses Outlined

"The freshman year involves a full course in cooking. The object is to familiarize students with the most healthful [and] attractive foods....

"A course in Domestic Science is given during the sophomore year. Among the other courses in the program are sewing, drawing, graphic arts, piano, floriculture, kitchen gardening, millinery, invalid [for disabled] cooking, dairying, and poultry raising."

Thirty-two Enroll

"On the fourth day after the opening of the term, thirty-two [women] enrolled in the women's course."[18]

Schedule Change

A second watershed change was the academic schedule.

"The long vacation was to come in summer instead of winter; some of the agriculture was to be taught earlier in the course; short winter special courses were agreed upon. The change ... is meeting the wants of the larger class of people than that accommodated by the old program."

Work Requirements Reduced

The schedule change was influential for another reason. It had the effect of lessening the work requirement of students and eventually eliminating it, which, according to Kuhn was a factor repelling some students from attending M.A.C.

Immediate Action

Both changes went into operation in September 1896.

One Other Lesson

Because of the substantial increase in enrollment after these changes, President Snyder noted, "The distribution of large numbers of *The M.A.C. RECORD*, started in '96 by the faculty, and the vigorous efforts of our field agent K.L. Butterfield, must have been influential in drawing students to the college."

Mary A. Mayo, lecturer in the Farmers' Institute, leader of the women's sections, and role model in broadening the life role of women in society.

Courtesy UAHC

Women's Program Begins

Courtesy UAHC

McDermott Heads Home Economics

Edith F. McDermott became the first person to head the Department of Home Economics at M.A.C. and was the first woman at M.A.C. to receive a professorial appointment. She grew up in Meadville, Pennsylvania, attended Allegheny College, and received her degree from Cornell. She served at M.A.C. from 1896 to1898.[19]

Women and Programs on the Campus

McDermott delivered her second annual report to the college president. Excerpts follow.

Women's Department

"[The goal is] to give a good college education in which the science and art of home making shall be a prominent feature. We endeavor to so train young women ... to apply science to the ordinary duties of the home. At the same time we give training in music, art, modern languages, literature ... to develop them into broadminded, cultured women."

Scientific and Practical Studies

"As long as ninety per cent or more of our young women, later in life, have to take charge of their own homes or some other body's home, why should not their education to some degree at least prepare them for this work? **Why should all that is practical be omitted from a young woman's education? Why should not science be compelled to relieve women of much of the drudgery of life, just as it has accomplished this for men?**" [Emphasis added.]

Abbot Hall is Home

"When the college was thrown open to young women, Abbot Hall was renovated and furnished for their use. An additional floor was added to the rear wing and fitted up as a cooking laboratory.

"At the beginning of the second year, three teachers were added — a matron, a teacher of sewing, and an instructor in music. There have been in attendance this year 82 young women. During the greater part of the year Abbot Hall has been full. It will not accommodate more than forty."[20]

Courtesy UAHC

Growth Necessitates More Space

McDermott closed her second report appealing for additional space: "The rapid growth of the department will make it necessary to provide more room in the near future or turn many young women away. A private boarding house is being erected on the delta north of the college. Arrangements have been made with the owner of this building, Mrs. Backus, to accommodate twelve young women next year."

Bids Excessive

In September the board opened the bids on the new Women's Hall. All were in excess of the legislative appropriations.

The board rejected all the bids and set a special meeting to receive new bids based on the elimination of the north wing of the building and a change in the brick.

The following week the board awarded the contract to A.W. Monke Co. of Grand Rapids.[21]

North Wing Cancelled

The building was thus constructed without the north wing, which would have been parallel to the wing on the southeast end of the building. As a consequence of the shortage of funds in 1899, the structure lacks the customary symmetry one might expect.

Continuing Adjustments

Good-by, *Speculum;* Hello, *M.A.C. RECORD*

Interpreting the Institution

The *Speculum* was a casualty of the enrollment committee's recommendations. It was essentially a student newspaper representing items of interest to the students. The committee's perspective was that the college newspaper should also reflect the views of the administration and faculty.

Faculty in Control

The first edition of *The M.A.C. RECORD* appeared in January 1896. Students remained on the paper's advisory board, but faculty members clearly dominated. Howard Edwards became the paper's editor.

The stated purpose of the new publication was specific. "The aims of the college and its courses ... [are] clear cut: a strenuous effort should be put forth to bring them to the attention of every farmer, indeed of every resident of the state."

Wide Distribution

"We take pleasure in recognizing the success of the weekly college paper originated at the instance of this committee, and would urge its continued support as a step in the right direction in carrying out this campaign." The college distributed *The M.A.C. RECORD* around the state as yet one more way to advance the reputation of the college and the loyalty of Michiganians.

Sole Voice for Years

The M.A.C. RECORD took over the cash reserves of the *Speculum* and became the sole newsprint voice of the college for the next dozen years.*

---

*Beal's explanation of the *Speculum* was a bit different. He wrote "The paper became unpopular, got in debt, and ceased to exist" (Beal, p. 239).

Yearbook Title: *The Wolverine*

The M.A.C. RECORD reported that the committee planning and designing a college yearbook had selected the title, *The Wolverine* for the annual 200-page (8.5- by 10-inch) publication. Earlier editions of the college annual were called the *Harrow, Heliostat,* and *Glück Auf.*[22]

Notre Dame Whips M.A.C.

On October 3, 1899, Notre Dame defeated the M.A.C. football team by a score of 40 to 0. *The M.A.C. RECORD* reported that was 13 points better than the prior year.[23]

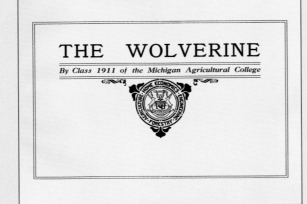

THE WOLVERINE

By Class 1911 of the Michigan Agricultural College

The Realm of Women

Excerpts from Pearl Kedzie's 1898 commencement address.

Home Appeals to All

"If there is one word in the English language which is dearer to us than any other, that word is 'home'. It enshrines all that is most precious, that is most sacred to the human heart...."

Training is Essential

"Knowing the influence of the home to be so powerful, can we give too much thought to perfecting it into an environment which shall give the conditions for the best development of our people?... For the demands of the household, who can be too well prepared? No doctor, lawyer, or minister would think of making a place in the world without years of study and training."

Woman's Education

"It has not been many years since a girl's education was thought to be completed with a knowledge of reading, writing, and arithmetic, together with what was termed the accomplishments, consisting of a little French, painting, and music. Mankind has at last awakened to the real needs of the woman's education.

Courtesy UAHC

"More is expected of the woman of today than ever before. Her education must give her high ideals and practical habits which will enable her to fill any position which the coming century may bring."

Goal

"The education ... aims to make of her the whole woman, whose influence shall be felt for good wherever she may be.... Whatever work she may afterwards undertake will only be helped because she has been made stronger for it by equal training of hand and mind."[24]

Forest Demo Sites

In 1894, the board asked the college farm to illustrate the "most advanced methods of proper handling of woodlots for continued and lasting profits." This decision was based in part on the assumption that timber in Michigan was inexhaustible.

Campus Demo Sites

Professors of agriculture and forestry were charged with the responsibility. They selected four sites —193.6 acres — for forest "laboratories." One parcel lay along the south bank of the Red Cedar River, east of the main farm. The second lay east of Hagadorn Road. Beal planted this parcel with white pines, thus giving rise to its designation, the "Pinetum."* The third and fourth plots included fields 17, 18, and 19.

Vulnerable to Fire

The first two sites required much preparation, in part to remove materials that made the sites vulnerable to burning. Several times while this work was progressing, fire escaped, "doing considerable damage to the young timber."

Natural Reforestation

The fields between the railroad tracks (18 and 19) were different because most of the large timber had been removed for fuel during 1892-93. The researchers cut the remaining large timber on this parcel, leaving only saplings and younger growth "...to exhibit as nearly as possible the natural method of reforestation...."[25]

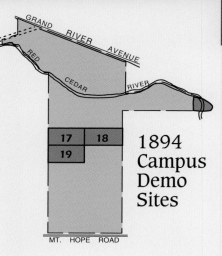

17 18
19

1894 Campus Demo Sites

GRAND RIVER AVENUE
RED CEDAR RIVER
MT. HOPE ROAD

*Beal's son, J.F. Beal, wrote concerning this site, "During the spring of 1896-97, Dr. Beal planted the white pines on the area across the road from the extreme eastern portion of the college farm.... This small patch of forest has many object lessons and should be preserved intact for all time, if for no other reason than to stand as a living monument to the labors of the man who may be justly called the Father of Michigan Forestry. He has been to the state of Michigan what Heinrick Van Cotta was to Saxony."

Understanding Tuberculosis

"Among the notable events in the history of the [experiment] station work for the year, the establishment of a bacteriological division of the veterinary department, principally for work in tuberculosis, may be mentioned."

Animals Tested for TB

"The tuberculin test was applied to the cattle of the college herd for the first time March 31, 1896, and again to part of the herd on the 11th of August.

"The method of applying the test is simple. By means of small but accurate thermometers graduated to tenths of a degree Fahrenheit, the temperature of the animal is taken frequently during a certain day.... Late in the evening of the same day there is injected under the skin behind the left shoulder a dose of tuberculin.... If there is a rise of two degrees or more, and especially if that rise [is] gradual and somewhat constant, it is certain that the disease is present...."

Seven Fail Test

"On the first application of the test on March 31, seven animals reacted so strongly as to be condemned by the veterinarian as surely tuberculous...."

Opportunity to Experiment

"The possession of so many animals known to be tuberculous offered a unique opportunity for carrying on experiments to aid in answering some of the perplexing questions that environ this dread disease...."[26]

Courtesy UAHC

Courtesy UAHC

Robert C. Kedzie, "Father of Sugar Beet Industry".

Sugar Beet Research

The interest of farmers in sugar beets got its start in 1891. Now, six years later, farmers are very interested and are "calling for experiments in growing this new crop."

Washington Sends Seeds

"Through the generosity of the USDA ... a large amount of beet seed was distributed to such farmers in the state as applied, promising to give decent care to the growing roots, and to report ... in the fall, sending samples of their beets for analysis."

Test Plots Needed

"Time has not allowed supervision of these growing plots ... [but] the widespread inter-

(Continued on page 88)

...On Campus and Off

U.P. is Home to 2nd Station

The north central Upper Peninsula became the location of the second experiment station in 1899. The site is near Chatham, about 18 miles southwest of Munising in Alger County.[27]

Gifted Land, State Funding

"The station was initiated with the donation of 160 acres from the Munising Railroad Company. The company also agreed to 'stump, clear, and grub' at least 20 acres so that immediate field demonstration work could begin."[28]

"An early report ... indicated the value of the property, at the time of donation, to be $4,000.[29]

The legislature appropriated $5,000 "to carry on such experiments pertaining to agriculture and horticulture as, in their judgment, will be most beneficial to the agricultural interests of the U.P."[30]

First Objective: Farm Crops

"Farm crops work started at the station in 1900. The plan was to spend the first five years in determining what could be grown ... in the U.P. After the fifth year, experimental work was to involve cultural practices and improvement of varieties.[31]

"About 10 years later the Cleveland Cliffs Iron Company donated 620 acres adjacent to the station. Since the timber had been removed, considerably more land was made available for experiments. It provided enough acres of cropland to start much-needed crops and livestock experiments.

"The goal of this station ... focuses on beef and dairy cattle research as well as feed quality and intake."[32]

Upper Peninsula
Experiment Station

T.T. Lyon, Pioneer Horticulturist

Long-term Supporter

T.T. Lyon had long been an advocate on behalf of the college. As early as 1860, his letter in the *Michigan Farmer* criticized the board's plan to change the college course to a two-year program.

Many Varieties

When the experiment station program began, Mr. Lyon rented 5 acres of land near South Haven to the college for experimental projects. Later, contributions from area growers expanded the site to 10 acres. Kuhn said Lyon was a "pioneer horticulturalist" who "reported each year with affectionate detail on the quality of his hundreds of varieties of peaches, apples, pears, grapes, strawberries, and even figs."[33]

At Lyon's retirement in 1898, Professor C.D. Smith, director of the farm and experiment station, noted T.T. Lyon's decision with the following comments:

Job Well Done

"The South Haven sub-station has made its important impress on the fruit growing interests of western Michigan, largely because of the unique ability of ex-President T.T. Lyon. It is painful to record the close of his life's work, and the necessary severing of the close bonds that have bound his genius to the work of the station."[34]

Lyon passed away on February 6, 1900, at the age of 87.[35]

Courtesy UAHC

T.T. Lyon

Policing Northern College Lands

M.A.C. Timber Stolen

"Last week Secretary Bird made a trip to Alcona and Oscoda Counties to assist the College trespass agent, F.E. Skeels, in collecting money for timber stolen from College lands."

Money Collected

"When he returned, he reported that they had collected $3,595 from the lumbering firm. Mr. Skeels spent his whole time on the college lands in the northern part of the state to detect every theft and assure that the trespasser is either prosecuted or brought to settlement."[36]

Booker T. Washington's Commencement Address

Customarily, commencement exercises included several orations. At the 1900 commencement, Booker T. Washington of Tuskegee Institute, a companion land-grant institution, gave the principal address.

Brick Mason Training

Washington was born a slave at Hales Ford, Virginia, in 1856. After attending mission and public schools in West Virginia, he studied at Hampton Institute. There he learned brick masonry. Teaching, however, was his real penchant, and he became a teacher in his family town and later at Hampton Institute.

Rise to President

When the time came to found and organize a new school at Tuskegee, B.T. Washington helped organize the institute. He served as its president from 1881 to 1915. Among his attributes were excellent oratory skills.

1900 Commencement

This skill, together with his role as a president of a southern land-grant institution, contributed to his attractiveness as a commencement speaker. Following are a few of his comments on June 15, 1900.

Training for Employment

"When I asked, why do you give this man or this woman training in this or that industry? the answer came that when these students come to us we ask in each case, what are the prevailing occupations of the people in the community where the students live? In a word, it is found out what the student can find to do in this immediate community, not what he ought to find to do, not what the instructors might desire him to do, but what the economic and other conditions prevailing in his neighborhood will permit him to do."

Building the Whole Person

"On this industrial foundation will grow habits of thrift, the love of work, economy, ownership in property, a bank account. Out of it in future generations will grow classical education, professional education, positions of public responsibility. Out of it will grow moral and religious strength. Out of it will grow that wealth which brings leisure, and with it the enjoyment of literature and the fine arts."

Courtesy M.A.C. Record

Booker T. Washington, President, Tuskegee Institute.

Institute a Strong Draw

"Beginning with thirty students, the number has grown [and now] connected with the institution are a thousand and more students from twenty-four states.

"During the nineteen years the institution has been in existence hundreds of students have finished the academic and industrial courses...."[37]

Women's Hall Dedication!

October 1900

The new Building for Women (now Morrill Hall) was available for use at the beginning of the 1900-01 academic year. The dedicatory program was held on October 25, 1900.

Large Audience

The facility and dedication had a great deal of symbolic significance. The event was planned to coincide with the annual meeting of the State Federation of Women's Clubs in Lansing. Some 250 club members attended, as did about 50 women from the granges and farmers' clubs. More than 1,000 attended.

Bountiful Banquet

The ceremony ended at noon and was followed by a "bountiful banquet" on the third floor. The reporters present were tempted to list the titles and names of the speakers after the banquet. Nearly a dozen persons from around Michigan and other Midwest states, including Ms. Maud R. Keller, dean of the women's department, made public comments.

Remarks Not Recorded

The remarks were not recorded, a regretted fact mentioned by President Snyder, who said, "They were of an unusually high order and would be read by future young women in this department with great interest and profit. This occasion was a notable one in the history of the college. There perhaps has never been before so large a gathering of representative women in the state."[38]

Courtesy UAHC

Women's Hall, now known as Morrill Hall.

Heritage Remembered

Pioneers and Proud!

Chicago Alumni

S.M. Millard (class of '64) addressed the third annual reunion in 1898, saying, "We do not worship any one man as the founder of our College — no John Harvard, no Hopkins, no Cornell — but in the beginning an idea appeared; a broad knowledge was demanded — a knowledge which would reach out into all walks of life, and elevate all pursuits and callings."

Practical Education

"Our alma mater was among the first colleges in the world to incorporate and crystallize the elements for a broad, practical education to men desiring to break away from the old curricula. The idea was at first crude.... They did not fully realize that the study of chemistry, botany, zoology, geology, and English literature might be as severely disciplinary as the dead languages."

Colleges Follow Plan

"Since our college had its birth, every college in the land has modified its curriculum, and has grafted into its requirements more or less of the sciences, mechanics, and practical arts in life...."

Pioneers' Dream?

"A college for a broad or practical education opened its doors, and our old boys walked in; little did we of the pioneer days dream of the present."[39]

Robert Clark Kedzie: College Hero Passes

The name "Kedzie" was well-known during the founding decades of M.A.C. One of this name, Frank S. Kedzie, along with his brothers, attended the college in the 1870s. F. S. Kedzie became college president in 1915, succeeding President Snyder.

Professor R.C. Kedzie

Preceding Frank at the college was Robert Clark Kedzie. He joined the college in 1863 as professor of chemistry. He had a degree in medicine from the University of Michigan. A professor for more than 39 years, Kedzie died at the college on November 7, 1902.[41]

Model Public Servant

R.C. Kedzie's dedication to public service is a model for all those who followed. He held numerous positions in the public sphere, including a seat in the Michigan House of Representatives (1867), the presidency of the Michigan Medical Society (1874), and the presidency of the Association of Agricultural Colleges and Experiment Stations (1899), among others.

Practical Questions

Many of his life's contributions stemmed from his application of science to practical questions and issues. Among them were his daily recordings of weather conditions, records that were published in the annual reports[42] and distributed throughout the state.[43]

Other research efforts involved the effects of lime, salt, muck, ashes, manure, and night-soil on crops of corn, potatoes, and clover. Later Kedzie went on to other research issues — the dangers of wallpaper tinted with arsenic, fertilizer standards, and the hazards of using volatile liquid in kerosene lamps. Some referred to him as the "father of the sugar beet industry."

Great Man, Great Work

President Snyder said of him, "Dr. Kedzie was a great man and did great work.... Can we not hope that the college, in the not distant future, may give to one of its new buildings the name which has for so many years brought honor and credit to the institution?"

Lasting Recognition

Robert C. Kedzie continues to be recognized by the buildings that carry his name — North and South Kedzie Hall. The north portion, constructed in 1913, was originally the "Kedzie Chemical Laboratory."[44]

Courtesy UAHC

Rock Painting Not New

Those familiar with the campus will readily recall the repaintings of the large rock on Farm Lane near the Red Cedar bridge. It gives notice daily to passers-by. Placing ads on large rocks is not a new phenomenon, at least not in the M.A.C. vicinity. In its October 2, 1900, issue, *The M.A.C. RECORD* included a brief report regarding its assessment of painting rocks in public places.

"The old half-way stone on the Lansing road has recently had its east face painted over with a glaring advertisement. What a shame that this ancient land-mark could not have been left undesecrated!"[40]

"The Rock" is a long-time friend on campus. The rock was once located in the "sacred space" near the Beaumont Tower. Shown with the rock are members of the class of 1871.

State Tax Advances Independence...

Background

Appropriations amounted to nearly $22,000 in 1883 and $13,000 the following year.

Land Sales Revenue Only

The 1885 legislature ended annual operating appropriations for the college on the premise that the Morrill land-grant earnings would be sufficient. Readers will recall that the land sale proceeds were to be endowed funds with interest earnings expended for general purposes.

But Insufficient

In 1890, Congress passed a second Morrill Act appropriating $25,000 to each land-grant institution. Nonetheless, with no appropriations for "current expenses," college resources would not fully meet the rising costs of an expanding student body in a growing economy.

U-M Funding is Model

What was to be done? The model was the way the legislature funded the state university — with a property tax levy. In 1873, the legislature imposed a property tax of 1/20th of a mill on taxable property in the state to fund the university. (The university levy had been increased three times during the 27-year period.)

One-fifteenth Mill Requested

"After careful deliberation the board decided to ask the legislature for a tax of 1/15th of a mill. The House committee, however, of whom Mr. B.A. Nevins — class of '74 — was chairman, decided to make an appeal for 1/10th of a mill.... It was decided later to limit the amount to $100,000. In this form the bill passed both Houses and received the signature of the governor."

The New Way of Getting Things Done

In 1902 then, college revenue, including the two Morrill acts and the Hatch Act proceeds, rose to $205,000. For the most part this significant increase in revenues eliminated the legislature's special appropriations for several years.[45]

Quality and Size are Priority

In 1902, President Snyder articulated a new approach to campus buildings. He said, "It is very much desired that the college cease the erection of cheap buildings to meet simply present demand.... The institution has reached that period in its development where only buildings of a substantial character should be erected. The size also should be such as to allow for future growth."

Bacteriology Need

The decision in 1902 revealed some of these priorities. Snyder reported. "The Board, realizing the important part which bacteriology must play in agricultural education and experimentation ... decided to erect a building devoted to this subject."

Marshall Hall

"The new building is a beautiful brick structure 59 by 76 feet, two stories high with a well lighted basement. When completed and furnished the cost will amount to about $30,000. It will be one of the best of its kind in the country." The structure on "laboratory row" is now known as Marshall Hall, honoring Professor Charles E. Marshall, who served as chairperson of the Department of Bacteriology and Hygiene.[46]

Marshall Hall underwent major renovations in 2004-05.

Building Needs Continue to Grow

As President Snyder closed his expressions of gratitude for the property tax solution to college funding, he indicated that "...there will be left for the present between sixty and seventy thousand dollars per annum for building purposes. This can be put to splendid use in meeting the following needs of the college."

Heating and Water Plant: Both systems were "inaugurated nineteen years ago.... Wooden pipes were used [in the water system]. It is estimated that a proper system would cost $60,000."

Mechanical Engineering: "In our mechanical engineering course we have 222 students ... the same shop room, drawing rooms, etc., as were thought necessary when it numbered only about 90 students...."

Auditorium and Library: "A fire-proof library and auditorium would cost about eighty thousand dollars."

Engineering: "[T]his department was satisfactory when the college had but 200 students, but at the present time there are 200 students studying chemistry, and 170 studying physics...."

Bacteriological: "Four years ago we began this work and assigned rooms for it in the veterinary building. The department has outgrown these rooms, and must have a new habitation soon."

Others: "Our botanical building is over-crowded and should have an addition. Our agricultural department should have a fine agricultural building. Ohio has an agricultural building, costing $100,000; and Wisconsin this year received $150,000 for the erection of such a building."[47]

...and Scholarship

Campus is Connected

Transportation was an ongoing problem. The campus was located 3 miles from downtown Lansing, and though a streetcar from Lansing to Harrison Road began running in 1894, the campus was still difficult to reach. Gradually, though, conditions improved.

Coal Delivery

In his report for 1900, President Snyder noted, "The Pere Marquette Railroad built a track from Trowbridge road to the college. The expense to the college was one thousand dollars. This was a very important improvement.

"The coal for the year ... was brought direct to the college campus. It has also proved very valuable by enabling the different railroads to run their excursion trains to the college without having to depend upon streetcar service."

Streetcar Improved

"By the turn of the century, the streetcar line was extended to the northeast corner of the arboretum. The streetcar line extension resulted in many more people coming to the campus, many of them attracted by the elk, deer, and angora goats kept in the arboretum."[48]

Courtesy UAHC

Michigan Avenue crossing the Grand River, early 1900s.

Academic Threshold Rises

Record Enrollment

President Snyder expressed great satisfaction at the new high for student enrollment when the total reached 552 in 1900.

He said, "It would have been larger had not the requirements for admission been more rigidly enforced. Quite a number were refused admission and others were advised to take one more year for further preparation in the public schools before endeavoring to enter the institution. In consequence of this action there were not so many failures as in previous years."

Low Performers Out

"It has been the aim of the institution to maintain a high standard of work. At the end of each term a committee on doubtful cases goes over the record of each student carefully, and those who have fallen below a reasonable standard are requested not to return.... It is now quite well understood among the students that if their work be of such a character as to call in question their ability to do successful work during the next term, they are liable to be requested not to continue in college longer."[49]

Student Government Out...

...Self-governance In

"For more than 20 years, 1876-1896, the discipline of the college was intrusted [sic] to the student body.

"At that time the college was well adapted for the successful carrying out of such a plan. The number of students — less than 200 — was not too large; there was but one course of study, hence their interests were the same; they nearly all lived in the dormitories on the grounds and could be summoned together quickly and easily; the isolation of the college rendered it free from outside influence...."

Students Lose Interest

"During the fall term of '96, the students' organization was at low ebb. The better element among students was willing to give it up. The faculty members were equally willing to assume control. During the winter term the faculty quietly exercised its authority and student government was a thing of the past at M.A.C."[50]

Reflections – the Campus and the Decade

One Student's Memories of Campus Life

"My dormitory, Williams Hall, stood four stories.... About sixty boys lived on the first three floors. Boarding clubs lodged in the basement.... Columbian, Hesperian, and Eclectic literary societies filled the fourth floor."

Multiple Use of Water

"All water for hazing, as well as that for washing, was drawn from a central water closet. There was a bathhouse back of Old Wells Hall. It required a miracle of adjustment — one simply had to be an artist — to draw a shower that was not either piping hot or ice cold, or alternately each...."

Room Furnishings

"The student furnished his room in the dormitory. Most students bought a kitchen table for $1.50, which they used as a desk, and a cot and mattress for $4.50. For my room my mother had stripped the parlor bedroom, heretofore kept sacrosanct for guests, of its best furnishings...."

Freshman-Sophomore Scrap

"When the freshmen met the first time early in the fall term a traditional class scrap took place between sophomores and freshmen. Juniors cheered the freshmen on, and seniors egged on the sophomores. It was a rough, unorganized, and unsupervised battle, ending when one side retreated from the field to avoid being ducked in the fountain near College Hall. Few boys emerged unscathed, or would care to, for bruises were symbols of class loyalty and were worn as badges...."[51]

1904 Enrollment

	Agric. (men)	Mech. (men)	Homemaking (women)	Total
Freshmen	73	131	36	240
Sophomores	16	52	15	83
Juniors	24	30	30	84
Seniors	35	23	13	71
Graduate students	1	1	2	4
Sub-freshmen	57	97	30	184
Special	18	19	83	120
Special courses students	137			137
Total	361	353	209	923[*]

[*]Deduct six repeated names for a total of 917. No students from foreign nations were reported.

The 1904 student body represented 58 counties and 14 states.[52]

Sugar Beet...

(Continued from page 82)

est taken in the matter leads us to hope that a goodly number of reports will be received ... and the question of adaptability of Michigan soil and climate ... may be settled, if the results of experiments of this year corroborate the work of 1891."

Processing Plant

"When it is remembered that it requires ... over $350,000 to build a factory for the manufacture of sugar from beets, the importance of being able to show ... that suitable beets can be grown and that the farmers know how to grow them, can be readily appreciated...."[53]

Period in Review

No doubt those at the college in 1904 would look back and say, "It was a good ten years." Several factors mark the success of the period.

Solid Enrollment Gains

Among them is the growth in student enrollment. In 1904, the student body grew to a total of 780 regular students. The number would reach 923 if one included the "special short course" students.

Women's Program and Hall

Establishment of the women's program and the construction of Women's Hall occurred in the period. The 209 women contributed significantly to the overall size of the student body.

Courtesy M.A.C. RECORD

M.A.C. logo.

New Financial Flexibility

The decision of the Michigan Legislature to fund the operating costs of the college with a statewide property tax millage was a major benchmark. The funding of $100,000 per year not only generated financial stability for the college but gave the college a degree of financial independence for a period.

Improved Relations with Public

The college enjoyed other marks of success. Promoting the college and building sound relations with the public by inviting visitors to the campus and by sending them information about the college helped the college overcome the challenges present at the beginning of the period.

Faculty Action Plan

Perhaps one factor not widely recognized was the work of the Special Faculty Committee, which prepared the plan of action for the decade. Its analysis and recommendations underlay most of the college actions that made the period successful.

"President Theodore Roosevelt stated ... his desire to make one address to the farmers of this country ... this would be the occasion ... the semi-centennial celebration of the Michigan Agricultural College."

President Snyder, 1906

"Much that was considered essential a few years ago has already, or will soon, give way to something better; but the preparation of young men and women for their places as members of society, as responsible citizens, as future leaders in their own communities, will not be lost sight of in the effort to make them exceptionally capable in their chosen lines of work."

President Snyder, 1906

"This agricultural extension movement is likely to prove the greatest work [the colleges] have ever done."

Senator Hoke Smith,
co-author of Smith-Lever Act, 1913

College is Confident...

Institutes Enthusiastically Received

The 1905-1914 period was one of great progress. Student enrollment grew steadily. Highlights for the period include the celebration of the 50th anniversary of the college's opening. Through a well coordinated campaign, the college was pleased to have President Theodore Roosevelt speak at the celebration and grant certificates to graduates.

Federal Support

Also marking the period was the enactment of the Smith-Lever Act. This federal statute provided funding for the establishment and operation of the Department of Extension. As is noted, extension services to Michigan farmers and farming communities had been provided for many years, and the Michigan model of having field agents give instruction around the state was very instrumental in getting the federal, state, and county governments to assist in funding these services.

New Ag Hall

Other changes included the construction of what was the largest building on the campus — Agriculture Hall — and the loss of Wells Hall to fire. Student life was begin-

ning to change as the area surrounding the campus began to develop and accommodate student residences. The decade also set the foundation for the institutional structure organizing departments into "divisions."

Engineering Dispute

A key dispute during the decade involved the issue of whether the state required two institutions to teach engineering. The college was fortunate in having influential friends around the state to support the appeal of college officials. A thoughtful judge also proved helpful.

Legislature Supportive

The legislature was very supportive of the college in 1895. The legislature appropriated funds for new buildings and special program support:

Northern Experiment Station	$ 9,000
Experimental work in livestock	20,000
New barn, moving, repairing existing units	15,000
New dormitory	55,000

In addition, the legislature removed the $100,000 ceiling on the college property tax.

The estimated increase resulting from this action on the mill tax was $15,000, which would be used for erecting and equipping an additional building.[1]

Founded at M.A.C.

Professors Kedzie, Beal, and Carpenter were key in establishing the Farmers' Institutes. The program consisted of lectures, essays, and discussions in various locations around the state during the winter. It became a model for agricultural colleges nationwide. Demand in Michigan was strong. The initial institutes were funded by the college with some state appropriations.

A Popular Program

"The current report [1906] reflects the development and challenges of continuing the program. Under the present law, institute societies are

Courtesy UAHC

Typical of traveling Farmers' Institutes.

formed in each county and upon their initiative one two-day institute, and where convenient, a few one-day meetings, are held in each county. Speakers are provided by the state, under direction of the college.... Last year [1905] there were 74 two-day institutes with a total attendance of 65,285 and 257 one-day institutes with a total attendance of 57,148; making a total attendance of 122,433."

Traveling Institutes

"In addition to these meetings, the college held 'railroad institutes' during the month of April in cooperation with the Lake Shore & Michigan Southern and the Michigan Central railroads.... Each road

furnished a special train consisting of two passenger coaches and one baggage car, and stops of from one hour to an hour and a quarter were made at each meeting.... These traveling institutes were accompanied by several newspaper reporters, railway officials, and representatives of leading farm journals. Governor [Fred M.] Warner [1905-1910] was with the 'corn train' one day and made several addresses."[2]

...and Moving Forward

New Infrastructure

Key utility system elements were put in place in 1906. At the center of the newly constructed system was a power plant with a large smokestack. The plant was located just north of the Red Cedar River. The facility generated power to the campus until the 1940s.

New Power Plant

"The building proper is 100 by 70 feet. The smokestack is 125 feet high, 6 feet in diameter inside at the base. It is built of vitrified hollow blocks.

"There are four 150-H.P. Scotch marine boilers equipped with the Jones Underfeed stokers. There are two 125-kilowatt dynamos.

These are duplicates, either one of which is ample to carry the entire load. A smaller 45-kilowatt dynamo carries the day load.

"A coal shed of 1,800 tons capacity is located back of the boiler house. The coal is transferred to hoppers automatically. The entire plant represents engineering skill of a high grade and will be of great educational value to all our engineering students."

Tunnels

"From this building, tunnels radiate to all the large buildings on the grounds. These tunnels are constructed of concrete, and are six feet wide and six and one-half feet high."[3]

1907 Enrollment[4]

	Agric.	Engin.	Home Ec.	Forestry	Total
Sub-freshmen	55	71	14	—	140
Freshmen	74	113	34	—	221
Sophomores	37	85	25	3	150
Juniors	32	42	19	3	96
Seniors	38	54	18	5	115
Postgraduates	2	—	3	—	5
Special students	14	14	48	—	76
Special courses	198	5	—	—	203
Totals	**450**	**384**	**161**	**11**	**1006**

Delete five repeated names.
Sixty-two counties, 11 states, and one foreign nation were represented.

Wells Hall Fire is a Shocker!

Early Morning Fire

Early on February 11, 1905, occupants discovered a fire in a partition between rooms in the basement of Wells Hall. President Snyder reported, "The hallways of the west ward were so full of smoke when the fire was discovered that the students living on the third floor were compelled to come down fire escapes."

Volunteer Firefighters Ready

"In ... not more than five or six minutes, our volunteer fire department had the hose stretched and was ready for action. Great credit is due our fire department....

"Our volunteer fire department consists of twelve young men, six for each line of hose. They drill one hour a day for three days per week. This work is taken in place of military drill and is under the direction and care of Mr. Thomas Gunson."

Water Supply Ample

"In our power house a large pump is kept in readiness for fire emergencies ... [and] water pressure of 150 pounds was immediately at the service of the fire department. Every precaution was taken

Courtesy UAHC

Wells Hall was destroyed by fire.

to guard against accidents to students and it is a pleasure to record that no one was injured." The building, however, was destroyed.

Student Relief Provided

"Immediately after the fire, a student relief fund was raised. [The intention was to give the money to] students who lost their clothing and books in the fire ... [but] it was their desire that the money be loaned to them with the expectation that it be returned after they were through college. About $1,100 was contributed to this fund...."[5]

Beal and Cook Honored

The college honored Dr. William J. Beal and Dr. A. J. Cook (then at Pasadena College, California) by awarding them honorary doctor of science degrees for their years of faithful service to the college. Beal was in his 35th year of service to the college at the time; Cook had been professor of zoology and entomology for 27 years.[6]

Woman's Building from front of President's Office

The Michigan Agricultural College

Offers Thorough Courses in

AGRICULTURE   ENGINEERING   HOME ECONOMICS
FORESTRY and VETERINARY MEDICINE

SOME advantages of M. A. C. are: Ideal location, pleasant surroundings, moral atmosphere, social advantages, sanitary conditions, a democratic spirit, splendidly equipped laboratories and thoroughly trained teachers

The graduates of this College readily find employment because they are prepared to solve the every day problems of life.   This is a practical age, and the demand is for men and women trained along practical lines

Are you prepared to enter college next year?   If so, you should plan at once to do so.   But before deciding upon *The College* send for catalog of M. A. C. and learn of the advantages offered there to earnest young people

J. L. SNYDER, *President*   ::   EAST LANSING, MICH.

M.A.C. promotion continues.

Changes in Student Social Life

Courtesy UAHC

Eclectic Society Room in Williams Hall.

Growth and Change

"The rapid increase in attendance during the recent years has [changed] the social life of the student body. Formerly, nearly all students lived in dormitories, took their meals in large boarding clubs, and seventy-five percent or more of the Literary Societies which occupied rooms were in the basement or upper story of one of the dormitories."

Life in Dorms

"Under these conditions student life was very democratic. Rich and poor were on the same level. Each student formed an intimate acquaintance with a large number of fellow students. If he completed a full course he could number his friends by the hundreds, if not by the thousands. In after life he appreciates these friends.... He values the friendships as one of the chief assets of his college life."

Buildings Erected

"There seems to be a very marked and strong tendency on the part of several of the older societies to erect their own buildings which will provide living rooms and boarding facilities for their members; in other words, to follow the fraternity house plan...."

Social Choices at Issue

"There is much in the fraternity house to be commended ... but the question is not the mode of student life they foster, but rather the advisability of changing from the free, democratic, wholesome social life which has characterized this college to the exclusive, expensive, and somewhat aristocratic ideas [in] the modern trend of fraternity life in larger institutions."[7]

Curriculum Review and Decisions

Broad Curriculum?

"The faculty has discussed ... our courses for agricultural and women students. The opinion of the faculty is practically unanimous that this college should retain in its [programs] certain general culture studies, such as English, history, political economy, etc."

Outside Profession?

"It does not look with favor upon the free elective system adopted by some distinguished agricultural schools, which makes it possible for a student to gain the bachelor's degree without mathematics beyond the rudiments of arithmetic, or without pursuing even to a limited extent those culture studies which give to the student a degree of ease in expressing his own thoughts, and a fair appreciation of the great fields of knowledge that lie outside his own narrow profession."

Goal: Capability

"Much that was considered essential a few years ago has already, or will soon, give way to something better; but the preparation of young men and women for their places as members of society, as responsible citizens, as future leaders in their own communities, will not be lost sight of in the effort to make them exceptionally capable in their chosen lines of work."[8]

...Brings on Change

Restructuring Ag Programs

By 1908, the new Agriculture Hall was nearly completed. Because many programs were to be housed there, it was reasonable to consolidate the programs administratively. President Snyder said, "The rapid development of the lines of agricultural instruction ... made it seem advisable for the board to place the lines of work, such as agriculture, horticulture, veterinary science, and forestry under one person as dean."

Shaw Appointed Dean

"Professor Robert S. Shaw, who has been the efficient head of our Agricultural Department for the past six years, was appointed to this responsible position."[9]

Organizational Refinements

Dean Shaw restructured the programs into "distinct departments as follows: Farm Crops, Soils, Animal Husbandry, Dairy Husbandry, Farm and Horses, Poultry, Farm Mechanics, Agricultural Education, and Agricultural Extension."

Shaw explained, "The new form of organization permits the concentration of effort, resulting in specialization and the exercise of specialized effort toward industries in the state of sufficient importance...."[10]

Three Lines

He noted, "The work of nearly all departments may be given a triple classification, viz.: education, experimentation, and extension. Only three of the ten departments receive federal appropriations for experimentation. The work of horticulture and crops is maintained in part from Hatch Act funds while the soil investigations receive support from the Adams Act revenues."[11]

Courtesy UAHC

Ag Hall Contract Awarded

"...[T]he board decided to erect a building for the agricultural department. E.A. Bowd, the college architect, is preparing plans. The contract will be let and the building well under way this fall [1907].

"This building will be the most expensive yet erected upon the campus and will cost not less than one hundred twenty-five thousand dollars. It will occupy the site at the southeastern corner of the campus formerly occupied by the original barns."[12]

New Building Needs

Expand Classrooms

The growing enrollment led to a need for more buildings. In 1906, President Snyder explained the need for more classroom space and a building for the agricultural department.

"The growth in attendance during the past few years," Snyder said, "has very much overcrowded our classrooms and laboratories."

Classes in Old Barn

"The engineering building, which is now under construction, will give some relief.... An old barn has been converted into classrooms, so great is the demand for room."

Library is at Risk

"Our library is not fire-proof and is very much overcrowded. Book shelves have been placed in many of the alcoves and room for students is ... less each year."

Gymnasium Needed

"The college has no gymnasium for young men. Formerly the armory was used, but with the large number in military drill, there is no space for gymnastic work."

Women's Wing

"The additional wing [that, was omitted from the women's building] and more space for botany should be provided."[13]

Courtesy Einer Olstrom collection

Site for the new Ag Hall — Marshall Hall is on the right along with cabbage plants in the foreground. The smokestack of the new power plant north of the Red Cedar River can be seen on the left.

Jubilee Celebration — 50 Years!

Planning the Anniversary

Anticipating the coming celebration, President Snyder appointed a faculty committee to develop a plan for the 50th anniversary.

Invite the President?

The prospect of inviting President Roosevelt and not knowing whether he would accept was cause for uncertainty. The issue was not only whether he would attend but the effect his presence would stimulate in the community.

M.A.C. Alumni Association

In addition, the M.A.C. Alumni Association had postponed its regular gathering so it could join the Jubilee Celebration. This association gathering would have a significant effect on the overall attendance.

Ag Colleges Association

Another factor was the American Association of Agricultural Colleges and Experiment Stations. This organization had planned for several years to hold its 1907 meeting at this time so it could participate in the Jubilee Celebration. Fortunately, the Downey House was recently rebuilt and agreed to reserve 140 of its best rooms for association members.

Paying Expenses

In addition, the committee had to decide how to pay the expenses of the celebration. The college possessed no funds for these purposes. Fortunately, the State Legislature appropriated $8,000 for the expenses. The board accepted the funds and directed the committee to plan the program within this amount.

When to Hold the Celebration

The date of the college's opening was May 13, 1857, but the committee felt uneasy about this date. The committee chose the last week of May, to have the baccalaureate graduation on the Sunday preceding the week of celebration and present the diplomas as part of the closing celebration ceremony.[14]

Getting Teddy to Town

While planning the jubilee celebration, someone suggested that "President Roosevelt might be induced to honor the jubilee of this college with his presence. The matter was taken up quietly."

How does one get the president to come to town?

1. The Hon. C.J. Monroe attended the M.A.C. alumni meeting in D.C., visited the president, and extended an invitation.

2. Governor Fred M. Warner, while in Washington, called on the president and urged him to come to Michigan.

3. The State Board invited Roosevelt and asked President Snyder to present the invitation in person.

4. "Accompanied by Senator Barrows, Congressman Gardner, and Professor Curtis, Snyder delivered the invitation on April 18, 1906. (Professor C.F. Curtis of Iowa represented the American Association of Agricultural Colleges and Experiment Stations, and assured the president that all the other agricultural colleges would send delegates and not press him to visit the other institutions.)"

5. Snyder also presented letters of invitation from the State Grange, the State Association of Farmers' Clubs, and the State Horticultural Society.

A Favorable Response

"Finally," wrote Snyder, "the president stated that it was his desire to make one address to the farmers of this country while he was in office, and probably this would be the proper occasion. In a few weeks his secretary opened communication with me as to the arrangement of the date, and the press dispatcher from the White House stated that the president had decided to speak at the semi-centennial celebration of the Michigan Agricultural College."[16]

Jubilee Activities

The Jubilee Celebration week in 1907 began with commencement exercises on Sunday. Monday and Tuesday were arrival days. Wednesday the day opened bright and warm. Snyder called the alumni meeting to order at 10 a.m. The afternoon was reserved for a baseball game. The final score was M.A.C.: 1, U of M: 2. The evening program offered a rendition by the college chorus of the "Elijah" accompanied by the Bach Orchestra.

Magnificent Light Display

"Considerable effort had been put forth in preparing for the illumination of the campus.... Rows of incandescent lights were run along the tops and edges of the roofs, down the corners, and all projections, until the buildings fairly glowed. Wires were stretched and ... every few feet Japanese lanterns lighted with electric bulbs."[15]

Michiganians Welcome President Teddy

Friday — Jubilee Celebration!

A Bright, Clear Day

"Friday morning opened bright and clear with every promise of fine weather.... Everybody looked forward to the Friday afternoon meeting as the climax of the Jubilee exercises. In anticipation of good weather and a great crowd, a platform [15 by 30 feet] had been erected overlooking the open space of ground southeast of the president's house. This platform was south of the road and west of the large elm."

Residents Join In

"The citizens of Lansing took great interest, not only in the visit of the president, but in the entire jubilee exercises, and rendered very valuable assistance. Upon arriving at the Capitol the president held a brief reception in the governor's parlors.... He then spoke a few words from the balcony to the large crowd on the front lawn, after which he spoke ... to an audience made up of state officials, members of the legislature and their friends."

The Reo Ride

"The trip from Lansing to the college was made in automobiles. The Reo Company furnished 10 cars to transport the president's party and special guests to the college, and the Olds Company a like number for the return trip."

T.R. Plants Elm Tree

"The battalion then quickly formed two lines from the steps of the residence to the platform from which he was to speak. Between these lines the president and other guests marched to the platform, halting for a moment midway while the president planted a tree. This young elm was about an inch and a quarter in diameter and seven feet tall."[17]

Courtesy UAHC

President Roosevelt and R.E. Olds (in the rear seat) leave the state Capitol for the campus.

Roosevelt Addresses College

"The platform was occupied by the candidates for the honorary degrees, the president's party, and a few distinguished citizens of Michigan. The president was given a hearty, cordial but dignified greeting by the audience [estimated to be from 20,000 to 25,000 persons]."

Standard Introduction

"The president of the college introduced the speaker in the following words, 'Ladies and gentlemen, the President of the United States of America, Theodore Roosevelt.'"

Energetic Speech

"The address was delivered from a small manuscript printed in large type on one side of the paper. The president held this in one hand and did not read it closely, quite frequently gesticulating with both hands. He spoke quite slowly, in a high penetrating tone of voice, and was heard by nearly all present. He was about one hour and fifteen minutes in delivering his address.... When he finished, the audience sang 'America.'"

Roosevelt Presents Diplomas

"The bachelor's degree was conferred on the senior class, ninety-six in number; they were requested to come forward and receive their diplomas. They were happily surprised to receive their parchments from the hand of President Roosevelt....

"The president of the college then conferred honorary degrees on delegates from sixteen agricultural colleges from around the nation."

Dismissal, Departure

"The audience was dismissed by the benediction. The president, his secretary, and Congressman S.W. Smith, occupying one automobile, were driven by Mr. Frederick Smith, one of the officials of the Olds Motor Car Company...."

Great Time

"During the evening the reunions, banquets, and parties of the various literary societies were held ... and an exceptionally happy time was reported by all concerned."[18]

Almost "College Park"

One Community — Two Units

The land selected for the campus in 1855 was located in both Meridian and Lansing townships. The boundary line parallels Abbot Street. The community, as they often do, developed without regard to governmental boundaries.

Plan: Organize a City

According to one source, the division of the community developing north of the campus often gave rise to "political conflicts and bureaucratic red tape."[19] These led to the conclusion that the community should be organized as a city.

"College Park City"?

As was done until 1909, a legislative act established the city entity. The legislative action took place in the 1907 session. The house approved the bill naming the city College Park.[20]

No, East Lansing

When the senate reviewed the bill, however, a majority thought the name East Lansing would be better. The house concurred, and with Governor Warner's signature, the city and name became official. C.D. Smith, dean of short courses, became mayor of the new city.*

*As it turned out, Smith served as mayor for less than one year. In April 1908, he resigned his professorship to become president of the Luiz de Queiroz College of Agriculture in Piracicaba, Brazil.

Campus Planning

Landscape Architect Advisor

"The board employed the noted landscape architect, Mr. Simons, of Chicago, to visit the college last spring and spend two or three days in looking over the campus.... This was done not with a view to any radical changes but rather, if possible, to settle upon some plan with reference to the location of buildings in the future."

"Sacred Space"

"He approved slight changes in a few of the old roads and removal of some unimportant trees. His suggestion that no new building be placed on the inner campus has been approved by the board and will, no doubt, be adhered to in the future. If this policy is followed, the M.A.C. campus will go down to future generations as a 'thing of beauty and joy forever.'

"His other important recommendation was that the new auditorium and administration building which we hope to erect in the near future be located near the public highway northeast of the horticultural building. This building will very naturally be a center of campus life, and the wisdom of placing it on the edge of the campus is doubted by some."[22]

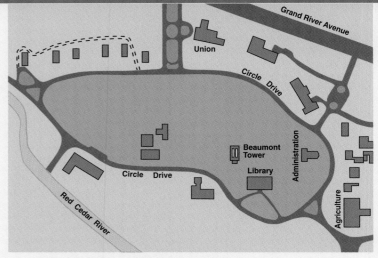

The "Sacred Ground" defined by Circle Drive.

People's Church Building

Worship Tradition

"On each Sunday during the attendance of students, a public meeting for worship has been held ever since the opening of the college in 1857. Some time in 1906, perhaps sooner, the subject of establishing a church in East Lansing was considered. Accordingly a church was organized and for a time services ... were conducted in the chapel."

College People Promote Church

"The chief promoters were college people. The cornerstone for a church building was laid on Sunday, October 23, 1909, on a lot north of the college.... The building is largely made of brick and cement and has four massive pillars in front with a dome in place of a steeple."[21]

Courtesy Michigan State Archives

The permit for construction of People's Church is posted (on left) along Grand River Avenue.

...College Decisions

Faculty Organization

The M.A.C. Record reported that the State Board had adopted a plan to establish divisions (colleges in today's terms). The purpose, according to the *Record*, was to enable the faculty to share responsibilities for teaching. The board authorized the president of the college to organize the faculty.

The general rules associated with the changes were:

- "At the beginning of each year the presiding officers shall appoint a secretary to keep careful minutes of all meetings.
- "All action taken by a division faculty must be approved by the [college] faculty before it can become operative. These divisional faculty shall have only advisory power....

- "Meetings may be called by the dean, or the body by vote of its members.

- "Any teacher whose name appears on the pay roll of the college is entitled to membership....

- "He shall also have the power to assign part of the teachers in a department to any one faculty and part to another in order that each department may have representation in the division in which its work lies."[23]

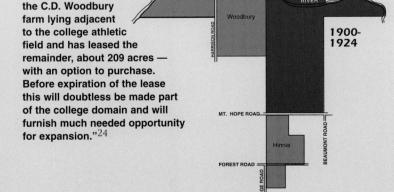

Land Purchases, 1912

"The Board of Agriculture, as by legislative authority, purchased 27 acres of the C.D. Woodbury farm lying adjacent to the college athletic field and has leased the remainder, about 209 acres — with an option to purchase. Before expiration of the lease this will doubtless be made part of the college domain and will furnish much needed opportunity for expansion."[24]

Veterinary Division Established

Pressures for Vet School

"For a number of years considerable pressure has been brought to bear upon the State Board, by the livestock interests of the state and the state veterinary associations, to establish a well-equipped veterinary school at this institution. The board finally acceded ... and has organized a veterinary division that will prepare young men to practice the profession of veterinary medicine."

Four-Year Course

"The veterinary students will receive the same instruction through the freshman year and part of the sophomore year as is given to the agricultural students. Beginning with the second term of the sophomore year, veterinary students will be given largely technical work.... The purpose is to maintain a school of veterinary science that will be of equal rank with the best institutions of this kind in the country.

"Dr. Richard P. Lyman has been placed in charge of this division of the college as dean. He is a graduate of Massachusetts Agricultural College and Harvard Veterinary School."[25]

M.A.C. Academic Divisions and Departments, 1912

Agriculture

Agricultural Education
Animal Husbandry
Dairy Husbandry
Experiment Station
Extension
Farm Crops
Farm and Horses
Farm Mechanics
Forestry
Horticulture
Poultry
Soils

Engineering

Civil Engineering
Drawing and Design
Mechanical Engineering
Physical and Electrical
  Engineering

Home Economics

Domestic Arts
Domestic Science

Science and Letters

Bacteriology
Botany
Chemistry
English
Entomology
History
Military Science
Physical Culture
Zoology

Veterinary Science

Ag Hall is Site for Short Courses

In December 1909, the college announced to prospective participants the short course offerings scheduled in the new Agriculture Hall in January.

Discovering Opportunities

"The short courses offer an opportunity to young men who have not the time or means to take a regular course of technical training.... It educates him to see his opportunities which are really the essence of modern education. The instruction is absolutely practical."[26]

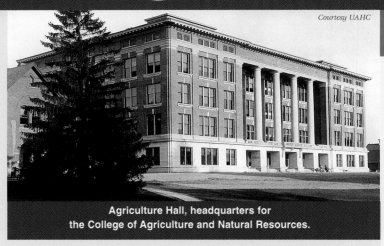

Courtesy UAHC

Agriculture Hall, headquarters for the College of Agriculture and Natural Resources.

The New Agriculture Hall

Most readers will not likely refer to Ag Hall as the new Agriculture Hall. It is the one they have always known. However, it did have a predecessor. The new Ag Hall was completed in 1909 and stands just south of the first "Ag Hall." The old one, now named Alfred J. Cook Hall, became the Entomology Building.[27]

Built on Barn Sites

Before construction began, the college cleared several barns from the site. The horse barn and cattle barn were removed to make room for the new structure.

New Structural Standard

No other college building was quite so large as the new Ag Hall. It and the counter-anchor of the "Laboratory Row" structures — the Women's Hall (Morrill Hall) — together began to project how the campus might develop.

Agriculture Hall was the largest building on the campus at the time. Its dimensions were 190 feet by 86 feet. As Beal stated, the building is "five stories high, including the basement and finished attic."[28]

Array of Uses

Present occupants of Ag Hall will likely marvel at how the building they now occupy was used. Beal reported that it "accommodates the work of farm mechanics, meat demonstration, farm machinery, instruction in the use of cement, animal husbandry, agronomy, work in soils, chemistry of the experiment station, a large assembly hall, and numerous offices and store rooms."[29]

Early Years of Soils Department

Only One Prof

The Soils Department in 1909 was getting organized and becoming involved with Michigan's citizens. Joseph A. Jeffrey, the department head; was the only faculty member until A.R. Potts, a member of the original Department of Agriculture, was appointed extension (field) agent for the two new departments, Soils and Crops.

The Soils Department moved into the agricultural building in 1910. Three classrooms, two student laboratories, a private laboratory, an apparatus room, and a stockroom were assigned to the Soils Department.

Long-term Prof

In 1911, the department hired G. J. Bouyocos as its first faculty member with a doctoral degree. His service in the department ended 53 years later in 1964. Heavily involved in research, he was the faculty member with the longest service record in the department.

Department chair Jeffrey reported strong demand for information about soils. In his annual report he reported strong demand for soils Extension specialists from the State Teachers Association, high school teachers of agriculture, Farmers' Institutes, boys involved in corn growing contests, county YMCAs, normal schools, and county commissioners.[30]

Department of Agricultural Education

Agriculture in Schools

"In recent years there has been a growing demand for the introduction of agricultural instruction into the public schools. The great obstacle in this way has been the lack of qualified teachers."

Train Teachers

"The responsibility of leadership in this new and desirable field of work seemed to lie with the Agricultural College. It is the only institution in the State prepared to give instruction in agriculture. It cannot, of course, train teachers for rural or graded schools, but it can pre-pare teachers for the county normal training schools, the high schools and the State normal schools."

Walter French Leader

"The College, ever ready to meet the responsibilities which come to it, has established a Department of Agricultural Education. Prof. Walter H. French, who has ably filled ... the position of State Department of Public Instruction Secretary, has been placed in charge...."[31]

Courtesy UAHC

Ag Hall Pavilion serves as auditorium.

Campus Life Issues

Keeping the Campus Democratic

More Dormitories, More Fraternities?

President Snyder in 1908 stated his views about "maintaining the democratic spirit" on the campus. The comments apparently stirred up a good deal of concern; enough so that the board chairman wrote a letter to alumni to learn of their opinions.

Societies Undemocratic?

The letter stated that the college "... has 10 literary societies for young men. The college has nine suites of rooms in Williams and Wells Halls which are available for use of these societies without charge. Two societies have built houses — one on the campus, which is used for social and literary purposes only — the other off the campus which is used as a home for its members.... It is in all respects a modern fraternity house."

On Other Campuses

"At least three or four other societies are anxious to build houses of the latter type, either on or off the campus. In their favor the claim is made that at the majority of our large universities fraternity houses are very common, permitted and sanctioned by the boards of control of these universities...."

Expensive and Exclusive?

"On the other hand it is claimed that these fraternity houses add very much to the cost of living; that only young men of considerable means can afford to live in a fraternity house; ... and naturally set a pace which the farmer boy or ordinary young man cannot follow...."

Key Question

"The question is, shall the college foster the fraternity idea of housing students and permit the building of fraternity houses with rooming and boarding facilities.... Will you not write me fully on this question? (Signed, R. D. Graham)"[32]

The college heard from 585 respondents, with most supporting the dormitory idea. The board then adopted a resolution to support the dormitory approach and not give its support for literary housing for student living.

Alums Reply and Board Responds

The college mailed the chairman's letter to alumni and received 585 responses. In summary the respondents:

- Almost unanimously endorsed the dormitory idea.
- Endorsed the type of literary society at this college.
- Believed strongly that this college should maintain a simple, wholesome social life within the means of the average student.
- Concluded that fraternity houses increase greatly the expense of students.
- Testified that "the moral life in fraternity houses is not free from censure."

The board resolution stated:

"RESOLVED: it shall be the policy ... to foster the dormitory system and increase quarters for social purposes.

"We conceive it to be the duty of the board to keep such an institution within the reach of the average student...."[33]

The Life of One M.A.C. Grad

Courtesy L.S. Brumm collection

Lynn S. Brumm (second from left) with his laboratory classmates.

Lynn S. Brumm grew up in Nashville, Michigan. Class valedictorian, he enrolled in M.A.C. in 1908.

First Farm Job

After college, he was farm manager for the Michigan School for the Deaf in Flint. He took his new bride to Ann Arbor to visit his "Uncle John", a professor at U of M. That day, M.A.C. won its first game against U of M, 12 to 7. Uncle John was not pleased.

The family moved to Sharon, Pennsylvania, to manage the largest farm between Pittsburg and Chicago. The owners wanted a "show place farm" and so sought a talented manager.

Farming Leadership

Brumm demonstrated his farming knowledge — he bought Ayrshire cattle and built the herd to 50 milking cows. The area had Ayrshire cattle well into the 1960s because of the Brumm herd.

Brumm's education at M.A.C. prepared him for leadership — he introduced crop rotation in Mercer County and was the first to use a tractor, hay loader, manure spreader, and milking machines.

Brumm was a member of the school board and the first farmer-member of the "downtown" Rotary Club. The Brumms were also members of the Hickory Grange. Brumm died in 1932 of complications of a heat stroke.

The teller of this story was but 5 years old at the time of his father's death.[34]

The Founding of Extension

When Did it Begin?

Field Agents Appointed

Early Roots

Readers of the earlier chapters of this writing perhaps will want to respond that college faculty members were "extension agents" from the very early years. In those early years and into the 1870s, professors such as William J. Beal, Robert C. Kedzie, and Albert J. Cook often reported on letters they had received asking for information on farm-related matters.

Indeed, Robert J. Baldwin, who was the first superintendent of the Department of Extension, cited these three as the "first extensionists ... who gave of their time ... not as a necessity, but by a desire to render a wider field of usefulness, influence, and experience."[35]

Farmers' Institutes?

Others might suggest extension services began with the Farmers' Institute movement. Ecklund cited Beal's writing: "Beal pointed out that institutes had the advantage over bulletins and reading courses in that they brought live men and women face to face where they can ask questions, talk back, gain enthusiasm, and form new resolutions."[36]

Butterfield's Efforts?

Alternatively, one might attribute the beginning to the work of Kenyon L. Butterfield, who worked as superintendent of the Farmers' Institutes. "In a paper on 'The Social Phase of Agricultural Education,' he described the need for vast enlargement of extension work among farmers, which 'should be conducted by a department of the college....'"[37]

Experiment Programs?

Some may wish to assert that the early works of the experiment stations under the Hatch Act were extension projects. The various experimental sites provided opportunity for faculty members and field agents to communicate with farmers face to face and to view various research demonstrations.

Field Agents?

A further response might be that the extension service began when the college appointed field agents to work directly with farmers in 1909. Ecklund stated, "This advent marked the genesis of a pattern in Michigan which would one day place full-time cooperative extension agents and their assisting staffs in every one of the eighty-three counties of the State."[38]

In 1909, the board appointed three field agents for the college. "The demand for expertise in the farmlands precipitated the action."

The three appointees were Walter Raven, a livestock specialist; Oliver K. White for the Horticulture Department; and Arthur R. Potts for the Crops and Soils departments.

White used the first year to teach spraying techniques, while Potts organized alfalfa clubs of 10 or more members, each of whom pledged to grow at least one acre of the forage. He visited each club and assisted in planting and caring for the crop. Raven's work of the first year was devoted to promoting livestock improvement projects throughout the state.

President Snyder, pleased with the farmers' responses, stated, "We could perhaps keep ten men busy as the demand is becoming more persistent each year. The state should be urged to furnish the funds for carrying on this work...." As it turned out, expansion of the field agent approach would not take place until the enactment of the Smith-Lever Act in 1914.[39]

One Agent's Impact

During 1908, W. F. Raven organized about 20 breeders' associations that were incorporated for a term of 30 years. "The object is to induce farmers and especially dairymen to use pure bred sires. Each association is required to purchase not less than three registered sires. These are shifted every two years....

"These associations have led to the purchase of registered sires by many.... It is probable that not less than 200 registered sires have been purchased this year as the result of Mr. Raven's work.

Courtesy UAHC

Regional breeders' associations, organized under the leadership of W.F. Raven, advanced information about livestock and encouraged selective breeding.

"The greatest good that will come from these organizations will be the result of continuous breeding by dairymen along one line. It is predicted that in a few years this movement will lead to the development of high-grade herds throughout the state."[40]

Congress Underwrites Extension

M.A.C. Leadership Essential

Thirty-two Bills

"The history of the congressional effort on behalf of extension is long and confusing. Between 1909 and 1914, the representatives and senators introduced 32 different bills to provide some form of aid. The act finally adopted was a combination of two measures."

Committee Compromise

"The Land-Grant College Association Executive Committee and its Extension Committee, which had been guided for almost a decade by President Butterfield, prepared a modified form of a bill which had been introduced in the House by Asbury F. Lever of South Carolina on June 12, 1911.

"Senator Hoke Smith of Georgia introduced the modification in the Senate on July 16, 1912. Its wording was the result of a study by both the colleges and the department. The bill, together with many other similar measures, was discussed ... in both branches of Congress.

"Congress passed the Smith-Lever Act, which President Woodrow Wilson signed on May 8, 1914."

Key Instruction of Law

The key directive of the act was contained in Section 2.

"...Cooperative agricultural extension work shall consist of the giving of instruction and practical demonstration in agriculture and home economics to persons not attending or resident in said colleges in the several communities, and imparting to such persons information on said subjects through field demonstrations, publications, and otherwise; and this work shall be carried on in such manner as may be mutually agreed upon by the Secretary of Agriculture and the State agricultural college or colleges receiving the benefits of the Act."[41]

Department Established

M.A.C. Did Not Wait

M.A.C. did not wait for Congress to enact the Smith-Lever Act. As President Snyder reported in 1913, the college already had field agents at work. He said, "Five men have been giving their full time to extension work, and will be increased by several men in the near future."

Formalized May 1, 1913

At the time of these statements, the extension services had not yet been established, but on May 1, 1913, at a joint meeting of the Division of Agriculture and the Experiment Station Council, participants adopted a resolution to organize the Extension Department.[43]

Features of the Smith-Lever Act

1. Provision was made for extension work in agriculture and home economics to be carried on by land-grant colleges in cooperation with the USDA. The local people acting through their state colleges were to initiate the plans for work in the respective states.

2. Extension work was "to aid in diffusing among the people of the U.S. useful and practical information on subjects relating to agriculture and home economics...."

3. Each state was to receive $10,000 annually and the following year additional amounts prorated on the basis of rural population from a federal fund.

4. These additional amounts of federal funds must be matched by state or local funds raised or contributed within the state.

5. Other provisions required that 75 percent of the funds would be spent for demonstrations and practical instruction in connection therewith; and no funds could be used for college teaching, agricultural trains, and permanent model or demonstration farms.[42]

Courtesy UAHC

M.A.C. laboratories, research, and Extension contributed actively to the fruit industry.

Progressivism and the College Board

Change in Board Role

Progressive Reform Era

With the beginning of the 20th century came the "Progressive Movement." A new vision of government — what to do, how to organize, and the role of the electorate — came onto the political agenda.

William Jennings Bryan, Theodore Roosevelt, and Woodrow Wilson were national-level names associated with this movement. California Governor Hiram Johnson and Wisconsin Governor Robert M. LaFollette were state leaders who "not only wanted government for the people but also government by the people."[44]

Key Reforms

Among the ideas of this era of government reform were those relating to separating administration from policy-making. Civil service, voter rights of initiative, referendum and recall, and the primary election process were all products of this reform era.

Constitutional Change

Popular demand led to a revision of the Michigan Constitution. Some of the changes affected the college.

Since the board's founding, board members were appointed by the governor, who also was an ex officio member. Under the new constitution, the board would consist of six members who would be elected in the spring biennial election to six-year terms. Two would be elected every other year.

President Becomes CEO

The new laws separating policy-making from administration designated the college president as the chief executive officer of the college, thus lessening "hands-on" involvement by board members. The college president "shall be the official channel of communication between the faculty and the State Board of Agriculture. He shall be the administrative head of the college and, as such, shall be responsible for carrying into effect the ordinances, rules, and regulations of the faculty and of the state board of agriculture."[45]

Courtesy UAHC

County, State, and National Population

1910		
	Number	Percent change, 1900-1910
Ingham County	53,310	33.9
Michigan	2,810,173	16.1
USA	92,228,406	17.4

"Greatest Game at M.A.C."

Readers may dispute this title. Each generation has its own idea of what was the greatest game played on this campus. *The M.A.C. Record* sports reporter and the crowd attending the football game between Marquette and M.A.C. on November 13, 1909, however, thought that the 10-0 win deserved this designation.

Solid M.A.C. Defense

"The ball was kept in Marquette's territory throughout, mainly by the use of the outside kick, the ball being recovered no less than three times during this half. After fighting on practically even terms, the first score came suddenly. Cortright caught a short kick and ran back to the 35-yard line, two plays took it to the 20-yard line when J. F. Campbell took the ball and through an opening made by Shedd, Lemmon, and Pattison ... went over for the first score."

Field Goal Seals Win

"The second half opened with M.A.C. having the advantage of the wind..., the ball was resting on Marquette's 40-yard line and [with three minutes to play] Shedd immediately took 15 yards from the other side; Frank Campbell tore off 15 more; Pattison went 8 to the 2 yard-line and Exebly planted the ball directly behind the goal posts for the final score of the game.

"It was a beautiful day, a splendid game, and the happiest crowd that ever crossed the Red Cedar wended its way homeward as the last whistle blew."[46]

Battle Over Engineering Course

Engineering Need Questioned

Two College Programs?

"For a good while there has appeared to be some prejudice against the existence of an engineering department at the college for the reason that engineering is also taught at the University. At the recent session of the legislature [1913] the feeling showed itself more strongly than heretofore and seemed likely to seriously embarrass the appropriation bill."

The issue arose in conjunction with legislative debate over the proposal to raise the college mill tax from one-tenth to one-fifth.

Notables Back M.A.C.

"When this situation came to the knowledge of the officers of the college, they asked for a hearing before the committee and this request was rather grudgingly granted. Accordingly, on the 13th of March, a considerable number of the most prominent men in the state met at the Capitol to present the needs of the college to the members of the Ways and Means Committee.... Altogether it was perhaps the most notable and representative body of men that ever addressed a legislative committee on the subject of an appropriation bill."

Spending Cap Imposed

"As a direct result of this hearing, the committee in a measure yielded to the demand made upon it and reported out the bill at one-sixth instead of one-fifth of a mill. The college officers felt that this was an unwarranted cut in the appropriation, yet this could have been overlooked had the committee not added, in the spirit of hostility to the engineering work, a proviso that the appropriation would be void if more than $35,000, no matter from what source derived, should be spent on the mechanical and engineering division.

"It is most unfortunate that two or three men, unacquainted with conditions, and with the assurance born of ignorance and prejudice, should be able to disturb the established policies of a great educational institution."[47]

Defending Engineering

Questions of Uninformed

"Very naturally the uninformed person asks — 'Why is engineering taught in an agricultural college?'" President Snyder prepared a lengthy defense, excerpts of which follow.

Just the Facts

"This answer is not in the form of an apology but simply a recital of facts." Snyder proceeded to recount how instruction in engineering developed on the campus, referring to the three laws — two Morrill Acts and the Nelson Act. "The three grants made by Congress specifically [require an engineering program] as do the three acts of the legislature in accepting these grants."

Board to Maintain Sufficient Instructors

"The mill tax," he stated, "passed by the legislature, which now provides the means for the carrying on of the college, stipulates that 'The Michigan State Board of Agriculture shall maintain at all times a sufficient corps of instructors in all the courses of study of the Agricultural College as presently constituted....'"

Legislature Obligated

"This would indicate plainly that the legislature fully recognized its obligation to maintain the engineering department and goes still further and enjoins the state board that it must not eliminate nor cripple this department in any way upon penalty of all funds from the state being withdrawn."

Michigan Needs It

"Since a large proportion of the people in Michigan are practically engaged in the manufacturing industry, it would seem only proper that the state should offer instruction of a high grade along engineering lines. If it prepares men for various professions, should it not also prepare them for that great basic profession, engineering?"[49]

Fears Revived and Resolved

The dispute between the legislature and the college over funding the engineering program created new fears at the close of the 1913-14 academic year. The Holcad published the following report in April.

Will the College Close?

"The question of whether or not M.A.C. will close before the end of the school year, because of the lack of funds, seems to be worrying many of us who are unfamiliar with the exact state of affairs and a little skeptical in regard to the various newspaper reports."

The reporter explained the issue regarding the $35,000 annual limit on spending for engineering and noted, "The amount specified has been overdrawn, and now Auditor General Fuller refuses to issue warrants on the state treasurer for M.A.C. financial needs."

Court Reviews

"Last Tuesday Judge Carpenter appeared for the college in the mandamus against Attorney General Fellows, declaring the proviso to be unconstitutional. The supreme court has not yet handed down its decision...."

Silver Lining?

"If any one should ask you whether M.A.C. is 'broke,' be as optimistic as you can, and trust that this threatening cloud has a silver lining."[48]

Split Rock Recalled

The split rock alongside the road from Lansing to the college often captured the attention of those walking by. Dr. Charles E. Bessey shared his recollections beginning with his first visit to the campus.

First Visit to Rock

"In ... June, 1866, I reached Lansing to enter the college. I stopped over night at a small hotel, and next morning walked to the college. On my way I saw ... a large boulder to which my attention was attracted by the fact that a little tree, not more than a foot and a half or two feet high and about a third of an inch in diameter of stem, was growing from a little crack in the top of the rock ... I climbed to the top of the stone, and [found] that the tree was a wild black cherry...."

Tree and Crack Grow

"I saw it again in January, 1870; the tree was much larger, and the crack had opened a good deal wider.... I was delighted when, in 1885, I found the crack had been extended entirely through the big boulder...."

Always in My Memory

"Then ... at the time of the semi-centennial celebration of the college I walked up again from the city to the college, and again I examined this boulder with the tree growing through the great crack....

"It has always seemed to me that this example of what plant growth can accomplish was placed here half way between the city of Lansing and the college especially in order that the hundreds of students going by might have a great object lesson in botany."[50]

Was it not also symbolic of the life, struggles, and vitality of M.A.C.?

1913 Enrollment[51]

	Agric.	Engin.	Home Ec.	Forestry	Veterinary	Total
Pre-freshmen	60	40	17	—	2	119
Freshmen	180	143	99	—	8	430
Sophomores	109	106	63	19	8	305
Juniors	66	89	48	14	2	219
Seniors	77	53	35	16	1	182
Graduate	4	—	—	—	—	4
Special students	42	3	10	4	3	62
Short course	326	—	—	—	—	326
Total	**864**	**434**	**272**	**53**	**24**	**1,647**

Four persons were counted twice.

Period in Review

Organizational Structure

The college made good progress during the 1905-1914 period. Several organizational and structural pieces were put into place during this time, and many of them remained 100 years later. The Smith-Lever Act, establishing what became known as the Cooperative Extension Service, proved to be durable legislation. It not only under-girded the outreach programs already in place but wove a fund webbing involving federal, state, and county governments.

Other organizational actions involved the establishment of "divisions" within the college. This action set the framework, if not the designations, for the major subdivision of the institution. Although the framework took some years to evolve, it established an organizational plan that is used in the present century. While giving cohesion to the growing agricultural programs, it also set the veterinary medicine program into its own division.

Physical Development

The period was also a positive time for the physical development of the college. Although a fire destroyed Wells Hall early in the period, other elements of the campus progressed. The advice of a campus planning consultant was instrumental in firming the descision to maintain the grounds inside Circle Drive as "sacred space." Ag Hall, opened in 1909, remains the "counter-anchor" to the Women's Hall (Morrill Hall) "protecting the historical structures in between."

One Fear Ended

The period probably marked the last time the college's survivability would come into question. The dispute between the college and the legislature over the college's desire for the mechanical engineering program became embittered. When college spending exceeded the statutory limit, the auditor general threatened to withhold all funds. Some feared that the college would close. The matter was resolved in court, and the fears ended.

Courtesy UAHC

"It is to the advantage of the plants not to shoot up all of their seeds at one time, but to retain a good portion alive in the soil to be ready for stocking the earth in successive years."

W.J. Beal, M.A.C. Professor, 1915

"So let us take the freedom from fear and superstition which science has given us. Let us take the power which the modern industrial revolution has placed in our hands. Let us hold to the joy of life, to the high hopes and aspirations which are ours today. With these we can construct a new and better world which shall stand as the expression of the spirit of the American college."

David Friday, President
Inaugural-Commencement Address, 1922

Change in Presidential Leadership

Extension Organized

Several themes characterize the decade for M.A.C. One was the implementation of the Cooperative Extension Service. The college was already engaged in the work before 1915, but new resources from the Smith-Lever Act enabled the college to reach out to the entire state.

World War I

A second theme occurred two years later as the nation began participating in World War I. The student body downsized, and the campus turned into a military training base. The federal government wasted little time in drawing on services from M.A.C. The Experiment Station and the Extension Service were called upon to guide the farming community to increase food production.

Adjusting to Normalcy

A third theme came with the postwar adjustment. The key was finding the path to normalcy. Farm communities experienced a difficult adjustment because of the oversupply of farm products and falling prices.

Changes in Presidents

Continuing turnover in the M.A.C. presidency brought instability to the college.

President Snyder retired in 1915 and was replaced by Frank S. Kedzie. Including the retiring Snyder and the two interim presidencies of Robert S. Shaw, the college had six presidencies in short order. Despite this instability, the period had a long-term impact on the college's curriculum — it broadened to a wider range of interests.

Another theme was development of a Union Memorial Building for the Alumni Association. Financing and constructing the building were challenging.

Snyder's Presidency Closes

President Snyder tendered his resignation in late 1915 after 20 years. He led the college through times that were challenging economically and perplexing because of lagging student enrollment.

Implemented Plan

Perhaps Snyder's most important decision was implementing the faculty report that outlined what the college would become. Snyder had little input in preparing the plan, but he had the insight to implement it.

State Tax Financing

Success of the plan and growing enrollment aided one of Snyder's other achievements

Courtesy UAHC

Jonathan L. Snyder

— persuading the legislature to finance college operations with a state property tax.

Law Overturned

As his career as president came to a close, Snyder had been waging a difficult battle over the college's right to determine what it should teach. As noted earlier, one of these related to the emerging engineering program. The legislature's annual spending limit and reduction in the annual funding led to Snyder's defense of the college and its challenge of the legislative action in court.

Decades of Achievements

In Madison Kuhn's words, "During the two decades the institution's prosperity more than justified the most sanguine hopes of those who elected Snyder."[1]

Courtesy UAHC

President Frank S. Kedzie in his office.

Frank S. Kedzie Appointed President

After Snyder resigned as president, the board appointed Frank S. Kedzie, then 58 years old, first as acting president, then permanently.

Son of R.C. Kedzie

The younger Kedzie grew up on "Faculty Row." He graduated from M.A.C. in 1877 and studied medicine. Frank took his brother Robert's place in the chemistry laboratory.

Department Chair

"In time, Frank took over some of the lecturing, inspiring and awing students by his vigorous presentation....

"Following his father's retirement in 1902, Frank guided the department. In the meantime he had earned a master's degree and received an honorary Doctor of Science in 1912."

Long Tenure at M.A.C.

He was known as "Uncle Frank." As Kuhn noted, "Although standards were high, former students grew increasingly fond of him through the passing years. And he remembered each of them. His election brought a flood of letters from alumni whose love for the school was renewed by the news."[2]

College Outlook Improves

As noted earlier, Snyder made vigorous arguments in the 1913 legislative debate over financial support for engineering programs at two state colleges. It appeared that his arguments had gone unheeded as the legislature limited the college's financial support to one-sixth of a mill and annual spending on the Engineering Division to $35,000.

Revenue Raised to One-fifth Mill

Given the intensity of the debate, it was surprising that the legislature in 1915 increased the tax to one-fifth mill. The action reflected strong support for continued growth. The legislature, however, imposed a new spending ceiling of $150,000 per year for "building or other extraordinary expenses before July 1, 1916."

Outreach Support

In passing that amendment, the legislature expressed support for the Experiment Station work and the Cooperative Extension programming, stating that the property tax allocation could be used to support these programs as well as the other college programs.

President Snyder expressed his gratitude for the legislature's revising the millage rate and his optimism regarding the overall estimated revenues of $869,000.

Financial Outlook Promising

Interestingly, the legislation provided some basis for increased revenues in the coming years. For example, the state property tax amount was to be revised every third and fifth year as property values were revised. In addition, the Smith-Lever Act provided for an annual increase of $15,000 each year for the next seven years.[3]

"The college appropriation bill providing more than $750,000 for the next two years was ready for Governor Albert E. Sleeper's signature.... Our part of the job is done and the sigh of relief that goes up from the scores of alumni who have taken an active part in the campaign is fairly audible."

Alumni Turn Tide

"The real fight on the issue was in the Senate and the last trench was taken by a committee of alumni headed by President Kedzie, '77, and President Prudden, '78, of the M.A.C. Alumni Association. College officers were given a hearing before the Senate Finance Committee and thrashed out the appropriation for the auditorium...."

"With the funds provided, agricultural extension work may go on unhampered. The library and administration building and the auditorium, buildings absolutely essential to the life of the college, are assured."

Join in the Rejoicing

"The future has brightened considerably during the week just past. It is indeed a time for rejoicing. Plan to rejoice with us [at] commencement. It is now clear sailing to the Union Memorial Building and a new dormitory."

A Birthday Gift!

The governor signed the bill on March 12, President Kedzie's birthday. At the time, it was the largest amount ever provided M.A.C. by a Michigan Legislature.[4]

Enrollment Falls

When the college dropped the summer term in the 1890s, graduate enrollments fell. Few teachers were able to undertake graduate studies at other times.

Graduate student instructors and experiment station assistants also discontinued studies because a new faculty rule required a year of full-time residency with no other responsibilities.[5]

Fixed Policy

In 1915, however, President Kedzie stated, "It has become the fixed policy of the college to develop graduate work." He mentioned that the college would grant eight scholarships for graduate students. Students assigning half of their time to the college would receive $400 per year; those allocating one-quarter of their time would be paid $200 per year.

Opportunities

"The College," he said, "with its extensive equipment and large number of able men in graduate work, offers splendid opportunities to a limited number who desire to pursue advanced work."[6]

	Agric.	Engin.	Home Ec.	Forestry	Vet. Sci.	Total
1915-16 Enrollment						
Freshmen	248	131	120	-	22	521
Sophomores	210	88	71	12	18	399
Juniors	140	83	60	12	12	307
Seniors	113	71	64	11	6	265
Graduates	20	-	2	-	-	22
Subtotal	**731**	**373**	**317**	**35**	**58**	**1,514**
Specials	15	-	13	-	-	28
Summer	81	35	38	12	9	175
Total	**827**	**408**	**368**	**47**	**67**	**1,717**

Extension Service Reaches Out...

Brody, M.A.C., and County Farm Bureau

Courtesy UAHC

Hog Cholera Problem

In 1914, Clark L. Brody worked as a part-time instructor with the Farmers' Institutes. Brody organized farmers in St. Joseph County to solicit state aid to battle hog cholera, a genuine pestilence for farmers. Brody himself had lost his hog crop for two years.

Disease is Manageable

Brody knew that the state Livestock Sanitary Commission had sent a veterinarian to Branch County to combat the virus. Serum and immunization materials were essential, but farmers would have to be informed about the need to vaccinate the hogs, something then not widely understood. He concluded, "The only way to control hog cholera was to organize a county farm bureau headed by a county agent who would be a public educator appointed by M.A.C."

County Farm Bureau

Brody continued, "I established October 12, 1914, as the day for a county-wide meeting of farmers in Centreville. Then I set out to persuade farmers to attend. I covered the county by horse and buggy, by car, and by train ... posted handbills ... wrote letters to everyone in the county, and [got local newspapers to publicize it]."

Farmers Respond

"A capacity audience turned out for the meeting.... I thought that once the reasons for a county farm bureau and the benefits were explained, I could get back to the farm. To my consternation George Fisher, an aged attorney from Sturgis, made a motion that I be elected president of the county farm bureau, asked for a vote, and declared me elected.... I had been railroaded and was effectively caught."[7]

WKAR Extends M.A.C.

Most have now heard of "virtual classes" — classes via the Internet. Few, however, recall courses by radio. The college began conducting classes via radio under the direction of Professor H.C. Rather.

Virtual Classes?

The first broadcasting from the campus was an unplanned event. "Ingenious students had used wireless equipment left from war-time instruction to broadcast ribald songs from Olds Hall to earphoned occupants of Wells Hall, only to discover from irate letters that they had reached a wider audience." Under the call letters of SYG more orthodox programs and a speech by President Friday were broadcast in the region.

WKAR Begins Broadcasting

"WKAR, as an official station, presented its first program in March 1923; it was a one- hour presentation from the Union Opera, 'Campus Nights.'"*[9]

*J. B. Hasselman became station director. He also broadcast basketball games from a telephone booth mounted above the running track.

One Year's Extension Work

Full Smith-Lever funding was not available during the 1914-15 fiscal year, but the Extension personnel were hard at work. The following summarizes the year's activities.

Work Category	Events	Attendance
Administration	6	625
Boys' and girls' clubs	-	4, 285
Horticulture meetings	8	816
Potatoes and vegetables meetings	45	4,185
Forestry meetings	67	2,800
Farm crops meetings	33	2,849
Home economics demos./lec.	181	9,272
Household engineering meetings	8	320
Demonstration car in U.P. towns	49	6,500
Farm mgmt. demonstrations, visits	-	524
Lectures, other than Extension staff	55	5,640
Bean marketing	22	1,163
Total		**38,979**

"In addition, agents visited 1,983 farms to give personal assistance to the owners. The figures do not include the activities of county agricultural agents nor Farmers' Institutes, which are reported separately."[8]

First-year Program Approval

The USDA reviewed the Extension Service plans. Each specialist was assigned to an approved plan before it was undertaken. The following activities were approved for the year ending June 30, 1916:

1. Administration
2. County agricultural agents
3. Home economics
4. Movable schools
5. Boys' and girls' clubs
6. Farm crops
7. Livestock
8. Potatoes and vegetables
9. Upper Peninsula
10. Control of insect pests
11. Household engineering
12. Forestry[10]

Snyder Praises Program Effort

Snyder Optimistic

President Snyder's last report to the board was strong in his praise for the rapid development of extension work. R.J. Baldwin, though, reported that "the extension service for the fiscal year ending June 20, 1915, [was] largely confined to projects already started before the year began. This was necessary because funds have not been available for further development."

Extension Funding

"The future development of extension work is largely determined by the terms of [the Smith-Lever Act]. This bill provides to the State a basal appropriation of $10,000 annually. An additional appropriation of $18,032.37 becomes available for the year ending June 20, 1916, provided that the state appropriates an equal amount for the same purposes. Each state receives amounts in proportion to the rural population residing within that state."

Each County

"The general policy agreed upon by the Office of Extension Work [USDA] and the Extension division of the college ... is to place an extension agent in each county ... if funds permit. The staff of local field men known as County Agricultural Agents is assisted and supported by an efficient staff of Extension specialists."

Extension Role

"Specialists work out from the various departments of the College. In counties where an agent is located, he is the leader and takes the initiative, calling in such assistants as are needed."[11]

Household Engineering

Dr. Giltner's 1915 report stated that 42 water samples from rural communities were examined during the year. "Of these, only three contained few enough organisms of a harmless type to render the water potable.... Sixty-seven per cent of all samples were polluted with soil bacteria and 55 percent with bacteria ... from both soil and sewage."

Extension Responds

In response to the problem Giltner devised a plan to deal with "the household engineering project ... in cooperation with the Office of Extension. The purpose ... was to improve the water systems and sewage disposal facilities in farm homes."

Family Economics

"In all cases recommendations were made in accordance with the financial and other conditions found. Whenever possible a community meeting was held to inspect installations made. Septic tanks and piping were left uncovered for neighbors to see and ask questions about."[13]

Lab Testing Service

"During the ... 31 days actually spent in the field, 75 farms were visited; 50 farmers were given advice; 18 sets of plans were furnished; five septic tanks were actually installed; eight meetings were held at which 320 were in attendance."[14]

"Yoopers" not Overlooked

Providing Extension services in the Upper Peninsula was especially challenging. The distance to the U.P., dispersion of farming communities, and diversity of agriculture were some of the challenges.

Assistance to U.P.

W.F. Raven and two colleagues, on a 23-day trip to seven counties, made 46 stops, conducted 98 demonstrations, and gave 97 lectures to 6,500 persons. They visited 802 farms to give instruction and collect data on the crops, the prevalence of diseases, and efforts to control diseases. They participated in county fairs and helped organize the Menominee Potato Growers Association.

Management Aid

Other efforts dealt with livestock management. They helped organize two new livestock associations for sharing purebred sires and to let settlers understand they need to "start with the right types of live stock.... "

Crop Improvement, Too

With respect to farm crops, Raven reported that the farmers were urged to plant better seed "and that the 1,500 bushels of Worthy oat seem to be well adapted to the region. By encouraging farmers to produce crops for seed purposes, it is hoped to produce seed within the region which is now being brought in from other states."[12]

Courtesy UAHC

Extension mobile unit for water and sewage systems education.

Serving a Wide Audience

Women's Institutes

Women's Sessions

"For nearly all of the county institutes held in the Lower Peninsula a woman speaker was furnished and in 53 counties a special women's congress arranged. In several of the counties, forenoon as well as afternoon sessions were held. A standard form of program ... was used at practically all of the meetings."

Food Preparation

"For the afternoon session the state speaker was generally assigned the topic, 'The Use of Eggs in the Diet.' The lecturer took up not only different methods of preparing eggs but also gave special attention to the consideration of the food value in eggs. Although it was in a measure incidental, the food value of milk in the diet was also considered in connection with the use of milk and eggs in certain dishes."

Household Utensils

"The topic most generally used by the local speakers at the afternoon sessions was the 'Selection and Care of Household Utensils.' Many valuable suggestions and helpful ideas were brought out, especially where they were able to secure exhibits of utensils not commonly found in farm homes."[15]

Local Schools Benefit

Walter H. French used his annual report to discuss his ideas for extending practical education in the public schools.

"The Department of Agricultural Education has proven its programs to be a way to reach the rural communities.... At the end of 1915 the department had 132 graduates, 90 from Agriculture and 42 from Home Economics. Many Ag-Ed students were taken around the state to observe and inspect actual school work."

Instruction in Agriculture

"During the year, the department added to its list of schools ... giving instruction in agriculture, thus bringing the total to 54 schools. In addition, other smaller schools scattered around the state were 'giving some instruction in agricultural subjects.'"

Valued Extension

"One other phase of this work seems to be vitally important. When we have the teachers of Secondary Agriculture employed by the year-end, these men will constitute a most valuable adjunct to the extension work in the college ... first, in connection with the one-week schools for farmers, and second, in connection with the county agents."

Visits and Lectures

Walter French also included several other activities in his report. He and his assistant visited all the schools teaching agriculture as well as some 40 or 50 others. One goal of the visits was to address students and meet with the boards of education and discuss agricultural and industrial education.[16]

Courtesy UAHC

Junior Farmers' Institutes

"For several years some counties have held special meetings for the boys, as separate sessions of the county institutes. These have generally been in connection with the Boys' Corn Clubs, and in addition ... the exhibition of products grown by members...."

Youth Presentations

"Separate sessions for the boys and girls were held on one afternoon, at which Mr. Spaulding and Miss Cowles discussed respectively, 'Club Work for Boys' and 'Sewing Club Work for Girls.'"

Satisfying Results

"Among the results of the institute has been a marked change in the feeling of the farmers toward the agricultural department in the high school, greater attention to Boys' and Girls' Clubs [by] both pupils and parents, and better work in the classes in agriculture."[17]

Wayne County 4-H club's election of officers.

Building Fires — Bad and Good Outcomes

Fire Resolves Hot Issue

Given the debate over the need for two engineering programs in Michigan, losing the engineering building to fire was an unfortunate event. It happened on Sunday morning, March 5, 1916. The fire destroyed the building and the shops. Yet, it had a good outcome.

The Request

That afternoon, President Kedzie called Ransom E. Olds of the REO Motor Car Co. and asked if he would provide assistance in coping with the loss. The request was critical to saving the M.A.C. engineering programs.

The Offer

On April 29, R.E. Olds delivered the following letter:

"Pres. Frank S. Kedzie
Michigan Agricultural College
East Lansing, Michigan

Dear Mr. Kedzie:

Confirming ... my statement that I would give One Hundred Thousand Dollars ($100,000) towards the reconstruction of the Engineering Building at the Michigan Agricultural College. It is my desire that you advise the Board of my action, and further advise them that in the near future I will deposit this amount in the Capital National Bank, of this city....

"I have great faith in the Michigan Agricultural College and see no reason why it should not become one of the foremost colleges in the United States."

Implications of Olds' Gift

"[T]his first great gift ... places the stamp of the highest approval upon the engineering work that has been done at this institution and forever closes the door of controversy. And this is not all, for it establishes the fact that M.A.C. as a state and national institution, is not beyond the pale of the private bequest...."

Memorable Deed

"To have one's name forever fresh in the hearts of the best youth of the land, to have given aid to struggling and worthy ambition, to have made possible a broader and better life for some of our fellows or those who may come after us, is a consummation that may add luster to the life and memory of any man."[18]

Courtesy UAHC

Williams Hall fire on January 1, 1919. When the site was cleared, the "sacred space" was enhanced. "It is surprising to a great many to see the relative location of the other buildings ... formerly hidden by old Williams."[19]

Oldest Building Aflame

"Williams Hall, the oldest building on the campus, was destroyed on New Year's Day [1919]. Only the walls remain standing, all the interior having been gutted by the flames."

Alarm Sounded at 1 O'clock

"Fire was discovered about one o'clock and a general alarm sounded, which brought out large numbers of spectators.... The flames were fought courageously by the college fire department, volunteers, and a truck from Lansing...."

Building Unoccupied

"Much as the loss will affect the college and, regrettable as it is, the burning of Williams Hall could not have occurred at a time when it could not have caused less inconvenience to the general administration of the institution. With the small enrollment of men students this term, it is not as difficult to find rooms for them as it would be in normal times.

"The sentiments expressed on the burning of Old Williams are many and varied. Among the older group of alumni the feeling towards Williams was something of that held for old College Hall."[20]

Courtesy UAHC

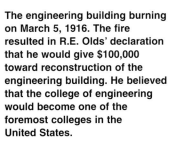

The engineering building burning on March 5, 1916. The fire resulted in R.E. Olds' declaration that he would give $100,000 toward reconstruction of the engineering building. He believed that the college of engineering would become one of the foremost colleges in the United States.

Call to Military Service

In 1917 President Kedzie noted, "For the third time ... since M.A.C. was founded, our College has been obliged to harmonize as best it could the demands of the class room and laboratory with the call to the patriotic citizen for service to the government."

War Declared

"The work of the fall and winter term was carried to successful completion without hindrance, but the opening of the spring term occurred simultaneously with the declaration of war by President Woodrow Wilson; it was natural, therefore, that the student body on assembling did so under a great deal of excitement. A mass meeting was called of the entire student body and faculty to consider the duties of M.A.C. under war conditions...."

How to Respond

"It was soon decided that Military Drill should be increased; that students who desired to enlist for the Officers' Training Camps who belonged to the senior class should be granted their diplomas and that members of the junior class entering the training camp should also be given credit for the spring term's work."

The report listed 55 students who left for military duty.

Quasi-military Camp

President Kedzie reported that by "act of the legislature an emergency fund of $5 million for protective purposes during the war led to the enlistment of a State Constabulary.... This camp site is now occupied by two hundred members of that organization including two hundred horses and complete military equipment."[21]

Courtesy UAHC

The military barracks site lay west of Harrison Road and south of the Cedar River.

Military/College Training Plan

Courtesy UAHC

Truck squad off for a "hike." M.A.C. training detachment, June 1918.

Now Training Fighters

"With the commencement of the fall term, M.A.C. has turned almost overnight from its sixty-year-old business of producing farmers, foresters, and engineers to training fighters.

"Those who are acquainted with the problems manufacturers faced when they changed their machines from peacetime production to take over a war order can appreciate the changes that have been going on at M.A.C. to put the college on a war order basis."

Brains and Brawn

"All summer the war department has been making preparations for an intensive use of colleges and higher educational institutions. War today is a series of scientific prob-

> *"All summer the war department has been making preparations for an intensive use of colleges and higher educational institutions. War today is a series of scientific problems — it takes brains as well as brawn."*

lems ... it takes brains as well as brawn. Emptying the colleges and universities was recognized as a deplorable situation.... But with a war program demanding five million fighting men by July next year how could these educational institutions be used?"

Students' Corps

"Many schemes were projected before the Students' Army Training Corps (S.A.T.C.) plan was hit upon.... While the war department was planning the S.A.T.C. the new draft law was passed, bringing further complications and eleventh hour changes."

War Order Production

"But now on the eve of registration day the changes have been arranged for and practically everything is ready. With 540 truck and tractor men, 25 horseshoers, 50 Jackies, and some 500 or more collegiate freshmen in uniform the college is on war order production of the highest type.

"As we begin this college year — one many feared would never begin — we find M.A.C. greatly changed, 'tis true, but back in the harness, straining every sinew, bent on quantity production of quality man power."[22]

...and Leaves Its Mark

War Ends; How Will College Be Affected?

World War I began in 1914, but the United States was not directly involved until 1917. It ended in November 1918. M.A.C. and other educational institutions were intensely involved in the training programs. Hence the question, "The end of the war — how will it affect us?"

Nation Grateful

In response to that question, the editor of *The M.A.C. RECORD* stated, "The war is over, and its ending means that hundreds of the sons of M.A.C. will soon be on their way back to the homes they have left.... The old college is proud of these loyal men who have upheld the honor of their country on the field of battle; she is proud, very proud of those who have made the supreme sacrifice and will wend their way back to the loved campus in spirit only. To one and all she extends her thanks, and to them all she holds out a warm, true welcome."

Will Students Return?

"An immediate question is raised regarding the status of the college during the rest of this year. Practically the entire male undergraduate body is composed of enlisted men who are enrolled in the S.A.T.C. Will this training unit be abolished by the government, and if so, will the college find itself virtually without students? These are the questions in the minds of many."[23]

Postwar Return to Normalcy

Military Needs Remain

"Military work as before the war, under the regulations of the Reserve Officer Training Corps, has been resumed at the college.... Owing to the fact that many of the upper classmen find it necessary to put in every available moment in academic work to make up credits lost last fall, there is a dearth of officer material and not more than half a dozen juniors and seniors are electing military work."

Training Still Offered

"'The men will be required to wear their uniforms seven days a week to give more dignity to military training and to accustom young men to military usages,' declared Major Wrightson...."

Veterans Excused if ...

"Individuals who have been in the service, however, will be permitted to take an examination in military subjects if they request it, and if they make the required grades, will be excused from drill."[24]

M.A.C. Alums Plan Welcome

"A Union Victory Mass Meeting at which the entire college will have an opportunity of doing honor to the returned soldiers of M.A.C. is being arranged by the Union.... The mass meeting will be held in the gymnasium in the afternoon of commencement day June 11."

Show Appreciation and Gratitude

"Because it is an all-college meeting for students, alumni, faculty, and friends, the arrangements are being handled by the Union.... It will be the first big 'all M.A.C.' mass meeting since the war and the only opportunity that the college community as a whole and alumni body will have to show their gratitude and appreciation of the deeds of M.A.C. heroes."

A few years later, those alums who died in military service would be memorialized on a plaque to be placed in the Student Union Building.[25]

Courtesy UAHC

War Affects Cost of Food

America's involvement in the war led to rising food prices.

Students Experience Effects

Some students were challenged by the increased costs and found their attendance at the college seriously threatened. Actions of the Student Boarding Club, however, helped to keep costs to individual students reasonable.

Extension Service Role

The Extension Service "during the current year [1917] has proved of the greatest value in carrying forward the campaign for greater food production."

Emergency Corps Appointed

"To attain the desired ends, funds were granted from the State Treasury on recommendation of the Committee, and [38] people were appointed as Emergency County Agents. These people, in addition to the regular county agents, assisted materially in the food production problem."[26]

Union Memorial Building Dream...

Don't Bury Union

College Hall not Alumni Home

"With the collapse of College Hall and the grinding of its old walls to a pathetic pile of ruins, there also crashed to earth the long cherished hopes and well matured plans of the M.A.C. Association for a campus home — a home that was to have been an all-college meeting place and stamping ground."

College Hall was Alma Mater

"The loss of College Hall has been a severe blow to alumni, akin to the loss of a dear old friend. Younger classes cannot appreciate the tenderness of feeling and the depth of love of the first fifty classes that have gone from M.A.C. for the old building. To many of them Alma Mater means College ... and all recognize the blow that has been dealt the student and alumni groups in the loss of the building as a home for the Union."

Union Must Go On

"The M.A.C. Union idea, however, is too big a notion to be smothered in the debris of College Hall. Already like Phoenix of old it is rising from the ashes. As we were recovering from the blow of losing College Hall, the first question asked was what will the Union do?"

Gifts are Welcome

"Very soon it will build a new home of its own. The building of it will be the most worthy undertaking that alumni of M.A.C. have ever had the opportunity of supporting."[27]

Building Campaign Commenced

Funding Campaign

"At the meeting of the executive committee of the [Alumni] Association held Monday afternoon it was decided to begin immediately a campaign for the Union Memorial Building. The committee resolved to ask the board to have the college architect 'draw up some sketch plans for the building.'"

Long-term Goal

"The M.A.C. Association has been behind the Union and the Union Building promotion ever since the Union was organized. They have been cognizant from the first of its centralizing and strengthening effect upon both students and alumni activities."

Union to be Memorial

"It was foremost in support of the rebuilding of College Hall as a home for the Union and when that building was found unsafe and had to be razed last summer [1917], individual members were resolved that a campaign for a new building must be immediately started. However, war conditions prevented any action at that time. Now the building as a Memorial to our men makes it a project especially appealing to every single alumnus and former student of M.A.C.

"In the course of the meeting one subscription of $5,000 with which to start the list was made known to the committee."

The Holcad, November 16, 1923

Union Memorial Building.

Alumni Work Influential

"Such a campaign as is proposed will do more to strengthen the alumni organization, renew interest in alma mater, and rejuvenate the old M.A.C. spirit than any other one thing alumni can undertake."[28]

U-M Alumnus is First Donor

"A check for $100 for the M.A.C. Union Memorial Building was received this week. It is the first real contribution ... and is unique in that it comes from an alumnus of the U of M."

How It Happened

"There is a little story ... worth telling. A Detroit alumnus was approached for a subscription for the Michigan Union at Ann Arbor. He replied ... that he was not a UM man but a graduate of M.A.C. and said that 'we have a little fund of that sort to raise ourselves.' Whereupon, Mr. John R. Russell offered to subscribe $100 to the M.A.C. Union building providing the other would subscribe an equal amount to the University building. This was agreed upon and the check was immediately forwarded."

Reputation Helped

"The honor of heading the list of subscribers to the M.A.C. Union Memorial Building falls to John R. Russell, U. of M. '71. Mr. Russell is president of the Great Lakes Engineering Works, one of the largest shipbuilding plants in the west."[29]

...Turns to Reality

Ground Broken | Construction Begins

W.K. Prudden, class of 1878, is shown turning the first spadeful of soil for the Union Memorial Building on Alumni Day, June 16, 1923. He was president of the association for three years and made the largest individual contribution to the Union Fund.

M.A.C. Union to Begin

After years of negotiating and planning, the construction of the M.A.C. Union Building is about to get underway. As *The Holcad* editor stated, "Dirt will fly fast when the gong sounds for work to begin on excavation for the Union Memorial Building."

Showing Progress

"A large thermometer, calibrated in cubic yards, will be erected on the site of the new building. As each half-day of labor is completed, the yards removed will be recorded on the big scale."

Work will be Fun

"Many interesting features have been planned by Harvey Prescott, President of the M.A.C. Association, and his co-workers. Notable among these will be the daily appearance of the varsity and Swartz Creek bands, the work of the girls, the serving of refreshments between shifts, and the digging that President Shaw and other campus officials will do."

Girls' Assignments

"The work of the girls [will be done under the leadership of] Ruth Abbott, Ruth Christopher and Marion Larkworthy.... Women will prepare and serve refreshments, and make out excuse slips for the workers, and keep a tally of the yards dug by each team."

Four Teams at Once

"Each half-day, three teams of men and one of girls will report to the foreman in charge. Work will begin at 8:00 sharp.... The teams will work in shifts in order that the wagons may be kept busy every minute."

Mementos

"Everyone who takes part in the Excavation Week will receive, in addition to an excuse from classes missed, a button of original design...."[30]

"Excavation Week" (November 1923) was the occasion for removing the soil so the foundation of the Union Memorial Building could be constructed. Approximately 7,000 cubic yards of soil had to be removed.

Union Memorial sculpture being placed.

Tradition Breaking and Making

Smoking Allowed

"Men will be allowed to smoke while engaged in the work of the excavating for the Union Memorial Building. This action, apparently setting aside one of the time-honored traditions of M.A.C., was passed by the student council at a recent meeting."

Set a Precedent?

"There is some question whether the council has the power to set aside traditions, even temporarily, without the consent of a majority of the students.

"A petition signed by 300 men and presented to the council will require it to submit the question to the students at the general election next March. At the same time it might be well to ask the question, 'Shall M.A.C. have any traditions at all any more?'"[31]

Meeting Campus Needs

Challenges in Campus Planning

Complexity and Uncertainty

Planning a college campus is a task in which few people have experience. Because past decisions constrain current decisions and because future needs cannot be defined precisely, the task of building a campus is challenging. The following portrays a glimpse of M.A.C.'s planning team discussion.

In the June 1919 meeting, the board asked its campus planning consultant to respond to two questions. "The first relates to the expediency of transferring land now included in the Campus to the People's Church as a site for a church building, and to the best location if expedient. The other related to the location of the Library and Auditorium."

Church on Campus?

"Bearing in mind the history of other educational institutions in regard to extension and contraction of the lands held by them for educational purposes, and bearing in mind the present logical and satisfactory boundary of the Campus ... we would advise against alienating any of the College land south of [Grand River and Michigan avenues]."

What is Board Policy?

"If it is the policy of the Board to enter into co-operation with ... the People's Church, or religious congregations which [may form] in East Lansing for the purpose of providing a common place of worship, it would seem that this end could be accomplished in either of two ways without the very serious risk of future complications."

Library and Auditorium Together?

"On the question of actually incorporating the Auditorium and Library in one structure, however, we beg to point out that there are three very serious complications in planning.

"First, it would make a very large building that would be difficult to fit into a general plan....

"Second, it might tend to restrict freedom of the architect in [designing] ... two structures of such radically different character....

"Third, it would materially reduce the flexibility of the library plan in regard to future extensions...."

Courtesy UAHC

Former M.A.C. hospital.

Preserve the Campus

"'The Campus Circle,' an organization of which Sam J. Kennedy, '01, is president, had its inception in the fertile brain of the Chicago M.A.C. Association. This organization advocates the preservation of the circle plan and opposes the placing of any buildings in the center of the campus."

Campaign for Support

"A folder which is being sent out to alumni all over the country asking their support, sets forth their ideas...."

Loss of Old Buildings

"We all regretted to see College Hall and Williams Hall go, but after their disappearance there came a revelation. The older campus was more beautiful than before. With the fine vistas in every direction across College Hall opened up, this became the supreme beauty spot of the campus."

Remain Distinctive

"If large new buildings were placed in the center of the Campus, they would dwarf the trees and open spaces and shut off the best vistas of the Campus. They would give M.A.C., which is today the most beautiful college in America, a nondescript character, throwing it into a common class with a hundred other colleges and universities."[32]

Spanish Influenza Hits Campus

Spanish influenza was reaching epidemic proportions.

To curb the spread of the disease, the college imposed a quarantine district. It included "all of the campus except Faculty Row and the Women's Building. There are but two 'ports of entry,' one between the post office and Abbot Hall and the other between the Women's Building and the library. Absent-minded faculty members are brought up quickly with the sharp 'halt' of the sentry if they wander from the beaten paths."

E.L. Women Assist

The same issue of the paper reported: "East Lansing women responded wonderfully in the emergency as the first grasp of the epidemic Spanish influenza fastened itself upon the college and the army training unit.... It was handled creditably."[33]

College Outreach Strengthened

Forestry Extension in Demand

The Department of Forestry experienced strong demand for assistance. Types of assistance provided are shown below. As Chairman H.H. Chittendon stated, specialist C.A. Tyler "has had all the work he could handle."[34]

Farm woodlots. In 53 farms Tyler visited, "Conservation has been most ardently advocated in the treatment of the woodlot. Better protection from fire, live stock, and from the farmer himself...."

Waste spaces. "Twenty-seven farmers have been induced to make plantings on unsightly and other waste places on their farms."

Windbreaks. "Efforts along this line have secured the planting of nine farm windbreaks. There is a great need for this form of planting, particularly in the fruit belt ... where destruction from unchecked winds is increasing."

Lakefronts, sand areas. "Five lake fronts and eleven sand areas ... have been given attention."

Municipal and others. "Assistance was given to seven Chambers of Commerce ... civic leagues, and eight different towns and cities ... 37 miles of roadside have been planted...."

Reforestation. "... the great opportunity open to the College ... is through reforestation of the larger areas now useless for agricultural purposes...."

Education. "Four weeks were given to extension school work, and one week to short course classes at the College. Sixty-seven public addresses have been given and 129 letters of an advisory nature written."[35]

Foresters in training.

Epidemic Wanes and Returns

No New Cases

By November 1918, the influenza epidemic was lessening. "There were 107 cases in the hospital...."

Quarantine Ended

"The guards, who for the last three weeks, have been ... maintaining the quarantine which forbade soldiers to leave or civilians to enter, have been drawn in."[36]

Sixteen Deaths

"Several severe cases of pneumonia are in the hospital.... Until Wednesday night, there have been but 13 deaths in the S.A.T.C. unit at M.A.C. and three in East Lansing."[37]

Belief that the infection had been eliminated was premature. "On Wednesday [December 4] 10 cases were reported among coeds, while a number of other persons in East Lansing were likewise ill...."[38]

John Hannah Attends M.A.C.

Early Responsibilities

John A. Hannah came to M.A.C. in the early 1920s. More accurately, he was recruited to M.A.C. As a youth, he managed the family's poultry business and said, "Very early I began to exhibit chickens at poultry shows around the state.... I made my first trip to Chicago alone by train when I was about thirteen, to exhibit Black Orpingtons at the poultry show in the Coliseum."

Recruited from Law School

It was because of that interest that E.C. Foreman, head of the Poultry Department at M.A.C., visited the young Hannah in Ann Arbor. Hannah was enrolled in the University's School of Law but he was also the president of the Michigan State Poultry Association.

M.A.C. Job Promised

Foreman asked Hannah about his plans when he finished law school. Hannah said he did not know. Foreman then suggested that he could come to M.A.C., take a degree in agriculture, and become an Extension poultry man at a salary of $2,500. Hannah discussed the offer with his father and explored the details as Dean Shaw and his assistant, Robert B. Hill, explored Hannah's background.

Demonstrate Course Knowledge

Hannah's memoir stated, "I would be held for all the required courses in agriculture, but I could either take them in class or, if I could convince the professors or department heads that I had the competence, I could pass some of them by examination. It was possible then to take an examination at the beginning of any term; if one passed it he could get full credit in the course."

Graduated After One Year

"As a result, in the fall of 1922 I came to East Lansing as a transfer student in the College of Agriculture, having taken no courses in agriculture before that time. To make a long story short ... in June of 1923, I graduated with the class of 1923 ... I went to work immediately for the Poultry Department...."[39]

Farm Bureau – From County to State

State Farm Bureau Formed

Tough Time Continues

World War I had come to a close. The difficulties of farmers in Michigan continued. Governmental price controls of the war years remained in effect. "Not only did [the farmer] not fare as well as industry, but the disparity between incomes had widened even further."[40]

State Association?

The 1919 Farmers' Week provided an occasion to discuss the proposal to form a state association.[41] On February 14, 82 delegates and 91 other members from 57 county farm bureaus gathered at M.A.C.[42]

How to Organize

"A lengthy and bitter discussion ensued.... The government had made postwar settlements with industry, but not with farmers. Moreover, at that moment, prices of farm products had declined, but the cost of many farm supplies remained high."

M.A.C. Involved

The leaders of M.A.C. — President Kedzie, Dean Shaw, and state county agent leader Dr. Eben Mumford — suggested that the county farm bureaus form a state farm bureau of which they would all be members. Article II of the adopted charter stated: "The object of this organization shall be to encourage, aid, and correlate the efforts of the county Farm Bureaus, to provide ways and means for concerted action in the solution of agricultural problems of state or national scope."

Close Ties with M.A.C.

The new state organization was to be independent of the M.A.C. However, as an organization having a strong educational component, the organization's departments implied a close alignment and affiliation with M.A.C.[43]

M.A.C. Welcomes Farm Bureau

Kedzie's Welcome

"It gives me great pleasure to greet so large a number of representatives of the newer movement in agriculture. This College ... has had the honor of inaugurating a number of movements for the development of practical agriculture in all its phases."

We Wish You Success

"The County Farm Bureau we feel has come to stay. Its help and influence is felt and acknowledged by us all at the college, and it is with great satisfaction that I greet you here this morning and bid you God-speed in your effort to organize the County Farm Bureau into a state organization."[44]

Social Life Supported

In its support for the construction of the M.A.C. Union, *The M.A.C. RECORD* quoted an editorial from the *Detroit Free Press* on the value of college social life.

Social Life not a Side Issue

"Whatever value may be set upon educational attainments, we must recognize they are not the whole business of life. Other things help toward recognition and success. It has been our fault to overestimate the work of 'book learning.' The social life of college or university is not a mere side issue; it is also a part of preparation for what is to come later."

Boorishness is Handicapping

"Many a young man has worked so hard to put himself through college on a minimum sum that he has ignored or disdained the social side of its life and has gone forth wiser intellectually but in a manner as uncouth as when he entered. A professional man is handicapped by a boorish manner."

Wholesome Spirit of Chivalry

"To promote the 'social welfare of the students of the M.A.C. and to foster a wholesome spirit of social chivalry' is the primary object of the M.A.C. Union. The Union idea and its purposes are not sprung from the minds of a few but are generally recognized as one of the greatest needs of our institution.

"It is in furtherance of this idea that plans are now going forward for a permanent home for the Union...."[45]

Courtesy UAHC

Framers of the State Farm Bureau.

County, State and National Population		
1920		
	Number	Percent change, 1910-1920
Ingham County	81,554	53.0
Michigan	3,668,412	30.6
USA	106,021,537	14.9

Time of Revolving Presidencies

F.S. Kedzie Relinquishes Presidency

President ("Uncle Frank") Kedzie resigned as president in September 1921, and thus began the decade of the revolving presidencies. Kedzie had indicated that he did not desire a long tenure.

Though his policies were not being attacked, some groups including the alumni were concerned that the college enrollment had again become static. *The Detroit News* published reports comparing M.A.C. enrollment with those of other land-grant colleges.

Kedzie was also caught up in concerns that the college was concentrating too much on academic studies at the expense of farmers, who were suffering from the postwar oversupply of farm products.

The board accepted his resignation immediately and began the search for a new campus leader.

Though the Kedzie presidency ended on a low note, he demonstrated leadership for and dedication to the health of the college.[46]

Dean Shaw Assumes Job Temporarily

Upon the resignation of Frank S. Kedzie as president and his subsequent appointment as dean of the Division of Applied Science, the board appointed David Friday to the position of president. At the time he was a consultant to a committee of Congress and could not leave that position for six months. The board then appointed Dean Robert S. Shaw to assume the position for the interim.

Shaw had worked for the Extension Service and as a professor in the Department of Agriculture, and later he was appointed to the position of dean of the Agricultural Division.

His interim presidency ended in February 1922 when Friday assumed the chair.

Political Bonfire Follows

As the board began seeking candidates to replace Kedzie, Hale Tennant urged appointment of David Friday, a professor of economics in Ann Arbor. (Tennant, a county agent and consultant to the Farm Bureau, and Friday were boyhood friends.)

Friday Recommended

M.B. McPherson and L.W. Watkins were on the executive committee of the state Farm Bureau. "Through these two men, Tennant prevailed upon the Executive Committee to express a wish to the board that David Friday be appointed president of M.A.C."

Friday's Mild Interest

According to C.L. Brody, David Friday "displayed no overwhelming desire to become president. Yet Tennant persisted in pushing Friday for the job."

Divided Board Acts

"In the summer of 1921, the board, by a majority of four votes, appointed Friday as president. Two men, John Beaumont, an attorney from Detroit, and William Wallace, general manager of the Michigan Sugar Company, resigned from the Board in protest of the appointment."[47]

Brief Friday Administration

President David Friday.

Courtesy UAHC

Unusual Preparation

As an 18-year-old, he ran the family farm near Benton Harbor after his father's death. At 29, he enrolled in the University of Michigan. After graduating in economics in 1908, he became an instructor.

Revive Agriculture

The board was attracted by his interests in economics and agriculture. Farmers increased food production during the war, but the oversupply after the war led to a drop in prices. The board saw the economist as a person who could "revive agriculture and the College alike."[48]

Change in Style

Friday brought with him a very different style. Although he served for little more than 18 months, his presidency was a time of broadened curriculum change. During this period the faculty changed the Applied Science Division to the Division of Science and Liberal Arts and added some 73 new courses.

Friday's View

"The American college which does not turn out 'highbrows' in the proper interpretation of that term as meaning well-rounded, cultivated students, is a failure."[49]

Faulty News Story

Ultimately, Friday resigned the position when a newspaper reported that his research assistant had accompanied him on a trip to Washington, D.C. The report turned out to be false — the young woman had been in East Lansing supervising the work of the office.

Presidential Changes

Shaw is Interim Again

Friday's presidency ended with the 1923 school year.[50] The board appointed Dean Robert S. Shaw for a second period as interim president.

It was a difficult period. The curriculum changes initiated by the Friday administration left the college with a budget deficit. The deficit resulted in part from the response of youth to pursue an applied science and liberal arts course of study.

Friday's Plan Continued

The Shaw administration, however, continued with the new courses and added some. For example, sociology and economics were separated. In addition, changes in the

English Department "to teach Christian solutions to contemporary problems led to the eventual formation of a department of religion."[51]

The liberal arts courses had expanded as well.

Shaw continued this interim administration until September 1924.

Butterfield Assumes Presidency

Kenyon L. Butterfield

Kenyon L. Butterfield became the fourth president of the period in September 1924. In the words of Kuhn, "In so unstable an atmosphere, the presidential voice was often a muffled one."[52]

Much of Butterfield's career involved land-grant colleges. To come to M.A.C., Butterfield had left a similar position at Massachusetts University. Previously, he had held the chair at Rhode Island State University.

Product of M.A.C.

His roots in land-grant institutions go even deeper, however. He graduated from M.A.C. in 1891 and was employed by the college. Recall that he was the person who planned and implemented the railroad excursions to the campus in 1897. He was also the first superintendent of the Farmers' Institutes and was a college field agent. As a student at M.A.C., he was an editor of the *Speculum*.[53]

4-H calf club leader demonstrates points.

Period in Review

National and state circumstances of the 1915-24 period played a significant role in the development of the college. Perhaps the most important was a combination of two factors: the financial crisis for farmers after the war's end and David Friday's reputation as an economist.

Friday Has Impact

Friday was president for only a short time, but he was at the right spot at the right time to enrich the college curriculum and that of the Division of Agriculture. He opened doorways for new courses and programs that in a few years would address a range of parental and student interests.

Union Memorial

The M.A.C. Alumni Association and its interest in building a "home" on the campus also has been a story

with long-term implications. It had the effect of forming a foundation of loyalty and dedication by those who attended M.A.C. The story of the Union Memorial Building was one of devotion.

R.E. Olds Precedent

The disputes between the college and the state legislators established some lasting principles about independent policy-making for the institution. The engineering building burned while arguments raged over the need for more than one school of engineering. President Kedzie's request of R.E. Olds and his favorable support helped continue engineering at M.A.C.

With the enrollment of 350 students in the summer school, the total enrollment of resident students for the year 1924 passed the 2,500 mark for the first time.

Forestry train exhibit: "Have Youth and Trees Grow Up Together."

Courtesy UAHC

"Representing the administration of the institution, the State Board of Agriculture, the advisory board of the college and the faculty, in accepting this wonderful gift, I want to assure you that every person concerned with the institution in an official way speaks with a heart full of the greatest appreciation."

Robert S. Shaw

"History is always deceiving when you are making it."

Frank S. Kedzie (Class of '77)

"The Tower is given ... with the hope that it will revive and preserve Old College Hall memories and be a spiritual inspiration to the present generation of graduates and students, and to those who may come after them."

William L. Carpenter (Class of '75)

(Comments were made at the dedication ceremony of Beaumont Tower, Alumni Day, 1929.)

Time of Change and Stress

Courtesy UAHC

Chapter Overview

As the 1925-34 period began, the Board of Agriculture had just appointed an experienced administrator and alumnus as the college president. Kenyon L. Butterfield had been president of two New York agricultural colleges. His interests in making college services available to a broad range of people seemed to fit very well the track the college had been on for the past several years.

College Name Changes

The Michigan Legislature changed the name of the college in recognition of the broadening curriculum. And renaming the "Aggies" the "Spartans" gave additional recognition to the changes taking place on the campus.

Continuing Education Goal

President Butterfield advocated greater college outreach through the concept of continuing education. The concept was not well received, however, and he was soon replaced as president by Robert S. Shaw.

Beaumont Tower

Perhaps one of the best remembered events of the period was the donation and construction of the Beaumont Tower on the site of Old College Hall.

Economic Stress

The Great Depression made life at the college very difficult.

Butterfield Pushes Concept of Community

President Kenyon L. Butterfield, addressing MAC students at the first convocation of the term, outlined the big problems facing the college in 1925 and advocated the application of the concept of community to the college.

Band Together

The president placed special emphasis on the great worth of the community idea that was fast spreading in modern life the world over. There was a great need for the people of the college to band together for the common interest of the institution.

Look Past "Local" Interests

"College honor and spirit built up after many years," he said, "could be destroyed by a small group of students in less than a week." Though the college was passing through a rapid transitional stage (as shown by a review of events for the past year), he said the college must be very thoughtful and careful in keeping the old ideals. Because there were some 80 activities on the campus reflecting a diversity of interests, the president said students must take special care to uphold the college as an institution above all these.

Unhindered Progress

President Butterfield forecast a year of optimism and unhindered progress if the legislature passed the board's provision for a $3.9 million building program and the freshman class of this year reached 1,000.[1]

Courtesy UAHC

Grand River Avenue Becomes Boulevard

The boulevard style of Grand River is taken for granted by most users and street crossers in the 21st century. A notice in *The M.A.C. RECORD* of 1925, however, reported "the new pavement south of the double row of elms along the north border of the Campus has become an established avenue to traffic from the Arboretum [on the west] to the eastern limits of the campus."

M.A.C. Renamed MSC

Legislature Changes Name

Alumni Legislators Influential

The Michigan Legislature, at the urging of two M.A.C. alumni legislators, changed the college name to Michigan State College of Agriculture and Applied Science. The operative name became MSC.

Rebirth of Purpose

President Butterfield spoke to the Alumni Association gathered to celebrate Anniversary Day. He said, "We also celebrate today what will become a new birthday for the College. Today the change in the College name ... becomes law. So it is off with the old and on with the new. The King is dead, long live the King!

"I like to think that this change of name is going to give us, not merely a change of name but a real rebirth of purpose. I think it is an excuse for making an inventory of what we have done, of what we have omitted to do, of what we are here for, and of resetting our course in the light of the changes that have come about in education and in the life and industry of the state of Michigan."

Assess College Values

"Moreover, shall we not use this new birthday as an excuse for assessing the real values of the College? Let us set our minds toward preserving all the good that has come through the past purposes, traditions, methods, spirit ... and push ahead under the banner of MSC."

In closing, Butterfield said, "Let me propose two toasts that I gave the students:

'Here's to the old M.A.C., Mother of Agricultural Colleges, and Alma Mater of a host of strong men and women.

'Here's to the new MSC, facing a great future with all the daring and adventure of youth.'"[2]

Students Celebrate Name Change

Celebrate!

Students and faculty members formally recognized the new college name at a special convocation in the gymnasium on May 13, 1925. The entire program was inaugurated by students.

Legislators Recognized

"President Butterfield gave a brief review of the events leading up to the celebration before giving way to the undergraduates. Senator Horton and Representative MacKinnon, for whom the Michigan State College bill was named, were introduced and cheered and then Eugene Davenport was given his place on the program."

Student Obligations

In his address, Davenport stressed the debt incurred by a student at a state-supported college. He warned his listeners that unless they became members of society who benefited the state because of their education, they were not fulfilling their contract.

Cake for "Uncle Frank"

Dean Frank Kedzie was born the day preceding the official opening of the college, so the students made the occasion one of special honor to him. He was called to the front and presented with a huge birthday cake decorated with 68 candles and the words "Uncle Frank."

Grand Finale!

At the closing a huge Michigan State College pennant was unfurled from over the beams of the speakers' platform. The Swartz Creek Band and the college orchestra provided music, and the crowd concluded the program by singing "Alma Mater."[3]

WKAR Outfitted

"Broadcasting from WKAR proved to be such a remarkable success that a larger and newer station has been erected during the fall term."

Varied Schedule

"The first 1924 programs were broadcast in January.... The programs consisted of dance music, vocal and instrumental solos, a concert by the M.A.C. varsity band, one by the college glee club, brief talks on agriculture, engineering, and other vocational and educational subjects and debates."

Equipment Donated

"The new tower, 182 feet high, a gift from the Consumers' Power Company, has been erected on the roof of the machine shop building.... A powerful Western Electric radio-phone transmitter, given to the college by the *Detroit News*, has been installed on the second floor of the new powerhouse."[4]

Courtesy UAHC

MSC stack and radio tower.

Student Numbers and Team Name

Enrollment Takes Jump

The increase in enrollment was seen by many as an exciting response to the academic program changes. The excitement is displayed by the *M.S.C. Record*.

Recruiting Pays

"The new attack on the high school graduates of the state by the publicity department was successful as evidenced by the registrar's report. The fall 1926 enrollment soared to 2,571.

"Correspondence between President Butterfield's office and high school principals of the state may have been responsible for the increased enrollment. It at least solicited the help of school officials in getting in touch with their most promising students."

Ag Outdrawn

"The fact that the liberal arts department claims one-third of the students on the campus, and the agricultural department, once the sole unit on the campus, has now dropped to third place, even though the foresters are counted in their number, seems to [point again to the] wisdom of calling this a State College rather than an agricultural institution."

Women and JC Add to Ranks

"The abundance of co-eds is one of the noticeable features of the incoming class. Last year approximately one-fourth of the students were girls; this year their number comes nearer to the one-third mark. Considerable talent is also coming into State College from the junior colleges of the state. Grand Rapids, Flint, and Detroit have made worthy contributions to the junior class in the past couple years."[5]

	1920	1925	1926	Percent change, 1920-1926
Enrollment changes since 1920.				
Men	1,093	1,621	1,843	68.8
Women	355	635	728	105.1
Total	**1,448**	**2,314**	**2,571**	**77.6**

How Spartans Were Named

"I happen to know the origin of the name, for I had a part in choosing it and, so far as I know, was the first to put it into print...."

"Aggies" Outgrown?

"With the curriculum broadening, the college name was changed on May 13, 1925. The name 'Aggies' was outgrown.

"A campus committee sponsored a contest and offered a $10 prize for a nickname.... The name of 'Michigan Staters' was the prize-winning selection."

What Else Suggested?

"I determined to make another effort in bestowing a nickname. Dale Stafford ... of the *Detroit Free Press* fell in with the suggestion.... We went to the college and asked ... to inspect the names submitted. We sought something original and settled on 'Spartans'. It was the name entered in the contest by Perry J. Fremont, then the catcher on the baseball team."

First Use: "SPARTONS"

"On April 2, 1926, [reporting on a] baseball game State had with the Fort Benning [Ga.] officers' team, the new nickname was first used.

'FORT BENNING, Ga., April 2 — The Michigan State College baseball team today waved menacing bats at the Fort Benning Infantry Officers team as it prepared to get revenge for a 7-to-5 defeat suffered in the opening game here yesterday. *THE SPARTONS FROM THE NORTH* were forced to bow yesterday although they actually out hit Uncle Sam's boys, 12 to 10.'"

Spelling Error Fixed

"Well, that was it. Note the incorrect spelling of the word. My carelessness...."[6]

"Spartan Welcome" Introduced

"In an impressive ceremony ... establishing a tradition on the Campus, the 'Spartan Welcome' [September 23, 1927] — upperclassmen extend a formal greeting to the more than 1,000 freshmen...."

Band Stirs Up March

"Classes were excused and promptly at 11:00 clock the band struck up a stirring march, bringing the sophomores, the juniors, seniors and faculty from the four corners of the drill field to the speakers' platform...."

Cavalry Escort

"A cavalry escort led the freshmen columns to the platform where the newcomers were extended greetings ... by L. Whitney Watkins, '93, chairman of the State Board of Agriculture. The program was opened with the singing of Alma Mater, led by the military band that made its first public appearance under the new director, Leonard Falcone."

Spirit, Living, Work

"In addition to Chairman Watkins, who gave a rousing talk on school spirit, clean living and hard work, the freshmen were greeted by Judge Emerson Boyles, deputy attorney general, representing the state; Coach Ralph Young, director of athletics; Miss Flossie Pangborn, Women's Self-Government Association; Clyde Olin, Student Council; and Ogden Grimes, president of the Union."

Singing of "America"

"The talks were concluded ... promptly at noon by the singing of 'America.'"[7]

Alumni Proud of Growing College

Alumni Association: Keep Standards High

On June 19, 1926, the MSC Alumni Association held its annual meeting. It was a time of renewed fellowship and of encouragement to the administration. The following resolutions were made.

Thanks to Governor

"Resolved: That we extend our grateful thanks to the Board of Agriculture and to the Honorable Alex J. Groesbeck, governor of the State of Michigan, for their guidance, work of cooperation, and understanding of the many problems arising to the performance of this great trust...."

Pride in Growth

"Resolved: That we have pardonable pride in the continued growth of the College and call attention to the fact that its student enrollment in 1925-26, over 2,300, was the largest in history."

Broader Curriculum

"Resolved: That we rejoice in the general broadening of the curriculum and in courses and appreciate that the greater usefulness of this College is enhanced thereby, and we favor the continuance of this policy."

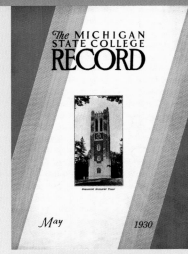

The M.S.C. Record was published monthly for alumni and students.

Union Building Debt

"Resolved: That we rejoice that the Union Memorial Building is nearing completion. However, we call attention to the heavy indebtedness of the $300,000 remaining, which must be paid, if we are to have an enduring Alumni Home.

"We urge the prompt collection of all unpaid subscriptions and recommend that a further campaign be now inaugurated among the sons, daughters, and friends of MSC with the view of reducing this indebtedness by at least $150,000."[8]

Butterfield Advocates Continuing Education

One of President Butterfield's favorite new programs was continuing education. The program was a new concept and required introduction. One of his discussions was reported in the *M.S.C. Record.*

Continuing Ed?

"I presume many alumni have been curious regarding our use of the words 'continuing education.' It is simply a phrase designed to include all types of educational work which the College does off-campus. One of the possibilities ... being developed in a number of American colleges, namely helping alumni to keep up their reading and study, both vocationally and for their leisure as well as to take leadership in their communities ...."

Benefit Community

"Arrange lectures (through your extension division, if you have one) through the first rate members of the faculty; utilize the local organizations; use local leaders; form discussion groups, forums, institutes; supply reading lists and reading courses, form reading circles — above all, convince the groups of alumni ... that theirs is the responsibility for the intellectual tenor of their own communities. The return will be great in the community itself."[9]

Butterfield was committed to advancing the role of education throughout the state's communities and, indeed, around the world. Continuing education did not have a high priority during a period of financial stress at the college, and the program suffered greatly, as did he when the board acted in May 1928.

Professors Publish Books

Joseph F. Cox, professor of farm crops, published a book on crop production and soil management. It was distinctive in that it was intended to serve as a textbook for high schools and college. As such, it was more "comprehensive than is offered in existing books of that nature."

"The work of a number of M.A.C. faculty members is noted. Professor Spragg's plant breeding experiments and the results of his efforts are referred to in many places." The book was published by John Wiley and Sons of New York.[10]

Property Design

The publication of a book on landscape gardening was an early indication of the college's interest in landscape architecture. The book, written by M.E. Bottomley and edited by Liberty Hyde Bailey, was published by the MacMillan Company.

"The book is designed to give specific advice and offer directions for laying out and planting the grounds of small properties, combining utility with beauty in order to give the greatest pleasure. Mr. Bottomley has 51 designs illustrating the points made concerning design of city and country properties."

Specific Plans Offered

"The chapter on design of city lots includes 39 plans for backyards, on lots from 30 to over 100 feet, of various shapes. These plans can be combined and modified to suit any particular property."[11]

Butterfield Presidency Challenged

Outlines College Policy

President Butterfield used a wide range of audiences such as Farmers' Week, the Michigan Federation of Labor, and others to outline his philosophy that would direct his role in shaping college policies.

Not Just Agriculture

"'It is true that the college started as a college for farming interests and those alone,' he said. 'It is still true to those interests but it has a wider range. The Morrill Act of 1862, which gave Federal support to the college, said that the purpose of these land grant colleges, among other things, was to educate the industrial classes in the several pursuits and professions of life.'

"'The college is a good place for your boy, for your girl. We have a democratic campus. There are many opportunities for self-help, and at least three-quarters of our students are working their way through in whole or in part. Your boy and girl can get ready in this college for almost any pursuit or profession in life.'

"'The college for 40 years has been maintaining engineering work and is now broadening that work so as to meet a wider range of industrial problems.'"

Agriculture in Focus

"But Dr. Butterfield is by no means neglecting agriculture," the article writer maintained. "He is blazing a new trail in extension work, one that promises to leave a profound and lasting effect upon the rural life of Michigan."

Broad View

"The institute of the future, however, is to be based upon the community as a unit. It will serve both as a connecting link between the college and the farmers and as a forum at which they may discuss all their problems, whether of production, marketing, or home and community phases of country life."[12]

Butterfield Administration Criticized

The board granted Mr. Butterfield a 10-week leave of absence in February 1928. His leave was to expire May 1. Dean Shaw again served as interim president during Butterfield's absence.

"It appears that the criticisms of his administration began to swell, enough so that at the April [1928] meeting, the board extended Butterfield's leave until July 1 without his knowledge or consent. He returned to the campus May 1, and was summoned before the board to make any defense of himself as he saw fit. The charges against him were never made public."

Spending by "Executive Order"

"They were known, unofficially, to center on his persistence in retaining the Department of Continuing Education after the 1927 legislature had at least tacitly told him to abandon it. The management of the funds of the institution also ... came under fire due to the fact that the comptroller of the College had stated, Mr. Butterfield was spending money 'on executive order' when there were no funds for such expenditures.

"The active history of the upheaval at MSC dates from the middle of January when the press was barred from the monthly meeting of the board. Reporters inspecting these minutes, found that the college had drifted into an impossible financial situation, having a financial deficit of $224,000 on its books."

Governor Keeps Hands Off

"Governor Fred W. Greene continued to maintain his 'hands off' position regarding the college pointing out that the State Board is a constitutional body and that previous attempts of a governor to interfere have been over-ruled."[14]

Alumni Urged to Support Butterfield

"The virtual dismissal of Mr. Butterfield was accomplished despite the efforts of Jason A. Hammond, of the Michigan Retail Dry Goods Association, to organize friends of the former president to stay the hand of the state board. Mr. Hammond sent about 150 telegrams asking MSC Alumni to protest to the state board with regard to its obvious intention of dropping Mr. Butterfield."

Support Fails

"L. Whitney Watkins, (Manchester) chairman of the state board, said that he had received just one complaint from any source, following the sending of the telegrams. Several other letters were written, each saying candidly, in substance that 'because I have been asked to write, I am doing so, but I trust the board will handle the matter without advice.'"[13]

Courtesy of UAHC

New Library Completed

"The new $400,000 library building designed by Edwin Bowd of Lansing is designed to serve students. The building is in the southeast corner of the campus proper. The structure is a beautiful example of the English Gothic Style."[15]

Another Presidential Change

Butterfield Meets with Board

Leave Extended

"President Butterfield, whose administration at MSC has aroused active opposition from the Board of Agriculture, culminating recently in the arbitrary extension of his leave from May 1 to July 1 ... was called before the board Wednesday morning, on his return to the campus, to 'talk things over.'"

Butterfield Confronted

"No official action was taken by the board, Chairman L. Whitney Watkins, Manchester, said early Wednesday afternoon. He explained that the meeting was merely one of discussion. Objections of the board to certain features, mainly financial, of Butterfield's administration, were presented. The president, who returned to the campus Wednesday from a trip to the Holy Land ... was given an opportunity to speak in his own defense."

Will He Resign?

"The board will act officially at the regular meeting, May 22, and not until then, Mr. Watkins said. President Butterfield, questioned as he was leaving the board meeting, refused to make any comment on the situation or to divulge his own plans."

High-paid Aides

"He had nothing to say, particularly with regard to adding former members of the Massachusetts Agricultural College staff to the MSC staff, with substantial salaries. The board cut three of these men, Dean John Phelan, J.D. Willard, director of continuing education, and R.W. Mayer, secretary to the president, from the college payroll, effective July 1."[16]

Deans Also Deposed

"With the elimination of Mr. Butterfield went his two 'vice-presidents,' who with him, were known unofficially as 'The Grand Triumvirate' of the campus. John Dayton Willard, Director of Continuing Education, one of the right-hand men of the deposed president, will cease to function at the end of the present fiscal year June 30. Leaving the campus with Butterfield and Willard will be Dean John Phelan, who had been termed 'Dean of the College' as well as 'Dean of Deans.' The salaries of both of these college officials cease June 30. They were not asked to resign but their offices were eliminated by the board."

"Buddies" Must Go

"The chief objections to these two men were that they were both imported by Mr. Butterfield from Massachusetts Agricultural College, at Amherst, from which the president had likewise come. Willard was paid $6,600 annually and Dean Phelan was on the pay roll at a salary of $7,600. With the exception of Mr. Butterfield's salary, these were the highest on the campus. There were other men, presumably more important, who were getting markedly less salary."[17]

Courtesy UAHC

President Robert S. Shaw

Butterfield Is Out, Shaw Is In

The long controversy over Butterfield's administration at MSC was settled on May 22, 1928. The State Board ended yet another college presidency — the fifth one of the 1920s — and initiated the sixth one.

Shaw Named

"The State Board of Agriculture, Tuesday afternoon, accepted the resignation of Kenyon L. Butterfield as president of MSC, effective immediately. At the same time it appointed Robert S. Shaw, who has been serving as acting president for the third time since his connection with the institution, as president."

Brody Negotiates Butterfield Settlement

"The resignation of President Butterfield was prepared earlier in the week, it was learned Tuesday. Clark L. Brody, Lansing member of the board, visited the president's home late in the afternoon and returned with the resignation.

"Butterfield's salary continues until Jan. 1, 1929, but his resignation is effective at once. There were no changes in the budget, which means that Dean John Phelan, and John D. Willard will be dropped July 1. Mr. Butterfield had been president since September 1924."[18]

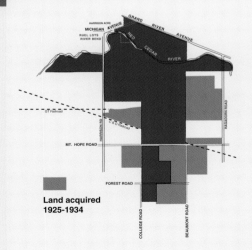

Campus Land Acquisitions

Land acquired 1925-1934

Shaw Administration Launches New Era

Shaw at the Helm

Newspaper Assesses Presidential Change

Robert S. Shaw, upon being named president of MSC, announced his intention to resign the positions of dean of agriculture and director of the Agricultural Experiment Station. Shaw said he would do this "in order to give his new position undivided attention."

Difficult Problems Ahead

"Never in all the 26 years that I have been here, have I seen as many big complicated problems facing the institution at any one time," said Shaw. "Any president, in order to conduct the college successfully, must also have the full support of faculty, students, alumni, and all friends of the institution."

Continue on Faculty Row

"Just how long he will retain the deanship and directorship of the experiment station, President Shaw was unable to state. He said the readjustments must be made as soon as possible. He could not announce his new office headquarters but said that the Shaws will continue to live in the house in Faculty Row, which has been their home for the past 21 years.

"President Shaw's permanent appointment followed the board's acceptance of Butterfield's resignation at the Tuesday afternoon meeting. Board action on the resignation was unanimous."[19]

Critical Time

"When informed of his election to the presidency, the face of Dean Shaw showed no elation. He made this statement, immediately after he had informed the board that he would accept the position: 'This means a radical change in my plans for later life, but if I can be of any service to the college, I'm glad to do so.'"[20]

Courtesy UAHC

Robert S. Shaw judging hogs.

Where Could Better Candidate Be Found?

"Since there was to be a new president, where could a man be found that better embodies the spirit, tendency and aim of the state for MSC than President Robert S. Shaw?"

MSC Momentum

"The college is bigger than any man likely to be brought to it. This institution has a momentum, a meaning all its own, acquired apart from whomever has been at its head. President Shaw is part of that meaning, part of that momentum. Under President Shaw the public may forget that the college has a president, but it will not forget the institution."

One Sits Behind

"The passing of the retiring president is exemplification of the old truism that where two ride horseback, one rides behind. Dr. Butterfield and the board were in a head-on collision. They did not harmonize or view the problems of the college from a common viewpoint."

Newspaper Neutral

"*The State Journal* has never been partisan on either side of the controversy. Its position throughout the late unpleasantness has been that of a reporter. It has merely told the situation as it was privileged to know it without any feeling toward either side."

Who is in Charge?

"The issue was not as to the character and ability of Dr. Butterfield, it was as to whether he or the Board of Agriculture, in the last resort, dominated the institution. Either one or the other, the issue being raised, had to go."[21]

Animal Husbandry under R.S. Shaw

With Robert S. Shaw's role in the MSC presidency, it is easy to overlook his other contributions to the college. He was invited to come to M.A.C. in 1902 to be a professor of agriculture and animal husbandry and to direct the Department of Practical Agriculture.

In 1908 when the college organized the Division of Agriculture, it named Shaw as dean. Over the next few years Shaw established seven departments. The first was Animal Husbandry under the direction of George A. Brown. Brown's classmate Ralph S. Hudson was hired as head of the Farm and Horse Department.

Departments Added

The Poultry Husbandry Department was added in 1909 and the dairy program in 1910, but it remained in Animal Husbandry until 1921.

Shaw's other department creations were Soils, Farm Crops, and Farm Mechanics. At the time, Horticulture and Forestry were separate divisions.

Breeders' Support

Under Shaw's leadership, the livestock program was strengthened by increasing the number of breeds, introducing pedigreed draft horses, and emphasizing marketing as well as production. He won the confidence of the Livestock Breeders Association, which helped secure appropriations for better facilities, improved livestock, and more research.[22]

Tower Dedication

Lifelong Dream

"Alumni Day took on a special significance this year with the dedication of the beautiful Memorial Tower, the gift of John Beaumont ('82) and Mrs. Beaumont of Detroit. The dedicatory exercise was the realization of a dream cherished by the Beaumonts for nearly a half-century, a fitting replacement for the pioneer hall of all the agricultural colleges of our country."

Several persons addressed the MSC Alumni Association. Come and experience their recollections.

Kedzie's Remarks

Dr. Frank S. Kedzie ('77), college historian, chairman of the program, said: "Seventy-two years ago the thirteenth of May, a large assembly met in what was known as 'Old College Hall'. That was the first college for the teaching of agriculture on this continent or in the world. Nobody recognized what that meant. History is always deceiving when you are making it."

Beaumont Architect

The architect of Beaumont Tower, John M. Donaldson, on behalf of the Beaumonts, who were not present, said:

"The significance and interest which this tower may possess lies largely in the spiritual influences which gave it birth. His gratitude and loyalty to his college he desired to express in some simple and dignified memorial, and this tower is his expression...."

Beaumont Friend

William L. Carpenter ('75) said: "We are at the site of Old College Hall. That hall which stood here ... is endeared to the old graduates of the college. For in it, all their recitations were conducted; in it they received the degrees conferred upon them. The place where it stood is to them hallowed ground."

Shaw's Gratitude

President Shaw said: "[We thank] the Beaumonts for this magnificent chimes-tower gift to Michigan State College.

"We greatly value this gift, coming, in the epoch-making period of the history of the institution. Our students and our faculty have been looking forward with great anticipation to seeing the statuary which has been carved on the side of the building, which carries a moral along with it."[23]

The Beaumonts Remembered

Alice and John Beaumont

Mr. Beaumont was born in Elizabeth, New Jersey, July 20, 1858. He came to Michigan in 1875 and graduated from M.A.C. in 1882. After studying law under private tutors, he was admitted to the bar in Saginaw in 1884. He was affiliated with many organizations, including the State Board of Agriculture, from 1912 to 1924. He died in July 1941.

Beaumont was ill and could not attend the dedication ceremony. His friend the Hon. William L. Carpenter ('75) spoke about the gift.

"Several years ago Mr. and Mrs. Beaumont determined to do something to testify their gratitude for what the college had done for Mr. Beaumont. This gift received long and careful consideration, and they finally decided it should be a memorial tower to be erected on this site. So this structure you behold was built...."

His Only View

"Mr. Beaumont's last visit to the campus was in 1937 when he saw his gift. He lived to realize that the gift he and Mrs. Beaumont had given became a source of inspiration to alumni, students, staff, and visitors.

"Mr. Beaumont received an honorary degree of Doctor of Letters, at the commencement exercise, June 13, 1932. The editors of the 1929 *Wolverine* dedicated the publication to Mr. and Mrs. Beaumont in appreciation of their gift."

Symbolic Tower

"Drawings and photographs of the Beaumont Tower are recognized today in nearly every campus publication, since the tower represents the 'spirit' of the college. The charm and beauty of the tower in its beautiful setting, its chimes of mellow bells and the sculptured 'Sower' over its entrance have echoed and will continue to spread the inspiration which Mr. Beaumont received early in life through his college teachers and associates."[24]

**Beaumont Tower sculpture —
"Whatsoever a man soweth."**

Research Broadened

W.K. Kellogg Bird Sanctuary Established, Donated to MSC

Courtesy UAHC

KBS bird researcher.

One of W.K. Kellogg's early bequests to the college was the Kellogg Bird Sanctuary, established in 1927. An early environmentalist, Kellogg modeled the sanctuary after one near Kingsville, Ontario. His objective was to preserve a safe harbor for geese as they migrated between Canada and the South.

Bird Sanctuary

Kellogg donated the site in 1928. It has since become a laboratory for professors in the Department of Fisheries and Wildlife and a destination center for naturalists. Eventually, the sanctuary, along with several other facilities, became elements of the Kellogg Biological Station. Altogether, the site consists of nearly 6.5 square miles.[25]

One Writer's Perspective

Fred Henshaw, editor of the *Magazine of Michigan,* reported some of his observations of the facility. "Here not only is American wildlife preserved, but that of other countries also, so that it is a very cosmopolitan feathered colony, indeed, which greets the visitor there."

Worldly Birds

"Living on the same tract as these members of a native variety — which were imported from Holland, the species having become extinct here — are groups of exotic birds from the ends of the earth — Green Java pea-fowls, Tasmanian geese, bar-headed geese from the Himalayas and aristocratic royal swans from the gardens of King George."[26]

Specialists Study Corn Borer Invasion

MSC Attacks Pest

"Michigan State has thrown herself into a fight to rid American agriculture of the merciless menace, the corn borer. In 1921, when the insects were found to have come across from Ontario, Prof. R.H. Pettit of the Entomology Department declared in a bulletin that the borer was the 'most serious menace that has ever threatened American agriculture.'"

Monroe Station Base

"Friends and graduates of the college may indeed be proud of the vigorous fight being waged by the alumni and representatives of the school. The work was begun by creating a 'corn borer' station at Monroe to meet the onslaught of the menace....

"Many departments of the college have focused their attention on work of relieving the situation. [Examples include] M.M. McCool of the Soils Department working on fertility problems which will hasten maturity and eliminate much of the trouble; R.J. Baldwin ... taking scores of farmers to infested areas so that they might realize the seriousness of the situation; Farm Mechanics students helping manufacturers create new devices to uproot the corn stubble and thus make it harder for the pests to winter in safety.

"Various hybrids of corn have been found to be practically free from the attack of the borer, but the task of purifying such strains and increasing them will be a matter of years."[27]

County, State, National Population		
1930		
	Number	Percent change, 1920-1930
Ingham County	116,587	42.9
Michigan	4,842,325	32.0
USA	123,202,624	16.2

Enrich Soils with Lime

"The use of lime in the program of building soil fertility is being adopted rapidly throughout the state, as a result of the intensive work of soils experts of the College, according to J.A. Porter, specialist in the Soils Department. Advance figures for the year just past indicate that 100,000 acres of Michigan farm land was limed in 1928."

Why Use Lime?

"Mr. Porter explains that through the use of lime, soils which formerly would not support a strong legume growth are now showing fine crops. This is enabling the farmer to raise a legume, such as sweet clover, to plow under as a green manure. This returns organic matter as a soil conditioner, and nitrogen from the air as food for following crops."

Makes Fertilizer Work

"On soils formerly lacking in lime the use of fertilizers and farm manures is giving a much greater increase in crop yields.... Over a period of eleven years the net return from the use of commercial fertilizers has been five times greater on the limed than on the unlimed soil."[28]

Extension Services Increased

MSC Extension Service Grows

Courtesy UAHC

R.J. Baldwin

Congress enacted the Smith-Lever act in 1915, but the college had many years' experience in providing services throughout the state by 1919. Coincidentally, the college also generated a number of people who followed lifetime careers in the Agricultural Extension Service.

"At present time, all members of the administrative staff but one are graduates of the institution, and fully two-thirds of the extension staff are State College alumni."

R.J. Baldwin, appointed to be the first head of Extension in 1908 at the founding of the program, was an M.A.C. alumnus. "The first actual extension project, called 'A Plan for the Improvement of Michigan Livestock,' was prepared by President Shaw in 1906. W.F. Raven was the specialist in charge. In 1913, Baldwin was placed formally in charge of extension work, and director after the Smith-Lever Act was passed."

4-H, Home Economics

"Now [1929] the extension service numbers 157 including an administrative staff of 7, 62 county agricultural agents, 9 home demonstration agents, 10 Boys' and Girls' Club agents, 12 home economics specialists, 44 agricultural specialists, 4 publications staff, and 9 Boys' and Girls' Club state staff."

More Federal Aid

"This work was made possible by the Capper-Ketcham bill, introduced by Congressman John C. Ketcham of Hastings. The law provides ... an additional $20,000 this year to Michigan ... to be increased to $33,000 next year for the expansion of extension work in the counties."[29]

Courtesy UAHC

4-H educator and member.

Shaw Administration Balances Budget

The financial condition of the college in 1927 was a key factor leading to Robert S. Shaw's appointment as president. Actions to eliminate the $250,000 deficit had priority in the early years of the Shaw administration.

Deficit Eliminated

An audit report showed that in a little less than two years, the deficit line was changed to a "rehabilitation fund" of nearly $100,000.

President Credits Staff

"President Shaw indicated that the college will continue to have a surplus as long as he is president. 'No one should try to run a business without a reserve fund of at least 3 per cent.'

"Credit for the present healthy condition of the college finances the president shares with the staff of the institution. 'When the members of the staff realized the financial condition they tried to help,' President Shaw asserted."

Three Key Factors

Three factors were instrumental in eliminating the deficit: reduction of administrative and overhead costs, voluntary curtailment of departmental expenditures, and the increase of receipts and enrollment.

Salaries Raised Moderately

"In the meantime [it was noted] that the staff and faculty members have not suffered salary reductions.... The public announcement of the surplus ... has given rise to a condition of smoothness on the campus. The college awaits the opening this fall with perfect accord existing throughout the entire organization."[30]

Courtesy UAHC

New Hort Building and Greenhouses

The new horticultural building was constructed in 1924 and was equipped with a special greenhouse for experimental and classroom work. The first greenhouse after that was a 'service greenhouse,' furnishing palms and ferns and flowers for campus functions, and also for state occasions such as the inauguration of governors, and sessions of the state legislature.

Courtesy UAHC

A Recurring Story

The story of uncertainty about state funding of higher education has been told many times. How the story played out in the years of the Great Depression, however, spurred special interest.

Special Session

"When Governor Wilber M. Brucker issued a proclamation on March 1, 1932, convening an extraordinary session starting March 29, he had just one thing in mind, balancing of the state budget."

Cut Mill Tax

"In his joint message to the legislature the governor stated that the state must accept leadership in balancing budgets and in his recommendation under the heading of 'State Governmental Expenses,' asked the legisla-

tors 'to reduce the ... Mill Tax acts of 1931 for the U of M and MSC fifteen percent....'"

College Share

"It seems to the *Record* that the state board has taken a fair stand on this vital question.... Whatever else the college receives, it must not lose too much of the income on its permanent endowment, the taxable property of the state of Michigan."

More than $250,000 Cut

"As we go to press, the lawmakers have cut fifteen percent from the mill tax $256,044.... It is hoped that little groups will not decide for themselves that the closing of courses and a department in which the opinion-holder is not interested would effect a panacea."[31]

Part-time Jobs Scarce for Freshmen

A Matter of Concern

"In times like these, many who advise young men and women to go to college often ask the question about opportunities for students to earn a part of their college expenses ... there are many more students desiring employment and somewhat fewer opportunities than usual."

Upper-level Students Advantaged

"Students who contemplate coming to MSC for the first time should recognize that they will have to compete in

securing employment with those who have been on the ground for at least a year and who will have made many contacts with prospective employers."

College Hires Some

"A very definite effort is being made by the College to turn as much work as possible over to students. As evidence ... building and grounds department employs about 90 students at part-time work. The agricultural department employs students about the farms, the barns, and in the laboratories.

"The rate of pay for student help varies from 30 cents to 50 cents per hour according to the type of work and the experience of the individual."

Housekeeping, Cooking

"Young women find employment in homes in East Lansing and Lansing. About 85 girls were able to earn room and board in this way. Several more girls find places in the College through the central stenographic office and as typists for individual members of the faculty."[32]

Bond Cancellation Denied

The alumni association continued to wrestle with its debt for the Union Memorial Building.

Bill to Cancel Bond

"For some months the alumni committee of the Union had worked with the governor ... to pave the way for cancellation of the bond issue. A bill was introduced in the house by A.C. MacKinnon ('95). This bill was referred to the College Committee [which] immediately returned it to the house requesting that it be passed."

Finance Committee Rejects Request

"As the bill carried a tax clause, it was necessarily referred to the Ways and Means Committee. Members of that committee deadlocked on reporting the bill out of committee. On Friday night before the session closed it was announced that no further consideration could be given the bill and it died...." [33]

Student Enrollment, 1932-33[34]

Agriculture	351
Forestry	49
Engineering	551
Liberal Arts	1,137
Home Economics	412
Applied Science	262
Veterinary Med.	114
Physical Educ.	169
Total Undergrads	**3,045**
Graduates	283
Summer Session	878
Ministers' Course	31
Short Courses	491
Total	**4,728***

*Exclusive of repeated names.

...to East Lansing, Campus, Students

Market Crash, Great Depression

Legislative Cuts

The stock market crashed October 29, 1929, the start of the Great Depression. As one result, the legislature cut appropriations by 16 percent in 1932 and an additional 27 percent in 1933.

Crops Department Accounts

One account regarding the Department of Crops illustrates the difficulties of the time. R.L. Cook, who was later to become head of the department, joined the staff in 1929 for an annual salary of $1,800. By 1931 his salary had risen to $1,910. Cook took a one-year leave of absence to pursue a Ph.D. in Wisconsin. Upon his return, he found his salary reduced to $1,600.[35]

The department lost other six faculty members as they moved on to other colleges, commercial organizations, and government agencies.[36]

E.L. Bank "Holiday"

Governor William Comstock decided on February 13, 1933, that he had no other choice but to close the banks in Michigan for 10 days. He later extended the "bank holiday" to prevent a panic run on the banking system.

The day after Franklin Roosevelt was inaugurated, he declared a national bank holiday, closing all banks in the nation. On March 9, Congress passed a law giving federal examiners the authority to decide which banks could remain open.[37]

Plan to Open

In May 1934, a reorganization plan permitted the East Lansing bank to reopen and receive a loan of about $80,000 to pay creditors and depositors 40 percent of the bank's obligations to them. They also agreed to wait until the bank could accumulate assets to pay the additional outstanding balance.

A Difficult Time

According to a newspaper account, "Bank officials spoke freely of the splendid spirit that [was] shown by the people of the community during the year ... but the foregoing does not describe the angst and stress that numerous individuals experienced.*

*Ultimately, the problem was resolved by Congress's establishment of the Federal Deposit Insurance Corporation — FDIC — which now insures depositor accounts up to $100,000.

Courtesy UAHC

Pine seedlings for reforestation.

Needy Students Helped

Student Jobs

"Steps to promote work were first taken in 1930 ... to give some needy students an opportunity to earn a part of their tuition. The work ... consists of general work around the building, in the library, and computing and cataloguing of different kinds of woods."

CCC Seedling Needs

"Another project ... is student labor at the Chittenden Nurseries where the students aid in the production of seedling forest trees that are sold to farmers to reforest wastelands. Since the beginning of the CCC [Civilian Conservation Corps] the demand for forest seedling trees has become so great that the nursery was forced to double its output ... over 3,500,000 seedling forest trees are grown annually at the nursery."

All Given Work

"No exceptions are made in choosing students for part-time work. Every forester who really needs financial aid is offered some sort of work.... As compensation the forestry heads are able to state that no forestry student has ever had to leave college because of financial difficulties."[38]

Federal Aid Supports Student Jobs

Lobbying Pays

"The *State News* recently received word that 255 students will be given jobs by the Federal Emergency Relief Association. About 185 students will be assigned work to help carry them through the term. This is the result of the efforts of organizations such as the Land Grant Colleges Association.... "

MSC Entitlement

"Each college is allotted ten per cent of the total number enrolled on October 15, 1933. Up to 75 per cent of the jobs may be given to students now enrolled in college. The allotment of men and women will be equalized according to attendance ratio giving State about two men to one co-ed."

"Dropouts" Supported

"The remaining 25 per cent of the jobs will be given to former students who have found it necessary to drop out of school.... Students will be paid from 30 to 50 cents an hour and the monthly salary will range from $10 to $20 with an average of $15."[39]

College Life and Service Continue

Nature Conservation

After forestlands in northern Michigan were devastated by harvesting, conserving natural resources became an active public policy issue. It became a major concern for MSC professors and the Extension Service.

Public Issue

As Professor P.A. Herbert observed, "The conservation of natural resources will occupy a more prominent part in the history of the last year than it has ever before. Our leaders of today realize that rugged individualism uncontrolled has resulted in the rapid deterioration of all natural resources and that our civilization cannot continue without these resources."

CCC Established

"The first conservation measure inaugurated by the new administration was the CCC [Civilian Conservation Corps], which combined the rehabilitation and conservation of our most vital resource, youth, with that of forests, land, water, and game."

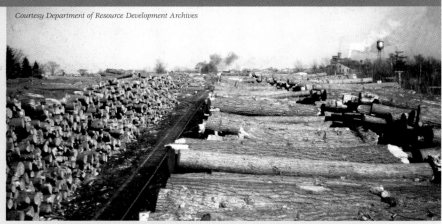

Courtesy Department of Resource Development Archives

Cut timber awaiting shipment and processing.

Public Ownership

"Then came the policy to expand the public ownership of our natural resources, particularly of forestland.... The federal forest service already has over 150 million acres of land and now it is proposed that it acquire 225 million acres more, thus putting in federal ownership over one-half of the forest land in the country."

Forests Protected

"But even such large public ownership of forestland is not enough; that remaining in private hands must be safeguarded from abuse. No longer can land be stripped of its lumber and allowed to revert to barren wastes so common in northern Michigan today."[40]

Jr. Farmers' Week Popular

"Approximately 1,700 junior farmers, representing 113 Michigan vocational high schools, journeyed to East Lansing ... to take part in the 15th annual Junior Farmers' Week held here."

Judging Contests

"Capacity crowds attended all lectures and exhibits [and] the judging contests. Entrants numbered 768 ... in the grain-judging meet, held in the pavilion of Agricultural Hall, and 728 contestants entered the dairy-judging contest which was held in Demonstration Hall."[41]

WKAR on the Air

Broader Listenership

"The voice is likely to be that of Keith Himebaugh, '28, announcer of the MSC radio station, but the program may be of any sort, for lately WKAR has widened its policy of service, and programs now not only interest the farmer, but as well the city dweller, the housewife, the high school children, and in fact all the members of any family."

Service for Farmers

"Because the Farm Service program is the most regular — 12:00 noon to 12:30 p.m., except Sunday — it is perhaps the one most known and most listened to. It includes the weather forecast and the latest livestock and grain quotations and information, in addition to two discussions daily relating to agriculture in some form."

MSC and USDA

"Since January 18, 1932, this program has also included the Michigan Farm Flashes, a new farm radio program service distributed by the College, in cooperation with the USDA."

Part of School Curricula

"A special feature for high school students includes talks given by agricultural staff members on farm crops and animal husbandry. It is estimated that 600 high school students, at least, listen to this program every week and discuss it in their classes."[42]

WKAR continues to say "Hello" to its listeners. This broadcast performance took place about 10 years after its first "Hello" in 1925.

Courtesy UAHC

MSC Respected

Shaw Recruits Hannah to Return

After graduating from the college, John Hannah was an Extension poultry specialist and was widely recognized for his insight and leadership. He was elected president of the International Baby Chick Association (I.B.C.A).

The college had granted Hannah a year's leave to become the managing director of the Poultry Industry Hatchery Breeder Code, headquartered in Kansas City.

Shaw Invites Him to Return

In the summer of 1934, President Shaw asked to meet Hannah in Chicago. Shaw invited him to become secretary of the board. Hannah said, "I told him I was interested, but I would have to first be released from my current responsibility. He offered me a salary of $4,200 per year, which was much less than I was receiving, and about one-fifth of what I would have received had I accepted an offer from a Chicago packing firm."

Choosing What is Important

Said Hannah, "I had already concluded that there were things more important to me than making money and I had about made up my mind that I would rather return to a university — particularly to Michigan State College — than do anything else."[43]

College Beef Experiment

College-Government Project

"To aid the butcher and housewife in obtaining high-grade beef, a seven-year project has been carried on by the Animal Husbandry Department under the direction of Prof. G.A. Brown, in cooperation with the Bureau of Animal Industry and Home Economics of the Department of Agriculture.

"At present, 12 steers and 12 heifers are to be put on a feeding period. As they gain in weight, they will be slaughtered in small groups during different parts of this period."

Quality Management

"After the carcass is analyzed, a prime rib cut and samples from different parts of the body will be sent to Washington for chemical analysis and palatability tests. The object of these experiments is to gain a desirable finish for the meat and to establish a point wherein steer and heifer carcasses are comparable in quality."[44]

High National Honors to Shaw

"Accorded one of the highest honors awarded in the field of agriculture, Robert Sidney Shaw, president of MSC, had the distinction of being chosen by the American Society of Animal Production to be its guest at a banquet given in his honor by the Saddle and Sirloin Club, and to have his portrait hung in the hall of celebrities in its club rooms."

25 years of Service

"President Shaw was born in Canada but has been connected with educational institutions in the United States since 1898 when he became an instructor in animal husbandry at the University of Montana. His connection with MSC began in 1902, when he was appointed professor of practical agriculture.

"Successive advancements through the posts of director of the experiment station, dean of agriculture, and acting president, culminated in the appointment of Mr. Shaw as president in 1928. During all this period Mr. Shaw has toiled to make this college an institution of practical benefit to Michigan agriculture."

Other MSC Alums are Prior Awardees

"Another source of pride for MSC in this ceremony at Chicago is that four former agricultural graduates and one former member of the college staff have been similarly honored since 1920. These men are Eugene Davenport, F.B. Mumford, E.A. Burnett, H.W. Mumford and Gordon H. True."[45]

Ag Men Aid Rural Power Survey

"The Agricultural Engineering Department has been notified that it will supervise the state work for a national survey of farm electrification ordered by the president through the federal power commission."

Rural Electrification

"Three Michigan counties, Clinton, Sanilac, and Macomb, are to be surveyed by a farm-to-farm canvass. The information on rural electrification obtained will furnish a cross-sectional view of this work in the Lower Peninsula. Information secured from the public utilities will supplement county reports in determining the future development in this field."

Two-month Project

"Prof. H.J. Gallagher of the Agricultural Engineering Department is to be supervising engineer, with Burr Foster of East Lansing and Elmer Berrine of Milford in charge of field men. The survey is to be in operation during April and May of this year 1934."[46]

Look around you, his legacy is here. To the end he delighted in the everyday expressions of biological complexity he knew surrounded us, if we would only look and patiently observe. For him, learning demanded time, perspective, and an open mind.

W.J. Beal, the Person

Beal was born near Adrian in the wilds of territorial Michigan in 1833. His life bridged the era of stump clearing to the dawn of commercial agriculture. His years at M.A.C. helped establish the foundation of the large, cosmopolitan university it would become.

Formal Education

After graduating from the State University in Ann Arbor, Beal went east to pursue his interest in natural history. He joined in scientific debate among the finest minds of science at Harvard University and chose the elements of investigation and teaching that resonated within him.

Emerging from Harvard in 1865, he taught in upstate New York, then in Chicago, before coming to Lansing in 1870 as professor of botany and horticulture.

Hands-on Teacher

He variously taught botany, horticulture, forestry, landscape gardening, plant physiology, and even history. He was one of the first in the country to provide compound microscopes for students to use in botany labs. His teaching combined the attention to systematic

detail of botanist Asa Gray with the independent observational learning from real-world organisms espoused by zoologist Louis Agassiz. His *The New Botany*, presented in 1880, outlined a hands-on, observational teaching philosophy, one rarely supplemented by lectures. A relentless scholar and teacher, Beal was also very personally involved with his students.

Frugal and Focused

Raised as a Quaker, Beal throughout his life was frugal and focused. He exercised daily, ate sparingly, and extolled physical labor and time spent outside.

He also took aim at "distractions" from higher education — alcohol, messy dormitories, smoking, spectator sports, and spoon-feeding lecturers. He was engaged with both campus life and town concerns, and he editorialized freely on topics that smacked of ineptness, inefficiency, or self-promotion.

What is now Cowles House was home to Beal and his wife, Hannah, for 38 years. It became a home-away-from-home for many students, where they came to eat and discuss campus issues. His primary legacy early on was the students' intense devotion to their teacher, mentor, and friend.

Plant and Garden Designer

Many know Beal best as founder of the botanical garden that bears his name. He reported it had "...a very modest beginning in 1877, or, if we include about 140 plots of grasses and clovers as a botanic garden, then the botanic garden was started in 1873." Now widely respected as a campus instructional and inspirational landmark, it is the oldest such facility in America in the same location.

W.J. Beal (right of child) and F.S. Kedzie (left of child) with faculty colleagues.

Bringing Up Botany

WILLIAM JAMES BEAL

PIONEER PLANT SCIENTIST AND BELOVED TEACHER, FOR THE FIRST TIME OF RECORD NEAR THIS SPOT IN 1879 CROSSED VARIETIES OF CORN FOR THE PURPOSE OF INCREASING YIELDS. A STUDENT OF AGASSIZ AND GRAY, DR. BEAL CAME TO MICHIGAN AGRICULTURAL COLLEGE IN 1870, WHERE HE SERVED IN VARIOUS CAPACITIES FOR A HALF-CENTURY. PLANTINGS IN THE BOTANIC GARDEN BEARING HIS NAME WERE BEGUN BY DR. BEAL IN 1873. FROM HIS ORIGINAL RESEARCHES HAS COME THE TWENTIETH CENTURY MIRACLE OF CROP PRODUCTION - HYBRID CORN.

The Innovator

One of the best known of Beal's investigations involved corn. His work is now generally recognized as the first controlled crosses made among several corn varieties. The experiment, born of scientific curiosity, was based on inferences drawn from published observations of Darwin himself. He wrote to Darwin and received a reply forever cherished by Beal in which Darwin noted, "I am glad that you intend to experiment." His work earned Beal a permanent, recognized role in the later miracles of increased yields from hybrid corn. Beal also pioneered turfgrass research and reforestation methods for timber harvested areas.

This plaque, south of the Red Cedar River and east of Hagadorn Road, memorializes Beal's experimental pine forest, called "The Pinetum."

The Experimenter

Widely known is Beal's seed viability study, which began in 1879 and is the longest continuously monitored experiment in the world. He buried 20 bottles, each containing 50 seeds from each of 21 species. The bottles have been opened and the seeds tested at gradually extending intervals — first 5, later 10, and now 20 years. The 120-year reporting of the work (published in 2002) details the continuing germination of several species. The next scheduled excavation will be in 2020.

Courtesy University Relations

Frank W. Telewski, curator of the Beal Gardens, displays the germinated seeds from bottle 15.

Presence Undiminished

Beal's campus presence has arguably not diminished in the past 80 years. The Beal Botanical Garden, the campus plantings that which he so fretted over and monitored ceaselessly, the seed dormancy study, the ongoing role of Cowles House as a beacon of campus warmth and welcome, and perhaps most subtle of all, the continuing ebb and flow of Bermudagrass intrusion throughout many parts of North Campus are continuing reminders of his contributions to science and the institution.

Community Builder

He believed deeply in the need to communicate and develop community among the few isolated scientists in applied botany and plant agriculture. He served as the key organizer and first head of many professional organizations, such as the Society for the Promotion of Agricultural Sciences, the Michigan Academy of Science, and the Botanists in the U.S. Agricultural Experiment Stations. He served as master of the State Grange of Michigan, director of the Michigan Forestry Commission, and school commissioner of Ingham County.[47]

Wiring Michigan's Farms

Extension Service Involved Early

Few readers have experienced life without electricity except during a temporary blackout. Of course, things were not always so. Given its record, it is not surprising that the Extension Service helped people make the transition to daily use of electricity. The Agricultural Engineering Department had been conducting workshops on the topic as early as 1914, but by 1923 only approximately 3,000 favorably located Michigan farm homes had access to electrical service.

National Committee Sponsors Experiment

A national committee on the relation of electricity to agriculture formed 26 state committees. Their task was to determine how the service could be extended to the farmer, how to use it on the farm, the economics of such power, and the sociological effect on agriculture.

Two MSC staff members on the Michigan committee "marked the first vital entrance of extension work in the field of farm electrification." The committee sponsored the creation of the

Courtesy John Gerrish Collection

Extending electricity to the countryside.

"Mason-Dansville" experimental line to serve these two communities.

MAES Gets Word Out

Researchers prepared an Experiment Station bulletin that got the word out quickly. In 1928 a program was established, and for five years a truck went about the state

carrying Extension Service electrification information to rural families. A four-wheel trailer, designed and built to carry a model electric kitchen, was added to the entourage about 1930. A home economics Extension specialist accompanied others in demonstrating household equipment and appliances."[48]

Period in Review

The 1925-34 period was a difficult time in the nation, in Michigan, and on the college campus. Beginning with the stock market crash in 1929, the years of economic depression were extremely challenging to all. Although many students were able to stay enrolled in the college, the economic stress of the time also meant that many young people would not receive a college education. Indeed, many would not even be able to complete high school.

College Mission Continues

Despite the economic difficulties of the period, the college continued to address its mission of serving the people of Michigan. College researchers continued to analyze the problems agriculture was facing. At the same time, technology such as the automobile, gasoline-powered tractors, and electrical service in rural areas held out promise of a better life even if financial resources were limited for a time.

Shaw's Stable Leadership

Robert S. Shaw, who had been on the campus for decades and who had served as interim president on three occasions, stepped into the role on a permanent basis just in time. His wise, strong, and stable leadership during this stressful period proved especially beneficial to all those associated with the college.

Return of John Hannah

Among his acts of wisdom was his effort to encourage John Hannah to come back to the campus as secretary to the college's governing board. Not only did that action prove helpful in gaining guidance through the rest of the Great Depression and the war that followed, but it gave Hannah experience that proved helpful in his subsequent decades of college administration.

Courtesy UAHC

"Those farsighted individuals, who laid the foundations for this institution and were cognizant of the necessity for beautiful surroundings, deserve a memoriam of praise. Today it is our duty to recognize this valuable inheritance, that has been handed down to us through the years, and carry forward in this program of beautification to a newer and greater Campus Beautiful."

Robert S. Shaw, President,
Michigan State College

"During the early days of my presidency, [World War II] was on and our faculty had few regular students. We had women students, some men ... and large numbers of military students from the Army and Air Force. All our facilities were fully used, and our dormitories, fraternities and sororities were taken over for military personnel. Many members of our faculty were teaching courses designed for the military...."

John A. Hannah
From *A Memoir*

National Recession in Full Bloom

Chapter Overview

Economic Stress

The 1935-44 period was one of continuing stress. The difficulties of the first half were rooted in the economics of the Great Depression. State government was hard pressed to fill the operating and capital needs of the college.

More students were finding their way to college, but state appropriators lagged resource needs. Administrators often noted the rising enrollments and contrasted them with falling appropriations.

Federal Aid Helped

During this time, the federal government played an increasing role in assisting the college and students. The WPA (Works Progress Administration) provided funding to compensate student laborers and the unemployed filling assignments on the campus.

The college also benefited from federal PWA (Public Works Administration) grants for new buildings and other capital improvements. The federal government's goal was increased employment. College administrators had to come up with matching funds. The construction of Jenison Fieldhouse in the late 1930s was one such project.

WWII Pressures

The second half of the period, while equally stressful or more so, was entirely different. The trials and changes on campus had to do with changes resulting from the war in Europe and the Pacific. For the second time in little more than 20 years, the college was asked to live up to its land-grant obligations to the federal government. In many ways the campus had again become a training station to prepare youth for war.

Despite these powerful economic and military pressures, the college continued to advance. Student enrollment grew, changes were made on the campus, leadership was stable, and the college research and extension services again demonstrated their usefulness in a time of need.

Academic Structure

The 1935-44 period for MSC began with the divisions of Agriculture, Home Economics, Liberal Arts, Applied Science, Engineering, and Veterinary Medicine plus a Graduate School. Each was headed by a dean. Within the Division of Agriculture were two general lines of study, agriculture and forestry.

Roosevelt's Search for Recovery?

Franklin D. Roosevelt became president in March 1933 and had been communicating with the American public through his "fire-side speeches." In one he described his plan to end the nation's economic despair.

Governing Principles

"Describing the nature of the $4.9 billion work relief program in his 'fire-side speech' Sunday night, President Roosevelt stated clearly that six fundamental principles would be followed in its administration:

- 'All projects will be useful;
- 'All will translate a considerable proportion of the fund into wages;
- 'Projects "which promote ultimate return to the federal treasury of a considerable proportion of the costs will be sought";
- 'Funds will be promptly spent;
- 'Employment created will be for those on relief;
- 'Projects will be allotted in relation to numbers on relief in areas.'"

Responsibility of Americans

"Then as an appeal for full co-operation with his aims, Roosevelt added that 'the most effective means of preventing such evils in this work relief program will be the eternal vigilance of the American people themselves.'"

Will Support or Jealousy Govern?

"Now Roosevelt has submitted another plan with a full explanation of its nature.... In its application he has asked for the support of the people of the United States. Will he be given it, or will it be stinted by petty jealousies that are interested solely in party activities? That remains to be seen."[1]

Hannah Informs the Legislature...

Courtesy UAHC

John A. Hannah in board secretary role.

For the past several decades, MSC had been receiving state funding on the basis of a state property tax millage. It now appears that the legislature will end this method of funding the state college and state university. In 1935, the legislature had before it a bill to substitute a biennial appropriations act that would spell out the funding provided over the coming two years.

Voice to Legislature

"Secretary to the State Board, John Hannah, had the responsibility for handling the college appropriation. In addressing the House Ways and Means Committee he stated, 'The request we are making for Michigan State College represents the most deliberate and conservative judgment of the administration and is tempered by an appreciation of state financial

Conditions are Stressful

Media Oppose State Cuts

As has happened previously and will likely do so again, state legislators confronted tough choices. In the 1935 session, the legislature was contemplating making cuts in appropriations for higher education. Building on the editorial comments of the *Detroit News,* the *State News* editor chastised the legislature for even considering such an action.

Unparalled and Reckless

"Commenting on budget cuts for the UM and MSC, the *Detroit News* says in part: 'To reduce the university's income and that of MSC would be false economy of the most reckless kind.' In the same editorial, the *News* states that the UM has but two alternatives: raise student fees and thus cut the enrollment, or to reduce the faculty."

UM Endowed, MSC Not

"But if UM is plunged into such severe straits because of cuts, what about Michigan State? The University is aided by generous endowments; this college has little support of that kind. Are we expected to make further retrenchments in the faculty, curtail our enrollment at the point when it is first beginning to show a substantial increase?"

Cut Past Progress?

"The answer obviously is no. Perhaps not immediately, but eventually the college will be given its due recognition. In jeopardizing the high standard of education in the state without apparent reason, the legislators have drawn upon themselves the condemnation of one of Michigan's foremost newspapers; others will follow. And there is always another election at which the people may express their feelings on important questions which their previous choices treated too lightly."[2]

Side Benefits of Stress

When asked to make a statement about the events of the previous year (1934), President Shaw was not hesitant to say that the economic stress "has brought about a changed attitude of the student body."

Students Stay Focused

"'Students today,' declared the president, 'are more purposeful, are thinking more correctly, and seeing more clearly than a year ago. From an administrative standpoint this means much, because need for disciplinary action has been entirely eliminated.'"

Financial Shortfall

"'The calendar year just ending has been a very busy and successful one for MSC. For the second successive year, operation on a greatly reduced budget has been necessary, but it has been made possible through the cooperation of the faculty, state administrative officials, the press, and the friends and supporters of the college in general. While curtailment of many activities has been necessary, increased demands, as indicated by a record enrollment of 3,326 students during the fall quarter, now warrant renewed activity.'"

Extension Busy

"'The extension organization ... has rendered a large and splendid service in aiding the execution of relief, re-adjustment, and recovery measures of the federal government. Many members of the instructional staff have likewise been called upon to aid in solving difficult problems involved in the recovery program.'"[4]

...Admissions Rising!

conditions.... We have lived within an income from legislative appropriations which declined from $1,640,218 per year for 1929-31 to $1,000,000 for the current biennium, a reduction of 39 percent.'"

"According to Miss Elida Yakeley, registrar, more applications for enrollment [were received] for next fall than her office has ever experienced. This registration curve, which started here last fall with a 17 percent increase, has apparently reached many other colleges and universities."

Teaching Load

"The burden which has been placed on the teaching staff through the policy pursued during the depression years of the non-replacement of staff members who have left will be materially increased. Classes are now practically at the saturation point."[3]

Courtesy UAHC

Cooperative Extension agents are kept busy providing relief and recovery assistance to families.

College Funding Erratic

Difficult financial conditions persisted and were destined to be played out in appropriations for higher education. MSC was not alone in having to deal with reduced state appropriations. *The State News* account provides added details.

Proposed Funding Inadequate

"Contending that funds recommended by the legislature are insufficient, state college officials condemned the appropriations approved by the Ways and Means Committee, with which to operate the institution during 1935 and 1936."

Board Requests Rejected

"Seeking $1,478,000, a slight increase over last year, college officials were disappointed when the legislative committee made drastic reductions in the bill, paring it to $1,178,000.... To this amount, approximately $20,000 in sales tax revenue is expected to be added, leaving an estimated amount of $1,200,000 derived from the general fund for college operations."[5]

"Secretary Hannah reported good news about college finances in the spring of 1936. He said an estimated $116,000 came into the college coffers for the next fiscal year from three additional sources last week."

Cuts Restored

"The new budget necessitated additional funds for next year if the college was to continue its present rate of growth. The largest source came from the state of Michigan. Governor Frank D. Fitzgerald ... granted a sum of $67,000 to the college primarily to restore a cut in appropriations in 1931."

Federal Assistance

"An additional $19,000 came from the Bankhead Jones Act providing federal funds for colleges and universities. Approximately $30,000 is expected from added enrollment funds next fall if the incoming students meet expectations for the increase."

Salary Restoration

"Major points of increase in the college budget call for $47,000 added to the faculty payroll, this being distinctly a salary restoration. In contemplation of the hiring of several faculty members, $25,000 has been set aside for this purpose.

"The remaining $27,000 ... will go toward increased maintenance arising from the added enrollment and costs of next year. From this will come new furnishings for the Union, including the new wing, laboratory equipment, and chemical engineering facilities."[6]

Courtesy UAHC

Ag Econ Meetings, Farmers' Week

Business people, including those related to the agricultural industry, are always concerned about the future. During the Great Depression, they must have been especially worried about what might not occur.

Coincide with Farmers' Week

"The 1935 Farmers' Week will include meetings for members of the commodity group organizations. The first session will deal with field crop specialties — potatoes, beans, and sugar beets; the Wednesday session with fruits and vegetables; and the Thursday morning session with livestock and dairy products."

Market Outlook

"R.V. Gunn, Extension Economist, who ... prepared the annual Michigan Agricultural Outlook Report, will discuss the 1935 outlook for farm products."

Marketing Changes

"Dr. G.N. Motts of the research section of the Economics Department ... will present some of his findings on out-of-state movement of Michigan fruits and vegetable and of imports into the state. Mr. Ulrey, Assistant Professor of Agricultural Economics, will discuss the results of investigations in direct marketing by farmers on the 19 public produce markets now operating in Michigan cities."[7]

Log-sawing contest at 1935 Farmers' Week.

Campus Changes

"Old No. 7": Lost To Faculty Row

Faculty Row Changes

"The little settlement of six campus dwellings that was reduced to three many years ago when the need for class space grew more rapidly than the ability of the college to construct new buildings, has now lost another member. Old No. 7, Faculty Row is now being converted into an administration building for the Education, Psychology, and Philosophy departments."

House on the Hill

"The brick dwelling ... was the president's home from 1857 until 1873 when the present college hospital was constructed as the 'prexy's' residence. The 'house on the hill' served this purpose until Frank S. Kedzie was appointed president in 1916 and he maintained his home in Lansing."

Shaw and Conrad Remain

"President Shaw and Elisabeth Conrad, Dean of Women, are now the only faculty members living on Faculty Row in college houses. One of the other faculty homes has been converted into a home economics practice house, another is used for the Economics Department, and a third house is the college health center."[8]

Old barns north of the Red Cedar.

Courtesy UAHC

Courtesy UAHC

"Old No. 7" faculty house.

Farm Buildings Moving South

"Gradually, but surely, earmarks of the agricultural program are being removed from the campus area north of the Red Cedar River."

Good-by, Tractor Barn

"One old landmark will be gone from the college with the removal of the tractor barn and the subsequent landscaping of the corner northeast of the Chemistry Building. Workmen will begin the razing of the old barn within the next two weeks, according to Secretary Hannah."

For Beauty and Safety

"According to Hannah, two reasons justify tearing down the tractor barn. It is unsightly and it is a serious fire hazard to the chemistry and dairy buildings. The tractor barn was one of the early farm buildings on the campus having been built sometime in the 1860s."[9]

Foresters Host Japanese Visitor

"Kakuri Oshima of the Department of Agriculture and Forestry at Tokyo, Japan, was a recent visitor of the forestry department of MSC. Mr. Oshima, who is on a study tour through the United States and other countries, has been visiting the places most notable for forestry study and research.

"Mr. Oshima ... was shown the various forestry activities including the woodlots, pinetum, sugar bush, Clark-McNary nursery, forestry cabin, and the experimental dry kiln. He was very much pleased and impressed with the methods of experiment and study that are in use here."[10]

County, State and National Population

	1940	
	Number	Percent change, 1930-1940
Ingham County	130,616	12.0
Michigan	5,256,106	8.5
USA	132,164,596	7.3

Land Abuse Crisis

Approach One: Conservation Institute

To some, the massive harvesting of timber in the late 19th century was seen as the glory days. Others would say these were days of shameful plundering.

Deforestation

Nonetheless, after our vast forests were felled to fuel Great Lakes steamers, provide lumber for Michigan's growing cities, and rebuild Chicago following the Great Fire of 1871, only 5 percent of the state remained forested at the turn of the century.

Plow Follows Axe?

At the time it had been assumed that the "plow would follow the axe"; that once cleared of timber, the cutover lands would change to productive farms.

Large segments of the cutover lands, however, were not suitable for commercial farming.

Land Abandoned

With no ready market for their cutover holdings, landowners found it expedient simply to abandon them. The problem worsened in the early 1930s when economic conditions led to wide-scale property tax delinquency. By 1932, some 17.6 million acres, almost half of the land area of the state, were reported as tax delinquent — lands repossessed by the state for nonpayment of property taxes.

Erosion

Severe erosion by wind and water ravaged the fragile exposed land located largely in 47 northern counties.[11]

Conservation Institute

In 1937, the State Board established the Conservation Institute in response to a recommendation submitted by a committee of deans and Director Gardner. Thus, the college became engaged in resource conservation and planning in an organized manner.

As early as 1925, Lee Roy Schoenmann was appointed staff director of the Michigan Economic Survey in the state Department of Conservation. This program, to evaluate the scope of Michigan's land crisis, was turned over to the Conservation Institute in 1937.

Conservation Districts

A particularly successful Extension function operating through the institute was the undertaking of Russell G. Hill and Leonard J. Braamse to organize soil conservation districts. (By 1948 the number of districts would reach 57.) Hill, with a joint appointment in the Michigan Department of Agriculture and serving as the executive secretary of the State Soil Conservation Committee, continued this work until soil conservation districts functioned in every county.

Courtesy Resource Development Archives

Abandoned lands and structures in northern Michigan.

These locally established districts provided a conduit through which the U.S. Soil Conservation Service could provide technical assistance to help landowners and local governments reduce the wind and water erosion problems in the north, and aid the growing farm operations and other land users in the south.[12]

Courtesy Resource Development Archives

Lakeshore lumbering took its toll on sandy soils.

Courtesy Resource Development Archives

Soil erosion was severe and widespread in some areas.

Approach Two: Land Use Planning

Though heroic measures were taken to get delinquent properties back on the tax rolls during the late 1930s, the efforts were not productive. By 1941, the state policy called for restoring areas suited for agricultural and commercial development use to private ownership and incorporating the remaining lands in public forest, wildlife, and recreational holdings.

College Help Requested

Local government officials and the Michigan Department of Conservation submitted requests to the college for help in classifying the reverted lands for their respective best uses. Professor J.O. Veach from the Soil Science Department and Schoenmann, now with the Conservation Institute, were early contributors to this land classification effort.

Classification of rural lands according to their supposed best use became a prime objective of the rural land use planning programs sponsored by the U.S. Department of Agriculture and the Michigan Agricultural Experiment Station between 1938 and 1941.[13]

Courtesy Resource Development Archives

Cutover lands, a daunting challenge.

Courtesy Resource Development Archives

Untended stump lands in northern Michigan.

Growing Knowledge Through Experience

Annual Foray

"The annual Botany Foray will be held as usual on Decoration Day, Wednesday, May 30. The Foray will start this year with the Kellogg Bird Sanctuary as the center and various woods and swamps in the vicinity will be visited under the guidance of Dr. Darlington and other members of the Botanical staff."

Registration and Fee

"It is essential that every person going register with the clerk in the Botany office by the early part of Monday afternoon, May 28, at the same time paying a fee of twenty-five cents a person. This will not be refunded unless on account of very heavy rain the trip is cancelled."

Student Car Drivers

"Students who have cars available would confer a favor on the Botany Department by indicating that fact and telling how many people can be carried in the car. Students who furnish cars will not be charged the twenty-five cents but must register so that it will be known how many persons are going in all."[14]

WPA Extends College Education

The federal government, under the leadership of President Franklin D. Roosevelt, initiated a variety of programs to alleviate pain of living during the depression.

One such program, sponsored by the Works Progress Administration, extended higher education opportunities to those who could not afford college. A key tool of the program was having MSC and six other state colleges support 27 "community colleges" around the state. Fourteen were located in Detroit. Several Detroit suburbs in Wayne and Oakland counties housed community colleges as did some smaller communities around the state.

Standard Courses

"These new colleges supply standard first-year college courses and college credits for high school graduates who are not financially able to attend regularly established institutions. In addition, other courses offered ... include accounting, political science, advanced chemistry and others that do not ordinarily appear in the first-year curriculum."

Practical Applications

"'Particular attention has been given to stimulate adult cooperative study of current problems having a practical and direct application in every day life,' Dr. Henry J. Ponitz, of WPA educational projects, declared."[15]

The new livestock judging pavilion.

Courtesy UAHC

Federal Support for Student Labor

"Working their way through college are some 1,500 MSC students who draw a monthly payroll of over $25,000. The maximum compensation any student may receive each semi-monthly payday is $20."

College and Community

"On campus, clerical work, painting, and cleaning are a few of the tasks being performed by students. Several serve as recreational leaders at Mason and Abbot Halls....

"Poultry research takes care of many poultry majors. Under the direction of the buildings and grounds department, men make signs used about the campus. And then there are always emergency jobs such as when a woman student was employed to bottle cough medicine and nose drops at the hospital.

"Among the most useful to students themselves are student mathematics tutors, who help nearly 100 persons each day to understand their geometry and calculus."[16]

The new Athletic Center, now named Jenison Fieldhouse. *Courtesy UAHC*

New Athletic Center

In September 1938, Governor Frank Murphy announced that the federal WPA approved a $337,500 grant to construct a $750,000 gymnasium and fieldhouse. It was funded to help revive the economy.

Fieldhouse Plan

"According to Ralph H. Young, athletic director, MSC will have one of the country's most modern athletic plants. The present men's gymnasium ... will be remodeled and used for a women's gymnasium.

"The gymnasium will house complete facilities for physical education and intramural athletics, with room for five basketball courts, wrestling, boxing, fencing, and other rooms on the second floor. A basement will house locker rooms and other equipment used in intramural and intercollegiate athletics."

Sports Arena

"The fieldhouse will have seating capacity for 8,500 persons for basketball games. The basketball court and first floor seats will be removable so the entire structure may be used for football, baseball, or other sports."[17]

... and Campus Development

WPA Crews Spruce Up Campus

In an effort to revitalize the national economy, many people were employed under the WPA and the PWA programs. Following is an account of how the college benefited directly.

Building Interiors Painted

"Approximately 300 WPA people continue to work on campus projects. One crew is painting the interior of all college buildings that need it and have completely redecorated the interior of Kedzie Chemical Laboratory, Engineering Building, Beaumont Tower, and the Bacteriology Building. Another crew has been installing farm drains and another has revamped a barn on one of the new college farms to be used by Dr. Hudleson in his work on Bang's disease and undulant fever."

New Sidewalks and Paved Roads

"A new crew is starting this week to pave the college drive extending from between Practice House No. 5 and No. 6 on Faculty Row in front of Mayo Hall and connecting with the new concrete drive at a point directly north of Alice Cowles Hall (the old hospital — formerly the president's home). This crew will soon be working on the new sidewalks about the auditorium and gymnasium. Many other sidewalks and service drives will be paved during the summer."[18]

Courtesy UAHC

Robert S. Shaw examining drainage infrastructure.

Campus Gets Federal Poultry Station

"The U.S. Department of Agriculture has accepted 50 acres of college land, donated by MSC, as the site for a new federal poultry research and experiment station. Several sites at land grant colleges were inspected before the plant was located here.

"The Federal government will pay construction costs of the proposed laboratory, totaling $85,000. An additional $100,000 will be appropriated later for operating expenses and for additional buildings, Federal representatives announced.

"Twenty-two states will cooperate in the poultry research to be conducted by the Department of Agriculture at the station. Each of the 22 states will be represented on the station's board of directors."[19]

Courtesy UAHC

Poultry Laboratory on Mt. Hope Road.

FDR Ends WPA Money

During the Great Depression, the national government brought work and money to the needy and funded numerous improvements, buildings on the campus, and work opportunities for many students. With World War II demanding national resources and workers, Roosevelt announced the end of the program. *The State News* informed the college community as follows.

War Renders WPA Needless

"Washington, Dec. 4 (AP) — The Works Progress Administration (WPA), which provided depression relief for millions and an ever bitter controversy for Congress, was ordered out of existence today by President Roosevelt.

"'War-time increases in private employment make the agency unnecessary now,' he said in a letter to Maj. Gen. Philip B. Fleming, the Federal Works administrator. Uncompleted building projects are to be taken over by other federal agencies.

"In 'many states' the death sentence is to become effective by February 1, in others 'as soon thereafter as feasible.' The whole is to be liquidated by June 30 at the latest.

"During its career, WPA spent more than $10 billion, providing relief for some 38 million people."[20]

First calf produced through use of artificial insemination, about 1940.

Still Good Investment

This *Michigan State News* editorial reflects student concerns about the value of a college education.

Quo Vadis?

"Millions of college students, on the road to something which they have no means of determining, are asking, 'Where am I headed?' — the modern version of the old Latin phrase 'Quo Vadis?'"

No Silver Lining

"It does not necessarily infer that a student is afflicted with pessimism when he asks the question and, after sizing up the situation, decides that the future destiny is dimmed by clouds that show no evidence of possessing that silver lining."

Beyond Breadlines

"After taking inventory of current conditions, it is impossible to come but to the conclusion that the road of higher education over which we trod leads only to a questionable destination. Although we cannot answer the question of where the college student is headed for, the one who can see beyond the breadlines is able to vision opportunities that transcend those of the past."

Good Investment

"Thus the answer of where we are headed can be answered only by the conclusion that our present course will lead to key positions of each one's special line of endeavor and that the road of higher education will be as good an investment as it has been in the past."[21]

Extension Federal Corn/Hog Program

Corn/Hog Production

"Under supervision of MSC Extension, the nationwide corn-hog program — part of the National Recovery Act — aims to bring the U.S. production of corn and hogs into balance with demand and give farmers a fair share of the national income."

Surplus Tariff Driven

"With the decline in exports of pork and lard, because of heavier hog production abroad and foreign tariffs, an excess of pork and lard must now find an outlet in the home market."

Federal Compensation

"In return for reduced production, farmers are paid $5 for each hog that remains after a reduction of 25 percent. For each acre of corn harvested is a payment of 30 cents a bushel based upon an estimate of this year's yield. In addition, farmers will receive an average of $100 to $150 each."

Spreading the Word

"The college Extension Service, directed by R.J. Baldwin, began an educational program in January to acquaint Michigan farmers with the benefits to be derived. With the support of the county agricultural agents and interested farmers, the preliminary steps were completed ... obtaining signatures upon the contracts was begun.

"The resultant increase in farmers' buying power will produce beneficial effects ... and makes the service of the college extension department valuable both to state and national recovery in agriculture."[22]

Co-eds Learn Child Care

"The nursery school, on the second floor of the Home Economics Building, has existed since June 1927. Its purpose was to teach child development. Later, it also became a childcare center."

Daily Schedule

"At 8:30 a general inspection is conducted, following which the children have free play. Then they are given cod liver oil (and believe it or not, they like it), so Miss Miller says. A period of music, and creative interests is followed by a morning walk or games in the playground. At 11:45 a lunch is served, and one hour later they are put to bed until 3, when they are given milk and do whatever they please until their mothers come for them."[23]

Courtesy UAHC

Children at play in childcare program.

...Activities Continue

Union Building Problems Ending?

Unpaid Pledges

In March 1935, the MSC Alumni Association concluded it could not pay its outstanding obligation of $300,000. The association and MSC Union asked the State Board to "take full control of the building."

Unpaid Bonds

"It was evident that the first mortgage bonds could not be retired in November. Only about $23,000 has been paid on the interest; it has been impossible to meet the balance. A vigorous and hopeful effort is being made to settle a contractor's lien.

"When complete data were placed before Governor Fitzgerald and the State Administrative Board last week, the matter was referred to the finance committee of that body."

State Assistance?

"The Union project was too large for the alumni to finish. Economic conditions of the past five years virtually stopped all pledge income, yet the building remained open and became more useful each year as a campus building. College authorities agree that the Union building has filled an important part of the institution.... If the contractor's lien can be removed and the state cancels the bonded indebtedness, the college authorities believe it possible to receive PWA [Public Works Administration] funds to complete the building."[24]

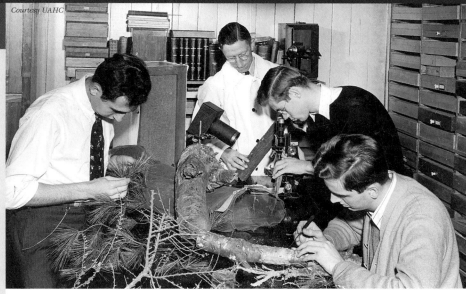

Courtesy UAHC

Forestry and entomology students study specimens.

Foresters Tour Companies

"On Wednesday, May 15, the senior foresters will leave for their annual spring field trip to southern and western parts of the state. The trip is an annual tour of companies whose products are made from types of raw wood."

Wood Mill

"On Wednesday the party will go to the Milligan Mill at Milligan, Michigan, where hardwood is cut. The Belding Basket Company comes next after which they will go to Grand Rapids to visit the Haskelite company and Grand Rapids Box Board."

Flooring Company

"The National Wood Products Company at Howard City and the Century Wood Preserving Company at Reed City will be visited on Thursday followed by a stop at the E.L. Bruce Company, where a study of hardwood flooring and progressive drying kilns will be made.

"The process of curing leather will be studied at the Eagle Ottawa Leather Company of Grand Haven where upholstered furniture and auto leather are manufactured. The Holland Furniture Company will be visited, where more drying kilns will be studied.

"On Saturday, the stop will be at Kalamazoo Parchment Company to view the paper-making."[26]

Big Ten Hopes Fade

"Hopes ran high that the Spartans might be elevated to ... the Big Ten, in the event that the University of Chicago and Northwestern University merger became a reality. Newspapers listed State, Notre Dame, and Nebraska as potential candidates to fill the vacancy."

MSC Chances Slim

It was said, however, that even if the two institutions merged, their athletic teams would continue as separate units. "This announcement indicates that ... State's chances to become a member of the Western Conference are completely blasted.

"A big break for MSC came in 1943 when Notre Dame agreed to play five football games against the Spartans. The agreement came when President Hannah and Father John Cavanaugh of Notre Dame met at the residence of Governor Harry Kelly. Kelly was a ND alum.

"When the topic arose, Hannah offered to play every ND game in South Bend; so critical was the relationship to MSC's athletic reputation. Father Cavanaugh, however, stated that alternating the sites would be more appropriate."

Groundwork Set

These episodes set the groundwork for joining the conference. "Many sports-writers in the Mid-west [said] MSC was the logical choice to fit into the Big Ten. They pointed to the fact that for two years the Spartans held Michigan, conference winners, to scoreless ties in football."[25]

Private Research Grant

In 1938, the college received its "largest private grant" ever. Income from the grant was dedicated to research in the general agricultural field with emphasis on finding industrial uses, other than food, for farm produce. The $500,000 grant came from Horace H. and Mary A. Rackham.

Governing Board

President R.S. Shaw and V.R. Gardner, director of the Experiment Station, along with persons from Ford Motor Company, the *Flint Journal*, and one from Ann Arbor were to constitute the board of trustees of the Horace H. Rackham Research Endowment of MSC.

Research Possibilities

"'Tentative plans,' Shaw explained, 'call for a study of the development and manufacture out of ordinary waste materials, such as straw or cornstalks, of a material that can be incorporated with the soil to increase soil porosity, give a more spongy texture and increase water absorbing and water holding capacity. Flood, drought, and soil erosion are involved — the three greatest problems.'"

Many Could Benefit

"'It is our hope,' said Shaw, 'that the income from the [fund] will provide for the beginning of a research program that eventually may utilize some of the best trained men in science for finding entire new and constructive uses for [the grower's] crops that will in turn provide new work for labor, new activities for industry, and new requisites and satisfactions for the consumer.'"[27]

College Board Approves Pension Plan

The college had never been a leader in compensating its faculty and staff. The level of compensation paid had long been a subject of complaint from both employees and administrative leaders.

As Secretary Hannah observed, the college was also one of the last educational institutions to provide a pension plan for employees. The Board of Agriculture, however, "tentatively okayed the retirement plan for the college faculty and employees."

All Employees to Benefit

"The plan, as it now stands, would include everyone on the college payroll from the janitors to the president, excepting student employees. The retirement age has been set at sixty-five. A scale to determine the amount of pension for each individual has not been arrived at, but it will be based on the length of service and the average salary, explained Hannah.

The money would not be taken from the salaries but would come from the general college fund granted by the legislature. 'Everything hinges on the passage of appropriation bills,' said Hannah.

"Already 105 educational institutions in the United States have set up retirement systems. 'We are the only college of major significance that doesn't have one,' said Hannah."[28]

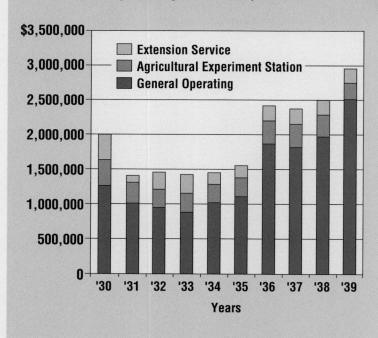

MSC Operating Revenues, 1930-39

Legend:
- Extension Service
- Agricultural Experiment Station
- General Operating

Y-axis: $3,500,000 / 3,000,000 / 2,500,000 / 2,000,000 / 1,500,000 / 1,000,000 / 500,000 / 0

X-axis (Years): '30 '31 '32 '33 '34 '35 '36 '37 '38 '39

Thanksgiving Holiday Issue Resolved

Students and faculty members had an ongoing dispute for nearly a decade. Students wanted a four-day holiday, but faculty members objected for fear students would skip Wednesday and Monday classes. In 1937, the faculty relented.

Four-day Holiday Break

"A Thanksgiving holiday was assured to MSC students for two years, Monday, when the faculty voted to approve the present year's calendar in accordance with an action of the administrative board taken Thursday.*

"This year the vacation will begin at 5 p.m. Wednesday, November 24, and extend to 8 a.m., Monday, November 29. The cooperation of all students is expected in attending classes Wednesday afternoon and Monday morning."[29]

*The administrative board consisted of the deans of divisions and the president, secretary, treasurer, registrar, dean of men, and dean of women. The faculty included members of the rank of associate professor and above.

...It Considers Demands of War

Long War Predicted

The war in Europe was gaining attention on the campus. The following account in late autumn 1939 reports the comments of one war correspondent.

"'Confusion and weakness of the French and English in the last three years culminated at Munich in a blunder that brought on the present war,' Vincent Sheean, noted war correspondent, explained in his lecture to State students in Peoples Church Thursday night.

"Blaming the English fear of leftist forces in Spain, the speaker accused the English and French of committing 'the worst blunder and the worst crime of their record' by refusing to aid the republican government in Spain. The Spanish Civil War was the first phase of the second World War, according to Sheean."

Chamberlain Errors

"Sheean asserted that Chamberlain's accentuation of the democratic weaknesses encouraged Hitler.

"In dealing with the Nazi technique, Sheean declared, 'the Nazi method consists of taking one thing at a time and declaring it to be the last. The way to tell where Hitler is going, is by where he promises not to go.'"

War Will be Long

"In conclusion, Sheean predicted that the war would last a long time."[30]

Members of the Women's Land Army on the MSC campus.

Courtesy UAHC

Students Will Fight if U.S. Invaded

The war in Europe was underway, but it was distant from the young men and women on the campus. Yet articles about the developing conflict continued to appear in the *Michigan State News*. Of concern to students was their involvement in the conflict.

Student Survey

One article in the student newspaper reported on a survey of student opinions regarding whether the young men were willing to participate in the war.

Want U.S. Neutrality

"Students are insistent that America remain neutral in the European conflict, with 96 percent voting 'yes' to the question, 'Should America remain neutral in the present European conflict?'

"Although a large majority of students stated they would not engage in a European war, slightly more than 19 percent indicated they would be willing to fight in Europe."

Fight Invasion

"A much greater percentage, however, agreed they would be willing to bear arms if a foreign country invaded the United States. Slightly more than 93 percent agreed they would be willing to fight under such circumstances. "The survey was conducted by students in the Department of Journalism."[31]

Abbot Hall becomes home for military students.

New President at the Helm...

Smooth Presidential Transition

Shaw Retires

President Shaw assumed the college presidency in 1928. In 1939, he told the Board of Agriculture that he intended to step down from the office. In January 1941, the *MSC Record* reported that Shaw would retire on July 1.

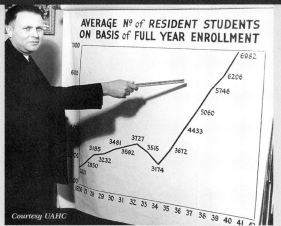

AVERAGE N° of RESIDENT STUDENTS ON BASIS of FULL YEAR ENROLLMENT

Courtesy UAHC

John A. Hannah explaining rise in enrollment.

Hannah Assumes Chair

John A. Hannah would become the 11th president. Hannah was the fourth alumnus to be president. Oscar Clute, '62, Frank Kedzie, '77, and Kenyon L. Butterfield, '91, were the others.

Hannah Skilled

Given the turnover in the president's chair in the 1920s, the move from Shaw to Hannah was unusually smooth. The transition was smooth in part because Hannah had been board secretary since 1935. The change-over was calm also because the duties assigned to him as secretary were significant.

The responsibilities included legislative relations on which the state appropriations for operating and building funds were so dependent. Thus, John Hannah was not only knowledgeable about the college funding and facilities; he also understood the administrative and leadership roles of the president's position.

Shaw Has Long, Successful Career

With his resignation, President Shaw could look back 39 years to the time he arrived on the campus to be professor of agriculture. Later he became the dean of agriculture, director of the Experiment Station, interim president (three times), and finally president.[32]

ROTC Classes Harvest Sugar Beets

"Highlighting the currently popular issue on campus — the sugar beet harvest — was the announcement made yesterday by Dean of Agriculture E.L. Anthony, stating that certain R.O.T.C. classes will be mobilized to work in nearby beet fields."

All Classes Excused If...

"According to the agreement between Anthony, Col. Stewart McLeod, and President Hannah, all classes, including military science, will be excused if the student presents a statement that he has been pulling sugar beets."

Regular Wages Paid

"However, under the new plan involving the military classes, students will report to their scheduled classes as usual. After roll call the college will transport cadets to areas where a definite labor shortage is apparent. Students will be paid regular rates for their afternoon labor."

Patriotic Duty

"Anthony expressed satisfaction with the response given to the beet field labor shortage by students, faculty, and the administration. 'It is the patriotic duty of every person to realize and act accordingly that this is not primarily a farmer's problem but also that of the consumer. America needs every bit of available sugar that she can produce.'"[34]

Sugarbeet harvesters excused from class.

Courtesy UAHC

Engineering on 24/7 Schedule

Engineering programs at the college encountered unusual demands brought on by the war. The demand for trained engineers came primarily from manufacturing plants that were being converted to production of war products.

"Classes are being held in several Michigan cities, in addition to those in our own engineering shops and laboratories. Incidentally, our engineering laboratories are working on a 24-hour a day basis — daytime for college students and with two night shifts in industry training courses from 6 p.m. to midnight and from midnight to 6 a.m."[33]

...As MSC Deals With War Demands

War Draws Male Students

The growing involvement of the United States in the war in Europe was having an increasing impact on the campus. From the fall of 1942 to the spring term of 1943, enrollment fell by 31.8 percent. The *State News* reported the drop as follows.

"Enrollment of students for spring term dropped to 3,714 as compared to an enrollment of 5,491 last spring term and an enrollment of 5,450 last term, Registrar R.S. Linton announced last night. The decrease was precipitated by the withdrawal of some 1,500 Army Enlisted Reserves at the end of winter term."

Women Students Become Majority

"Of the total enrollment, 1,669 are men and 2,045 are women while last year's figures were 3,467 men and 2,024 women. The former ratio of three men to two women is now reversed to one civilian man to two women."[35]

Conscientious Objectors Camp

"MSC's Dairy Department will soon have the service of six conscientious objectors to serving in the military. Prof. Earl Weaver, head of the Department of Dairy Science, made the announcement following Lewis B. Hershey's naming MSC as recipient of a Camp for Conscientious Objectors. Hershey was Director of Selective Service in Washington.

"Requests for the men to cure a severe campus labor short-age were filed in May, Weaver said."

To Get Dairy Jobs

"The six men were to be assigned to dairy work to consist normally of handling and milking cows in the dairy barns, and pasteurizing, butter-making, cheese-making, and ice cream-making in the creamery. Dean E.L. Anthony, head of the Agriculture Department, said they would be coming from a camp near Pellston."

More May Be Obtained

"If six men do not prove sufficient in carrying out the needs of the department in solving labor problems which have arisen in the campus barns, more will be obtained, Weaver said. They will be paid $60 per month and will be provided with room and board."[37]

Courtesy UAHC

Military Involvement Pervasive

A year has passed since the Pearl Harbor attack. Major adjustments were made to prepare young people to defend the nation.

Military Training

"Army enrollment at MSC from April 1 to November 30 has been 7,200. Of this number, 3,700 have received their training in classrooms and laboratories at MSC and are now receiving advanced training in more specialized army posts or are on the bat-tlefronts in the South Pacific or Europe. About 3,500 men are on the campus daily as members of the Army Specialized Training Program, the ROTC, and the 310th College Training (aircrew) Detachment."

13,000 Involved

"In addition ... about 5,000 State graduates and former students are serving in the armed forces, more than 50 of whom have already paid the supreme price. About 200 members of the faculty are serving their country in a vital war activity.

"Summarizing, about 13,000 men and women attached to MSC are using their abilities to bring peace to the world."[36]

Women's War Responsibility

"'Women today face a greater responsibility than any other generation of college students,' said John Hannah to an audience of 2,000 at the women's convocation."

Urges Fitness for War Effort

"'Any wise woman will fit herself for some field that will help in the war effort and that will be valuable to her after the war. Women should continue in their present course of study, adapting it, in the best possible way, to the war effort. This is no time for any woman to do less than she can.'"

Looks to Women for Leaders

"'Women have a great opportunity to produce the leadership and background to win the war and maintain a secure peace,' Hannah said."[38]

Victory garden promo.

Men in Uniform Welcome

In one of President Hannah's presentations, "Much of his speech was devoted to discussion of social problems next term concerning the men in uniform on campus. 'They will be allowed to attend every social function within their military hours,' he pointed out. 'There will be no USO. This college will not be an army camp ... no 'little Custer.'"*

*The "Custer" reference is to Fort Custer near Battle Creek, Michigan.

Dandelions, a Rubber Source?

During World War II, rubber, like gasoline, was scarce. Both products were rationed by law. With that background, the following *State News* story takes on more meaning.

"While no college professors are planning to run for Congress on a 'Tires for Everybody' platform, experiments at the college muck plot on Mt. Hope Road have succeeded in growing Russian dandelions that may some day be used as a source of rubber."

Experimental Stage

"From a batch of seed received from the USDA last winter, the Experiment Station has procured favorable results, Prof. K.C. Barrons of the Horticulture Department announced. But the whole matter of growing rubber on Michigan farms is still in the 'early experimental stage,' he emphasized."

Roots are source

"Rubber is obtained from the plant by harvesting and processing its roots. This rubber is of a good quality, but large yields are not forthcoming. About 5,000 pounds of root per acre were obtained from the college muck plot on Mt. Hope Road."[39]

Freshmen Competitive

"Michigan State freshmen have reason to puff out their chests. Collectively, they are above the average in general achievement, tests conducted by the college reveal.

"Scores made by MSC first-year students were considerably higher than those achieved by 19,600 'frosh' in 133 other universities and colleges. Their percentages dropped, however, in vocabulary examinations, while it was much higher in reading and English tests."[40]

Period in Review

Life on the campus was marked both by the Great Depression and World War II. The war led the nation out of the difficult economic times but pulled everyone under a new umbrella of fear and uncertainty.

Difficult but Good

On balance, the period was a good one for the college. Both the uncertainty of the Great Depression and the war in Europe brought about a degree of unity and collaboration. Conditions were difficult, but students, administrators, and faculty members joined forces to support one another and the well-being of the institution.

Military instruction on MSC campus.

The period was a time of maturation for the college. Even though state appropriations for operations and facilities were rock-bottom, few doubted that the college would survive. Enrollment increased steadily except for the war period, when many young men were called away to war.

Conservation Institute

The Experiment Station and the Extension Service demonstrated their responsiveness to the state's agricultural communities and economies. The college established the Conservation Institute to deal with the travesties of deforestation and soil erosion and thereby demonstrated their capacity to address serious and practical problems. The period is marked by numerous instances when the college performed its duties and responsibilities as a land-grant institution.

Leadership

This period is also marked by sound leadership. Robert Shaw, installed as president in 1928, gave the institution solid direction for the next 12 years. He was also wise in selecting John A. Hannah as secretary to the board and giving him the responsibility for legislative relations. That experience benefited the college then, and for the several decades that were to follow as well.

Courtesy UAHC

President Hannah congratulates 2-year-old Richard Larsen, who is wearing the Silver Star awarded posthumously to Capt. Irven T. Larsen. Mrs. Larsen was a Farm Crops staff member. Col. John L. Whitehead, chair of the Military Department, presented the medal.

"We are gathered here ... to honor the brave dead who fought and suffered and died ... in order that you and I may have an opportunity to enjoy the rights and privileges of free [people]."

John A. Hannah at the V-E Day Memorial Service

"The program that is now being thought through [in the School of Agriculture] in cooperation with leading farm organizations and farmers in the state, will, if properly encouraged, bring about greater stability and a more satisfactory living...."

John A. Hannah, President, MSC

The war in Europe and the Pacific was still going on as 1945 opened. Conditions around the world were stressful, but it was becoming clear that the Allies would prevail.

Work and Plan

President Hannah and others on the campus continued to fulfill obligations of land-grant colleges to the national government. Despite the complexity of overseeing a campus that was both military and civilian, Hannah envisioned and planned for life on the campus when the noise of war ceased and the joy of peace prevailed.

As the college began addressing the adjustments needed in the postwar period, it would find that major transformational changes had occurred since the years of the Great Depression. The changes would affect virtually every aspect of life.

Enrollment Demand

Upon the war's end, the campus would suddenly be confronted with unparalleled demand for a college educa-tion. Not only would this new student body be much larger but it would be a complex mix of recent high school graduates and mature, seasoned veterans, many of them married and new parents.

The war's end also brought other changes for the college. With the massive changes in technology, the Experiment Station and Extension Services would face new challenges in applying the technologies to a broad range of circumstances and problems. The new technologies provided numerous new opportunities for guidance in making the transitions.

International Aid

In addition, millions of people around the world would be addressing issues of reconstruction and postwar hardships. For MSC it would open nearly limitless opportunities to provide assistance. Faculty and staff members went abroad to provide assistance, and the campus became a place of learning and preparation for international students and visitors.

The college held a memorial service on the morning of May 29, 1952, to honor the more than 240 MSC men killed in World War II. The program included a tribute to those who gave their lives by President John A. Hannah, excerpts of which follow:

"We are gathered here this morning to honor the brave dead who fought and suffered and died ... in order that you and I may have an opportunity to enjoy the rights and privileges of free [people].

"It is entirely fitting and proper that we pause to honor our brave dead."

Zeal for Justice

"Through them America may have a rebirth of zeal for the advantages of democracy, a fervor for honesty and integrity in government at all levels, and an insistence upon morality, integrity, and fundamental honesty on the part of all persons in whom we are to place our trust.

"There can be no peace unless it is a peace for the world. There must be a willingness on the part of each and every one of us to dedicate ourselves for our part, great or small, not only in a military defeat for the enemy but in winning a peace for ourselves and for the world."

Courtesy UAHC

The Veterans Memorial Chapel was constructed and dedicated in memory of those from the institution who served and those who gave the supreme sacrifice.

Died for Our Liberty

"These heroes are dead; they died for liberty; they died for us. They are at rest; they sleep under the flag they rendered stainless for the land that they kept free. They sleep in far off lands under desert sands, under tropical palms, in unfriendly clay, some of them on the bottom of the sea.

"Wherever they sleep, it is beneath the shadows of the clouds, careless alike of sunshine or storm, each in the windowless palace of rest."[1]

Hannah Outlines Postwar Challenges

World War II had not yet ended in January 1945, but the outcome was becoming clear. President Hannah began articulating the implications of the war's end for MSC. His thoughts, reflected in excerpts from a *M.S.C. RECORD* report, are summarized below.

G.I. Bill of Rights

"The federal government is encouraging all members of the armed services to seek more educational training after their discharge. The so-called G.I. Bill of Rights offers to pay tuition, provide books, and pay $50 a month of the living expenses for these men and women during the time they are enrolled at college."

Enrollment Forecast

"The following statistical tabulation shows the actual and anticipated enrollment of students at MSC.... Added to these estimated enrollments must be the returning war veterans, estimated to be ... between 4,000 and 5,000.

ENROLLMENT FIGURES	
Year	**Enrollment**
1940	8,457
1943-44	11,347*
1950	12,220
1955	15,000
1960	20,200

*Includes 4,753 military, 6,594 civilians.

Coming Challenge

"This great anticipated increase in enrollment presents very serious problems. There have been no gifts or appropriations for this purpose [increased enrollments] since 1929. The buildings that have been built on this campus since 1930 have been built on a self-financing basis."

Postwar View

"Every activity at MSC today is geared to the war effort. In dedicating itself to help win this war in the least possible time, MSC has not lost sight of a program for postwar. The college was established, developed, and is maintained by the people of Michigan. It must stand or fall upon its ability to serve the public that supports it."[2]

Hannah States MSC Priorities

Classrooms Essential

"MSC has now reached the point where it is unable to schedule final examinations because of lack of classrooms. Unless a major classroom building with a large number of teaching classrooms is made available immediately after the war, the college will not be able to offer reasonable educational opportunities for [those] who will come to the campus."

Highest Priority

"[MSC] must ever be mindful that the most important component is the quality of its teaching and research staff. A substantial number of additional staff members is now required, and these ... must be of the highest quality obtainable."

Pay Must Compete

"MSC has found itself being the training ground for other colleges and universities. Competent people demonstrate their worth as teachers or scientific research workers, and other institutions attract them away. MSC ... must be able to pay salaries comparable to those paid by other similar colleges and universities."

"Women's Land Army" doing chores on campus as war comes to a close.

New Ag Problems

"The post-war period is going to bring new problems to agriculture. The war has greatly stimulated total production of agricultural produce. There may be a demand for that increased production in the devastated areas but that demand will be shortly curtailed as they struggle to place themselves on a self-sustaining basis. When that occurs American agriculture will be faced again with a great problem."

Research Needed

"Meeting these impacts requires the expenditure now of substantial sums in various types of research and educational activities for and in cooperation with the farmers of the state. The program that is now being thought through by Dean E.L. Anthony and members of his staff in cooperation with leading farm organizations and farmers in the state, will, if properly encouraged, bring about greater stability and a more satisfactory living to farmers."[3]

MSC Served in the War

"**Editors' note**: With the world once more at peace and Michigan State's campus returning again to a peacetime basis, it is well to pause for a moment to review ways in which MSC men and women served their country during the war."*

Clips about the service follow on this and the next page.

---

* The article clips on this and the next page were excerpted from *The M.S.C. RECORD*, September 1945, pp. 17-18.

MSC Goal: Just, Enduring Peace

"The college immediately established new wartime courses, revised others to meet the demands of war, and began training men and women for the armed services and related fields. MSC did not lose sight of the war's prime objective — a just, enduring peace. One of its major responsibilities was to offer to men and women not in uniform a broad liberal education to equip them for useful postwar roles."

Many Teaching Adjustments

"The arrival of the army men necessitated shifts in teaching personnel from one department to another. Members from one department were lent to another to handle increased teaching responsibilities. For example, the teaching load in the department of physics increased five-fold. Five members of the chemistry department worked on the atomic bomb project."

Courtesy UAHC

Students in dormitory waiting to call loved ones.

Military Training Center

"MSC became one of the most important military training centers in the country. Since March 25, 1943, when the first army students arrived on the campus, approximately 10,000 men have received training. Peak enrollment of trainees during this period was 3,500 which represented more than one-half the total registration of 6,441."

War Industries Training

"MSC cooperated with the federal government in developing courses for the Engineering Science Management War Training Program. After it began in 1940, MSC offered 114 courses to 4,592 men and women seeking training to do better work on the industrial production front. Courses were conducted in about a dozen cities for war industries needing technical training for their employees."

Public Informed by MSC

"During World War II years, nearly 10 million copies of publications were printed by the Extension Service. Many were targeted to aid the war effort for increased production, labor saving, and conservation."

Women Aircraft Engineers

"Women, too, were trained for specialized wartime activities. During their senior year in college, 36 received $1,200 scholarships from the Pratt-Whitney Aircraft Corporation. Upon graduation the women engineers were employed by industry."

Linton Hall scene in winter time.

Courtesy UAHC

...Teaching, Research and Extension

Labor Shortage Solutions

"Early in the war, the federal government gave the MSC Extension Service the responsibility to direct the Emergency Farm Labor program to aid farmers with labor shortage problems. During the first year of its operation, 151,000 placements were made for farm labor assistance."

Labor-saving Devices

"To farmers goes a constant procession of bulletins telling how to make such devices as motor-driven grain conveyor elevators, portable ear-corn elevators, baled hay elevators, buck rakes, electric-heated chicken brooders, and infra-red pig brooders. Other bulletins deal with the use of lumber from jack pine and poplar, floor finishes, and farm home remodeling."

Courtesy UAHC

Efficient and labor-saving hay baling machinery was demonstrated by the Extension Service.

Needed Products

"Plant pathologists and other college specialists developed methods to speed up production of the raw material from which the new drug, penicillin, is derived. Other research dealt with finding ways to alleviate the food shortage. Special research centered around attractive ways to prepare game food, to plan dishes with soybeans, and many other new ways to use products of the soil."

4-H Clubs Serving

"They were often called upon to replace older brothers and sisters to carry on farming operations during the war years. They helped neighbors and trained their city cousins for farm work in harvest seasons. Clubs organized salvage drives for scrap iron, paper, fats, tin, and other metals. They assisted in war bond sale drives and practiced conservation."

Solving Technical Problems

"Technical problems of production were solved during the war years. From the high point of helping produce record-breaking crops, the Extension Service dispensed information on substitute crops, and told city families how to patch clothing and preserve garden crops...."

Food Preservation

"In the field of research MSC assumed additional responsibilities. Considerable investigation centered around food production and preservation. Specialists in horticulture searched for the substance which caused spoilage in dehydrated vegetables and fruits, thereby assisting materially in saving more food for battle fronts where food must be stored in hot climates."

Families Aided

"Another contribution to the war effort came from the Home Economics Extension Service, whose members assisted in programs in nutrition, family health, and clothing. Also, in one year, Extension groups reported making nearly 50,000 mattresses and 28,000 comforters. Many families were able to have bedding otherwise unavailable during the war years."[4]

Courtesy UAHC

World War II veteran and family in married student housing.

Students taking exams at crowded college.

Courtesy UAHC

Enrollment Exploding

Women Majority

As the war in Europe continued to draw male students, male enrollment for spring 1945 dropped to 946. The number of women grew to 2,705, accounting for almost one-third of the majors in agriculture and pre-medicine; 15 were in veterinary medicine, six in engineering.

Madison Kuhn wrote that the prosperity of the war made it financially possible for more parents to send their daughters to college.

G.I. Bill

"The G.I. Bill of Rights provided money for fees, books, and $65 per month for subsistence for a single veteran to attend college. Married couples received a $90 subsistence allowance. Returning troops wasted little time to enroll. The 1946 winter term saw the college enroll some 2,000 and in the spring nearly 4,000 men and women veterans."

Enrollment Records Toppled

That set new records, but more were to come. In the fall of 1947, more than 9,000 veterans, of whom 168 were women, were knocking on the doors. Was it crowded? *Total* enrollment for 1947 rose to 15,000 and to 16,000 in 1949. That changed the college enrollment status from 22nd to ninth in the nation.[7]

Hannah Battles for Funding

Firsthand View

In response to the postwar demands for capital funds, the legislature held a special session in February 1946. On the agenda was a bill to appropriate $12 million for new buildings. MSC, U of M, and state mental hospitals were contending for the funds.

Firsthand View

To advance MSC's cause, President Hannah invited legislators to tour the campus and observe the crowded conditions. "They had a chance to see the 387 veterans jammed into the not-so-homelike atmosphere of Jenison Field House, the unsightly trailer houses for married veterans and their wives, students packed into

living quarters in the Union Building, and the crowded dormitories. They learned how students were having noon and night classes because of over-crowded conditions."[5]

Hannah's Appeal

"MSC had requested nearly $12 million but its share of the bill being considered was $3 million. Hannah's priorities were $700,000 for a new classroom building and $1,075,000 for veteran housing. The balance of the initial request was for instructional buildings.... Hannah underscored his case by pointing out that the legislature had appropriated no capital funds since the late 1920s."[6]

Grants for Emergency Housing

"With the closure of WW II and the expected use of the G.I. benefit program, the state's colleges and universities were pressing the legislature for assistance for emergency housing for veterans. The legislature approved a grant of $211,000 [in October 1945] for this purpose.

"The grant will be used for family units and service buildings with toilet and bath facilities. Trailers for this purpose to be obtained through the federal housing authority have not been selected."[8]

Courtesy UAHC

"Quonset Village" and trailer park near Kalamazoo and Harrison intersection.

Creative Innovations Follow

Making Room for Vets

"Unlike most other institutions, MSC has not yet turned down a veteran because it had no room for him, Dean of Students S.E. Crowe revealed."

Classes and Housing

"Noon and night classes have overcome the classroom shortage, and returning vets have helped swell the faculty. The biggest problem, according to the dean, has been housing. But so far the college has provided a 'sack in every student's curriculum.'

"Large increases in enrollment have proven that the vets plan to make good use of their educational opportunity. MSC is rushing to complete several permanent and temporary housing facilities."

"Huts" Hold 700

"Quonset huts with a capacity of 700 will all be ready at the beginning of summer quarter. Two new men's dorms will be ready fall term. They are Glenn T. Phillips hall, named after a former college architect, and Jonathan L. Snyder hall. These buildings will house 1,320 men."

Homes for Families

"The apartment building for married veterans, at the corner of Harrison and Shaw Lane, will be ready for Mr. and Mrs. Spartan and Jr. fall quarter. They will house 108 families in addition to the 560-unit trailer camp, now partially occupied.

"All told, Dean Crowe stated, the college will have campus housing for 4,500 men. This figure does not include Union dorm and Jenison fieldhouse ... temporary units to be returned to their former uses as soon as possible."[9]

General Studies Curriculum Introduced

Freshmen in the 1944-45 school year were the first at MSC to experience the new curriculum. It consisted of a two-year basic plan requiring students to take four comprehensive courses each year. The courses were English, social sciences, literature, fine arts, psychology, philosophy, natural sciences, and mathematics.

Broadened Education

President Hannah recommended the new program because it "provides opportunity for personal, educational, and vocational guidance to assist students in making an adjustment to college and training for a more useful and satisfactory life after college. The plan also prepares students for immediate entrance into the professional fields of study such as engineering, veterinary medicine, agriculture, home economics, and others."

Two-year Course

Provisions were "made for a two-year terminal course for those students having no desire, or being unable, to complete degree requirements. These students will be permitted to take selected courses of a technical type in their field of interest along with more general courses. At the end of two years they will receive a certificate recognizing satisfactory completion of the work."

Special Exams

"Students were permitted to take comprehensive examinations when they felt qualified to pass the tests. Through special examinations it was possible for students to complete degree requirements early."[10]

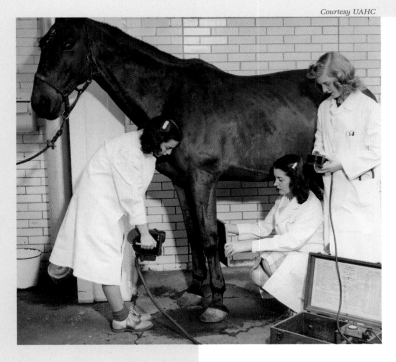

Courtesy UAHC

Women Crash Vet School

"Nineteen women's professed love of animals has led them into a realm of work once reserved for men. They make up the largest group of women enrolled in any of the 10 veterinary schools in the country. Many colleges still do not consider veterinary work a field for women...."

Dean Explains

"As Dean Ward Giltner, head of the division, explained, every student signs up for what is in the catalog. It is all there and they know what will be required of them.

"At State skirts or trousers are not a basis for discrimination. The Veterinary Division does not recognize any difference between men and women students. This confidence placed in women's ability has been fulfilled by an admirable record."

Aspirations

"Usually women veterinary graduates take positions in clinics, universities or colleges with veterinary programs."[11]

Vision and Support for Future

Ag-CES Connection Challenged, Reaffirmed

Strong, Unified Program

"President Hannah believed strongly in the basic charter of the college calling for 'the dissemination of all education work of [MSC] to all people of the state.' All was the key word. Hannah envisaged a strong, unified program.

"How to do this was the question. Consultant Reeves had an answer. Set up an all-inclusive extension service outside the School of Agriculture."

Die is Cast — Extension Stays

"The idea would not fly. Agriculture won out. The reorganization committee voted to leave CES under the Dean of Agriculture. Later, even a vice-president could not garner support for a single off-campus division. Agriculture prevails. Extension remained in the 'ag' domain."[12]

Extension Funding Enhanced

New Federal Acts

New legislation bolstered funds for CES. Following the war, Congress passed a law in 1945 to provide $4.5 million for 1946 and an additional $4 million for 1947 in payments to states.

"Other federal legislation in the decade granted federal retirement benefits to CES employees. A 1944 law granted the 'penalty mail privilege' allowing all official mailings of the CES to be made, in effect, postage free."

Ag Marketing Act

"The Agricultural Marketing Act of 1946 provided for expansion of marketing education efforts. Federal funds of $2.5 million were appropriated for 1947. An additional $2.5 million was allocated for 1948. Beyond that, an additional $5 million was specified for each of three years with a total of $20 million for 1951 and subsequent years."[13]

National Recommendations for Extension

Hannah Leads Study

"USDA Secretary Clinton P. Anderson proposed a joint committee to recommend programs, policies and goals for the Cooperative Extension Service....

"MSC President John A. Hannah was named to the committee and elected chairman. The final report, submitted in 1948, became known as the 'Kepner Report.'"

Recommendations

"The committee, consisting of college presidents, deans, and directors, made several major recommendations, including:

- "Meet growing demands from nonfarm rural and urban residents as resources permit.

- "Improve coordination of teaching, research, and extension functions.

- "Adapt educational methods maximizing both the numbers of persons served and effectiveness of programs.

- "Raise state and federal funding for Extension work and avoid earmarking funds."

Rural and Urban

"The committee noted, 'The search must be intensified for more effective ways of stimulating rural people to seek and find solutions to their problems.... Extension can see a growing need for its services ... a challenging opportunity ... to make a continuingly greater contribution to the welfare of both rural and urban people."

Implications

"It seemed clear that Extension at mid-century should look beyond the traditional audiences; e.g., farmers, farm families and rural communities."[14]

Teaching and testing youth skills in 4-H tractor contest.

Courtesy Einer Olstrom collection

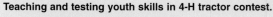

College and International Assistance

International Development Assistance

Land-grant Becomes Model

President Hannah, speaking for the land-grant colleges, proposed to President Harry Truman that these colleges should participate in U.S. efforts to restore global food systems that had been disrupted and damaged by the war. Hannah not only led the collective land-grant institutions but made it clear to his own faculty that participation in "international development" would be recognized and rewarded similarly to the traditional faculty roles.

Federal Involvement

Early commitments between the U.S. government and MSC focused largely on developing institutions of higher learning abroad that would embody the principles that evolved in the U.S. land-grant universities. Because food was a primary need, those early efforts placed great emphasis on agriculture.

The first undertaking for MSC was at the University of the Ryukyus on Okinawa. Typically the U.S. Department of State or the U.N. Food and Agriculture Organization (FAO) identified the need and furnished support for assistance through the USDA, which had a history of working with the land-grant institutions.

Primary Effort

The primary focus was training indigenous faculty members to assume new institutional roles as both extension educators and administrators. This led to an influx of foreign graduate students to the college.

New needs arose to cope with the special funding sources, visa requirements, language skills acquisition, health problems, housing — all those elements associated with foreign student study and life in the college.

Students and Departments assisted

MSC hired John Stone in 1951 to provide support for the college departments and faculty to address these needs. Ms. Patricia Riley, who was then working elsewhere on the campus, joined him in this effort. Together they assisted departments in meeting needs of new foreign students.[15]

MSC Soldiers of Peace

Staff Enlisted

"The late forties began a steady procession of staff enlisting for foreign assistance. Potato specialist E.J. 'Ernie' Wheeler went to Japan; dairy specialist George Parsons helped develop an artificial insemination project in Germany. Harold R. Clark delivered a shipment of Holstein cattle to Venezuela and reported the primitive conditions."

Many Foreign Visitors

"There was a steady parade of foreign visitors to MSC and tours of duty by MSC members to foreign nations.

"At Christmas 1948, Muskegon agent Carl Knopf arranged for 14 foreign visitors to observe the holiday in Muskegon homes."[16]

Chinese Technicians Aided

Eleven Chinese technicians, part of a contingent of 600 sent to this country for study by the United Nations Relief and Rehabilitation Administration, were at MSC for a year of intensive training in veterinary medicine.

International Dimension Grows

Foreign Visitors

"Throughout the postwar period, many foreign visitors came to the campus and CES staff hosted dozens of them in local communities. Both agents and specialists were to take assignments to aid in reconstruction, food production, and aid to underdeveloped countries.

"Over the next decade, major college projects would be undertaken in Okinawa, Colombia, Pakistan, and Latin America."

IFYE Program

"For a dozen years the International Farm Youth Exchange (IFYE) sent rural young people abroad to live with host families. In a reciprocal project, many foreign youth lived on American farms. Michigan's first 'IFYE' delegate was Russell G. Mawby, who went to Great Britain in 1948. Later, he became state 4-H club leader at age 28."

Courtesy UAHC

Members of the MSC International Club, organized in 1945.

International Leadership

"MSC would be a major contributor to international education. And 20 years later, MSU President John A. Hannah would head the Agency for International Development (AID)."[17]

The Sugar Beet Industry...

Launching the Industry in Michigan

Editors' Note: *The relationship of the CANR to the sugar beet industry has deep roots. Chapter 4 briefly summarized Professor R.C. Kedzie's role in introducing the farming community to planting and harvesting sugar beets.*

The stories on these two pages provide additional perspectives on the beginning of the industry in Michigan and the role of MSC researchers in addressing problems experienced by farmers. The solutions developed by MSC faculty members have been essential to the success of the Michigan sugar beet industry.

The close association to the sugar beet industry is best seen as one of many examples of the college's close working relationships with commodity groups and other segments of the agriculture and natural resource industries.

Seeds to Industry

The tenacity of a German transplant to America, combined with the drive of a far-sighted professor at M.A.C., gave birth to Michigan's sugar beet industry. In 2005, that industry encompasses 180,000 acres farmed by 2,100 farmers who also own five sugar beet processing factories. Two are located in the Saginaw Valley communities of Carrollton and Bay City and three in the Thumb cities of Croswell, Caro and Sebewaing.

Publisher's Role

Joseph Seemann first stepped ashore in New York in 1857 at the age of 12. He re-crossed the Atlantic 25 years later to visit his mother. He was enjoying the success of founding Saginaw's *Evening News*. While in Bohemia, Seemann discovered many small farms growing sugar beets. He marveled at the similarities of soils and climate between Bohemia and Michigan.

Seeds from Europe

Seemann mailed a kilo of sugar beet seeds from Bohemia to his business partner, Charles Peters. Peters then sent them to Dr. Robert C. Kedzie, at M.A.C. Kedzie launched a statewide study of the feasibility of sugar beets as a crop that could replace the fading lumber industry.

Experiments Underway

Professor Kedzie's experiments occurred in 28 Michigan counties. The sugar content put Michigan on par with Europe's successful beet-growing regions. Kedzie and Seemann had an answer.

Legislators Assist

Michigan legislators, aware by 1897 of the need to replace lumber as a mainstay of the economy, provided a bounty of one cent for each pound of sugar produced in Michigan from sugar beets. Interest surged!

First Factory

The first factory came to life in 1898 on a riverbank in Essexville, near Bay City. The next year, the Saginaw Valley blossomed with foundations for new processing factories. Farmers lined up to sign beet contracts, excited by the promise of $4 per ton.

Twenty-four to Five

Within a few years, 24 sugar beet factories reposed on riverbanks from Rochester to Menominee. Time and circumstance winnowed that number to five. Those remaining factories, however, slice nearly twice as many sugar beets as did the original 24.[18]

For its sugar industry Michigan can thank a printer who had no stake in the industry and a college professor whose zeal for agricultural advancement knew no bounds.[19]

Courtesy Clarence M. Hansen

Courtesy Clarence M. Hansen

This early mechanical harvester had to stop and drop the beets in piles on the ground, where they would be picked up and placed on a truck.

This equipment conveys the harvested beets directly to the truck.

Professor Clarence Hansen inspects fan assembly ventilating stored sugar beets.

Courtesy Clarence M. Hansen

Clarence Hansen joined the Agricultural Engineering Department in 1945 and soon became involved with a research project sponsored by the Farmers and Manufacturers Beet Sugar Association, headquartered in Saginaw. The goal of the project: improve the mechanical harvesting of sugar beets.

Research Projects

Ag Engineering staff members and Crop and Soil Sciences Department colleagues were working on 11 research projects concerned with sugar beet harvesting. Six focused on mechanical harvesting, and the others, on storage.

Findings

- Data collected in 1945 concerned the tare — crowns and dirt remaining on beets. It ranged from 6 to 14 percent. Other data showed harvesters missed up to 1.3 tons of beets per acre, with yield per acre between 6.8 and 16.5 tons.

- Data from 1946 assessed the effectiveness of a rotating wire brush in the elevator raising beets from the harvester to a truck. Without brushes, the pounds of dirt ranged from 104 to 519 pounds per ton of clean beets. With rotating brushes, the ratio was 66 to 349 pounds per ton.

- The 1946 MSC sugar beet storage experiment showed that trash should be removed from beets before they are placed in storage, that the stockpiles should have movement of air, and that improperly topped beets do not keep well in storage.

- The 1948 experiments recommended that forced ventilation to maintain the stockpile be used only under specified temperature and humidity conditions.

- Ventilating a sugar beet stockpile can be accomplished by using 50-gallon steel barrels or 16- to 18-gauge 18-inch-diameter road culverts.

- Sugar beet processing varies with the type of soil in which they were grown. The four soils used to grow beets in Michigan were Salkirk, Brookston loam, Brookston clay, and Carlisle muck. The last two were the most difficult to remove from the beets.[20]

Courtesy Clarence M. Hansen

One version of dirt-removing device.

Research Enhances Industry and Economy

Ag Research Benefits

This article appeared in the *Detroit Free Press* and was reproduced by *The M.S.C. RECORD* in 1945.

"Throughout Michigan the story is the same. Farmers regard the East Lansing institution with a respect bordering on reverence."

Sound Investment

"For 57 years [MSC] has been building up this respect through its extensive agricultural research program. The cost to taxpayers has been minutely low. The returns to Michigan agriculture have been staggeringly high. Just six improved varieties and farming techniques developed at M.S.C. have added $16,370,000 annually to Michigan farm income. These half dozen projects cost but $76,000."

Income Milestone

"Farming improved to such a point that its 1944 income hit $500 million. Of course, much of this total was due to stepped-up production. But the greatest portion was the cumulative result of patient research."

No Agricultural Collapse

"Many farmers fear the coming of peace will cut their profits. 'That's where MSC is stepping in. It now has 230 research projects under way. All will mean more dollars for farmers. These projects are costing less than $500,000 annually. That means one-tenth of one per cent of the annual gross farm income.'"[21]

Research Costs; Production Rewards

In its laudatory report about MSC's contribution to Michigan's agricultural economy, the *Detroit Free Press* included 25 examples of research projects to improve agricultural productivity. Some are listed below.

- "ALFALFA - BROMEGRASS. This project cost only $15,000. Its introduction has poured an additional $7.5 million each year into farmers' pockets.

- "MICHELITE WHITE BEANS. Michigan leads the nation in the production of white beans. Eighty-five percent of the crop consists of the Michelite variety, developed by MSC specialists. Because of Michelite, bean growers reap an extra $8.1 million every year.

- "HALE HAVEN PEACHES. Introduced by Michigan State in 1930, Hale Haven has become the second commercial variety east of the Rockies. Results of the research [are] a peach crop worth up to $7 million annually. Peach research cost $50,000.

- "POTATOES. Katahdin, Chippewa, Pontiac and New Menominee varieties from M.S.C. have jumped the crop value $1,695,000 a year, at a cost of less than $5,000 annually.

- "GREAT LAKES HEAD LETTUCE. The U.S. Department of Agriculture previously had discarded the head stock which a Michigan State man developed into one of the nation's best varieties. Costing less than $4,000, the lettuce is worth $1 million annually in Michigan.

- "MUCK. Michigan State converted 200 acres of 'worthless' muck land into an area which produces one-thousand-bushel-per-acre yields of onions and characteristically huge crops of mint, spinach, lettuce, dill, carrots, parsnips and cabbage."[22]

Courtesy UAHC

College use of tandem tractor.

MSU "Whips" Illinois in Fertilizer

Drs. Cook and Robertson of the Department of Soil Science and Clarence M. Hansen, Agricultural Engineering Department, researched the placement of fertilizer with respect to corn seed for about three years. The common method by mechanical corn planters at that time (1948-53) was to place fertilizer on each side of the corn seed near the surface of the soil.

New Machine

Ag Engineering faculty members then designed a machine for a small farm machinery manufacturer in Fort Wayne, Indiana. It was a two-row corn planter that placed the fertilizer 2 inches below and 2 inches to the side of the corn seed. This method produced excellent results.

Findings Shared

Later, Cook, Robertson, and Hansen went to a fertilizer conference in Chicago where they discussed this process for fertilizing corn. The esteemed colleagues from the Department of Agronomy of the University of Illinois made light of the fertilizer placement idea.

Widespread Adoption

Not long after the conference virtually all of the commercial corn followed the pattern of the MSC method. The consensus was that it was a more efficient way to fertilize corn.[23]

Service and Innovation Continue

Ag Engineering for Better Farm Living

Repair & Electrification

"In the war years, availability of farm equipment was at a premium. Limited farm machinery was manufactured as industry was tooled for the war arsenal. There was a renewed interest in equipment repair. Extension staff conducted hundreds of training sessions to assist farmers in maintaining and repairing implements. As labor became even more scarce, use of electricity as a farm power source increased dramatically."

Many Applications

"With the war's end, engineering programs turned to 'Better Planning for Better Farm Living' with projects in irrigation, drainage, electrification, tractor maintenance, and farm building construction.

"To promote new ideas, 'Rural Progress Caravans' of education exhibits visited almost every county."[24]

Early Years of Meat Science

An Early Beginning

Professor George Brown initiated the meat science program at M.A.C. He taught the first courses while serving as department head of Animal Husbandry. When the Livestock Pavilion was completed in 1938, "Slaughter and Meat-Cutting" was taught there, moved from the Ag Hall annex.

Lasting Findings

In 1946, Lyman Bratzler joined the MSC faculty. He had received a master's degree at Kansas State College, where he improved a shear device used for measuring meat tenderness. This device, known as the Warner-Bratzler (W-B) Shear, is still widely used for tenderness measurements at universities and in industry.

Bratzler developed a strong research program that included studies in meat quality, especially tenderness and meat color, meat cookery, meat emulsions, chemical isolation of wood smoke constituents, and quality and preservation of coho salmon.

Team Expands

Al Pearson, who had a keen interest in methods of measuring fatness and leanness in live animals and carcasses, joined the team in 1954. In later years the meat science group grew to four full-time staff members who taught, conducted research, and disseminated information to advance the mission of the Department of Animal Husbandry (and later that of the departments of Animal Science and Food Science and Human Nutrition).[26]

Tourism/Resort Management

Surge in Tourism

"Following the war the interest in tourist and resort business surged. Tourist accommodations, camp sites, marinas, and many allied businesses sprang up.

"Owners and operators wanted help and came to the college to make their requests. The result was the establishment of a tourism/resort program in the Conservation Institute."

Institute Responded

"Staff provided assistance to motel and resort owners, builders and food services. Specialists prepared publications and held hundreds of training sessions dealing with topics such as site selection, construction, sewage disposal, food preparation, ordinances and regulations — going all the way to advertising and public relations.

"The pioneering effort drew national attention and played no small part in the development of Michigan's tourist and recreation industry."[25]

Nematology

Ernst Athearn Bessey (1877-1957) became professor of botany at M.A.C. in 1910.*

In 1911, he published a classic on the science of nematology entitled *Root-knot Nematode and its Control*. It was popularized as a farmer's bulletin in 1915.

In 1942, the foliar-feeding nematode *Aphelenchoides besseyi* was described in honor of E.A. Bessey. It was not until 1948 that the sugar beet cyst nematode was detected (Bockstahler, 1950). The eminent B.G. Chitwood was commissioned by the MSU Experiment Station in 1953 to evaluate the significance of plant-parasitic nematodes in Michigan. This resulted in identification of three high priority research areas: muck soil, field crop, and fruit/forest/nursery enterprise nematology.[27]

Courtesy UAHC

Plant and soils experiment by Agricultural Engineering using electronic measuring device.

*Bessey's father, Charles E. Bessey (1845-1915), graduated from M.A.C. in 1869 and served as a botany professor at Iowa State University and an administrator at the University of Nebraska.

New Units are Organized

Resource Development

Conservation Institute

As reported in the previous chapter, in 1937 the State Board of Agriculture established the Conservation Institute as part of the School of Agriculture. In 1938, the institute began offering courses relating to natural resource management.

Through the leadership of Leonard J. Braamse, who held a joint appointment in the Soil Science Department and the U.S. Soil Conservation Service, and Russell G. Hill of the Department of Zoology, the institute organized the 57 soil conservation districts in the state by 1948.

Land and Water Department

The success of the institute, coupled with its expanding work in teaching, research, and extension, led to its designation as a department in 1950. Roy Schoenmann was named head. The new Department of Land and Water Conservation became one of four departments included in a new Division of Conservation in the School of Agriculture. The others were Fisheries and Wildlife, Forestry, and Wood Utilization.

Resource Development Department

The "Conservation Department" would undergo reorganization in 1956 and emerge as the Department of Resource Development. In 1959, Raleigh Barlowe would be named to chair the department. Under his leadership the department would regain strength and became a nationally recognized place for integrated transdisciplinary study of natural, environmental, and community resources.[28]

Ag Econ Department Established

From Section to Department

In 1949, agricultural economics, a section of the Department of Economics in the MSC School of Science and Arts, and farm management in the School of Agriculture were merged to form the Department of Aricultural Economics.

Clifford M. Hardin, who had headed the agricultural economics section since 1946, later became director of the Agricultural Experiment Station. He became dean of agriculture in 1953.

T.K. "Tom" Cowden, director of research for the American Farm Bureau Federation, was named the first head of the new department. Cowden was later (1955) to follow Hardin to become dean of agriculture.[29]

Creating the School of Packaging

As was true of many units, the School of Packaging went through several iterations before the program found its "base."

Stage One

It began in 1950 as Dr. Alexis J. Panshin, Forest Products Department chair, and John Ladd of the General Box Company discussed the idea of a university packaging course that would attract young people to careers in packaging.

Courtesy UAHC

David Seagrave (L), the first Packaging School graduate, works with Dr. James Goff (R) on a triangle-shaped box.

Their hope was to provide packaging firms with new talent. The "wooden box" program was expected to increase the number of students in the Forest Products Department.

The program began in September 1952 as part of Forest Products under the direction of Dr. Paul Herbert. James Goff, a graduate student working as an instructor, had the assignment of developing the program of three courses.

Stage Two

During that year, Dr. Larry Burton conducted a survey to help define the needs further. With the help of the program's first Industrial Advisory Committee, a new four-year packaging program was proposed with curriculum including seven new courses and 12 weeks of practical experience in the industry.

The institute hosted two military-industry packaging conferences along with an exhibit at the National Packaging Exposition at Chicago's Navy Pier, and articles in *Modern Packaging* gave the institute a needed public relations boost.

The first student, David Seagrave, enrolled in spring 1953. His friends and articles in the *State News* and *Lansing State Journal* provided support for recruiting students. The following September, 17 students enrolled in the program's first course.[30]

Many Dimensions of Change

Gigantic Contributions

Baldwin Leadership

Director R.J. Baldwin turned over the reins of Cooperative Extension in 1948, after heading the off-campus program for its entire history. He led a contribution to America's war effort of gigantic proportions.

Rapid Mechanization

From the war years would emerge an agriculture that was to move rapidly into mechanization with a productivity that was to become the envy of the world. Michigan's rural scene would be forever transformed.

Campus-field Liaison

"In the 1940s, Extension programs continued to be organized under three divisions: County Agricultural Agents, Boys' and Girls' Club Work, and Home Demonstration programs. Each program was directed by a state leader responsible for programming and personnel management."

Marketing, Resources and Communities

"Clinton Ballard became Extension director in 1948. He had served as an assistant leader and as state leader of county agricultural agents for more than 25 years. He was responsible for agricultural programs and the beginnings of evolving educational efforts in marketing, community development and natural resources educational programs."

District Supervisors

"For supervision, the state was organized in five districts of 15 to 18 counties....

In 1947 each downstate district had a supervisor with certain implied geographical loyalties patterned after the Upper Peninsula regional office."

Perform Peacefully

"Employment of the first district supervisors took place in early 1947. Gradually, assignments of program leaders were transferred to the newly appointed supervisors. The director's mandate was firm: 'Your job is to keep a peaceful Extension family and get a job done! You are to develop a team within your district.' The appointments were to mark a milestone in organization."[31]

The study, maintenance, and improvement of mechanical labor-saving equipment was part of the curriculum in Agricultural Engineering.

Courtesy UAHC

Changes in Home Economics and 4-H

"In the reorganization of 1945, Home Demonstration Work was to undergo irreversible changes. Its successors, Home Economics and Family Living, were to expand rapidly."

Specialists into Departments

"Home economics specialists became faculty members in departments in the School of Home Economics. Specialists in agriculture had been departmental staff members for years, and the system appeared to work admirably.

Since 1946, specialists have remained in departments through Extension program title changes, first to Home Economics, then to Family Living Education, and finally to Family and Consumer Sciences."

4-H Clubs Expand

"The children of the Depression years became the 4-H members of the war years. More than 55,000 youngsters were enrolled in some 7,200 clubs in 1940 but enrollment dipped because of labor shortages, movement of families to urban areas, and lack of 4-H staff. By 1949 the enrollment had climbed to about the pre-war level."

4-H Club Origin

4-H club work in the state traces its beginnings to 1908. A Muskegon congressman, J.C. McLaughlin, fostered Michigan's first boys' and girls' agricultural clubs. By the end of the 1930s, yearly enrollments surpassed 50,000.

Into M.A.C. Extension

After the passage of the Smith-Lever Act, Boys' and Girls' Club Work became a part of M.A.C.'s Extension. E.C. Lindeman was appointed the first state leader in 1914.

Arne G. Kettunen

A young MAC graduate, Arne G. Kettunen, became a state poultry club leader in 1917. He had earlier served as a 4-H agent in Houghton County. "Kett" went on to spend nearly 40 years with Extension youth programs.[32]

Mawby Enrolls in 4-H

"During the 1940s, Russell G. Mawby enrolled as a 4-H member in Kent County. After high school he came to MSC and received his agricultural degree in 1949. In his junior year he was selected as the first Michigan delegate for the International Farm Youth Exchange (IFYE) in Great Britain.[33]

An Active College Serves

Interdepartmental Grass Days

Courtesy UAHC

"Forages took on a new importance in farm crops during the 1940s. Alfalfa and legume mixtures helped to boost livestock production and reduce feed costs."

Regional and Statewide Events

"To spur the interest in forages, Extension staff members organized regional and statewide 'Grass Days.' More than 1,000 attended the first such event, held in Mason County in 1947. The field days were interdepartmental efforts and continued throughout the 1950s. The USDA 1948 yearbook was titled *Grassland Agriculture*."

How Idea Grew

The first "Grass Day" resulted from a request from the Mason Soil Conservation District to agent Harold Larsen. Specialist Russ Hill got the original idea from Wisconsin. Larsen and local committees planned the Mason event as an experiment. Based on the day's success, a new grass program was announced for 1948.

Attendance: 25,000

"Twelve Grass Days were held the second year to emphasize the need for better forage production. More than 25,000 farmers attended the sessions despite bad weather, which often hampered hay-making demonstrations.

"Before the regional events ended, plans were underway for future Grass Days. Staff members concluded that these Extension programs ... were popular with farmers and created much visibility for Michigan agriculture."[34]

4-H Club Week

"4-H Club Week continued to be held on the East Lansing campus each summer. The yearly event began in 1919 and attracted as many as 1,000 youngsters each year. In 1949, club week attendants were housed in Quonset Village, and general sessions were held in Jenison Field House."[35]

MSC Alums are Legislators

Nine of the people taking office in the 1945 Michigan Legislature were alumni of MSC. They were:

Senator G. Elwood Bonine, '23, Vandalia

Senator Harold Tripp, '16, Allegan

Senator Carl F. DeLano, '12, Kalamazoo

Senator George Girrbach, '24, Sault Ste. Marie

Representative John W. Thompson, '00, Midland

Representative Albert W. Dimmers, '26, Hillsdale

Representative Dora Stockman, '34, East Lansing

Representative Howard Estes, '17, Birmingham

Representative Arthur C. MacKinnon, '95, Bay City[36]

County, State, and National Population

1950

	Number	Percent change, 1940-1950
Ingham County	172,941	32.4
Michigan	6,371,766	21.2
USA	151,325,798	14.5

U.S. Bureau of Census

Women's Week

"The annual week, held each summer, was cancelled for the war years 1943-45. An abbreviated week resumed in 1946 when 300 attended sessions held in Campbell Hall. The dormitory had been named for Louise Hathaway Campbell, who served as state home demonstration leader in the twenties.

"The 1947 sessions were held at two locations. U.P. women convened at Camp Shaw at Chatham, and downstate delegates came to the campus in East Lansing. The yearly event continued to be 'College Week for Women' and later 'College Week.'"[37]

Agents Enjoy Serving

Another Job for County Agent

County Agent Highly Visible

In the early 1950s, the county Extension office was a highly visible county office, especially in a lightly populated, agriculturally oriented county.

"The family farm was a significant part of rural America. It was a way of life that contributed to a productive community as it provided real-life tasks for all family members."

Supervisor Seeks Help

"It was mid-morning on a mild February day that the township supervisor came down to our office. He asked, 'Would you two be willing to witness a marriage?' I looked at Bernice and she responded, 'We might as well, we do everything else around here.'"

Couple is Introduced

"The supervisor quickly turned around, went out the door. Two minutes later he was back with a couple in their mid-forties. They looked as if they had just completed their morning chores. We led them into the temporary courtroom, the supervisor introduced us all around, and Bernice asked the man to take off his worn and dirty cap."

Lifetime Commitment

"Bernice stood next to the not unattractive woman and I lined up beside the unkempt man. The supervisor brought forth a Bible and proceeded with the ceremony. They repeated their vows in the usual fashion. The supervisor pronounced them man and wife, but skipped the part about kissing the bride."

Marriage Certificate Signed and Farewells Expressed

"We shook hands all around. Bernice and I signed the marriage certificate. We were thanked and they all turned around and paraded out and up the basement stairs. Their chance to live happily ever after seemed quite remote, but who were we to not give them that chance?"[38]

Durwood B. "Woody" Varner (left) became CES director in September 1952 to replace Clinton V. Ballard (right).

Clinton V. Ballard retired as director of Extension at MSC in 1952. His career began as a high school teacher followed by 37 years in Extension. His friends published a booklet of Ballard's poems, one of which is below.

THE COUNTY AGENT'S DATE BOOK

Sometimes, oh boy, in the evening
When the weather's cold and raw
And I've dined with the wife and kiddies
—And my chair I've planned to draw
Close to the cheery fire
To smoke a friendly pipe,
And tell the world: "Go hang yourself!"
I've turned in for the night!"-

I think of a book I'd like to read
—Then wake with a sudden start;
The thought has reminded me of a book
I carry close to my heart:
There in my upper vest-pocket
The treasure so modestly lies,
That thrills my soul like a comet
Shooting cross midsummer skies.

I race to the hall and seize it,
(*DeLaval's* compliments slight)
Turn to the date it happens to be,
Read twice to make sure that I'm right.
—My soul is at peace with creation,
My slippers and jacket I seek.
Thank God for the little notation:
"Meeting postponed till next week!"

Home Demonstration Programs

Began in 1912

"Home demonstration programs were an early addition in the history of M.A.C. Extension work. An early history noted: 'Not to be outdone by their male coworkers, those on the distaff side took food and nutrition Extension work into the home as early as 1912.'"

State Coverage

By 1949, 39 counties had county home demonstration agents with an additional 13 serving multicounty areas or districts. The staff also included campus specialists.[39]

Campus band shell, built in 1938, was used for many outdoor performances, including commencements and pep rallies.

WKAR Goes Visual

January 15, 1954, WKAR began broadcasting on UHF Channel 60. WKAR was the first public station east of the Mississippi River and, 50 years later, was the second oldest operating public TV facility.

Pioneer in Public TV

The studios were located in Quonset huts on Kalamazoo Avenue near the present Breslin Center. Bob Page, '54, began his career with WKAR as a student and eventually became the station's general manager. He noted the quarters "looked nice and bright in the '50s. That was before chipmunks built nests inside the walls and plants came up through the floor. At the time, however, the facility was considered state-of-the-art, and the National Association of Educational Broadcasters held workshops at the station, making it a showplace among broadcasting peers."

Challenging Task

"Those who put the television station into operation found it challenging. Few people had UHF tuners, the WKAR-TV audience was limited even though the tower had a signal radius of 60 miles. Page noted

Courtesy UAHC

WKAR staff producing TV program at the Beaumont site.

that President Hannah was unable to receive the broadcasts in the president's residence.

"In addition, the nation did not yet have PBS (the Public Broadcasting System). That meant the local station had to produce up to 80 percent of this programming. The station provided television courses in French, Spanish, and social studies and broadcast nightly news and entertainment programs."[40]

Period in Review

The 1945-54 period was a time of growing maturity as the college completed its first 100 years. The official anniversary date was still weeks away as 1954 ended.

As World War II ended, society in general and the college in particular began to take on a whole new perspective. The war period was a time of transition from the disappointments and struggles of the Great Depression to a new environment of economic strength, numerous family formations, extensive development, amazing technologies, and personal optimism.

These social and economic changes had a significant impact on the development of the college. No longer were officials concerned that the college would not survive. The focus turned to how the college and its various units would address the demand from returning veterans and many others for a quality education from a highly respected institution.

With excellent leadership, energetic faculty and staff members, and an enthused student body, the college created its pathway through the unprecedented maze. The period was one of establishing a new firm foundation for the college's second century of teaching, research, and service.

Spartans Admitted to Big Ten

Hoped-for Membership

The MSC Spartans, for several decades, had been hoping to join the Western Athletic Conference (the Big Ten). Earlier, it appeared that the University of Chicago and Northwestern University were going to merge, making room for MSC. That did not happen.

MSC had become too competitive for teams from the Michigan Intercollegiate Athletic Association, and generating a schedule with competitive Midwest colleges was nearly impossible. In six seasons (1944-1949), Michigan was the only Big Ten football team the Spartans played.[41]

As mentioned earlier, in 1943, Notre Dame agreed to a five-year football contract. It came when Hannah and Father John Cavanaugh of Notre Dame met with N.D. alumnus Governor Harry Kelly. Hannah offered to play every N.D. game in South Bend, but Cavanaugh said that alternating sites would be better.[42]

Drive for Integrity

The Spartans' admission to the conference came about largely because of Hannah's leadership. According to Kuhn, Hannah gave a speech to the NCAA in 1946 proposing new standards for athletic scholarships. He said, "If there is not to be the highest degree of honor, and ethics, and integrity, and fundamental honesty found without equivocation and without weaseling on the part of our public ... colleges and universities, where is such integrity to be found?"

The conference admitted MSC in 1948 to fill the vacancy created by the University of Chicago's withdrawal from the conference.[43]

Courtesy MAES

"Michigan State's founders were men of prophetic vision. How else do we account for the fact that in establishing here a college to meet the needs of that day they laid foundations of strength and adaptability sufficient for a university of size and scope to meet the needs of an expanding economy and a society growing constantly more complex and diversified?"

John A. Hannah, President

"The loftiness of Beaumont's chimes reminds us of the vigor of the university's pioneer spirit, its most sacred tradition. Proud of the past, we stand as Spartans, confident of our ability to attain our goals."

Jennings T. Bird, Editor
The Wolverine, 1960

Overview of the north campus printed in the *1956 Wolverine*.

Founders' Day — February 12, 1955

Harlan M. Hatcher, president of the University of Michigan (R), and Governor G. Mennen Williams (C) with President Hannah at the Founders' Day Convocation.*

"'We recognize,' affirmed President John A. Hannah on that occasion, 'that we are observing, not the one hundredth birthday of Michigan State alone, but the centennial of the putting into practice a great, a new, a revolutionary idea in higher education.'

"Founders' Day itself represented not only the anniversary of the date ... Michigan's Governor Kinsley S. Bingham had signed the authorization of a Michigan Agricultural College into law in 1855, but the birthday of President Abraham Lincoln, who set his seal upon the Morrill Act in 1862.

"From ... this Founders' Day would evolve ... academic and commemorative events ... to sustain the ideals and accomplishments of the past as inspiration for Michigan State's second century. Among the distinguished Founders' Day gathering were leaders in education, science, business, government, agriculture, industry, and other fields."[1]

Founders' Day Convocation

Dr. James B. Conant, then U.S. high commissioner for Germany and president emeritus of Harvard University, was the key speaker. Governor G. Mennen Williams and others "'paid tribute to the manner in which Michigan State has discharged its historic responsibilities and looked forward to its future undertaking of problems with 'resolution, confidence, and wisdom.'

Dr. James B. Conant

"Dr. Conant observed, 'What was going on a hundred years ago involved even more than the transformation of a university; it involved the development of a totally new educational tradition.

"'If in the changing world of 1855,' he continued, 'it was necessary to examine old educational concepts and alter them drastically to obtain equality of opportunity and equality of respect, so might it be necessary in 1955 for higher education to adapt itself to a new world — the constricted globe of the mid-twentieth century.'"

Agriculture College Symposium

This symposium addressed "Nutrition of Plants, Animals, and Man" and continued for three days, February 14-16, 1955. It was the first of 10 university symposia.

It drew upon a 10-year nutrition project at MSU and was "directed at people of technical competence in the field of nutrition." The project involved the College of Home Economics, the Agricultural Experiment Station, and the College of Agriculture.

"Speakers from off-campus provided leadership in each

of the project fields and to supplement the reports of the highly skilled MSU project supervisors and researchers."

Considered were the relationships of "soil fertility, fertilizer practices, use of growth regulators upon the nutritional value of crops, and indirectly, of cows' milk." Also considered were "relationships with health, reproduction, and production of animals, with applications to human nutrition. An attendance of 382 persons was recorded."[2]

This birthday cake, decorated with events from the university's history, was featured at the Founders' Day banquet.*

Courtesy UAHC

President Hannah receives souvenir plates from Ralph T. Wills, deputy secretary of state, October 28, 1954.

*Photos were published in *The Michigan State University Centennial...Its Planning and Execution* (Michigan State University, 1955), p. 19.

Agriculture's "feature act" for the centennial was a gigantic mechanical exhibition in August 1955. It was billed as "the most complete exhibit of engineering in agriculture ever attempted."

Campus and More

Hundreds of associations, organizations, and equipment manufacturers took part. The exposition utilized five buildings on campus, as well as a

were attracted to the drama depicting progress in American farm and family life. Realism was accomplished with the aid of a large cast, authentic historical costumes, some 75 historical items, and a simulated farmhouse in century-old style.[3]

This aerial view shows the 100-acre outdoor exhibit area located just south of the university campus.

Courtesy UAHC

Allen B. Kline, president of the American Farm Bureau Federation, opened the Centennial of Farm Mechanization.

Courtesy UAHC

Reviewing gateway are (L-R) A.W. Farrall, head, Extension agricultural engineer; Sig Larsen, Equipment Dealers Assn.; Robert Maddex, Extension agricultural engineer; Dean Marie Dye, Home Economics.

Huge Participation

The Centennial of Farm Mechanization included virtually all kinds of machinery in the farm and home. The value of exhibits approached $20,000,000. About 300,000 persons attended, including a Russian farm delegation. People from every state attended, as did many Michigan farmers who had long supported the institution.

special exposition area of 100 acres on the university farm, and the dining and sleeping facilities of four dormitories. Hundreds of Extension staff members, rural leaders, and members of farm organizations helped. Exhibitions filled some 600 booths.

Daily Pageant

Each day a pageant, "Land of Plenty," was presented in a special arena. Nearly 44,000

Courtesy UAHC

175

Legislature Approves Name Change

As is evident from the two preceding pages, the security and confidence of the university are not only intact but strong. The struggle to accommodate the demands of the first decade after World War II was a maturing experience for the institution. The name change from "college" to "university" — approved by the state legislature and the governor — was an official recognition of the institution's progress. It provided a sound footing for the decades to come.

Enriched Growth

The first decade of the new century was one of enriched growth and development. The ever expanding enrollment drove the addition of new residence halls, academic buildings, and infrastructure. The expansion of classroom and research buildings generated the removal of earlier symbols of the "agricultural college" and their movement to the southern reaches of the campus.

Technological Change

Social and technological changes also had their impact on the practice of agriculture and the economic change farmers would experience. The automobile, of course, had a major impact on communities and the way people lived. Other changes, such as the home refrigerator, also changed the lifestyle. The supermarket, not the farm, became the source of food for most people. The number of farms declined; the average size of farms increased.

Farming Business

This new breed of farmers expressed new needs to researchers in the CANR and to CES agents. Farmers had become business people now engaged in marketing and using new equipment and other techniques in agricultural operations. The people of the college were responsive to these changing conditions and resulting needs.

Campus Life

Life on the campus also underwent change. The growth of the student body outpaced the ability to provide facilities. Most came from Michigan, but more than one in five came from other states or nations.

The year 1955 was a significant marker for the institution. It was a time to look back to commemorate the 100 years the institution had been operating. It was also a time to look to the challenges ahead.

The year had another significant marker — a name change to Michigan State University. On April 14, 1955, the Michigan Senate approved a bill to change the name. As the accompanying *State News* headline shows, the Senate vote was 23 ayes and two nays.

A few more days would pass before the bill would be signed. As it turned out, Governor G. Mennen Williams was away when the bill was ready for signature. Consequently, the signature task was left to Lieutenant Governor Philip A. Hart. The bill became law on April 21 with the effective date of July 1, 1955.

Significance

The "university" designation was significant because it recognized the growing and already complex institution and enabled it to structure its numerous components and employ titles customarily used in comparable institutions. The change enabled the newly established MSU Board of Trustees to substitute "college" for "division" and "dean" for "director," terms consistent with comparable positions in other complex universities.[4]

Michigan State News, April 14, 1955.

Celebrate the University

Circle Drive (Union Building in background), 1955.

Courtesy UAHC

Honorary Degrees

Thirteen honorary degrees were awarded. Among those receiving degrees were the Canadian ambassador to the United States; representatives of land-grant universities, other public and private universities and colleges; and Dr. James B. Conant, Harvard University's president emeritus and speaker of the day.

In "recognition of the part agriculture played in the development of MSU, a citation was awarded the week before Founders' Day to Ezra Taft Benson, the U.S. Secretary of Agriculture, the chief speaker at the annual Farmers' Week."[6]

Whew! Centennial Year Ends!

"A cross-section of the nation's outstanding educators were gathered in November for the 69th annual convention of the Association of Land-Grant Colleges and Universities."

"Representing colleges and universities enrolling about 450,000 students, they formulated basic policies governing the land-grant schools.

"About 1,200 National Flying Farmers came to East Lansing in 400 planes for their annual conference in August.

"Such mass visits to the campus posed major housing problems throughout the year, as Butterfield dorm residents soon found out. The university set aside 100 rooms in Butterfield Hall during the entire year for guests because Kellogg Center could not accommodate all visitors.

"In November, the entire dorm was taken over by Land-Grant conference guests.

"MSU, a tired but successful host, said goodbye to its last Centennial visitors in December, 1955."[7]

Commemorative Stamp Presented

"More than 700 guests, delegates, and friends of the university attended the presentation, on the morning of Founders' Day, of a commemorative stamp honoring 'The First of the Land-Grant Colleges': Michigan [Agricultural] College and Pennsylvania State University.

"Representing the U.S. Government on this occasion was Assistant Postmaster General Albert J. Robertson. Accepting the souvenir albums on behalf of the honored institutions were President John A. Hannah of MSU and President Milton S. Eisenhower of PSU."[5]

...and a New One Begins

Courtesy UAHC

The 1955 Rose Bowl parade marks the beginning of a new era.

MSU Develops Leaders

New Generation Takes Over | Short Tenure for Extension Directors

"The 1950s were indeed a shift from the old to the new. While President Hannah remained 'in command' for the entire decade, there were dozens of new university appointments. After university status was achieved in 1955, the State Board of Agriculture was dissolved and replaced by a new board of trustees, so named in 1959."

Veterans Depart

"The era also marked the passing of a number of key figures in MSU history. Death claimed President Emeritus Robert Shaw, retired [Extension] Director Ballard, and veteran state 4-H leader A.G. Kettunen. Pioneer agents of the Depression 1930s and the war years retired or left to be replaced by younger staff."

Extension Administrators

"It was a dynamic era. Four CES [Cooperative Extension Service] leaders in the decade became college presidents, and one, president of the W.K. Kellogg Foundation. An information services editor entered law school and was later to be elected chief justice of the Michigan Supreme Court. Rapid university growth and upward advancements were the order of the day. It was no less so for the CES, which launched into new areas and expanded into new horizons for 'Better Living Through Learning.'"[8]

College Leaders Change

"The 1950s was also a time of change in the administration of the School of Agriculture. E.L. Anthony, long-time dean, retired after 20 years. Clifford M. Hardin replaced him in that post. Prior to becoming dean, Hardin had moved from agricultural economics to be director of the Agricultural Experiment Station.

"Hardin's term as dean was brief. In less than a year the University of Nebraska offered him the position of chancellor. He remained on the 'Cornhusker' campus until 1969 when President Richard Nixon appointed him to be Secretary of Agriculture. Replacing Hardin as dean in 1954 was Thomas K. Cowden, chair of agricultural economics."[9]

Ballard to Varner

"With Director Ballard's retirement in 1952, many changes in the CES were to occur during the centennial years. Durwood B. 'Woody' Varner, a dynamic ag economist who had come to Michigan from Texas, was selected new director of Extension to replace Ballard. Varner had the respect of many through his statewide programs in public policy."

Paul Miller

Varner to Miller

"Varner was at the Extension helm for less than three years. In 1955 he became the university's first vice president with the title vice president for off-campus education. Six months before this appointment, Varner brought in sociologist Paul Miller as the deputy director for Extension. In preparation for the university's opening of MSU-Oakland near Rochester, Michigan, in 1960, the board appointed Varner to be the chancellor of the new institution. Later, MSU-O would gain independence and be renamed, 'Oakland University'.

"On April 1, 1955, Miller was named Michigan's fourth director to succeed Varner. Miller headed the Extension Service until early 1959, when he was appointed MSU's first provost."

N.P. "Pat" Ralston

Miller to Ralston

"Succeeding Miller was N.P. 'Pat' Ralston, head of the dairy department. As the fourth director of the 1950's and a newcomer to Extension, he was the first administrator in 45 years who had not risen from Extension ranks. Ralston served until the mid-sixties, when he accepted a post with the Federal Extension Service."[10]

Agriculture Continues to be Well Served

Gibberellins Research and Plant Growth

Courtesy Crop and Soil Sciences Department

Martin John Bukovac, professor of horticulture.

Martin John Bukovac's first exposure to agriculture came at age 10, when he moved with his family from southern Illinois to a fruit farm in Paw Paw, Michigan. His father was a mining technician. The fruit orchards stimulated his interest enough for him to enroll at Michigan State College, where he eventually earned three degrees in horticulture during the 1950s and became a professor of horticulture.

At the time of his graduate studies, plant hormone research was among the hot new fields of scientific investigation. Sylvan Wittwer, professor of horticulture, was conducting extensive experiments on the value of foliar-applied nutrients. Bukovac, a graduate student under Wittwer, studied the absorption and movement of such compounds by plant species in his Ph.D. research.

International Exchange

Soon after completing his doctorate in horticulture at MSU in 1957, Bukovac visited Tokyo to present a series of lectures on autoradiography. While there he visited Prof. Sumiki, professor of agricultural chemistry at the University of Tokyo where the gas gibberellic acid* (GA) had been isolated by Dr. Kurosawa in the 1920s. He had been studying a fungal disease that caused extensive elongation of rice plants and demonstrated that the fungus produced chemicals that stimulated the plants' growth.

At the time of Bukovac's visit, the work on elucidation of the GA structure was in progress. Members of Sumiki's group were primarily chemists and had little concern for the potential of these compounds for agriculture. Bukovac was given a small sample of GA. Wittwer obtained another 100 milligrams of a mixture of GA allowing the two CANR scientists to "get in on the ground floor" in developing practical applications of gibberellins. The results of experiments with a range of horticultural plants were dramatic. This became the basis for a concerted effort by Bukovac to determine how leaves absorb various compounds, especially growth regulators.[11]

*Substances of plant origin such as gibberellic acid, used to produce plant stem growth (*American Heritage Dictionary, 1985*, p. 558).

Project '80 — Survey Future

Target 1980

The College of Agriculture undertook a major survey to project the future, 'what rural Michigan would be like in 1980.' Ag economist John "Jake" Ferris was named to direct "Project 80."

"The ambitious project was guided by a steering committee headed by L.L. 'Larry' Boger, chairman of the Department of Agricultural Economics. He was to become dean of agriculture, MSU provost, and a land-grant president by 1980."

Courtesy UAHC

Lawrence L. Boger

Sixteen Reports

Summaries and recommendations from 16 major reports were to be presented at a 2-day seminar of the state's agricultural leaders in April 1965.

Growth Projections

"Projections were for a state population increase of 2 million, and the number of rural farm residents was projected to drop by more than half. The report forecast 40,000 fewer farms in the state, with 32,000 commercial units to account for 95 percent of all farm product sales. Farming would become big business.

"Other forecasts were for a dramatic increase in farm size and 3 million acres to be shifted out of farmland operations. The average farm of 1980 was projected to have an investment of $72,000. Other calculations were that commercial farms would average more than 500 acres and have gross returns exceeding $70,000 per year.

"The Project 80 report concluded: 'This will be the kind of agriculture that will have a big stake in feeding the state's 10.4 million residents in 1980. Population increase will mean adding the equivalent of a city approximately the size of Detroit.'"[12]

Technology Changes Agriculture

Technology and Farming

"Agriculture of the 1950s was marked by gradual, certain, and irreversible change. The technology that brought victory in World War II was spilling at an unparalleled rate into U.S. industry and on America's farms. 'Efficiency' became the key word. Reduce labor inputs, expand land and capital — with the result, increased productivity [and] lower prices.

"In 1950 the farm economy was on the brink of rapid change. Individual farms were growing larger with increased investments. During the war years the value of the average farm had doubled. By the end of the '50s, the figure would double again."

Acres and Values Up

"At the end of the 1950s, the average-size farm had grown to 131 acres and had a market value of about $25,000. [However,] Michigan lost over 40,000 farms during the decade, and only 59,000 reported sales of $2,500 or more in the 1959 census."

Farm Boom Over

Not unlike conditions following WW I, "the post-war farm boom of the late 1940's was short-lived. Productivity geared up to fulfill the 'Food Will Win the War' slogan continued but demand evaporated."

Government Efforts

"Charles F. Brannan, USDA secretary, proposed [a plan] to bolster the agricultural economy. His plan would permit no production cut-backs. Price differentials were to be made up in direct payments to farmers — from the U.S. Government. 'Heresy!' many cried, and in the 1952 elections, voters returned Republicans to power.

"Ezra Taft Benson, a champion of free enterprise and staunch supporter of agricultural research and education, took over as Secretary of Agriculture. His appointment had a sharp impact on U.S. agriculture for the next 8 years."[13]

Graduates parade to auditorium.

New Marketing Emphasis

During the 1950s, the sagging commodity prices and a downturn in the agricultural economy brought stress to the farming community. With increasing use of technology, agricultural productivity rose and often outstripped demand. These conditions gave rise to a renewed interest in agricultural marketing. With state and federal funds reaching as much as $585,000, CES launched a new marketing program.

Ambitious Venture

"A bold new emphasis was given to marketing education. In the course of a year, some 20 specialists and district agents were hired for consumer marketing information, retailer education, and commodity marketing."

Target Groups

"The tri-focal marketing effort included three target groups: producers, market firms, and consumers. New specialists were employed in agricultural economics, food science, agricultural engineering, and foods/nutrition. Across the state, district marketing agents were placed in areas of concentrated production.

"Those agents developed specialists in marketing cherries, potatoes, vegetables, grain, poultry, and livestock. In the 1955 annual report, Director Miller noted that among significant changes for the year was 'the introduction of the largest coordinated marketing education program in the nation.'"[15]

Latest Farming Techniques

The first institution to teach agriculture as a science, MSU has always been a source for the latest in farming techniques and research. Some 40,000 attended the 41st annual Farmers' Week in January 1956. Speakers, banquets, demonstrations, meetings, and contests rounded out a full week of activities centered around the theme 'Science Serves Agriculture.' Educators, philosophers, welders, restaurant operators, scientists from all walks of life traveled to the campus during the Centennial year for major conferences.[14]

Courtesy UAHC

University is Responsive

Goal: More Prosperous Agriculture

For Farms and Agribusiness

A major Extension objective of the 1950s was the development of a more prosperous agriculture. Prosperity was to accrue to farm families and to the state's agribusiness industry. For farmers, the goal was increased farm income; for farm suppliers and marketing firms, improved efficiency of the market system — and, hence, profits.

"'Michigan agriculture,' one summary concluded, 'is directly in the path of the second largest and fastest moving wave of population growth of the 48 states — in a region which already contains 90 percent of the people and which will have to accommodate virtually all the growth of the next 10 years.'"

Township Program

"In 1953 the W.K. Kellogg Foundation granted $270,000 for a 5-year experimental program in intensive agricultural management. The project was designed to test whether a concentrated effort could result in greater educational impacts. Results were to be measured by increased incomes, practice adoptions, and knowledge gained by participants. Another objective was to determine if small governmental units would vote financial support for such ventures if these demonstrated results for local people."

Offset Price Slides

"Trends of the 1950s were clearly toward fewer and larger farms. But even the combination of expanded size, greater efficiency, and available technology could not offset farm price slides.

"Unwittingly, the educational programs and technology adoptions designed to aid farmers frequently resulted in production levels beyond current markets; the end product — surpluses and depressed prices."[16]

Varner Appointed VP for Off-campus Education

"The appointment of Extension Director 'Woody' Varner as MSC vice president in 1955 was a landmark in campus history. Since the days of President Butterfield, various attempts were made to coordinate and develop off-campus programs."

Separate Administrations

In his new assignment, Varner was to coordinate all off-campus education, including the Extension Service. That directive was threatening to some, and the School of Agriculture mustered strong opposition to the proposal.

Durwood B. "Woody" Varner conferring with Federal Extension Director C.M. Ferguson.[17]

Nor was there great enthusiasm among deans of other colleges to relegate extension activities to agriculture and the director of Extension. The end result was the creation of the Continuing Education Service, answerable to the president.[18]

Varner and Miller Innovate

New Leadership

"Both Varner and Paul E. Miller spurred many innovative and dramatic developments in Extension. Additional funds from both state and federal sources rapidly expanded both programs and personnel."

Spurred Growth

"In 10 years, more than 100 agent and specialist positions were added to the CES staff. At no other time in history had Extension experienced such growth, nor — as pointed out elsewhere — had the student body, the campus and the entire university community."

State and Kellogg

"State appropriations were generous, and the first of numerous grants from the W.K. Kellogg Foundation provided for bold new programs."

Mechanization Explosion

"Interspersed in this seven-year span (1952-59) came the MSU centennial celebration with the mechanization exposition ... and a new era for the land of the Spartans."[19]

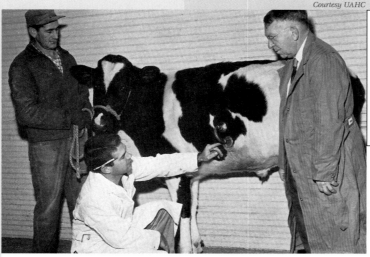

Courtesy UAHC

Researchers examine "access" to cow's digestive tract.

Courtesy UAHC

These three magnets were used to collect pieces of metal in the stomachs of a trio of cows. The magnets prevented serious injury to animals in dairy herds.

Pioneering Breakthroughs...

Meat Science Developments

Animal Husbandry in the '50s and '60s

MSU Meat Lab

In support of the meat science program, the university completed the meat laboratory in 1956. It had a well-equipped abattoir (slaughtering facility), coolers, processing equipment, and teaching and research spaces. The team focused on quality aspects of meat that could be influenced by breeding, diet, and handling of animals. They looked at a variety of methods for determining backfat thickness and carcass cutout, measurements on live cattle and their carcasses for predicting cutout yields, and use of bone weights as an index of carcass muscling.

Pioneers in Flavor

These meat researchers were pioneers in meat flavor information. They demonstrated that major meat flavor components were water extractable. They were among the first to demonstrate the influence of gender on carcass composition of swine and that "boar/gender odor" in both gender groups, albeit at

lower incidence. These findings led the Federal Meat Inspection Division to liberalize regulations on the use of meat from boars.

These meat scientists studied animal nutritional treatments on meat quality and the relationship of marbling and naturally occurring enzymes on meat tenderness. Albert Pearson and Robert Merkel were among the first to study the effect of carcass fatness on cold-induced shortening and tenderness of beef. Factors influencing meat color and lipid oxidation were of interest, with emphasis on the benefits of vitamin E. This group coined the term "warmed-over flavor" and pioneered studies relating lipid oxidation in meat to this adverse flavor.

This team provided the impetus for numerous studies by others, nationally and internationally, to advance the scientific body of knowledge in meat science. They provided the basis for many of today's industry practices.[20]

The 1950s and '60s were good years for the Department of Animal Husbandry, a department officially formed in 1908. Enrollment was strong, and the department received resources to meet the demands. During an 11-year period, Ronald Nelson was successful in employing 12 new faculty members and brought the total to 21. Moreover, ground was broken in 1954 for the construction of Anthony Hall and a meat laboratory near the Farm Lane and Shaw Lane intersection. To make space for the new building, a new beef cattle barn was constructed.

New Facilities

Upon completion of Anthony Hall in 1956, the Animal Husbandry, Dairy, and Poultry departments moved from Ag Hall into the new facilities complete with modern research laboratories. Further improvements came with the construction of new dairy and sheep barns on south campus sites. The facilities made MSU attractive to top graduate student prospects. The animal departments at MSU were becoming recognized among the nation's best.

Courtesy UAHC

The animal industries building, Anthony Hall, was completed in 1956. It marked the beginning of south campus expansion.

Extension Outreach

Michigan's beef industry received a significant boost in 1964, when the Beef Cattle Research Center (BCRC) was dedicated. Hugh Henderson and Terry Greathouse, who had split appointments in research and Extension, provided dynamic leadership to MSU's beef cattle program. Hugh Henderson's research

showed Midwest cattlemen how to make optimal use of corn silage in feedlot diets.

In 1964, Harlan Ritchie received his Ph.D. at MSU. He was asked to take charge of the beef cattle teaching center and coordinate the undergraduate teaching program in place of Harold Henneman, who had earlier been named director of the Agricultural Short Courses program.[21]

Other Brief Insights

Veterans to Grad School

"On the Michigan State campus, World War II veterans in record numbers were completing degrees or continuing in graduate school. Enrollments continued to climb steadily to reach nearly 30,000 in 1959."

Rapid Growth

"Building classrooms, laboratories, a new library, and dormitories continued at an unprecedented pace. The college was becoming a major university. Faculty and staff members were recruited from across the nation as enrollments spiraled....."[22]

...Researching and Solving Problems

Effective Plant Growth Regulators

Spraying Goals

One purpose of spraying plants is to rid them of insects, fungi, and bacteria that are active on the surface of the plants. A second purpose is to "thin" or reduce the crop load and improve the fruit size. Compounds used as growth regulators (GRs) must penetrate the leaves and/or fruits. A natural cuticle, consisting of a waxy deposit on the plant surface, limits water loss and penetration of chemicals from aqueous solutions.

Growth-regulating compounds, however, involve a second challenge — their effects are dose-dependent. When apple trees are sprayed with GRs to reduce crop load and improve fruit size, the response varies from the top to the bottom of the tree.

Challenge One

John Bukovac's earlier research employed both physical and chemical methods, combined with electron microscopy, in both field and laboratory studies. He and his co-workers analyzed the composition, structure, and cuticles of several plant species, and measured penetration by both GRs and other compounds.

Bukovac and co-workers developed laboratory techniques that are now standard for similar studies. This research led to the publication of a series of 10 papers on the penetration of octylphenoxy surfactants through such cuticles.

Challenge Two

Bukovac also worked with ag engineering colleagues to study differences in spraying equipment so as to maximize the uniformity of application and increase the absorption of GRs. This work resulted in improved sprayers that deliver chemicals more uniformly.

This two-pronged approach resulted in contributions to both applied and theoretical areas. Laboratory studies provided the knowledge for solutions to practical problems.[23]

Courtesy UAHC

Building the Michigan Potato Industry

Joint Effort

Many Michigan potato growers realized a century ago that diseased seed menaced their future. The education-oriented Michigan State Potato Association (MSPA) in 1920 decided it could improve seed quality by providing inspection and certification services. MSPA's secretary, Henry C. Moore, was M.A.C.'s "potato man." A specialist in the Farm Crops unit, Moore expanded industry-college collaboration by becoming chief of the seed program.

He headed the MSPA for 30 years while also conducting potato research, much of it with potato breeder Ernie Wheeler at the Potato Experiment Station near Lake City.

MCIA Responsible

Organizations responsible for seed certification changed over the years. By 1924, the college had full charge through its Extension Division. The Michigan Crop Improvement Association (MCIA) started sharing authority with the college in 1926. In 1944, MCIA established a separate seed potato inspection service and became the sole formal certifying agency. In 1950, Moore handed the duties to Dennis Clanahan, a U.P. Extension potato expert. Moore retired in 1958 after 41 years on the faculty.

In 1959, the legislature brought the Michigan Department of Agriculture into co-responsibility with the MCIA. Two years later, supervision began shifting to MSU's new potato specialist, Dr. Richard Chase. In 1968, MCIA staff people took over, working out of the Department of Crop Science in Ag Hall.[24]

Examining potato quality.

Making Pickle Picking Efficient

Stanley Ries was a professor of horticulture with a 50 percent Extension appointment emphasizing food processing. One aspect of his work involved working with pickle growers who generally had small fields; the farmer's spouse would have a couple of acres of cukes with rows 5 feet apart and plants 3 feet apart in the row. The plots yielded 50 to 90 bushels per acre (bu/A).

Success and Challenge

Ries began experimenting with close plantings, a pattern that yielded 200 to 300 bu/A. With a shortage of labor, however, the new question was how to harvest all those cucumbers?

Harvester Needed

William Stout, in Ag Engineering, worked with Ries to develop a machine for multiple harvesting — seven or eight harvests per season. The H.J. Heinz Company strongly backed the research. Stout and Ries received sufficient funds, but they failed to come up with a harvester to address the usual pattern of planting. Stout calculated that, even with an effective machine, the costs would be excessive. Needed was a machine for once-over harvest.

New Variety Needed

The team had data to show that close spacing gave high yield and began pursuing a machine and cultural methods for once-over harvest. The existing once-over varieties set few fruit, so the need was for a variety that set many fruit.

"Spartan Dawn"

Clinton Peterson, a vegetable breeder in Horticulture, addressed the problem by developing the gynoecious cucumber. This plant has all female flowers and sets many fruits at a time, thus allowing once-over harvesting. Peterson also developed methods for its reproduction and development of hybrid seed. This resulted in the 1960 release of the first F_1 hybrid pickling cucumber, "Spartan Dawn."

Industry Innovations

The university patented the machine, but MSU did not pursue compensation for it. Nonetheless, the team came up with a cucumber plant and harvester that laid the foundation for machine harvesting cucumbers today.[25]

Clinton E. (Pete) Peterson, USDA horticultural scientist stationed at the college.

Courtesy UAHC

Lessons for Tomatoes

Growers harvesting tomatoes mechanically were experiencing problems similar to those of the pickling cucumber industry. The early pickle harvesters shook the fruit off the plants. This method did not work well for pickles, but Professor Stanley Ries, of the Department of Horticulture, suggested to William Stout, of Ag Engineering, that it might work for tomatoes.

Testing Harvester

They started with an old potato digger and modified it to shake and remove tomatoes for once-over harvesting. Tomato breeders at Purdue had developed a tomato (B52) that had concentrated fruit set. They tried the machine on some plots at Purdue. The machine took the fruits off but threw some of them 30 feet out!

Meanwhile, in California, Jack Hanna had developed high quality tomato cultivars that were firm, like Romas, and did not bruise easily. The Blackwelder Company (of California) developed a tomato-harvesting machine that operated on a different principle — it did not shake off the fruit.

Shaker Widely Accepted

MSU got a patent on the shaking machine, and Blackwelder adapted its tomato harvester to shake the vines. FMC Corporation built a prototype harvester based on the Stout design but never sold any. As was the case with the pickle harvester, the professors did not receive any royalties from the patent. Nonetheless, today about two-thirds of processing tomatoes in the United States are harvested by machine.

Designing Tomato Bins

Other work related to tomatoes involved the use of bulk bins — 4 by 2 by 3 feet — purchased with a grant from U.S. Steel to test various designs. Bulk bins similar to those used for apples are now used for tomatoes. In addition, to compare and evaluate the quality of hand-harvested with machine-harvested tomatoes, Ries and his colleague would take machine-harvested tomatoes to the Campbell Soup Company plant in Napoleon, Ohio, and process them.[26]

...Get Answers

New Peach Varieties Stimulate the Industry

Stanley Johnston and his wife by marker commemorating peach-breeding accomplishments.

The MSU peach breeding program is steeped in the tradition of the Department of Horticulture. The university is known for the "Haven" varieties, so-named because the breeding program was centered at South Haven, Michigan, birthplace of the world famous botanist Liberty Hyde Bailey.

Peaches Well-liked

Stanley Johnston, the first "dean" of peach breeders, initiated the program. Johnston crossed and released eight fresh market varieties during the period from the 1940s through the 1960s. The names of the varieties are well known. The "Haven" peaches provided an orderly supply of red-blushed peaches over an extended ripening period. Previously, peach harvests were limited to a three-week period. Robert Andersen would release three more selections — Jayhaven, Sweethaven, and Newhaven — from the Johnston program in the 1970s.

Redhaven Best Known

The most famous Haven variety is Redhaven. It is the most widely planted freestone variety in the world. The cultivars that Johnston released, particularly Redhaven and Halehaven, were used as "parents" by other breeders, not only in the United States and Canada but in other nations as well, to produce nearly 60 named selections.[27]

Peach Varieties Developed by MSU[28]	
Halehaven	1936
Kalhaven	1938
Redhaven	1946
Fairhaven	1946
Richhaven	1955
Sunhaven	1955
Suncling	1961
Cresthaven	1963
Glohaven	1963
Jayhaven	1976
Spartancling	1976
Sweethaven	1976
Newhaven	1978
Beaumont	2005

G. Malcolm Trout, the "father of homogenized milk."

G. Malcolm Trout — A Legend

Judge

G. Malcolm Trout started his dairy products career as a student in 1922 as he sought a place on the Iowa State College Dairy Products Judging Team. He did not make the team. Still, he developed abilities as a judge of dairy products that carried him through his career at MSU.

Scholar

In 1934, John Nelson, a member of the 1921 Iowa State College Dairy Products Judging Team, and Trout collaborated to write *Judging Dairy Products*. It was the standard for training industry personnel as well as product judging teams. Through five editions, the framework and intent were maintained. One edition is likely to be found in the library of any serious dairy products judge.[29]

Historian

Trout coached several MSC judging teams and stayed involved, making sure that hard work and accomplishments not be forgotten by acting as historian for the Collegiate Dairy Products Contest.

Friend

Trout continued to be a friend to judging teams as long as he was able to attend a practice or an annual contest. In the 1980s, he would take several of John Partridge's teams to a victory celebration after the contest. As attested to by his own illustrious career as a teacher and researcher, one did not have to bring home the trophies to gain from the experience.

The college and university honored Dr. Trout, the "father of homogenized milk," by naming the Food Science and Human Nutrition building as a lasting memorial to his service.[30]

Scientific Farming in Spotlight

Home Demos on Traffic Safety

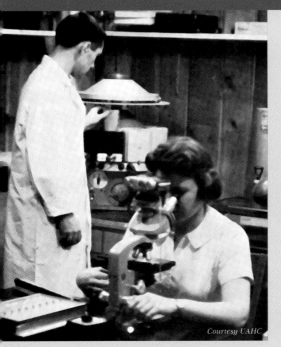

Courtesy UAHC

"Farm families from all over the state began arriving on campus as the 48th Annual Farmer's Week opened [on January 28, 1963]. The event annually attracts more visitors than any other meeting of its kind in the nation, Byron Good, general chairman, said."

Farmers' Event

"The program is planned as an educational event for Michigan farmers, T.K. Cowden, dean of the College of Agriculture, said. 'While everyone is invited to attend,' this is the one time of the year that the university holds open house for farmers, a vital force in the state's economy.

"Today's farmer is both a technician and manager. New technology often increases production to a point which temporarily outstrips demand."

Economics Focus

"Nearly 50 economists will offer tips for making sound farm business decisions in Thursday's farm management day program. Farmers will also hear how a European Common Market can be a big factor in the price of wheat or a pound of beef.

"As farms grow larger and more complex, labor costs are critical. Engineers will outline developments in new equipment for materials handling, tillage, field machinery and livestock buildings. Hundreds of pieces of equipment will be on display...."

Homemakers, Youths

"Homemakers can visit a space kitchen designed for interplanetary flight, hear the latest on new foods and consider housing for modern families. 'Expanding Horizons for Youths' will feature career choices for high school graduates....''[31]

"Millions of homemakers will be joined in the battle against highway traffic carnage in the next few months."

MSU Hosts Meetings

"The 125 home demonstration leaders from 42 states, including Hawaii and Puerto Rico, who have been participating in the first National Home Demonstration Council conference on highway traffic safety at MSU were en route home Saturday armed with plans which will explode to encompass upwards of 7 million homemakers within the next seven months.

"The conferees were safety and program chairmen of state organizations with a million and a quarter enrolled members whose programs open up to touch untold millions in a year's time.

"The home demonstration women's motivation in the march against highway traffic maiming and death is two-fold.

• "They learned well from MSU Highway Traffic Safety Center experts that the attitudes and poor driving habits of their hometown drivers are responsible for the killing and maiming of their hometown folks.

• "The All-State foundation gave $20,000 to finance the three-day conference at MSU and also offered a $200 reward to local home demonstration group in the nation which by August has set up the best safety program...."

State, Local Recommendations

"Recommendations coming out of four regional conferences at Kellogg Center Friday afternoon called for setting up a state conference in each state...."[32]

CES Challenged and Changed

"It was the best of times, it was the worst of times...." A quotation from a Dickens novel could characterize the early 1960s for the Extension Service. The decade began with new leadership and an agenda for action.

Critics Abound

Critics appeared and asked whether CES was following its original mandate. Extension's line-item budget was under attack. A single vote spared a 25 percent cut from a $4 million state appropriation.

Legislators often used harsh words: "Get your act together and we'll see what the future brings." CES responded with a "back to basics" move. County directors were reassigned as agricultural or natural resource agents. Thirty positions were eliminated, and those remaining were placed on multicounty or area assignments. Other positions remained vacant. In what some saw as a political move, George S. McIntyre of the state Department of Agriculture was hired as associate CES director under N.P. "Pat" Ralston.

Tensions Ease

"As the 1960s progressed, tensions eased. Budgets improved, and steadily the positions cut in 1965 were restored. The 31 multi-county areas remained for 4-H Youth and Family Living programming.... In 1969, the 'county Extension director' title was returned, and it has remained.[33]

...and Off Campus

Statewide "Ag-Ed" Events Popular

Farm Tour

"The first state Farm Management Tour was held in 1949. More than 150,000 attended the annual event rotated around the state. One tour featured a talk by Extension economist D.B. 'Woody' Varner, 'What the Economists See Ahead.'

"Agricultural engineering programs were concerned with mechanization, farm buildings, drainage irrigation, rural electrification and crop drying."

Crops and Livestock

"Agents continued to devote a high percentage of time to crop and livestock production. The 'grass days' were held each June to emphasize use of forages. Animal disease programs focused on eradication of brucellosis and mastitis in Michigan dairy herds.

"The year 1957 was a record crop year. The state had its first 100 million-bushel corn crop. An average yield of 1,080 pounds of field beans set another record. In the same year 56,500 soil samples were tested in Extension labs."[34]

Programs for Local Officials

With the dramatic increase in family formations and housing in the suburban areas and planning of the national freeway system, the faculty of the Department of Agricultural Economics saw rural Michigan was about to face dramatic change.

In response, they developed an educational and technical assistance program to prepare and motivate township board members to develop land use policies, services, and ordinances. The program targeted townships with agricultural industries and their supporting businesses and communities. Dale Hathaway was a leader of the team, along with Arthur Mauch, policy specialist in agricultural economics.

New Position in Extension

Township boards welcomed the new program. But team members saw an urgent need to include county boards as well. Mauch, Hathaway, and Einer Olstrom, a CES program administrator, worked to establish a position in Agricultural Economics to expand educational and technical services to these governments. In September 1963, the department hired Alvin House to fill the position.

House began studying state government and state agency interactions with county and local officials. He initiated outreach with presentations to groups such as the League of Women Voters, local service clubs, CES staff members, and township boards. Close working relationships with county boards of supervisors and township boards evolved, mainly because of these relationships.

Taxation and Public Finance

Later House began working with Raleigh Barlowe (Resource Development) and Milton Taylor (Economics) in studying Michigan tax systems, consulting with state legislative and administrative groups and public interest groups around the state. Local officials and CES staff members were particularly interested in the taxation of agricultural land and various alternatives for supporting schools.[35]

The Michigan 4-H Foundation constructed Camp Kett (later Kettunen Center) at Tustin in 1961. In May 1962, a group of MSU Extension employees constructed a pavilion at Kettunen Center in memory of Robert Dancer, Ionia County 4-H agent. As the work proceeded, Charles Lang drew a pencil sketch of the workers as humorous characters.

Community Development Evolves

Roots of Resource Development

During the 1950s, the role of the college in natural resource management broadened significantly. Under its aegis, the Division of Conservation was established. It included the new Department of Land and Water Conservation, along with the departments of Fisheries and Wildlife, Forestry, and Wood Utilization.

Resource Development

In 1956, Land and Water Conservation became the Department of Resource Development with Frank Suggitt as director. In 1959, Raleigh Barlowe assumed the responsibility. Under his leadership, the department gained strength and achieved recognition for its integrated, transdisciplinary study of natural, environmental, and community resources.

Legacy for Future

Who could have imagined that Michigan's logging boom a half-century earlier would lead to the birth of an academic unit? The department and its predecessor units sprang from the need to heal a wounded landscape and avert a monumental land crisis.

Entwined in this evolutionary process were numerous cooperative ventures between institutes, departments, and state and local governments. Together they changed the Michigan landscape in many ways, healing the scars left by logging. And to the credit of the unit's early leaders, the department had the ability to be nimble and foresighted in addressing contemporary issues.[36]

R.D. Sets New Pattern

R.D. Quandary

During the mid-1960s, the programs of Park and Recreational Development were organized into a free-standing department. This left the Department of Resource Development (R.D.) with only a few undergraduate students, although the department had a goodly number of graduate students.

While considering the alternatives, someone noted that the bachelor's degree programs of every CANR department were career-oriented. Yet many MSU graduates were finding employment in fields unrelated to their collegiate majors.

Experiment?

This led to discussion about the relative merits of pursuing broad educational programs rather than specific majors. Discussions with the dean of the University College indicated that university rules required students to declare specialized majors before they completed their sophomore years.

The idea that R.D. might offer a general educational curriculum stressing broad grounding in the sciences and arts with emphasis on resource and environmental concerns was endorsed by University College. Dean Cowden agreed to treat the proposal as an experiment for 5 years.

Courtesy Department of CARRS

Raleigh Barlowe

The number of students enrolled in the program jumped from six to around 150. The program became a model for other departments, which introduced comparable broad educational programs so that more students could complete their collegiate programs in the CANR.[37]

Community Development Formalized in CES

From the beginning, M.A.C. personnel assisted with community problems. Rural residents sought help in dealing with concerns such as education, health services, transportation, and water supplies.

In the early '50s, efforts focused on improving living conditions.

New Impetus

The 1955 addition of the Rural Development Section to the Smith-Lever Act formed a new foundation for community development efforts. A new nationwide Extension thrust called Program Projection soon followed. CES staff members were expected to lead efforts in community long-range planning.

In 1959, a fourth program area — Community Resource Development and Public Affairs — was created in CES to complement Agriculture, Home Economics and 4-H.

In July (1959), William Kimball of the Resource Development Department became the first leader in this area.

Kellogg Support

At the time of these efforts, outreach — especially in urban areas — was given a big push with the establishment of the Institute for Community Development. A Kellogg Foundation grant of $500,000 funded the startup of this unit in Continuing Education. Specialists from Political Science, Geography, Engineering, and Labor and Industrial Relations became available to assist in Michigan communities.

In the '60s, a new array of programs for community assistance was launched through federal support. Specialists, working with county personnel, produced a format for community planning, zoning, and development in many counties.[38]

Life on Campus

Enrollment Drives Space Needs

"'MSU may have to close its doors to hundreds, perhaps thousands of qualified students in 1965,' President John A. Hannah [said] Tuesday. Freshmen are expected to number 7,800 in 1965, he said. This year's freshman enrollment is 5,300.

"'How will we take care of that many students?' he asked. 'The answer is we don't know, and we are not sure that we can. The time and energy of people can be stretched only so far, and buildings cannot be stretched at all.

"'For 15 years we have been warning our fellow citizens about the coming crisis. We have not yet made adequate preparations for the eager youngsters who will be seeking admission in the fall of 1965 and thereafter.'"

Need New Structures

"With the increased enrollment, Hannah said, the University will be faced with many problems both physical and academic which must be met with outside funds.

"'One of the most pressing immediate needs is for a building containing a number of large lecture halls and auditoria equipped with all of the modern learning resources — television, visual aids of all kinds,' Hannah said.

"Power plant facilities are another pressing, problem, Hannah said. 'We are now using all of our available steam and are purchasing much electricity from outside generating plants. We can't buy steam, and without steam we cannot heat the buildings we are about to build.'"[39]

Bus service is available.

Parking and Driving Rules

"Times change and so do campus driving and parking regulations. Students, take note or a golden opportunity may be missed or a pocket may be emptied."

Change One

"Lt. Allen Andrews of the Department of Public Safety emphasized, 'every student driving on campus must register his car...'

"A student carrying less than seven credits may register the car free. Others must pay a $6 fee."

Change Two

"A second change involves a step process in parking fines. [The fine for the first violation is $2; for the fifth and subsequent violations the fine is $25.]"

Change Three

"Students are forbidden from driving on the campus (north of the Red Cedar) between 7:30 a.m. and 6 p.m. Monday through Friday except for the six university holidays."[40]

The fountain in the center of the early horticulture garden was a gift of the class of 1883.

Coat and Tie Optional at Dinner

"The coat and tie required for dinner in men's residence halls since World War II have become optional. Recommendations of the Faculty Committee on Student Affairs specify dress slacks and dress shirts, omitting the more formal coat and tie.

"According to the committee, the regulations were originally intended to 'teach self-discipline and etiquette, foster a mature atmosphere, and instill some degree of social expectations in MSU students.'"

Student Initiated

"MHA President Jim Chandler, Ann Arbor senior, said, 'By relaxing the regulations, I think the effect will be that the student will feel that this new set of regulations is a little more realistic.'"

New Regulations

Trousers: Dress slacks, clean, neat.

Shirts: Conventional dress shirt.

Tie and coat: Optional (but no lumber jackets, golfer's jackets, etc.).

Shoes: Conventional dress shoes (including bucks) adequately clean.[41]

Extension Celebrates 50th Year of Service

CES Mission Broadens and Expands

Courtesy UAHC

Governor George Romney signs Extension Day proclamation.

The Cooperative Extension Service (CES), founded in 1914 with the enactment of the Smith-Lever Act, was recognized for its 50 years of service in 1964.

Those 50 years were a time of reaching out to residents of Michigan, bringing to them the knowledge developing on the campus and helping farmers apply the evolving technologies.

Over time, the understanding of the CES mission grew. In 1928, a new law supported program expansion to 4-H and home economics. During the following years, the federal government, as well as state and local governments, relied on Extension educators to help communities get through the crises of the Great Depression and World War II.

Following these periods, Extension helped society to cope with yet another large social transformation — urbanization, natural resource consumption, mechanization of farming, and a variety of other social and economic changes.

The Cooperative Extension Service, like M.A.C, had no model. However, it did have a strong sense of mission and discovered ways to carry on the duties assigned to it.

The contributions of all those affiliated with CES are entitled to recognition, but the guidance of two founding heroes — Director Robert J. Baldwin (1914-1948) and C.V. Ballard (1921-1952) — are especially entitled to our gratitude.

Period in Review

The first decade of the university's second century was one of great progress. Building on the foundations of the decades of the first century and especially on the accomplishments of the post-World War II decade, the institution made great strides in preparing itself to serve the people of Michigan, the nation, and, indeed, the world.

The period following WW II was a time of making temporary accommodations to meet the growing demands of veterans and others for a college education. In the following decade, social change continued to propel the desire for both undergraduate and graduate education. The new understanding of the need for advanced education and the ever expanding enrollment warranted permanent facilities and programs. The post-WW II period was no longer seen as just a "rush" by veterans with federal support. Going to college had become a widely recognized way of preparing oneself for the years ahead.

The implications of this understanding had significant ramifications for the newly named university. No longer was it only a "cow college." Rather, it had become a home for the science of agriculture and a host of other disciplines advancing knowledge.

Its roots, however, were not forgotten. It remained a land-grant university dedicated to serving people.

The Population of Michigan Continues to Grow

1960

	Number	Percent change, 1950-1960
Ingham County	211,296	8.18
Michigan	7,823,194	8.14
USA	179,323,175	8.43

U.S. Bureau of Census

Courtesy IIA

The Nigerian Agricultural Project took MSU faculty members to Africa to assist residents of Nigeria.

I think the record indicates that such success as I had probably resulted in part, at least, from good fortune, hard work, and perhaps some skill.

John A. Hannah, quoted in Richard O. Niehoff, *John A. Hannah, Versatile Administrator and Distinguished Public Servant* (Lanham, Md.: University Press of America, 1989).

It is no exaggeration to say that at Michigan State University, breaking with traditions is a tradition.

Former President Gerald R. Ford at the 1998 Michigan State University-Detroit College of Law founding.

The late, legendary Dr. John A. Hannah, MSU President 1941-1969, validated the innovative culture by encouraging faculty, administrators, and students to try new ideas; to take chances, to create new educational vistas, and to work cooperatively.

Bruce J. McCristal, Historian

Chapter Overview

Plant Research Laboratory History

Political and Social Issues

The 1965-74 period marked the third consecutive decade in which the United States was at war. The Vietnam War set the tone on the campus and off. But it was not the only issue society was dealing with. At issue was the implementation of a major social change — operationalizing the new U.S. Civil Rights Act. Both of the issues gave rise to various protests and demonstrations. The activity created an environment that challenged university and community leaders.

International Programming

The period was also a time, however, of growing awareness of poverty and hunger in Third World nations. Under the leadership and encouragement of President Hannah, many elements of the university responded by applying their knowledge and skills to these conditions. The Extension Service and research scientists reached out in a variety of ways. Collaborating with other land-grant institutions, the travelers sought to transplant the land-grant philosophy and methods to colleges and universities overseas.

Presidential Changes

Midway through the 1965-74 period, the university underwent a series of presidential changes. After 29 years of service and leadership, John Hannah left the university for service in Washington, D.C.

Throughout the 1950s and 1960s, Hannah had been occupying various federal and United Nations offices; in at least one instance, he took leave from the university to provide leadership in the nation's capital.

After Hannah's departure, Walter Adams, professor of economics, served as interim president. Nine months later, Clifton Wharton, Jr., a person with extensive international experience, came to occupy the presidential chair.

University Progress

Despite the leadership change and stresses of the time, the institution proceeded apace. While many changes were taking place in agriculture — fewer but larger farms and pressures of urbanization — CANR faculty members continued to address with success the problems and opportunities presented to them in a variety of arenas.

AEC and Plant Research

In the early 1950s, the U.S. Atomic Energy Commission (AEC) considered research on plants to be part of its mission. The commission thought that the effect of radiation on plants was important and that studying such effects would first require intensive research on basic plant processes. Therefore, the AEC decided to promote experimental plant research.

Land-grant U Preferred

The AEC preferred to support a plant research program at a land-grant university. The AEC staff invited expressions of interest and qualifications and found that 42 universities met the criteria. Four Big Ten institutions – Illinois, Minnesota, Wisconsin, and MSU – were selected for further consideration.

MSU Chosen

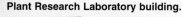

After site visits and discussions with administrators and faculty members, the AEC staff invited MSU to submit a proposal. In 1964, the parties signed a contract to establish what came to be known as the MSU-AEC Plant Research Laboratory (PRL) within the colleges of Agriculture and Natural Resources and Natural Science.

Plant Lab Constructed

The next step was constructing a laboratory building on Wilson Road. In May 1965, the MSU Board of Trustees appointed Anton Lang as PRL director. Lang hired the first 13 faculty members to conduct research on general biological systems.

The early research interests included:

- Biosynthesis and mode of action of plant hormones.
- Photosynthetic reactions and gas exchange.
- Biochemical genetics.
- Cell wall biochemistry.
- Biochemistry of nitrate and sulfate assimilation.
- Cyan bacteria as developmental model systems.

Research Highlights

Of the lab's many research accomplishments, some stand out as landmarks in the field. Gregory Varner and co-workers elucidated the hormonal basis for the degradation of reserve substances such as starch in cereal grains. This had practical implications for the brewing industry. Hans Kende's group worked out steps in ethylene biosynthesis, which was significant for fruit ripening. Pioneering work on establishing *Arabidopsis* as the model plant for molecular genetics was performed by Chris Somerville and co-workers.[1]

Plant Research Laboratory building.

Courtesy UAHC

...Widening and Diversifying

Forest Genetics

CCC Established New Era

The science of managing American forests was still in its formative years when President Roosevelt's New Deal program created the Civilian Conservation Corps (CCC) and spurred a massive reforestation program. The CCC planted an estimated 3 billion trees between 1933 and 1942.

Questions Unanswered

The CCC efforts revealed a dearth of knowledge about the genetics of American forest trees.

In the late 1940s, the MSU Department of Forestry cooperated with area state land-grant universities and the U.S. Forest Service to address the questions and describe quantitatively the genetic variation in commercially and ecologically important species. From 1947 to 1970, MSU Forestry established provenance (common garden tree seed derivation or origin) tests for more than 20 species across Michigan. Jonathan Wright directed these tests, consisting of more than 130 experimental plantations. His efforts earned him international renown as a pioneer in forest genetics.

Tree Selection Steps

The geographic patterns in genetic variation revealed that local seed sources were not always the hardiest or fastest growing. Forest planting stock could be genetically improved through selection and breeding methods traditionally associated with agricultural crops. In the mid-1960s, MSU Forestry took the first steps toward capturing these genetic gains by initiating tree improvement programs for species important to Michigan's wood industries. Wright began several of these programs, and his successor, James Hanover, continued the development.

Expand Tree Quality

Hanover built the existing foundation of research plantings into one of the most extensive tree improvement programs in the nation and expanded tree improvement work to include non-traditional forest products such as Christmas trees, ornamentals, and short-rotation energy plantings. MSU Forestry's tree improvement programs would manage 40 species in more than 300 test plantings, including 50 acres of seed orchards designed to produce genetically improved seed for Michigan's forest industries.[2]

Courtesy Einer Olstrom collection

More than 1,300 farmers were sending electronic data into the TelFarm computer program. John C. Doneth (L), farm management specialist, and Arlene King, Agricultural Economics computer supervisor, examine records just processed. The system was an attractive exhibit at Farmers' Week on the campus.

Electronic Farm Management

"Computer technology began being used to analyze farm business options. In the 1960's, Kellogg Foundation grants had catalyzed the development of 'TelFarm' and 'TelPlan' for farm record keeping and decision making. Specialist John Doneth became the 'father' of Michigan's computerized system. Each year more than 1,300 farm records were summarized by TelFarm. Ag economists Doneth, Leonard Kyle, Everett Elwood, M.P. 'Mike' Kelsey, Ralph Hepp, Stephen Harsh and Roy Black gave leadership to the use of new computer applications.

William Ruble, W.A. 'Bill' Dexter and James Mulvaney managed the data processing details at MSU's Computer Center.

"Harsh and Black created more than 30 programs ranging from determining least-cost ratios to projecting farm cash flows. District farm management staff and agricultural agents could access a U of M computer via a touch tone telephone. From a farm kitchen phone jack, an agent could input data and obtain answers on 'Synthia,' U of M's voice response computer."

Access Extended

"In 1970, 19 counties could access the computer by phone or teletype. Ten years later more than 40 offices had direct connections and their own terminals. District agents assisted county staff in the computerized management project, which drew national attention. Farm management agents worked closely with campus specialists in farm management.... In a dozen years, Michigan's farm management project had become one of the most respected in the nation."[3]

Experiment Station Leadership...

MSU's Experiment Station Dynamo

Courtesy UAHC

Professor Sylvan Wittwer, talented researcher and leader.

"Sylvan Wittwer brought his talents and fervor to MSC in 1946 as an assistant professor of horticulture. Born in Hurricane, Utah, he was sometimes known as a 'constructive hurricane.'"

Research Contributions

"His early scientific work on measuring plant growth in greenhouses gassed with higher levels of carbon dioxide ... was applied to commercial greenhouses for tomatoes and other crops.

"In the late '40s and '50s, Wittwer was a leading researcher studying the effects of the plant growth hormones called gibberellins. He has long emphasized the need for adequate nitrogen nutrition for plant growth. His association in the '50s with MSU programs on foliar application of nitrogen fertilizer brought him international recognition.

"In addition to his early work as a scientist, Wittwer was a dedicated teacher interested in education programs ranging from formal classroom instruction to specialized training institutes. The honor society of Alpha Zeta named him as the outstanding teacher of undergraduates in 1957."

Leadership Talent

"In 1965, Wittwer became director of the MSU Agricultural Experiment Station and assistant dean of CANR. In this position his speaking skills brought him to the forefront as a missionary for agricultural research. He also served 4 years as guest lecturer for the NSF [National Science Foundation] and as visiting lecturer in the Esso Science Lecture Series for high school teachers.

"A man with the energy, dedication, and interests of MSU's benevolent hurricane from Utah will never retire. He'll step into other challenges and other fields of interest that will continue to serve the cause of agricultural research and his beloved Agricultural Experiment Station."[4]

Dunbar Forest Experiment Station

The Dunbar Station lies about 15 miles south of Sault Ste. Marie along the Saint Mary's River. In 1910, Chippewa County established a co-ed agricultural school on a farm donated by Harris T. Dunbar (a local businessman). Dunbar wanted to provide an opportunity for rural students who were limited to an eighth grade school. After graduating only 50 students, the school closed in 1921. Dunbar and the county gave the site to MSC in 1925, when it was designated the Dunbar Forest Experiment Station (DFES).

A Ready Market

Michigan's foresters were busy reforesting the vast lands denuded by logging. The DFES began producing a variety of pine and spruce seedlings. In 1933, the CCC established a camp at the station, and nursery production increased. Production continued until 1960, when the nursery was closed. The DFES nursery produced more than 26 million seedlings and transplants for reforestation work in Michigan.

Study Site

The forestry curriculum included extended sessions for students at DFES beginning in 1946. Students participated in maintaining the forest and operating the nursery and a new sawmill.

Students of MSU's Civil Engineering Department used the site for surveying and road building from 1953 through 1962.

The 1966 forestry summer camp for students was the last one, although students continued to use the station for research and to assist with forest management as interns.

Additional purchases and gifts over the years brought the station size to 5,700 acres. Forest research projects at DFES are maintained and monitored by university staff members based at the U.P. Tree Improvement Center in Escanaba.[5]

...and Development

Saginaw Valley Station — Cooperative Venture

Transition to New Site

Since 1936, the key site for research on dry edible beans and sugar beets was the Ferden Farm near Chesaning. The site was on the southern edge of the growing region and grower and industry groups preferred a more centrally located site.

New Research Site

A group of representatives from farms, industry, and MSU began exploring alternatives in 1967. The Farmers and Manufacturers Beet Sugar Association, the Michigan Bean Shippers Association, and the Michigan Bean Commission reached an agreement to estab-

lish the Saginaw Valley Bean and Beet Research Farm (SVB-BRF) in January 1971.

They purchased the land and leased it to MSU to operate a branch experiment station. It was organized to provide on-site research on dry edible beans, sugar beets, and other related cash crops.

Shared Responsibilities

The current owners of the farm — the Michigan Sugar Company, the Michigan Bean Shippers Association, and the Michigan Bean Commission — share administration of the property and help determine research priorities through an advisory board. MAES provides funds to operate the station.

The Department of Crop and Soil Sciences (CSS) provides a faculty coordinator and manager. The departments of CSS, Entomology, and Plant Pathology, as well as the USDA, conduct research along with scientists from the bean and beet industries.

Effort Rewarding

Information generated on the site is disseminated directly to farmers by a network of MSU and industry personnel. The research is also extended to cooperative on-farm sites so farmers can see the same results in their own backyards.[6]

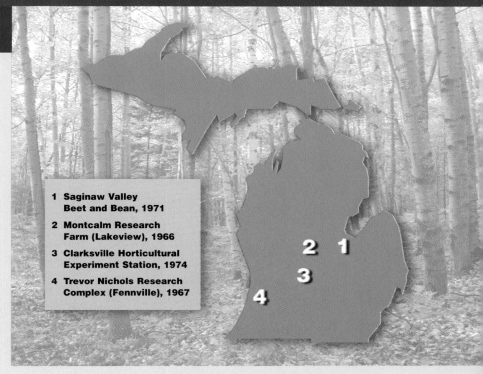

1 **Saginaw Valley Beet and Bean, 1971**

2 **Montcalm Research Farm (Lakeview), 1966**

3 **Clarksville Horticultural Experiment Station, 1974**

4 **Trevor Nichols Research Complex (Fennville), 1967**

The 1965-74 period saw the establishment of four new stations.

Forestry students learn to identify good utility poles in a red pine thinning study at Dunbar Forest Experiment Station.

Switch to Bedding Plants Initiated

In the early 1960s, many greenhouse growers were raising vegetables but faced shrinking markets. They had small greenhouses and were challenged by growers in California, who grew vegetables year round and were very competitive.

It was suggested that Michigan growers switch to producing bedding plants and that a conference be held to provide information helpful to making the transition. The

meeting in the Kellogg Center was very successful and was followed by two additional meetings.

New Organization

With this encouragement, a new organization — Bedding Plants Inc. (BPI) — was formed in 1969. William Carlson, Department of Horticulture, served as executive secretary and ran the operation out of his home with his wife as secretary.

Great Success

BPI gave MSU programs high visibility and increased contacts among growers and the industry. The name would be changed to Professional Plant Growers in the 1980s, and later to Bedding Plants International. Later, BPI had a spinoff called Floriculture Industry Research and Scholarship Trust (FIRST), which provided research grants and scholarships totaling $100,000 in 2001.[7]

Times of Stress

The chemical DDT became an issue at MSU when it was used to control Dutch elm disease, which is spread by a beetle.

Research Discoveries

Researchers at Princeton University and the Patuxent wildlife research refuge in Maryland said that DDT (dichloro-diphenyl-trichloro-ethane) was harmful to birds. John Mehner, a doctoral student in zoology at MSU, picked up on the claim for his dissertation. He and his advisor, professor of ornithology George Wallace, were concerned about the dead robins they inventoried on the campus.

With a research grant from Cranbrook Institute of Science, Wallace began pursuing the question along with Richard Bernard, another zoological doctoral student with a background in chemistry. Their analyses showed that dead robins had lethal doses of DDT. Earthworms often absorbed large amounts of DDT and transmitted the chemical to birds that fed on them.

Ag Community Objects

As risks of the chemical gained national attention, Wallace testified before a congressional committee, angering some leaders of the Michigan Department of Agriculture. The state commission adopted a resolution asking the university to speak with a single voice on the matter. That was a difficult request, given the disagreement among the involved scientists.

MSU Responds

In 1963, after the publication of Rachel Carson's *Silent Spring*, President Hannah established a committee to review use of DDT. In the end, the committee suggested a different pesticide may be as effective and less harmful. A week later, Hannah established the Pesticide Research Center (PRC) with the assignment to coordinate, across disciplines, efforts to study how pesticides interact with the environment. Five years later, the PRC issued a report indicating a willingness to phase out chlorinated hydrocarbon pesticides such as DDT.

True Pioneer

"The episode did not make Wallace popular. Later he wrote in his memoirs that his DDT work engendered animosity among elements in the campus community. Gordon Guyer, head of the entomology department at the time, agreed, recalling years later that he had been on the other side in those days.

"Over the years, what remained of those ill feelings faded away, leaving behind a different kind of legacy within the agricultural college...."

Wallace Recognized

In 1993, MSU conferred posthumously upon George Wallace a special commendation. None other than Gordon Guyer, then university president, referred to Wallace at that spring's commencement ceremonies as a true pioneer at the land-grant university.[8]

Courtesy UAHC

While visiting MSU, Dr. Martin Luther King, Jr., talked with graduate student Laura L. Leichliter (C) and Lenore Romney.

Dr. M.L. King Addresses Students

A thunderous standing ovation welcomed Dr. Martin Luther King, Jr., as he addressed an overflow crowd at the MSU Auditorium on February 11, 1965.

"Dr. King's reception ... was impressive as more than 4,000 students and townspeople turned out to hear him speak...."

Ensure Rights of All

"He rejected what he called the 'myth of time,' the view that racial justice will 'work itself out' if given enough time, and called for 'massive action programs' to insure all citizens of their basic constitutional rights.

"King also rejected the idea that legislation to help end racial injustices cannot really work, because it cannot change what is in people's hearts.

"'It may be true that morality cannot be legislated, but behavior can be regulated,' he declared, noting that minority groups still face such problems as above-average unemployment, housing bias, and inadequate education."

Praises Project, Hannah

"King had high praise for the MSU All-University Student Government plan to organize an education project for culturally deprived youngsters in Marshall County, Mississippi. King also lauded the work of MSU President John Hannah, who he said had served in a 'magnificent manner' as chairman of the federal civil rights commission."[9]

Changes in University Presidents

Hannah Goes to Washington

Longest Serving

Hannah was the institution's longest serving president. On April 1, 1969, John Hannah brought his 29-year presidency to a close, leaving MSU to administer the U.S. International Development Agency at the request of President Nixon.

Adams Selected

"MSU's Board of Trustees selected professor of economics Walter Adams as interim president on April 1, 1969. Adams reluctantly took the helm for the waning months of the decade and indicated that he would not be a candidate for the permanent appointment."

His nine months in the position came at a time of intense social upheaval in Michigan and throughout the U.S. Among these events were "confrontations by white radicals, sit-ins by black students, Vietnam demonstrations, ROTC protests, a strike by university employees, heated debates over open admission and quota policies, angry demands by alumni, parents, and legislators, and attacks by the news media."[10]

Returns to Teaching

At the end of the year, Adams returned to the classroom despite a campus petition of 17,000 signatures supporting him as a presidential candidate.

"'I have never deviated from my inflexible game plan,' he told the trustees, 'I have tried to serve the best interests of the university without ever entertaining the possibility of becoming its permanent chief executive.'"[11]

Courtesy UAHC

President Walter Adams flashing the peace sign while leading a march to the state Capitol.

Courtesy UAHC

Wharton Named 14th President

Clifton R. Wharton, Jr., was named president of Michigan State University in October 1969 and took office on January 1, 1970.

"An expert on economic development problems of Latin America and Southern Asia, Wharton said his professional interest is 'the economics of poverty — how to ... raise the quality of life of those who now suffer grievous poverty.'

"'Wharton had an uncanny knack for getting at things that were relevant to the people of Malaya and Singapore,' an MSU faculty member, who worked with Wharton in Asia, said. 'He didn't go in with a blueprint but sought the thinking of the Malayas.'

"Wharton also served last summer on Governor Nelson Rockefeller's presidential mission to Latin America. He was asked to recommend implementation procedures for the International Education Act of 1966 in rural and agricultural development because of his knowledge of the international role of U.S. universities.

He earned a bachelor's degree in history at Harvard. He earned other degrees at Johns Hopkins University (M.A. in advanced international studies) and University of Chicago (M.A. and Ph.D. in economics).[12]

Clifton Wharton, the 14th president, with his spouse, Dolores.

Sharing CES with Students

Some students on campus have little awareness of the university outreach efforts. The following article from the *Michigan State News* in 1966 informed students about one aspect of the outreach: the Cooperative Extension Service.

"You won't find course numbers listed in the catalog, but a division of the College of Agriculture held more than 30,000 class sessions last year."

"Field Faculty" of 230!

"Across the state, the Cooperative Extension Service (CES) conducts one of MSU's off-campus programs with a motto of 'Better Living Through Learning.'

The 'field faculty' conducts training sessions ranging from farm management to child development, from marketing timber to career exploration for teen-agers.

"The 'county agents,' as this staff is commonly known, are faculty members. They get an assist from a corps of nearly 100 'extension specialists.' Specialists are campus-based but spend a great deal of time in counties as a kind of 'visiting professor.'

"During the annual Farmers' Week, the process is somewhat reversed. CES, in fact, the entire staff of the College of Agriculture, entertains some 20,000-25,000 'visiting students.'"

People's Colleges

"The CES is the unique feature of land-grant universities. The land-grant schools have the most far-reaching off-campus programs. CES conducts programs along five major lines: agriculture, natural resources, marketing, family living, and youth development."[13]

Courtesy Einer Olstrom collection

Professor Edward Pleva (Western Ontario University) (L), greets James Neal (C) and Einer Olstrom (R), Shiawassee County New Horizon Study-Travelers to Canada.

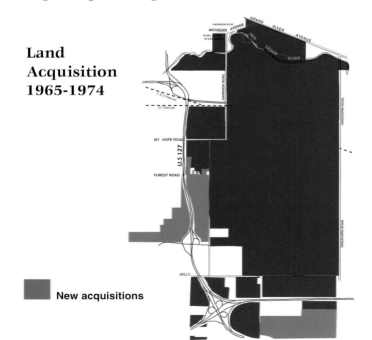

Land Acquisition 1965-1974

New acquisitions

Iron–Dickinson County 4-H Experiment

The 1960s and '70s were a time of stress for residents in the U.P. Locally, the iron mines were closing. Communities were experiencing population losses. School consolidations and new community programs competed for existing youths. To survive in such an environment, 4-H had to practice a cliché popular at the time: "Different strokes for different folks."

Teen Leader Program

Replacing lost leadership was the No. 1 problem. Developing a strong teen leader program was the solution. To attract and retain teens, the local 4-H councils, after some reluctance to change the traditional program, became enthusiastic supporters of diverse offerings.

The turning point developed over participation in downstate programs. Traditionally the entire U.P. would send just two busloads of 4-H'ers to state Exploration Days as a reward.

The proposal was to send as many county youths as wanted to attend. The two counties ended up sending two busloads.

Give It a Try!

Upon their return, attendee enthusiasm convinced the county councils to be creative in developing new programs while also improving the traditional ones.

Contributing to Community

The teens became involved in the community. They moved a historic barn to the local museum to preserve it, participated in a weekend camping program involving mentally handicapped adults, and produced a play on the history of 4-H in Iron County.

The investment in the teen program paid significant dividends. The teens enthusiastically recruited young members, led local 4-H clubs, and became counselors and workers at the county fair. 4-H is most significant when it relates to the people it serves.[14]

...and Expanding

Extension's Management Information System

"Annual plans of work and periodic reports have always been a 'way of life' for CES staff and have never been popular with agents or specialists.... Plans of work provided budget justification; yearly reports enabled accountability for accomplishment."

Launched in 1968

"A national Extension Management Information System (EMIS) was launched by the Federal Extension Service. All states were mandated to submit plans of work and an annual report which would reflect both planned and expended time inputs of all staff.

"Audience numbers were reported for all Extension program objectives. Reflecting an affirmative action influence, all audience contacts were reported by race and sex to be tabulated at the end of the year."

Computer-assisted

Howard Miller of Information Services was appointed to direct the new management system. He held the post for 12 years. To handle the enormous database which the system generated, all inputs were summarized by computer. Each of 400 staff members reported total time spent in hours on program objectives.[15]

Courtesy UAHC

Promo for 1965 ACWW conference.

Nutrition Education

Congressional Act

"In 1968, Congress appropriated funds from overseas food exports for a mammoth nutrition education effort — the Expanded Nutrition Program (ENP). The total exceeded $50 million. Extension was delegated to manage it."

Family Living and 4-H

"Michigan qualified for nearly $1.5 million in the first year....

"ENP was a major addition to Family Living. It would forever alter future programs. 4-H geared up for a youth component in ENP, as speci-

fied in the federal grant. Its philosophy and mode of operation would also have an impact on the total Extension Service."

Local Aides Employed

"Two key provisions gave impetus to CES' first major effort to reach the disadvantaged. Recipients of the nutrition program had to be low-income families and program aides were to be employed wherever possible from local neighborhoods. At first, funds could be used only for salaries of aides or other 'paraprofessionals.' By mid-1969, some 136 aides were employed in 16 counties."[16]

Associated Country Women of the World

ACWW Meets at MSU

"In 1968, Michigan women hosted an international event. More than 2,500 delegates to the Associated Country Women of the World attended their 12th triennial conference at MSU.

"Committees from the U.S. organization were more than a year planning the high-level event. Program leader Anne Wolford supervised local arrangements.

"The president of the world group, Ms. Aroti Dutt of India, visited the campus in 1967 and returned for the conference in September of the following year."

Fifty Countries

"Delegates attended from more than 50 countries. Initially, Governor George Romney could not attend, but later, on opening day, he made a surprise appearance and received a standing ovation. Mrs. Romney also was a conference speaker."

Spectacular Event

"USA Day in Jenison Fieldhouse featured participants from 32 countries and an address by Mrs. Eugenia Anderson, special assistant to the U.S. Secretary of State. Other speakers included MSU President Hannah and

Charles Shuman, president of the American Farm Bureau. A review of the conference was published in England for distribution to all delegates."

Hallmark Success

"The conference logistics were immense. When campus food services backed away from a chicken barbecue for 10,000 on USA Day, President Hannah himself interceded. The ACWW conclave was clearly one of the most ambitious projects undertaken by the Family Living staff in the 1960s or any other decade. It was a stellar accomplishment."[17]

Visionary

Even before the end of WW II, John Hannah was urging educators and policy-makers to prepare for increased student enrollments. He led the growth in facilities, faculty, and staff, transforming MSC into a major university of nearly 40,000 students.[18]

Enjoyed Students

President Hannah maintained active interactions with students and was forward-looking about their needs and potentials. The high regard students had for him was evident.

Caring Family

Mr. and Mrs. Hannah and their four children out for a stroll. Mr. Hannah and Mrs. Sarah (Shaw) Hannah are with (L-R) Robert Wilford, Thomas Arthur, David Harold, and Mary Elizabeth. Their caring extended to those within the academic civic community and far beyond.

Mrs. Sarah (Shaw) Hannah was the daughter of President Robert Shaw. She was reared on the campus. When she married John, together they reared their four children in the Cowles House. She joined Dr. Hannah in many roles on the campus and in the state, nation, and world.

International Outreach

President Hannah visits with Vladimier V. Matskovich (L), head of the 12-member Russian farm delegation. Matskovich told Hannah that attending the Centennial Farm Mechanization display at MSU was the highlight of their U.S. visit.

Strong Agricultural Roots

President Hannah with 4-H club members at 1951 state club show. His roots included leadership with poultry associations and service as a county agricultural agent and poultry Extension specialist for MSC.

"*I do the very best I know how, the very best I can, and I mean to keep on doing so until the end. If the end brings me out all right, what is said against me won't amount to anything. If the end brings me out wrong, 10 angels swearing I was right would make no difference.*"

Hannah reminded himself of President Lincoln's motto, posted on the picture frame behind his desk.

Students Were Central

President Hannah signing a student's "organization paddle." At his retirement party, Dr. Varner stated, "... of the 98,492 diplomas awarded in the history of this institution ... our honored guest tonight has personally signed 89,662 of them.[19]

International Leader

Administrator John A. Hannah, accompanied by Mrs. Hannah, disembarking from a China Airlines flight from Taiwan for a two-day visit of USAID-assisted projects in the Philippines. Earlier, he served President Truman as a member of the International Development Advisory Board, which formulated policies for the Point Four Program.

Legacy Endures

President Hannah walking in front of MSU's new administration building in 1969. The name "Hannah Administration Building" was given by the Board of Trustees. Hannah asked that his name not be used on a building until after he left MSU.

Academic Leader

Dr. Ernest Boyer, President of the Carnegie Foundation for the Advancement in Teaching, identified Dr. John Hannah "as a leader in this century who did more for higher education than any other person."[20]

Honored and Beloved

A bronze sculpture was dedicated Sept. 17, 2004, honoring John A. Hannah. MSU President Peter McPherson observed that Hannah led the transformation of M.A.C. to an MSU that is "truly global in every sense and acknowledged throughout the world as the pioneering land-grant university."

Stage One: Irrigation System

Devastating Drought

For growers in St. Joseph County, the 1966 drought was a disaster. With little industry, towns lose their economic base if farming collapses. With an average of 35 bushels of corn per acre, the question in the growers' minds, as they came to see the county Extension director Fred Henningsen, was "How can we assure a consistent income?"

Reliable Water Source

They wanted Henningsen to help them determine what could happen if they had a consistent water supply. At the time, only 1,000 acres in the county were under irrigation, a labor-intensive, high-maintenance process that relied on a solid-set pipe that had to be moved manually from one field lane to another. Elwood Russell, Emo Barney, Phil Cupp, and others told Fred that the county had the right corn hybrids, soils, farm ponds, and good growers. All they lacked was a consistent water supply.

Axle, Hub, and Rim

Fred was not an expert in irrigation, but he listened carefully. He knew where to go to find information and resources. Ernie Kidder, an ag economics specialist at MSU, agreed to assist Fred and the growers. Maury Vitosh, from the MSU Department of Crop and Soil Sciences, came in to do additional research. Joseph Mueller, who had worked on irrigation with specialty crops in Indiana, also came to assist.

Together, they developed the first soft hose traveler. The soft hose still needed access to surface water and required lane changes. The key, though, was eliminating the manual labor by creating a pulley made from a steel plate, a car axle, a hub, and a rim. They hooked this assembly to a wagon to change lanes.[21]

Courtesy of Sara A. Stuby and Fred Henningsen.

John Barclay (L), of the Soil Conservation Service, and Theodore (Ted) Loudon, Professor Emeritus, Department of Biosystems and Agricultural Engineering, measure the irrigation flow with a rain gauge.

Stage Two: Financially Feasible

Financing Irrigation

In the early 1970s, Ezra Graber asked Henningson, "Why not grow seed corn in the county?" He explained that such a crop would have a higher profit margin than corn grain. It was a new idea. Fred told Ezra to contact DeKalb Seed Company for a meeting with the growers. DeKalb, with a plant nearby in Ohio, met with the growers and left with 4,000 acres under seed corn contracts.

Seminar Overflows

In 1972, Pioneer Company representatives came to talk to Henningson about building a processing plant in the area.

About the same time, he and Kidder scheduled a meeting at Glen Oaks Community College. More than 100 people gathered to hear a professor from the University of Nebraska, a leader in irrigation.

Pivot Technology

Pivot sprinkler technology began maturing during the 1970s, and growers in St. Joseph County bought their first sprinklers, used, from Nebraska. This technology, which is a laterally moving irrigation system that rotates around a fixed pivot point, began to have an impact.

Extension's Irrigation Specialist

In the 1980s, well drillers mapped the area for industrial and municipal wells. The growing irrigation industry, dealers, well drillers, MSUE, growers, Farm Bureau, and seed companies put information together and held meetings. The growers pointed the way. MSUE facilitated. It was during this time that MSU came to be considered a world leader in irrigation, and Henningsen became known as Michigan's Extension irrigation specialist.

...and Helping the Economy Thrive

Stage Three: Protecting Water Resources

Pioneer Research Grant

A related problem surfaced. Growers were unsure of how much nitrogen to use under irrigation. Some thought that excessive use could cause leaching. Ted Loudon and Joe Ritchie from MSU prepared a proposal to present to the Pioneer Company. Pioneer responded with a $300,000 grant to install lysimeters. Funding rose to $600,000, and for the next five years Pioneer conducted research with MSU. Based on their findings, Henry Miller agreed to reduce his use of nitrogen. Others soon followed suit.

Additionally, Al Herseg of the Soil Conservation District worked with Henningsen to create irrigation schedules that regulated water usage and timing to minimize leaching. Loudon, Vitosh, and one of their graduate students developed a computer program to increase irrigation schedule efficiency.

Courtesy Einer Olstrom collection

Joe Ostanek (L) demonstrates a strawberry irrigation system to farm management specialist Rick Hartwig (C) and Arvid Norlin (R), county Extension director.

Stage Four: Economic Benefits

Economic Benefit

With the combination of commercial and specialty crops, the technology of irrigation, and the presence of the seed corn companies, growers started showing increased profits in a broad spectrum of crops. Detasseling corn provided new and profitable summer employment opportunities for 3,500 young people.

An Industry and Community Saved

Today the 60,000-acre seed corn industry in southwestern Michigan generates over $125 million in local economic activity. It also directly provides more than 5,000 people with full- or part-time employment. Another 2,800 people are employed either directly or indirectly as a result of the industry, and these jobs generate over $20 million in wages. Land values have increased from $250 per acre in the 1970s to an average of $2,500 per acre today (with or without irrigation.) Currently, 100,000 acres are irrigated in St. Joseph County.

Stage Five: Other Benefits

Contributions Continue

Henningsen is now retired from MSUE but not from active participation in water issues. After he retired, Governor John Engler appointed him to the Great Lakes and Water Resources Planning Commission. The committee found that water levels in 30-year-old wells are still within range of where they started. He is currently on the Michigan Groundwater Conservation Advisory Council, studying water use, irrigation programs, and economic impact.

Later, MSU received a gift to establish an endowed chair — the Homer Nowlin Chair of Water in Agricultural and Natural Resource Systems. Dr. Joseph Ritchie, with his strong interest in water conservation, became the first to occupy the position.

Broad Benefit

As for the growers in St. Joseph County, their interest, determination, and partnership with MSUE and others helped to develop a consistent water supply. They played a key role in St. Joseph County's economic survival and vitality.

International Service and Benefits

Hannah Advocates International Outreach

President Hannah, speaking for the land-grant colleges, proposed to President Truman that these colleges should participate in U.S. efforts to restore global food systems that had been disrupted and damaged during World War II.

Land-grant Obligations

Early commitments between the U.S. government and MSC focused largely on the development of institutions of higher learning abroad which would embody the principles of the U.S. land-grant universities. Because food was a primary need, especially where surges in population were occurring, they placed a great emphasis on agriculture in those early efforts.

Contracts Complex

Typically the Food and Agriculture Organization (FAO) of the United Nations identified the need and furnished support for assistance through the USDA, which had extensive experience with land-grant institutions. The early contractual documents were simple and short, but as time progressed and government became a more complex process, the contractual documentation grew. The Office of Contracts and Grants developed its competence and became an essential partner with the dean, departments, and faculty. The strains of administering the programs led also to the creation of the Institute of International Agriculture in 1964 to cope with the increasingly complex opportunities and obligations.

Programs

The college programs made an impression on many areas benefiting from the program. Professor George Petrides left his mark on many overseas national parks because of his involvement. Agricultural economists assisted Nigeria in developing agricultural policy, a legacy that continues in several African nations. Foresters, animal scientists, agricultural engineers, fisheries and wildlife specialists, agronomists, and horticulturists were deployed in overseas assignments.

Extension Involved

Early in the creation of development assistance, special interest in providing agricultural extension specialists developed in the hope they would be effective in teaching indigenous "extensionists" new methods for transferring technology to residents in developing countries. In retrospect, it became apparent that appropriate technology and resources to fuel the transfer process were often unavailable in the areas of greatest need. The Rockefeller, Ford, and other foundations became involved by recruiting college staff members to assist in the effort to stimulate development.[22]

Varied International Assignments

MSU now had dozens of staff members with wide-ranging international experience. The ambitious institution-building efforts of the 1950s and 1960s gave way to developments that were more problem-oriented and less related to a single institution or country.

MSU worked more closely with other universities in cooperative agreements or consortia such as MUCIA (Midwest University Consortium for International Assistance). Former CES staffer George Axinn served as MUCIA director for a number of years.

In the 1970s, fewer MSU staff members served extended periods abroad and more went on short-term assignments. The University of Nigeria contract ended in July 1969 and brought to a close an outstanding example of "institution building" — the largest that MSU, and perhaps any American university, had attempted. Extension staff members were a major resource in the project.[23]

Courtesy Einer Olstrom collection

Leyton Nelson, farm crops Extension specialist, discusses crops at a village in East Pakistan. Work with the Pakistan Extension Service was financed by the Ford Foundation and was undertaken in 1974. The Pakistan Extension Service had been established some years earlier but needed more worker training and improved information transfer. Garland Wood of Ag Economics took the lead in the Pakistan project.

...In Numerous Ways

John Hannah greets Nigerian officials on a rice/maize tour in August 1971.

4-H Leads Belize Program

Extension had a major commitment to assist Belize and other Central American nations through a "partners" venture. Mary Woodward of the state 4-H staff coordinated the early Belize effort when the country was called British Honduras. In 1970, she helped organize local 4-H clubs. International Farm Youth Exchange's Kay Siegrist and Harold Schmidt were also early workers. Some 26 clubs were formed in the first 18 months in the country of 130,000.

4-H was the lead program in Belize, and the program benefited from repeated visits and consultantships by MSU faculty members, specialists, and agents.

A feeder pig program was started to improve pork production and increase incomes of small farms. Each farmer selected received 10 baby pigs and funds for a feeding facility. Program leader Tom Thorburn and Gratiot agent "Van" Varner were consultants. Robert Deans of Animal Science assisted in crop and livestock development.[24]

Subsurface Asphalt Water Barriers Studied

Will an asphalt barrier below the ground surface benefit vegetation growth in areas of modest rainfall and sandy soils? Professors Earl Erickson (Department of Crop and Soil Sciences) and Clarence Hansen (Department of Ag Engineering) were conducting research on this question. It gradually gained international interest. Below is a brief account of the experiment in Taiwan.

Tenan, Taiwan

Erickson supervised the construction of an asphalt barrier as an earlier experiment in Tenan, Taiwan. A tractor-mounted applicator was not available in Taiwan, so the work was done manually on sugarcane plots 8.75 meters wide and 25 meters long. Workers removed and replaced the soil over the sprayed asphalt at three depths.

Step two in the research project involved planting and growing sugarcane in plots irrigated by a sprinkler system. The amount of water provided was based on the known moisture needs of the sugarcane. The plots were irrigated in March in five increments. All the F-156 sugarcane was planted at the prescribed depth. The germination of the sugarcane was 92 percent.

Findings

With sandy conditions at the site, they concluded that 75 centimeters was the optimal depth for the asphalt barrier. Because the Taiwan Sugar Corporation had large areas of sand and a scarcity of irrigation water, this field experiment with sugarcane was well received and placed on many corporate farms.

The final question discussed was whether the barriers were cost effective. The researchers concluded that the barriers "can be machine installed and paid for in three years .... A conservative estimate was that the useful life of a barrier is 15 years. The future of the barriers for improving sugarcane production in Taiwan looks very promising.*[25]

---

*Subsurface Asphalt Barriers for the Improvement of Sugarcane Production (A.E. Erickson, C.M. Hansen, et al., 1968).

Another dimension of international programming involved 4-H student exchanges. 4-H's Mary Woodward (L) coordinated the program.

CANR and Cherry Industry...

CANR and Cherry Industry Partnership

Ruby-red tart cherries are jewels of Michigan agriculture. Cherry trees were first planted in the late 1800s in the Traverse City area. By the early 1900s, cherries had become a commercial crop. Today Michigan produces 70 to 75 percent of the nation's tart cherry crop and 20 percent of its sweet cherry production.

Michigan Cherry Committee

The legislature established the Michigan Cherry Committee (MCC) to allow growers to work together in funding research and market development activities. Over the years, the cherry industry and MCC have relied on the CANR for research and innovation. This partnership grew stronger as MSU researchers worked to address growers' needs.

Mechanizing Harvesting

A key achievement of the relationship was the development of the mechanical harvester. This began in the 1950s, with the first cherry harvesters (or shakers) being purchased by growers about 1965. By 1968, many growers had adopted this revolutionary technology. Previously the cherries were picked by hand. Developing the harvester involved the Ag Engineering Department, the USDA Agricultural Research Service unit at MSU, private companies such as the Friday Shaker Co., and cherry growers, who tested the equipment.

Dramatic Change

Mechanical harvesters dramatically changed the cherry industry. Millions of pounds of cherries could be harvested quickly by machine. The need for a large seasonal labor force to pick cherries was diminished.

The shakers themselves underwent change. The first mechanical harvesters were limb shakers that shook each limb individually. Later, trunk shakers were developed to shake cherries from a tree in seconds.

The cherry industry is proud of its affiliation with the CANR and looks to the future with enthusiasm for this winning partnership.[26]

Courtesy Michigan Cherry Committee

Modern cherry harvester.

CANR Addresses Other Needs

New Tree Style Need

Mechanical harvesters led to new research by the Horticulture Department. Traditionally, cherry trees had limbs close to the ground, but that made it difficult to clamp the tree trunk with a trunk shaker. Horticulturists worked with cherry growers to develop a new style of tree to minimize injury to the trunk and increase harvesting speed.

Other Research

Ag Engineering researchers also developed new sprayer technology. Other CANR departments also helped advance the cherry industry.

- The Horticulture Department developed new cherry varieties, pruning techniques, and production systems.

- The Entomology Department played a key role in the early adoption of integrated pest management, teaching growers how to trap and monitor insects and diseases in orchards and use science to determine when spraying was necessary.

- The Plant Pathology Department discovered new ways to control weather-related plant diseases.

- The Food Science Department helped develop new products and, more recently, information on the health benefits of cherries.

- The Department of Agricultural Economics contributed to domestic and international cherry marketing.

Joint Research Station

Need for Research Station

Another important MSU-CMI (Cherry Marketing Institute) relationship — the effort of cherry growers to establish a university research presence — resulted in the establishment of a research station in the heart of cherry country on the Leelanau Peninsula.

The idea for a research facility in northwestern Michigan began in the 1960s. Growers commented that southern Michigan research stations did not address the problems of Michigan's northwestern cherry industry, where most of the sweet cherries and a high percentage of the tart cherries are grown.

New Station

In 1978, growers in five northwestern Michigan counties organized the Northwest Michigan Horticulture Research Foundation. The foundation raised funds to purchase an 80-acre farm in Leelanau County and build an office, conference center, and storage facility on the site. A year later, the founda-

(Continued on page 207)

Joint Research...

(Continued from page 206)

tion leased the station to MSU for $1 per year for 99 years, thus developing a new partnership. MSUE and the Ag Experiment Station provide funding and personnel to conduct research and organize educational sessions in the conference facility.

Winning Partnership

The station celebrated its 25th anniversary in 2004 as a multidisciplinary horticultural facility with research projects focused on agricultural production and related environmental issues. The station is a blend of MSU research and Extension programming combined with the active participation of the cherry industry and the support of the Michigan Department of Agriculture.[27]

Making Trees Amenable to Shakers

Shakers and Tree Damage

A problem of using shakers to harvest cherries was damage to trees. That led to the question common to mechanical harvesting: can the plant be changed to make the mechanical harvesting more effective?

The critical question was whether the fruit could be loosened so more fruit would be removed with the same or less force. M. John Bukovac, professor of horticulture, pursued an answer. He asked chemical companies whether they were screening chemicals for fruit abscission. Virtually none was.

Exploration Underway

Bukovac invited Robert Beatty of AmChem to give a seminar in the Horticulture Garden. When Beatty was asked if he had any chemicals that had promise for fruit loosening, he replied, "We're not sure, but we'd be happy to send you samples for testing."

Early branch shaker harvesters.

Ethephon Shows Promise

One of the compounds, later referred to as ethephon, decomposes in the plant tissue and releases the gaseous, naturally occurring plant hormone ethylene. When Bukovac saw the first response, he asked his colleague, Arthur Mitchell, an Extension specialist, to come and see. Mitchell agreed that the compound might have potential. Bukovac took another sample to Traverse City, where cherries ripen later, and tried the compound on Ozzie Herkner's orchard with identical results. They made plans for extensive trials the following spring.

A drawback with ethephon was temperature sensitivity. If the temperature rose 10 degrees Centigrade, the plant released about eight times as much ethylene. Thus, a greater response occurs when it is applied at high temperature.

Chemical and Mechanical Knowledge Productive

Bukovac and his colleagues conducted experiments over several years on the physiology of fruit abscission, coupled with evaluation of the effects of ethephon concentration and time of application on fruit removal force, quality of the harvested product, etc., to

Courtesy Olstrom collection

develop recommendations for commercial use in the fruit industry.

Cherry growers now apply ethephon as a standard practice in the mechanical harvesting of cherries in Michigan. Today, virtually all cherries mechanically harvested in the eastern United States are treated with ethephon.[28]

New Program Activities

Local Government Program

Taxation Policy

Ag Econ's local government program continued to expand as the years passed. In the later 1960s, Alvin House was working with Raleigh Barlowe (Resource Development) and Milton Taylor (Economics) focusing on Michigan tax systems. Local officials and MSUE staff members were especially interested in agricultural land taxation and alternatives for supporting schools.

About the same time, Congress appropriated large grant funds to finance local sewer and water projects. These federal programs led to even more demand for programs for which House recruited representatives from key state agencies, bond and financial consulting firms, and engineering firms.

County Commissioner Training

Under the new state constitution, township supervisors no longer also served on county boards of commissioners. Instead, county commissioners were directly elected from districts. At the request of some CEDs, House organized regional training sessions for new commissioners after the November biennial elections.

House selected program presenters and discussion leaders who were among the most experienced and best informed county board members in the state. To add some flavor, House asked Governor William Milliken to record a welcome message, which they played at the beginning of each session.

Following the 1970 elections, the county association joined the program. Kenneth VerBurg, MSU Institute of Community Development (ICD) specialist in county and local government, joined the NCCT (New County Commissioner Training) team. VerBurg had been writing both topical papers and books focusing on the problems and opportunities of county and local officials.

By 1974, the team, sponsored by the Michigan Association of Counties, MSUE, and ICD, had developed three manuals for the program. Eugene G. Wanger, an attorney with thorough knowledge of county government affairs, was also a member of the team.[29]

Environmental Policy and Law

Concerns and issues about human effects on the environment were growing in the 1960s. State and federal governments would enact legislation addressing the problems. In 1969, Congress passed the National Environmental Protection Act.

How to Respond

How should the Department of Resource Development respond? Leaders in the department concluded that if its graduates were to be effective administrators in the state and federal environmental management agencies, they would have to know the law and also the natural context of these policies.

Establish Program

If the department was going to prepare students for professional work in these areas, it would need faculty members with legal training and knowledge about the environmental issues. Establishing the Environmental Policy and Law (EPL) program was seen to be the appropriate action.

An early action was the hiring of the department's first lawyer, Leighton L. Leighty, in 1970. That same year, the first master's and doctoral candidates entered the program. In 1972, the department added another lawyer, Daniel A. Bronstein, to the faculty. M. Rupert Cutler joined the faculty in 1973.*

Daniel A. Bronstein

The coming decades would reveal the insightfulness of this response to developing environmental issues.[30]

*With the advent of the College of Law at MSU, Resource Development was one of the first departments to establish a joint (M.S./J.D.) degree program.

Courtesy Eugene G. Wanger

New county commissioner workshops were held every other year following the fall elections. From left to right are the early instructional team members: Eugene G. Wanger, an attorney; Alvin E. House, professor of Agricultural Economics; James Callahan, executive director, Michigan Association of Counties; and Kenneth VerBurg, professor, Institute for Community Development.

Other Campus Dynamics

Crop Science and Soil Science Merge

When Robert S. Shaw reorganized the Division of Agriculture into departments, Soils was designated a department in 1909 and Crops in 1910.

Nearly 60 years later, in 1969, the departments of Crop Science and Soil Science were combined to form the Crop and Soil Sciences Department. The new combined department continues in the tradition established in the 19th century of addressing challenges of research, teaching, and extension.

Moves South Great for Agriculture

"As competitors vied for campus space, agriculture moved south — each time with newer and more modern facilities.

"When Agriculture Dean T.K. Cowden left in 1969, the venerable Ag Hall, crops and soils labs in the old dairy building, and the horticulture building and greenhouses were the only ANR facilities remaining north of the river. Entomology, under the joint leadership of the colleges of Agriculture and Natural Sciences, remained on the north campus.

"To the south were impressive multimillion dollar research and teaching centers for dairy on College Road and beef cattle on Bennett. A sheep facility was built on Hagadorn Road, and a greatly expanded poultry center opened on Jolly Road."[32]

Student Regulations

Well before he left office, President Hannah expressed his concern that student rules and regulations were outdated. In a letter to the Student Affairs Committee of the Academic Council, he said:

"As I have indicated at meetings of the Academic Council and the Faculty Senate for nearly a year, I have a growing concern about the relationships of students at MSU with other members of the university community, and with those beyond the campus." This concern had been "stimulated by events both within our own university and without."

He also told committee chairperson Fred Williams that he thought that it was "high time we reviewed the rules and regulations affecting students to see whether they are sound and practicable... because the society we serve has changed in many ways and is continuing to change."

Full-scale Review

"All the rules and structures of the university which affect the academic freedom of students are being reviewed by a standing faculty committee of the Academic Council.

"The Committee on Student Affairs called on all members of the university community and greater Lansing area for aid in carrying out its assignment. It plans to evaluate all pertinent university regulations, written policies, and unwritten customs, in classrooms and outside them, on and off campus."[31]

New Hort Research Site

The decision to begin a medical college at MSU led to the movement of horticulture's home on the campus. The horticulture teaching and research farm was located near Hagadorn Road and the railroad tracks until the mid-1960s.

New South Campus Site

The new site for horticulture research consisted of 110 acres south of Jolly Road and west of College Road. The university purchased these lands in 1963. Later, the 72-acre parcel on the east side of College Road was acquired. That brought the university holdings south to Sandhill Road.

The board of trustees approved the expenditure of $224,000 to prepare the land for the Department of Horticulture. The existing buildings were destroyed. Fences, trees, and tree rows were removed, and the land was plowed. Trenches were dug in 1964 to install irrigation pipes.

Ready for Business

Other improvements included the planting of apple, peach, plum, and apricot trees, drilling a 12-inch well (372 feet deep), and clearing land and constructing new buildings. A new plant laboratory building housed a large room for equipment repair and seven refrigerated storages for nursery stock, seeds, herbaceous plant material, and vegetables. A pole barn for equipment and supplies completed the complex.

The complex was dedicated on August 2, 1967.[33]

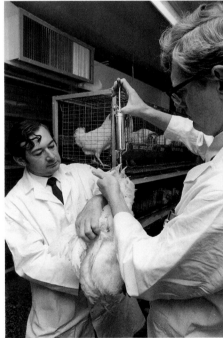

Courtesy Einer Olstrom collection

Poultry scientists Donald Polin and John Wolford found that limiting diets can prevent disease in hens.

In 1959, to bring more focus to outreach effort, a fourth program area — Community Resource Development and Public Affairs — was created in the Extension Service. In July 1959, William Kimball of the Resource Development Department was named the program leader.

Federal Grants Provide Impetus

Federal Extension grants to the Resource Development Department supported four national workshops in community development for training field workers in Extension and related units. The workshops, held at MSU from 1965 to 1969, involved numerous national experts and participants from nearly every state and Canadian province.

Economic Excellence

Governor James Blanchard's new program — Communities of Economic Excellence — generated demand for Extension assistance in community development in the early 1980s. Cooperation between field personnel from the Michigan Department of Commerce and Extension staff members had significant impact in numerous Michigan communities.[34]

Community Leadership Emphasis

Increasingly, Extension workers began to realize that community development was highly dependent on community leadership, something often missing. Beginning in the 1970s, the emphasis gradually shifted to leadership development.

One example of integrated community and leadership development was the new Leadership and Local Government Education Project for Southwest Michigan, which the Kellogg Foundation funded in the later 1980s. This also generated new collaborative efforts between the departments of Agricultural Economics and Resource Development.[35]

Ag Economists Address Issues

Technology and Lower Prices

"On January 1, 1960, corn was $1 per bushel; wheat, $1.83. Choice steers in Chicago were $26.03/cwt., and the milk price was $3.99. Ten years later, corn was $1.07; wheat $1.29. Choice steers sold for $29.27, and milk in the super pool was $5.78/cwt.

"Economist Lester Mandersheid in December 1969 forecast that 1970 looked like a year of adjustment. 'After nine years of economic expansion, there is real concern about a recession.'

"As the 1960s ended, and the conflict in Vietnam was winding down, there were signs of inflation and forecasts that farm prices would reach new highs."

Overproduction?

"Prior to his retirement in 1970, policy specialist Arthur Mauch concluded: 'Past farm programs have been legislated and administered on the assumption that a higher price would cure the ills of all farmers. It is time we recognize the nature of the problem and treat its cause of overproduction and low prices.'"[36]

Period in Review

Socially and politically, the university experienced a difficult and trying time on the campus. But it was also an exciting time, and the institution gained the respect and confidence of the general public.

The period was a trying time because of social and economic changes. The state and nation were experiencing continued high growth in population and rapidly changing technology. These changes led to increased mobility and widespread suburbanization, raising concerns about community building and planning.

Such social and economic change necessitated adjustment by some elements of the agricultural and natural resource communities. The faculty and staff were called upon to provide advice and assistance as those affected sought solutions to the changing conditions and growing challenges. CANR work with the seed corn industry in southwestern Michigan, collaboration with the cherry industry in northwestern portions of the state, and the founding of community development and land use planning are but a few examples of how the college and university applied knowledge and counsel for those undergoing change.

With the help of the W. K. Kellogg Foundation, one other major innovation was achieved. With the emergence of computer technology, various elements of the CANR were able to collaborate and apply the new technology to farmers around the state.

The decade involved substantial change in leadership. President John Hannah had been a beacon of leadership for nearly three decades.

County, State, and National Population

1970		
	Number	Percent change, 1960-1970
Ingham County	261,039	23.5
Michigan	8,881,828	13.5
USA	203,302,031	13.4

U.S. Bureau of Census

Courtesy Sandra J. Allen

"The University is the focal point for creativity in civilization. It is the mind which is creative. The university is dedicated to the mind.

"Students aware and sensitive to the fact that Michigan State is one of the few institutions that is dedicated both to the mind and to nurturing of the creative spirit of each individual can make the greatest possible use of their creativity."

Clifton R. Wharton, Jr.
President

Natural Resource Studies Grow

Chapter Overview

The qualities of stability and maturity of the university and the college marked the 1975-84 period. The university enrollment rose, curricula broadened, and state funding was generally stable except for the challenge of the 1980-81 economic downturn.

Lands Affected

For the college, the period was different. Economic, social, and technological changes continued to make an impact on the agricultural community. The dominance of the automobile as the means of travel fueled suburbanization and conversion of farmlands to residential and commercial uses.

Farming Changed

One effect of these changes was a decline in the number of full-time farmers. The increases in mechanization of farming and a reduction in the reliance on human labor added to this change. Thus, the number of farms dropped while the size of the farms rose.

Natural Resources Highlighted

The period stimulated greater attention to study and management of natural resources. The increasing suburbaniza-

tion and farmland conversion gave rise to questions about land use and how to balance the competing demands.

Similarly, the social and technological changes stimulated questions about the steps that society and government should take to manage and protect water resources.

These factors expanded the role of local governments and increased the complexity of challenges facing local officials.

Pandisciplinary

The departments of the college responded in a number of innovative ways. Researchers on the campus collaborated across departments to deepen the understanding of the complex challenges. Similarly, the Extension Service found itself dealing with an ever increasing range of questions.

As a consequence of these changes in the broader environment, the departments of the college became more environmentally focused and more pandisciplinary in their orientation and approaches.

Resource Economics Specialization for Society's Benefit

Sons of Henry George

Professors Robert Manthy and Robert Marty noted that a large concentration of faculty members and students at MSU had a strong interest in resource economics. However, they did not see themselves as a "community."

To build community, Manthy and Marty organized the Sons of Henry George. (George was a 19th century social reformer.)

Interdepartmental Specialization

From informal conversations in the 1970s came a proposal for an interdepartmental graduate program led by professors Milton Steinmueller (Resource Development), Donald Holecek (Park and Recreation Resources), and Allan Schmid (Agricultural Economics). Professor Larry Libby guided the proposal through the academic community. It appeared in the catalog in 1984.

Courtesy MAES

A. Allan Schmid, University Distinguished Professor, Agricultural Economics.

Resource Economics

The purpose was to provide an opportunity for graduate students to obtain a comprehensive and contemporary academic experience, to be sensitive to professional obligations and responsibilities, and to develop an intellectual environment fostering growth of research and public service.

Early Core Faculty

The program included faculty members from the departments of Forestry, Resource Development, Park and Recreation Resources, Fisheries and Wildlife, and Agricultural Economics. The specialization was later broadened to include the College of Business and the Department of Economics.

Specialization Demand

The specialization attracted many international students who went on to make substantial contributions to resource economics. Among the first graduates was Juan Carlos Seijo, who became rector of Marista University in the Yucatan, Mexico.

Other graduates have gone into leadership roles in government, industry, universities, and other pursuits across the United States and internationally.[1]

Courtesy Resource Development Department

Milton Steinmueller, Professor Emeritus, Resource Development.

Water Quality Research Project

Water Quality Facility

While driving on College Road south of Jolly Road, you may have noticed four lakes, two on each side of the road. Why are they there? The original purpose was to conduct research on the use of natural ecological systems to treat wastewater.

Vision for Site

In 1973, with funding from the U.S. Environmental Protection Agency, the state of Michigan, and the Ford, Kresge, and Rockefeller foundations, MSU scientists had the facility constructed at a cost of $2.3 million and named it the Water Quality Management Facility (WQMF). Professors Robert Ball and Howard Tanner envisioned the facility, which provided a setting for the research of more than 30 faculty members during the next 7 years.

Site Specifications

The facility consisted of four constructed lakes ranging from 8 to 12 acres, three 1-acre marshes, 325 acres of land for irrigation, and a pumping station to control the movement of water. Piping — 4.5 miles — connected the facility to the East Lansing wastewater treatment plant.

Movement of Water

The project involved pumping 500,000 gallons of partially treated wastewater per day through the pipeline. Effluent treated at the second level entered the first lake and moved through underground pipes to the succeeding lakes. The project goal was to provide a combined aquatic/earthly system to treat wastewater with maximum recovery, reuse of resources, and conservation of energy.[2]

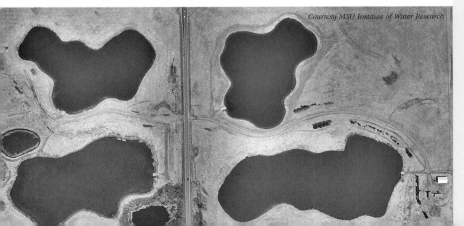

Aerial view of the research lakes. The inflow of wastewater continued until 1980. The site was converted into an inland lakes research and education study center for faculty members and students at the university.

Courtesy MSU Institute of Water Research

Lake System Research

Researchers learned much about the ecology, economics, and efficacy of this type of system. They collected and analyzed baseline data on water chemistry, sediments, animal and plant diversity, and production.

Other studies assessed nutrient concentration in plants, nutrient recycling, reduction of human pathogens, management of fish populations in lakes of this type, utilization of harvested plants as dietary supplements for livestock or aquaculture, and economic and energy evaluations of the system.

Summary of Findings

- The lakes were efficient at removing nitrogen from the wastewater, mainly through chemical transformations. They were less efficient at removing phosphorus, especially when the lake sediments became saturated with phosphorus.

- The lake-land system was efficient at stripping nitrogen and phosphorus from incoming wastewater. Response of the vegetation to irrigation water varied by plant type. Crops, grasses, and old-field plants were efficient at removing both phosphorus and nitrogen during the growing season.

Courtesy MSU Institute of Water Research

Joseph Ervin, Inland Lakes Research and Study Center manager, and Lois Wolfson, aquatic ecologist, measure dissolved oxygen in Lake Four.[3]

- In combination with lakes, excellent efficiencies were obtained for removal of both nutrients. Winter irrigation was proven to be feasible, but removing nutrients under winter conditions was primarily a function of sorption on soils.

- Researchers found that the marsh plants in three 1-acre marshes were very efficient at nutrient uptake, though too much nitrogen could actually cause a decrease in uptake rates in some wetland species.

The studies led to numerous scientific publications. The research provided state-of-the-art information on use of natural ecological systems for treating secondary effluent.[4]

Land-grant is Model for Sea Grant...

Partnering with U of M

Treasures in the Depths Bring Tourists

Michigan has 3,288 miles of Great Lakes shoreline and 11,000 inland lakes larger than 5 acres. It is truly a water wonderland, and Michiganians enjoy these widespread natural resources. Not all, though, think about the hazards associated with the lakes and whether anything can be done to reduce negative outcomes.

Sea Grant Program

Congress established the Sea Grant Program in 1969 at the University of Michigan to help the state take advantage of its Great Lakes opportunities and deal with its Great Lakes issues.

The program founders envisioned the Sea Grant Program to be the oceans and Great Lakes counterpart to the land-grant and funded the program to conduct research, education, and outreach as part of a national program.

In 1977, the Michigan program became a U of M-MSU partnership, with MSU assuming responsibility for the outreach aspects of the project and placing Sea Grant Extension agents in several coastal communities.

Reduce Drownings

Many Michigan residents and visitors spend time on, near, or under the water for their livelihoods and/or recreation — boating, skiing, fishing, swimming, snorkeling, and diving. Unfortunately, many drownings occur each year, and boating accidents result in numerous fatalities.

To prevent this tragic loss of lives, Sea Grant sponsored research on drowning accidents at the U of M College of Medicine in the 1970s. Martin J. Nemiroff discovered that people who drown in water 70 degrees F or cooler can survive much longer than the few minutes experts had previously thought.

Nemiroff developed techniques that benefit people who have been submerged for more than an hour. In Michigan's climate, many bodies of water, especially the largest, deepest lakes, seldom warm to more than 70 degrees F. Therefore, the potential for cold-water near-drowning accidents is great.[5]

Building Linkages

Sea Grant agents helped form the Michigan Underwater Preserves Council to facilitate communication among the widely scattered preserve communities. One of the promotional strategies of the council is reaching potential users through cooperative advertising.

Economic Effects

Campus researchers and Michigan Sea Grant agents have collaborated in conducting several studies to document the economic benefits of diving activities for coastal communities. One study documented that at least 6,000 divers visited the preserves during a 2-year period and spent an average of $250 per person. The study indicated an economic stimulus of at least $1.5 million for nearby small towns.

Advancing Diver Safety

Sea Grant sponsored diving safety research at the University of Michigan, and other universities provided guidance to preserve committees in developing vital diver education programs and coordinated dive accident management plans. Michigan Sea Grant's diving specialist also trained dive rescue personnel and emergency medical technicians in proper rescue techniques and emergency treatment procedures.

Model Goes International

These Michigan Sea Grant efforts have produced an internationally respected model for the management of underwater cultural resources and the stimulation of coastal economies. Several other Great Lakes states, Florida, and the nations of Belize and Malaysia have used the Michigan Sea Grant model in underwater preserve establishment, development, marketing, and safety.[6]

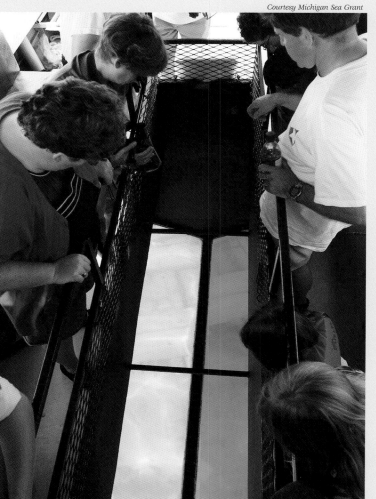

Courtesy Michigan Sea Grant

Great Lakes shipwreck sites attract tourists.

Underwater Preserves

Historical Remnants

Forty percent of Michigan territory — 38,575 square miles — lies within the Great Lakes. The lakes' cold fresh water preserves the remnants of prehistoric cultures and the many shipwrecks scattered on the bottom, all elements of maritime history.

These priceless artifacts attract thousands of recreational divers and many archeologists to the region.

Early Research

Sea Grant research at MSU in the 1970s demonstrated the archeological, recreational, and economic desirability of establishing preserves to protect these artifacts.

The preserves would stimulate recreational scuba-diving and associated tourist spending in coastal communities. These findings led to state designation of bottomland or underwater preserves.

A second task for Sea Grant agents was to assist coastal communities in proposing nine of the 11 designated preserves. The agents also helped with legislation to expand the area to be desig-nated as preserves and provided for placing additional historic vessels.

Thunder Bay Sanctuary

The U.S. Department of Commerce and Michigan in 2000 designated an area of Lake Huron including the Thunder Bay Underwater Preserve as the Great Lakes' first national marine sanctuary.

Michigan Sea Grant nominated the area as a sanctuary in the early 1980s and supported inventory work and educational initiatives in succeeding years.

Facilitating Searches

Sea Grant agents have helped communities secure financial resources for important projects such as buoying shipwrecks so they can be found easily and protected from damage.

Preserve communities have received assistance in using such research technologies as remotely operated vehicles and video mosaic imaging to search for undiscovered wrecks and to map and document them.[7]

Cold-water Near-drowning Revolution

Michigan Sea Grant Extension agents played a significant role in informing medical professionals about cold-water near-drowning by using a "train the trainer" approach. They conducted workshops for thousands of emergency medical technicians, nurses, and physicians, who learned the appropriate rescue protocol. Participants receive continuing education credits through the state health department.

Training Efforts

The training programs would lead to an international revolution in the treatment of cold-water near-drowning victims over the next 30 years. Many emergency medical professionals would change their approach to treating such accidents and succeed in reviving victims, citing Sea Grant as the provider of vital information. Cold-water near-drowning rescue techniques entered the mainstream of water rescue practices and are taught in medical schools and in emergency response training throughout this country and abroad.

Sea Grant Extension has helped the Coast Guard Auxiliary and other organizations conduct cold-water safety programs.

Courtesy Michigan Sea Grant

Drowning rescuer prepares for action.

Cold-water Safety Programs

Michigan Sea Grant publicized the problem and also published, promoted, and distributed materials for first responders at the scene of cold-water near-drownings. Many staff members and volunteers involved in the Great Lakes Education Program since 1991 have learned the basics of cold-water survival from Michigan Sea Grant Extension. Every year in Manistee County, fifth graders learn about cold-water near-drowning through a Sea Grant Extension presentation coordinated with 4-H events.

Lives Being Saved

The result of this classic Sea Grant effort in research and outreach? Thousands of lives have been saved.[8]

The 1970s saw many units in the CANR grow. The teaching program was vibrant. Research targeted social issues. Extension addressed a wide range of public needs.

Performance Central

The RD team did not worry about the lines between research, extension, and teaching – faculty members could be involved in each to make their contributions. Graduate students were involved in applied research with Extension colleagues as well as in research with faculty members who carried only teaching and research appointments. Together, faculty members planned to expand capabilities to meet the emerging public challenges of the 1970s.

New Capabilities Built

The department's environmental policy and law program was launched. "Natural resource management and development" was expanded. "Natural resource information systems" was established as a vital new capability.

The department's "community and leadership development" program was expand-ed. Faculty members provided vital land use programs throughout the state as well as conservation education for soil conservation districts, governmental officials, school children, and the public.

Reputation Grows

RD collaborated with other departments on a number of programs. The departments of RD and Forestry were national leaders in forest management modeling. The National Science Foundation funded several units including RD in a land use modeling program. In cooperation with the Institute for Community Development, faculty members helped organize and develop the Community Development Society of America. Faculty members led the formation of the International Association for Impact Assessment and participated in the National Academy of Science Committee on Environmental Quality Indices. One of RD's outstanding contributions was Professor Raleigh Barlowe's world-renowned book, *Land Resource Economics.*[9]

What is IPM?

In the early 1970s, MSU organized an Extension integrated pest management (IPM) fruit scouting program to help improve control practices and lessen grower expenses.

The core principles of IPM include:

- Identify the pest correctly.
- Monitor the population size.
- Know the pest's biology and seasonal development.
- Apply economic injury thresholds when necessary.

Apple Programs

An early objective was to teach college students, growers' children, or other "scouts" how to check orchards for insect, mite, and disease pests, and to give weekly reports to farm managers. These reports provided information for improved pest management and enabled growers to spray only when necessary. More than 200 growers benefited and paid the scouting costs of $10 per acre.

Expanded Program

As the program matured, it expanded to include all fruit trees, vegetables, field crops, and forests. The scouting program was reduced and supplemented with the Pest Management Field Assistant program (PMFA). Field assistants provided a more general educational pest management service to the entire industry. They prepared weekly 3-minute recorded telephone messages so growers could learn about current pest information, the weather forecast, and how best to affect pest development.

Benefits

This program reduced spraying costs (one grower reported over $2,000 in savings for apple maggot control alone). It improved the quality of harvested fruit and yielded immeasurable environmental benefits from reduced insecticide use.

Courtesy Larry G. Olsen collection

James Nugent examining asparagus fern.

An unexpected outcome of the program was the training and experience provided to scouts and PMFAs. Many of them now hold important positions in industry and at the university.[10]

> *"IPM is like one big cooperative. We're all working together with the farmer to help him be the best possible agricultural producer and steward of our natural resources."*
>
> Dale Mutch, Extension Program Leader for field crop IPM.

...Orchards and Fields

IPM—Improving Pest Management

Mite Control

Brian Croft discovered a way for growers to achieve biological control of mites. By modifying the insecticides used, a grower could preserve predatory (good) mites in his orchard. Then, by determining the ratio of good mites to bad mites per leaf, a model predicted how well biological control would work. Researchers discovered that 82 percent of the orchards had good mites present. Some 34 percent achieved biological control as good mites fed on bad ones. This program saved growers many expensive sprays and provided better and longer lasting mite control.

Plant Disease Forecasting

Alan Jones developed a disease reduction program to aid growers in controlling apple scab. The program was based on weather conditions and the developmental stage of the trees. In wet weather, spores are released and scab develops on the leaves and fruit.

This model indicated when a spray was needed on the basis of temperature and how long leaves remained wet. The prediction allowed growers to make timely applications when needed rather than spraying weekly as they had been doing.[11]

Armyworm War in Clinton County

Casual Encounter

It was a Friday afternoon in 1978 when Clinton County CES agent Mark Hansen found armyworms in a field near Westphalia. Hansen majored in entomology and worked as a student in the department and readily identified these insects. He told county Extension Director Jim Pelham, and they thought it was just a random pest outbreak. Little did they know that this first sighting of armyworm would be the start of a 3-week ordeal.

Armyworms Marching

By the next day, armyworms had destroyed an entire 5-acre field near St. Johns. Residents said they saw worms "marching across the lawn of the farmhouse." On Monday, Hansen alerted entomology specialist Robert Ruppel. The battle was on!

A Busy Time Recalled

"The secretaries were taking calls, filling out telephone slips with producer names and farm addresses. Jim and I would make a few visits and then return to the office to pick up more telephone slips. I was determined to get to every farm on my list. My final farm visit one day was about 10 p.m. near Elsie. It was dark when I pulled into the drive. The farmer was sitting on the front porch in his pajamas, waiting for me. He was surprised to see me still out making farm visits, but he grabbed his pants and we headed for the field."

5,000 Acres Treated

When the armyworm outbreak subsided, much of the corn crop and a few small-grain fields in the county had been affected. A telephone survey of aerial and surface pesticide applicators showed that when it was all over, more than 5,000 acres of cropland had been treated.[12]

Phillip Schwallier checks for mites. As a master's degree student, he was fulfilling a requirement of 6 months' field study with the horticulture agent.

Extension Responds to Energy Crunch

In 1977, Director Gordon Guyer appointed a CES Energy Task Force to address the growing concern among farmers about the 1973 oil embargo. Agricultural engineer William Stout, department chair 1970-75, chaired the panel. Other members were agent Paul Thompson, specialists Lee Schull and Alvin Rippen, and Agricultural Economics chairman Larry Connor. First on the agenda was building awareness. Many farmers were not convinced there really was an energy shortage.

Building Awareness

Stout and the energy specialists used a variety of media — meetings, radio and TV, publications, and exhibits — to get their message out.

"Conservation is the first and simplest step," Stout contended. "It's relatively easy to limit energy demands by increased efficiency and reduction of waste."

Energy awareness days were held in more than 30 counties. Energy considerations were fundamental to all agricultural practices, and energy became a main topic for conferences.[13]

Subsurface Resources in Spotlight

Extension and Oil and Gas Production

With a growing environmental movement and skyrocketing oil prices brought on by the Middle East oil embargo in 1973, questions arose about the role of the college in these areas. The chair of the Department of Resource Development, Ray Vlasin, employed Peter Kakela to develop programs in "mineral land development, energy requirements, and environmental impacts."

Reaching Out to Oil/Gas Issues

A *Wall Street Journal* report, "Gas Fever Hits Michigan," underscored the increasingly growing issue of oil and gas drilling to many lower Michigan landowners. Kakela responded to individual requests but quickly scheduled Extension meetings.

One early presentation to 200 landowners in Kalkaska County was especially memorable. Kakela's presentation emphasized environmental concerns associated with oil spills and gas leaks, and the legal risks of granting access to buried resources. He urged the audience to be cautious if a "landsman" offered to lease their mineral rights.

Learning on the Job

Feeling content with the cautionary message, Kakela called for questions. One rather burly landowner stood right up and said, "Now son, I'm wondering how I can get a-hold of one of those landsmen to offer me a lease on my land."

Turning on a dime, Kakela had to rethink the issues, including access and protections for eager landowners. One outcome was preparation of an Extension bulletin, "Oil and Gas Facts," written with graduate student William Patrick. Another outcome was the preparation of several longer Extension bulletins, "Oil and Gas Royalties" and "Look Before You Lease," which provided the core for subsequent programs.[14]

Courtesy Michigan Sea Grant

Modern Great Lakes ore transporting vessel.

Mining Research: Minerals No Longer Ignored

Mineral resources such as iron ore and copper were being mined and shipped to Detroit, Chicago, Cleveland, and Burns Harbor in the 1840s. Mining has been important to the state economy ever since. In 2000, major mineral and fuel resources contributed more than $2.9 billion to the state's economy.

Focus is Mine Resources

In the 1980s, Professor Peter Kakela's study began to include mining minerals as well as oil and gas drilling. Mining and drilling involve taking non-renewable resources, an act often labeled as not sustainable. However, consumers continue to drive cars and trucks made of steel, chrome, copper, and other minerals. They use barrels and barrels of oil. They drive on roads made of cement and steel reinforcing rods webbed over layers of gravel and crushed stone and so forth. These non-renewable resources bring us the life we enjoy.

Industry and Landowners Benefit

Many of Kakela's contributions have come through publications, a willingness to work closely with practitioners, and media interviewers. He gained national recognition as an expert on the iron ore industry and authored more than 125 publications on energy, mining, and other natural resource topics.

Is the college service to the mining industry valued by the industry? One executive wrote, "Many years ago Kakela pioneered a detailed cost analysis of mines, which came to be the universal measure for evaluating the performances of individual mines. His work was used in setting productivity goals, determining mine viability, and negotiating contracts.... He became the industry's outside expert."

Courtesy Peter Kakela collection

Early open-pit mining.

A key result is that the CANR units are seen as impartial aids to many in the state's mineral industries as well as to landowners who might be affected by local mineral production.[15]

Service Extended to Local Governments

Kellogg Foundation Support

The fledgling Extension state and local government program received a boost in 1971 by way of a grant from the W.K. Kellogg Foundation to the Center for Rural Manpower and Public Affairs. The grant provided resources to hire Extension's first district Extension agent in public policy.

Public Policy Agent

Thomas Martin, appointed to the public policy position, served a five-county area in southern Michigan. He became a well-known expert in federal revenue sharing and assisted local governments in securing federal funding. In 1974, Martin joined Governor William Milliken's staff.

Providing Technical Assistance

Lynn Harvey served as a field-based district agent from 1974 until 1979, when the position was changed to an "Extension specialist" and assigned to campus. Harvey developed the position to provide technical assistance to local governments in taxation and finance, intergovernmental contracting, administration, and property tax education.

Courtesy MSU Extension

Lynn R. Harvey, professor and local government specialist, delivers a presentation at a local government officials' conference.

In 1977, Harvey joined the county commissioner training team consisting of Alvin House, Kenneth VerBurg, and Eugene G. "Gil" Wanger, a lawyer affiliated with Ingham County government. Experience about problems and solutions were shared, enabling the team to develop a degree of reliability and expertise in presentations to new Michigan county commissioners. The new county commissioner program series has reached about 80 percent of the newly elected county commissioners each time it has been offered.[16]

Helping Small Communities Succeed

Small Towns Vulnerable

The recession of the early 1980s changed the complexion and economic stability of many Michigan communities. The changing land use and migration patterns took a toll on smaller communities — those that historically brought residents of rural Michigan together through commerce and education.

MSU Extension addressed these challenges by conducting educational programs for leaders of small towns. The USDA Fund for Rural America Project supported the program.

Hands-on Learning

A focus group of community leaders used a two-pronged approach: first, identify "best practice" communities that successfully addressed the challenges identified by the focus group; second, conduct site visits to allow community leaders to observe successful models.

What Others Learned

A program, "Small Town Success Strategies," was used to improve local economic and land use decision making and promote sustainable communities. Building the knowledge base and capacity of local leaders was key to the program.

Best Practice

The "workshop-on-the-move" to best-practice communities gave opportunity for participants to discuss local challenges and opportunities. Guests from the state Economic Development Corporation and MSU faculty members accompanied three regional trips to facilitate discussions before and after each local stop.

Statewide Initiative

Program leaders then conducted a statewide seminar, "Small Town Success Strategies," in cooperation with the Michigan Municipal League (MML).

Information gleaned from the best-practice communities was used to create a "Planning for Economic Development" module for the successful Citizen Planner education program.[17]

Expanded Programs

Beginning in 1978, unrest over property taxes generated numerous proposed amendments to the state constitution. The state and local government team sponsored educational programs, developed support materials, and traveled the state educating the public and local officials of the policy choices.

MSU Extension distributed its ballot issues bulletin in printed form. Elizabeth Moore, an Extension public policy specialist, provided the leadership for this bulletin. The analyses and programs offered educators increased Extension's visibility as the team utilized radio, television, and satellite downlinks to deliver educational information.

Public Services Collaboration

Increasing the efficiency in the delivery of community services became a focal point for Extension's state and local government program. It assisted communities in creating joint service production arrangements, special public service authorities, and new intergovernmental service arrangements.[18]

Extension Leadership in Communities

Roots of Michigan Ag Expo

The roots of Michigan Ag Expo started in the Thumb of Michigan, Tuscola County, in 1976. It took a lot of courage to establish something new and different, especially an event the size and scale of a farm show.

Volunteer Committee

The enthusiastic Tuscola County farmers had a vision and elected to move forward. Equally important was the support of agribusiness. More than 420 farmers and agribusiness people volunteered their time serving on 100 committees. They planned the event and made sure the work was carried out.

1976 and 1977

The first Expo, held on the Richard Donahue farm, attracted 115 exhibitors and more than 10,000 agriculture participants, even as rain ruined one of its two days. The following year, the committee coordinated the event on the John Homakie and Son farm. This time, 35,000 agiculturalists came from all sections of the United States. The exhibitors numbered 214.

For Farmers' Benefit

"Those two farmers — Donahue and Homakie — were never paid a dime," said Extension Director William L. Bortel. "They did get some corn and sugar beets harvested, but still they had people rambling through their fields and tramping them down, and they did it for the farming community without a thought about damages."

After no show was held in 1978, Bortel said Extension Director Gordon Guyer "recognized the demand from the agricultural industry for a farm show" and decided that MSU would pick up the pieces and host a show in 1979. Tuscola County would have liked to keep the show going, but it had outgrown the county setting. One individual county Extension office had no chance of carrying on an exhibition and doing the extension work. It was obvious that the show should be more centrally located and it should be linked to MSU.[19]

Blue Water bridge lighting. *Courtesy Mark F. Hansen*

Extension and Blue Water Bridge

Mark Hansen, county Extension director of St. Clair County in 1980, realized that the Blue Water Bridge between Port Huron, Michigan, and Sarnia, Ontario, and the continuous passing of ships were hidden from many Michigan residents. He decided to assess tourism needs for the area to see if Extension could assist.

Survey Area

He sent a survey to tourism-related agencies on both sides of the bridge and suggested a joint international tourism group to address tourism enhancement. From this emerged the Bluewater International Tourism Council (BITC).

The BITC generated an idea: to beautify the Blue Water Bridge with decorative lighting. Carol VanCamp, director of the downtown Port Huron business association, brought the idea to the group after seeing the lighted Ambassador Bridge.

Idea Takes Hold

Midstream in the project, the Port Huron-based tourism bureau was organized and the BITC dissolved. By this time, though, the Blue Water Bridge Authority and MDOT were leading and funding the effort to light the bridge. On October 1, 1988, the Blue Water Bridge received white lighting for the 50th year celebration of the bridge. In 1997, the southern span

(continued on next page)

Corn and Sugar Beet Exposition in Tuscola County, 1976.

Courtesy William Bortel

New Horizons Leadership Development

Communitywide

As an outgrowth of favorable reactions to the Kellogg Farmers Program, a New Horizons Leadership Development Program was started in 1969. It expanded the community leadership capacity of participants.

Extension conducted the New Horizons programs on a multicounty basis, with participants selected from the total community. Each group consisted of 30 to 40 individuals, both men and women.

Broad Experiences

Participants improved their understanding of the economic, political, and social framework of their communities, identified local issues, and advanced communication and problem-solving skills. Each group was scheduled over a three-year period. The sessions typically were held in the autumn and winter.

Groups traveled to view another community's accomplishments. For example, a U.P. group traveled to Detroit, a southern Michigan group visited the Traverse City area, and several groups visited Lansing to learn about Michigan's governmental processes.

Department Assisted

An Extension specialist from the departments of Agricultural Economics, Resource Development, or Forestry guided each group. The initial series of New Horizons programs included 63 county groups and one four-county group over the period 1969-75.

Positive Outcomes

Participants increased their knowledge of community affairs. Some pursued local elected office or other public positions. Their participation benefited schools, churches, and professional groups.[20]

Extension... *(continued from page 220)*

would be outfitted with blue lighting. The spirit of Extension's role in tourism and economic development lives on in the beauty of the Blue Water Bridge at twilight.[21]

Mackinac Island's Pesky Flies

Courtesy U.S. Environmental Protection Agency

Mackinac Island is a famous tourist attraction in Michigan. The island's turn-of-the-century atmosphere results from Victorian architecture and horse-filled streets. But this is not without drawbacks. The 500 to 600 horses used for transportation produce an enormous amount of manure. The manure, in turn, provided breeding sites for two nasty pests, the housefly *(Musca domestica)* and the biting stable fly *(Stomoxys calcitrans)*.

Houseflies were more than a nuisance to fudge shops. Outbreaks of dysentery were common on Mackinac Island, and public health officials and Extension entomologist Herman King discovered in 1945 the excessive housefly population was a contributing factor.

Reputation at Stake

The National Governors Association had scheduled its annual conference at the Grand Hotel for summer of 1945. About then, the insecticide DDT became available for experimental civilian use, and local health officers quickly chose to test it for fly control. It appeared to be very effective.

Resistant to Chemicals

By 1949, the fly population became resistant to DDT. Other similar chemicals were used until 1964, when MSU entomologists Gordon Guyer and Roger Hoopingarner showed fly populations had become resistant to them, too. Cygon (dimethoate) became the pesticide of choice until 1977.

Second Problem

A second serious pest problem that emerged in the late 1970s was the European fruit lecanium scale (LS).

This got Keith Kennedy, an ornamental entomologist, and Richard Merritt, a medical entomologist, from MSU involved. They wondered whether something on Mackinac Island reduced the LS's natural enemies?

They discovered that the LS-infested trees occured where Cygon spray was being used. It was eliminating the LS's natural enemies without affecting the LS itself. Without the natural controls, the LS increased to outbreak levels.

The island was also slowly losing its chemical war against flies.

IPM Program Works

In 1977, the Mackinac Island authorities invited Merritt and Kennedy to study the fly problem. Ultimately, they proposed an integrated pest management (IPM) program placing primary emphasis on sanitation, composting manure, poison panel traps, parasitoid releases, and localized spraying. It achieved a marked reduction.

At the end of the program in 1982, the Mackinac Island City Council passed a fly control ordinance and accepted Merritt and Kennedy's protocol on fly control. This protocol continues in use.[22]

Courtesy Richard Ledebuhr and Clarence M. Hansen

The NIAE in England designed the long tines and applied them to a machine built at MSU. The rods mounted on the toe pieces of the tines carried the plant and cluster cuttings into the machine for processing.

During the early 1970s, Clarence Hansen, Burton Cargill, and Richard Ledebuhr of the Agricultural Engineering Department continued pursuing their goal of mechanizing strawberry harvesting. Not having engineered a satisfactory harvester during the 1960s, they turned to a second avenue of strawberry research.

This second approach involved investigating ways to remove stems and caps from machine-harvested fruit. After concluding that no existing machinery could decap machine-harvested strawberries, they undertook new research.

They began by testing a promising prototypical decapping machine. It captured the strawberry stems between hundreds of pairs of counter-rotating rollers configured as a continuous belt. Fruits were sliced from their caps and stems and directed to further processing.

International Ties

The next phase of the project resulted in a cooperative effort among Smallfords of England, the National Institute of Agricultural Engineering of England (NIAE), Canners Machinery Ltd. of Canada, and MSU. The U.K. cooperators had extensive field experience with a prototypical harvester, while CANR researchers and Canadians had made significant progress in developing a machine for decapping strawberries. These mutual interests brought the technologies together as part of an overall systems approach to strawberry mechanization.

Gaining Efficiencies

This design accommodated both tractor and self-propelled chassis layout and increased the capacity of the machines significantly.

Another change included bulk handling of the fruit in pallet boxes. As the productivity of the machines improved, handling the product in small boxes was not efficient. Bulk box handling was less labor-intensive. Forklift equipment readily moved the product onto trucks headed for the processing plants.

Patents

From the first attempts to harvest strawberries by machine to the present, the research teams discovered many new developments and processes. Several patents were issued to MSU researchers for development of the equipment.

Later, several of the components developed for this research found their way into machine systems for other crops.

The processing market for strawberries was crushed by low-priced imports several years ago. It made the economics of growing strawberries for processing impossible. The processing strawberries that are produced in the United States are a byproduct of fresh picked production. Though the strawberry harvesters caused some damage to the fruit, this did not affect their use for processed products.[23]

Courtesy Ledebuhr and Hansen

The Ford Tractor Division provided tractors with special low speed transmissions for use in developing strawberry harvesters. As the reliability and capacity of the machines increased, engineers added material handling systems.

Courtesy Ledebuhr and Hansen

This machine operated at Robert Krieger Farms in Leelanau, Mich. This prototype was the most advanced design built at MSU and was widely used thereafter. The total redesign of the harvester head permitted the cutting mechanism to "float" on the ground and produced a much more precise cut of fruit and foliage.

Small Farms Benefit, Too

Boost for Small Farmers

The trend toward larger commercial farms was strong, but nearly three-fourths of all Michigan farms were small or part-time operations in 1976. CES Director Gordon Guyer named Ralph Hepp to head a 2-year program to assist such farm operators. The goals were to improve the efficiency of small units, increase production, and raise the standard of life for all residents.

From Small Farms ...

Guyer appointed a task force to work with Hepp — specialists Myron "Mike" Kelsey (Agricultural Economics), Milton Erdmann (Crop and Soil Sciences), Steven Baertsche (Animal Husbandry), and agricultural agents from counties with many small and part-time farmers.

...To Home Gardening

Other small-farm activities focused on migrant workers, residents of Indian reservations, and African Americans in areas such as Cass, Lake, and Muskegon counties. Agents also assisted with urban gardening projects spawned by Expanded Nutrition Program grants. Some counties employed program assistants to work with home gardeners. Across the state, volunteers gave many hours of gardening know-how.[24]

Enjoying Summers and Small-farm Living

In 1965, Gerald Huizenga married his college girlfriend and began his public school teaching career. In 1971, he bought a 12-acre muck farm. Farming would be his summer job.

MSUE Agents Assist

Along the way, county agents and the people at MSU told him how to take soil samples and order fertilizer. He learned about the importance of foliar fertilizing on his soil.

Weevils and Radishes

One year his radishes started normally but then stopped growing. He called the county agent who came out with an entomologist from MSU. He quickly identified the microscopic weevils burrowing into the radish bulbs. He told Huizenga this weevil could not fly well, and that he could grow radishes a few hundred feet away. The season was saved!

Growing Herbs

County agent Thomas A. Dudek also gave good advice on growing herbs. After trying several species, Huizenga began growing dill, which soon became a major crop.

A Way of Life

Here they raised their family and taught them and several hundred neighborhood children the value of work. Now the grandchildren come over for tractor rides to see the biggest pumpkin and help Grandpa plant his garden. They, too, can see the miracle of life as seeds turn into plants and well-tended plants produce food. The hope is that they, too, will come to know that farming is not only everyone's bread and butter, it is a wonderful way of life.[25]

Wharton to Take SUNY Post

In October 1977, President Wharton announced that he would accept the chancellorship of the State University of New York (SUNY), the largest centralized education system in the nation, with 365,000 students at 64 campuses.

"Announcing his decision at a press conference, Wharton said, 'The excitement and challenge of heading the higher education system of the nation's second largest state made the offer of the SUNY Board of Trustees most attractive.'"

Regrets Leaving MSU

"'That excitement is tempered, however, by the deep regret I will have in leaving MSU. The opportunity for the past eight years to serve this university, which I truly believe is one of the finest in the nation, if not the world, has meant a great deal to Mrs. Wharton and me.'

"'... The invitation from SUNY provides the opportunity to continue the support of educational excellence in a new setting.'

"Wharton said he would stay at MSU until the completion of the $17 million enrichment program, which has been a pet project of the Whartons since their arrival."[26]

Courtesy UAHC

President Wharton presents an American spruce to Governor William Milliken for planting on the Capitol lawn. James Hanover (R), professor of forestry, developed the spruce. Forestry Department chair Lee James is on the left.

Presidential Changes

Harden No Stranger to MSU

"MSU's new president — the 15th — while known for his business expertise is no stranger to education or MSU. Edgar L. Harden officially took over the MSU presidency from Clifton R. Wharton, Jr. on January 2, 1978. Harden had been an MSU faculty member from 1946 until 1955.

"The director of continuing education in 1950, Harden assisted in developing the Kellogg Center for Continuing Education. He held that post until 1955, when he entered private business."

President Edgar L. Harden.

NMU President

"After a year with a firm in Cleveland, he became the president of Northern Michigan University. While at NMU, the student enrollment rose 10-fold to about 8,000. He left NMU in 1967 to become president of the automotive firm Story, Inc., in East Lansing.

"... Harden began his career when he graduated from Iowa State Teachers College in 1930. He earned his master's degree at the University of Iowa in 1937 and his doctor of education degree at Wayne State University in 1951."

Michigan has been home for the Hardens since he was hired as principal of Battle Creek High School in 1945.[27]

MSU Set to Name Mackey President

"The stage has been set to name Cecil M. Mackey president of Michigan State University, the current president of Texas Tech University. Sources say that ... Mackey, 50, will be appointed at a special meeting of the MSU Board of Trustees on Thursday."

Lengthy Search

"This action would end the search that began in November 1977 when former President Wharton announced he was resigning his post at MSU to become chancellor of the State University of New York."

Experienced Candidate

"The search and selection committee says Mackey ... has been effective with the Texas legislature and the executive branch of Texas government. He went to Texas Tech at Lubbock in 1976 after five years as president of the University of South Florida in Tampa.

"He had been executive vice president ... at Florida State University from 1969 to 1971. Previously, he held positions with the U.S. Department of Commerce and in the U.S. Department of Transportation.

President Mackey and family.

"An Alabama native, Mackey received his B.A. from the University of Alabama in 1949 and a master's, law, and doctoral degrees from the University of Illinois. He also did postgraduate work at Harvard University.

"He taught economics at the University of Illinois and the U.S. Air Force Academy, and law at the University of Alabama."[28]

County, State and National Population

1980

	Number	Percent change, 1970-1980
Ingham County	275,520	5.5
Michigan	9,262,044	4.3
USA	226,542,199	11.4

U.S. Bureau of Census

A New Tradition is Born

Ag Expo Makes Way to Campus

Statewide Show

Ag Expo, first held on the MSU campus in 1979 on an experimental basis, soon became the major agricultural equipment show in Michigan. The Michigan Corn and Sugar Beet Exposition (1976) and the Michigan Farm Exposition (1977) made the transition to MSU in 1979 on a 35-acre exhibit area.

Ag Expo provides a focal point for agriculture in Michigan. People attend Ag Expo to learn of new developments in agricultural equipment and technology and the latest about the science and practice of farming. A partnership between MSU and Michigan's agricultural industry, Ag Expo provides farmers with educational opportunities not readily available elsewhere.

Numerous Displays

The central exhibit area is filled with more than 225 displays highlighting the latest technology in farm equipment, products, services, and supplies. In addition, Ag Expo has featured daily field demonstrations on subjects ranging from tillage to tile drainage to forage harvesting to manure application.

Learning Opportunity

Representatives from the various CANR departments are on hand in "Education Row" to answer questions about animal health care, farm security, beneficial effects of soil quality, water quality, gardening, farm business software, etc. Special features such as demonstrations on animal handling and displays of antique tractors and steam engines offer additional educational opportunities.

Sesquicentennial Special

Ag Expo 2005 included a special celebration of MSU's sesquicentennial anniversary and a ceremony marking the completion of the Natural Resources Conservation Service's soil survey of the entire state.

Ag Expo, originally organized and coordinated by the Agricultural Engineering Department, is now sponsored by the CANR, MAES, and MSUE.[29]

William Bickert, Ag Expo chairperson (L), and Barbara Brochu, Ag Expo coordinator, greet John Hannah, president emeritus, at the 1982 Agriculture Exposition.

Courtesy Department of Biosystems and Agricultural Engineering

Gast Named Director of AES

Dean James Anderson announced the appointment of Robert Gast to the directorship of the MSU Agricultural Experiment Station. He succeeded Sylvan Wittwer in the position.

"Gast will be leaving his position as chairperson of the Department of Agronomy at the University of Nebraska and assume the new position in April 1983. As Experiment Station director, he will administer research programs being conducted by 160 faculty members in 30 departments and eight colleges on campus, as well as the 13 field research stations throughout the state.

"James Anderson, CANR dean, said, 'Bob Gast is a person who has demonstrated his ability to conduct research, who understands the land-grant system and how it interacts with the federal government. He has the ability to relate to a wide range of audiences.'"

Background

"Gast earned his Ph.D. degree in soil chemistry from the University of Missouri. As a research associate at MSU during the 1968-69 academic year, he worked ... on a National Science Foundation project examining movement and retention of organic

Courtesy UAHC

New MAES director, Robert Gast.

materials in clay mineral surfaces.

"Prior to his work at U. of Nebraska, Gast was a soil science professor at the University of Minnesota and the University of Tennessee/ Atomic Energy commission agricultural research laboratory at Oak Ridge."

One of the Best

"Gast said the MAES is among the most respected in the U.S. and he considers his primary challenge as director to be demonstrating the contributions of AES research to boosting Michigan's economy. 'I see an opportunity for the Agricultural Experiment Station director to work with key leaders throughout the state to broaden the state's economic base,' Gast said."[30]

Hancock Turfgrass Center Dedicated

Courtesy MAES

Some 300 people attended the Robert W. Hancock Turfgrass Research Center dedication as President Cecil Mackey and Mrs. Hancock cut the ribbon. Vice President Jack Breslin holds the ribbon as David Diehl (R), Michigan Agricultural Commission chair, looks on.

Several things came together enabling the Turfgrass Research Center to open September 10, 1982. Jack W. Breslin, university vice president for administration and public affairs, said he had been working on the project since 1975. The center was located on a parcel between Farm Lane and Beaumont Road and south of Mt. Hope Road.

Industry and Research Interests Merge

Linking factors that made the facility possible were the research interest on the part of the college and the financial support of Michigan's turfgrass industry. The late Robert W. Hancock's gift of $160,000 initiated the industry's joining to fund the project. The cost of developing the 10-acre site was about $500,000.

"What we see here today is evidence of confidence in MSU research. This is the

bringing together of the researcher and the businessman for the benefit of the citizen," said Sylvan Wittwer, MAES director.

Ribbon Cutting

Joining the dedicatory ceremony were Mrs. Hancock and Cecil Mackey, MSU president. David Diehl, chairman of the Michigan Agricultural Commission, said at the ceremony that "all of agriculture should be looking at this as an example of what could be done and that most of Michigan agriculture had not taken a positive enough attitude toward what they can do to help universities help them."

Research Information to be Extended

"The goal is to get information from research conducted here to the community people," said turfgrass researcher Paul Rieke. "The expansion of our Extension education effort will occur primarily through county Extension staff members."[31]

Food Industry Institute to Aid Food Professors

"No groundbreaking or ribbon cutting ceremonies have been planned.

"The new Food Industry Institute is not a bricks and mortar establishment. Rather, it's an organizational structure ... with the mission of helping food processors and distributors enhance their efficiency."

Expand Food Industry

"The institute's designated director is Thayne Dutson, chairperson of the MSU Department of Food Science and Human Nutrition. He explained that the institute is part of a state government plan to expand Michigan's food processing industry.

"'The Food Industry Institute will be a sort of one-stop shopping center where any segment of the food industry can get assistance,' Dutson says. 'Providing this type of technical assistance will be an asset to the state in attracting new food companies to locate in Michigan.'"

Add Value to Ag

"The potential for economic development in the food sector is great. Farmers in the state produce $3 billion in food each year, but a third of it is sent out of the state for processing. Michigan food processors sell about $7 billion of goods annually, but most food consumed here is shipped into the state.

"MSU has a long history of assisting the food industry with product research and development feasibility studies and processing plant design. Campus researchers have expertise in food production, processing, packaging, marketing, and distribution as well as consumer nutrition."

Cooperative Funding

"The institute is being established for a 5-year period, with a program review scheduled after 3 years.

"A first-year operating budget of $70,000 will be funded by the MSU Agricultural Experiment Station, Cooperative Extension Service, and the Michigan departments of Agriculture and Commerce."[32]

...and Have Many Dimensions

IT and Animal Disease

Electronic Tracking

"A pioneering program developed at MSU called FAHRMX (Food Animal Health Resource Management System) is a computerized animal health management program being tested by a group of Michigan dairy farmers and veterinarians. FAHRMX maintains animal records and provides daily management information. It promises to be most useful in analyzing complex factors involved in raising healthy animals and putting a price tag on disease control.

"As FAHRMX director Ed Mather explains, the cost of drugs and veterinary care is only a small part of animal disease costs. Larger economic losses result when diseased animals become less productive...."

Animal Disease Costly

"John Judy, professor and associate dean of the College of Veterinary Medicine, says animal disease is a multi-million dollar problem in Michigan and a multibillion dollar problem in the U.S. Research conducted at MSU is helping to reduce the magnitude of animal disease problems."

Chicken Vaccine

"According to Sylvan Wittwer, MAES director, one of the most significant recent breakthroughs in animal disease control was a vaccine for Marek's disease by scientists at the USDA Regional Poultry Research Laboratory. It has greatly reduced poultry production costs for farmers."[33]

Dr. Jacob Hoefer answers a question by an animal sciences student.

Change Rain Schedule or Bean Plant

Dry beans grown in the early days of the Ferden Farm had a prostrate vine growth habit that made them susceptible to the "Saginaw County Fair Week" rains, which occurred after Labor Day as the beans ripened. The rain discolored the beans and lowered their quality and price.

New Bean Variety

During the 1960s, a bush-type bean was developed. It had short vines and improved harvesting – all beans were mechanically pulled and windrowed before harvesting. The bush beans, however, let some bean pods touch the ground, resulting in reduced quality and low price.

During the late 1970s at the Saginaw Valley Bean and Beet Research Farm, researchers introduced an upright short-vine dry bean plant that kept most of its beans off the ground. This bean has been introduced into most of the edible dry bean classes currently grown in Michigan.[34]

First Packaging School

James W. Goff, a long-term director of the School of Packaging, began working with wooden boxes in the military during World War II. It was not until he was at MSU working on a master's degree in forest products, while the packaging program was being formed here, did he realize he knew something about packaging. Goff was hired as the first teacher of packaging because of his knowledge of forest products.

Goff was Available

"In speaking of his job Goff said, 'They needed somebody to teach packaging. I was available, I needed a job. I was cheap enough so they could afford me, and I really did know something about it – even though I didn't know I did and I really didn't have any great aspirations for it.' In 1957, with the founding of the first school of packaging in the world, Goff helped change the main concept of packaging from merely a use for wood products to a functional service for consumers."

Sought-after Speaker

"As director of the first and leading school of packaging in the world, Goff is much in demand to give talks at packaging conferences worldwide. When speaking, he stresses that 'everyone is a package user; even the most primitive cultures in existence use packages.'"

James W. Goff, Packaging Professor Emeritus, and Diana Twede, Associate Professor of packaging, illustrate the importance of sound packaging.

Educate People

"In addition to speaking activities, Goff enthusiastically teaches and recruits new students into the packaging program at MSU and takes an active part in research done here. Goff's goal is to educate people to buy, sell, and use packaging materials and containers more effectively."[35]

Center for Remote Sensing

To generate data for land use analysis and planning, the departments of Resource Development and Urban Planning and Landscape Architecture collaborated to explore the use of remote sensing technology — first photographic information gathered from airplane fly-overs and, later, satellite imagery. With numerous research grants from NASA, the CANR and the College of Social Sciences established the Center for Remote Sensing (CRS). The CRS advanced applications of remote sensing in Michigan in four core areas:

Aerial Photography

The center staff analyzed low-altitude aerial photos for many projects, including a land use assessment of the Detroit riverfront, forest inventory, crop disease and stress, mosquito abatement, and Great Lakes shoreline bluff recession.

Satellite Imagery

Using the first microcomputer image analysis systems, CRS researchers processed data from NASA's first Landsat satellite. Jon Bartholic and Stuart Gage analyzed meteorological satellite data depicting surface temperatures and solar reflectance to determine temperature patterns for freeze forecasting. CRS, in partnership with the Environmental Research Institute of Michigan, merged Landsat satellite imagery, aerial photography, and map sources to improve the accuracy of land cover classification.

Land Cover and Forest Inventories

The CRS conducted the first of many land cover/use inventories in Michigan through photo interpretation of high-altitude aerial photography. Such maps were created for most of southern Michigan, and detailed forest inventory mapping of northern lower Michigan was done.

Computerized Applications

CRS staff members developed two of the first microcomputer-based geographic information system (GIS) programs: Steven Tillman's "Resource Analysis Program" for computer analysis of soils data, and William Enslin's "C-Map," were used to digitize soil survey maps and construct early digital parcel maps.[36]

Period in Review

Presidential Changes

Perhaps among the notable changes during the period were the shifts in university presidencies. The period began with Clifton R. Wharton, Jr., in the president's chair. In contrast to John Hannah's tenure of nearly three decades, Wharton's term of 8 years was brief. It set the pattern for the coming decades.

Like Wharton's predecessor (Walter Adams), Wharton's successor, Edgar L. Harden, would serve an interim one-year term. The MSU Board of Trustees then chose Cecil Mackey to take the post.

Other Leadership Changes

Lawrence L. Boger was the CANR dean at the beginning of the period but left the college to become provost of the university. Jacob Hoefer served as acting dean until James Anderson began his term in the position.

Other leadership changes involved the departure of Sylvan Wittwer, after an admirable career as MAES director. Robert Gast assumed the duties in 1982. Leadership in Extension was stable; Gordon E. Guyer, director since 1973, remained director until 1985.

Programs Established

The period was marked by programs addressing the changing conditions in the state. CANR departments responded — Turfgrass Center and the Center for Remote Sensing and Sea Grant were established, and Ag Expo came to campus. Leadership development and assistance to local government became priorities.

At the same time, the MAES and MSUE continued to address needs related to other social, economic, and technological changes. The land-grant mission was faithfully addressed during the period.

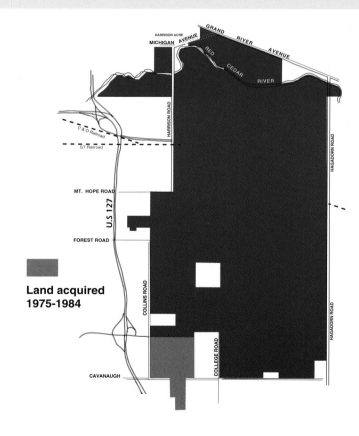

Land acquired 1975-1984

Courtesy KBS

"Here are a few [things] one can see: 68 varieties of geraniums, 98 varieties of petunias, 26 varieties of dianthus, 150 varieties of roses and more than 1,000 varieties of bedding plants. In the 4-H Children's Garden are 50 mini-gardens, including an Alice in Wonderland maze leading to a secret garden, a walk-in sundial, an amphitheater, a butterfly garden, an African-American garden, topiary bears and a pizza garden containing peppers, tomatoes, onions, basil, oregano and thyme."

Lansing State Journal, August 8, 1993

"Our students heard and saw things [in the Michigan 4-H China Project] they will remember for the rest of their lives."

Elementary school teacher, Calhoun County

"The Michigan 4-H China Project, a global education program, could actually have been conducted in China....This was a very direct experience."

Public school principal, Midland County

Challenges and Growth...

Chapter Overview

Presidential Changes

The 1985-94 period was a decade of exciting transitions for the university and the college. Presidential transitions again marked the period. John DiBiaggio assumed the leadership post vacated by Cecil Mackey. At the end of the period, DiBiaggio left and Gordon Guyer served in the post for one year until M. Peter McPherson was appointed president.

Facilities Modernized

The CANR also experienced a change in leadership as James Anderson stepped down from the dean's role and Fred Poston took over. The decade was a time of genuine growth in facilities and programs.

With support of the state legislature, the Animal Initiative transformed the Animal Science Department and modernized its facilities. A bit later, program development advanced with implementation of Project GREEEN.

Programs Grow and Advance

Other changes in the college involved "the second revolution" of biotechnology, and scientists at the Kellogg Biological Station advanced the development of sustainable agriculture. College programs, research, and Extension became more diverse and complex on the campus, throughout the state and nation, and indeed, the world.

New 'U' Chief Faces Immediate Challenges

Courtesy MAES

John DiBiaggio, MSU's 17th President.

"When MSU President John DiBiaggio took over the reins of power [July 1, 1985], he hit the ground running. The 52-year-old executive immediately faced two major issues that his predecessors tackled year in and year out – the university's more than $300 million budget and the possibility of a tuition increase."

Tuition Increase?

"Administrators and trustees ... have said any potential tuition increase will be based on the amount of funds the state legislature appropriates for MSU.

"Meanwhile, two student organizations, the Council of Graduate Students and Associated Students of MSU, have been actively campaigning against a tuition increase since spring term.

"Although university administrators refused to comment on the major issues DiBiaggio faces ... several professors active in MSU's academic governance system offered their opinions. The legislature has shown strong resistance to tuition increases, 'yet the university needs additional funds to make progress,' said Zolton Ferency, a criminal justice professor."

Faculty Relations

"Zolton Ferency said DiBiaggio 'has already put his finger on one of the challenges — improving the financial resources of the university.'

He said the new president also will have to improve his administration's relations with [the] MSU faculty."[1]

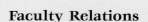

Courtesy UAHC

The Plant and Soil Sciences Building, 1986.

Addition to Campus Plant Science Complex

"The new Plant and Soil Sciences Building at Bogue Street and Wilson Road provides ... a first-class research facility to enhance MSU's role in agricultural research and education.

"After 10 years of planning and two years of construction, the $29.5 million structure was dedicated September 9 [1986] by Governor James Blanchard and MSU officials."

Teaching and Research

"The five-story building consolidates teaching and research from five locations into 6.5 acres of floor space. It improves communication and collaboration among professors in research and gives proximity to the Plant Biology Building, Pesticide Research Center, and the greenhouses.

"The teaching greenhouse complex is a state-of-the-art facility for plant production technology."

Competes Worldwide

"These first-class facilities will enable MSU to compete in agriculture with the rest of the world, said James Anderson, vice provost and dean of CANR.

"Citing the Michigan Farm Bureau's 1986 policy book, President Elton Smith said, 'Michigan is in direct competition with not only other states, [but] other countries. To be competitive, we must have up-to-date research.....'"[2]

...Initiatives and Actions

The Animal Initiative

A Mega-department

In 1980, James Anderson, dean of the CANR, formed the Department of Animal Science by merging the departments of Animal Husbandry, Dairy Science, and Poultry Science. He selected Ronald Nelson to chair the new department. Nelson retired in 1984 after an illustrious 35-year career. Maynard Hogberg succeeded Nelson.

Department Advisory Council

After a few years, Hogberg asked for nominations of industry leaders to serve on an advisory council for the department. The council, representing all facets of the animal industry, elected Larry Cotton, an Animal Science alumnus, as chair. Council members foresaw the need for new and updated animal science facilities and for new faculty and staff members in molecular biology.

Council discussions were instrumental in fostering the Animal Agriculture Initiative. A four-member committee of industry leaders met to discuss plans for a livestock exposition center and eventually evolved into a steering committee for the Animal Initiative.

Members were Jack Laurie, Michigan Farm Bureau; Tom Reed, Michigan Livestock Exchange; Elwood Kirkpatrick, Michigan Milk Producers Association; and Frank Merriman, Michigan Animal Breeders Cooperative. Much earlier, Ron Nelson and later, Jerry Haarer, director of land management, envisioned the possibility of a Michigan exposition center.

Legislature Approves $70 Million

In 1993-94, the Michigan Legislature passed the "Revitalization of Animal Agriculture in Michigan Initiative," which Governor John Engler signed. The Animal Initiative provided $70 million for new facilities, including an exposition center, and improvement of Anthony Hall and farm units. It also provided $4 million for programs and 12 new faculty positions in Animal Science. Work on facilities started in 1995.[3]

Computers Take Over

Converting communications operations to computer technology is history, and few give it much thought. People such as Maxine Ferris, director of MSUE Outreach Communications in the early 1990s, however, know the dilemmas she and others faced as the technology came alive.

"One thing I've concluded," Ferris said, "is that there are a lot of bells and whistles out there. The hardest thing to do is to make reasonable decisions about which to purchase. There are so many options and prices are coming down. You can't wait forever ... but you don't want to put yourself in a situation where equipment will quickly become obsolete...."[4]

Courtesy MAES

Maxine Ferris, MSUE Outreach Communications director.

Initiative Advances Meat Science

Changing Practices

During the 1980s, meat science at MSU operated in a meat laboratory behind industry standards. Changes in the industry included the development of boxed meat, rather than whole carcasses, merchandised at retail stores, and the variety of ready-to-eat foods available today. Poultry meat had expanded to become a significant portion of the consumer diet.

Cross-contamination from research laboratories to food produced in the MSU facility was also a potential problem. Similar observations applied to Anthony Hall, housing the Department of Animal Science.

New Leadership

The vision of Maynard Hogberg, Animal Science chairperson since 1984, included renovating the facilities of the department, now the elite animal science programs in the nation. The renovations plan included the meat laboratory and poultry meat facilities in Anthony Hall. The muscle foods handled in the meat laboratory included Great Lakes fish after MSU became part of the National Sea Grant College Program in the late 1970s.

The department benefited from the Animal Initiative bill approved and funded by the legislature. The $70 million appropriation included funding to raze the existing laboratory and build a state-of-the-art facility. The new facility is a USDA-inspected teaching, research, and outreach facility.

Planning Committee Goals

The vision of the planning group was to advance science and technology by integrating teaching, research, and Extension in the food and animal industry. The departments of Animal Science and Food Science and Human Nutrition manage the new facility.[5]

Kellogg Farm: Model R and D Site

Demonstration Farm

Cereal magnate W.K. Kellogg established and equipped a 600-acre model demonstration farm near his Gull Lake manor in the 1920s. He gave the farm to MSC in 1928, a gift celebrated in a public ceremony attended by 1,500 people.

Kellogg's gift came with one stipulation — whenever the Kellogg family was in residence at the Gull Lake home, they were to be supplied with farm-fresh eggs, chickens, and milk for the Manor House table.

For more than 50 years, Guernsey cows were queens of the Kellogg Farm. By the 1970s, the herd, under the supervision of MSU animal science professor Clinton Meadows, was recognized as a premier Guernsey herd. It played a major role in improving Michigan dairy production.

New Dairy Farm

During the 1970s, a new Kellogg Dairy Farm consisting of 1,100 acres and a new modern milking facility was established a mile north of the original farm. A Holstein herd replaced the Guernsey herd. In August 1985, more than 3,000 visitors attended an open house and dedication ceremony.

Goal: Sustainability

Since its early days, Kellogg dairy research focused on improving farming systems. In keeping with W.K. Kellogg's conservation ethic, the future of the Kellogg Dairy lies in the study of dairy farm management together with the ecological processes that control productivity and environmental sustainability.[6]

Courtesy Kellogg Biological Station

Portrait of W.K. Kellogg.

Courtesy KBS

Aerial view of Gull Lake.

Gull Lake — A Gem Restored

W.K. Kellogg's summer estate, built in the 1920s, overlooks Gull Lake, once one of the highest quality lakes in southwestern Michigan — a true gem! In the 1950s, the estate became part of the W.K. Kellogg Biological Station (KBS), a world-renowned center. In the 1960s and '70s, something started to go wrong with Gull Lake — nuisance aquatic plants were increasing and water clarity was diminishing.

Search for Cause

KBS scientists and graduate students found oxygen levels were decreasing because of high algae populations. Research indicated that the culprit was excess nutrients, especially phosphorus from septic system waste and lawn fertilization.

Restoration Campaign

A newly formed lake association began educating residents to the threats. Work of committed citizens backed by university research generated support for a new $12 million sewer system. Also many lakefront homeowners were persuaded to switch to zero-phosphorus fertilizer. After the sewer system became operational in 1984, water clarity improved.

Lessons Learned

The models created led to an expanding educational role for KBS faculty members and Extension specialists—helping people understand their role in protecting Michigan's lakes.[7]

Agricultural Research at KBS

Ecological, Sustainable

By the 1980s, KBS had established itself as a premier center for ecological research. A major grant from the W.K. Kellogg Foundation in 1982 established the Farming Systems Center (FSC).

Emphasis was placed on productive, profitable, resource-conserving, environmentally sound, and socially acceptable practices. An organic apple orchard planted in 1983 has been used to study integrated pest management techniques for horticultural operations.

The Nowlin Chair

Joseph Ritchie, first appointee to MSU's Homer Nowlin chair in water research, constructed the world's largest automatic rain control shelter at the FSC in 1984. The 60- by 250-foot shelter enabled the monitoring of crop growth under controlled moisture conditions. Studies examined various field crops and vegetables so researchers would understand the water needs of various plants and which ones could be grown under drought conditions.[8]

...Research and Demonstration Model

The Kellogg Manor House at KBS. *Courtesy KBS*

Endowed Chair Leads

MSU boasts a lot of firsts. One is MSU's Charles Stewart Mott distinguished professor of sustainable agriculture. This position was established through a gift from the C.S. Mott Foundation in 1989, with additional support from MSU, the MAES, and MSUE.

Harwood First

Richard Harwood was the first appointed to the C.S. Mott endowed chair. He completed degrees in vegetable production and plant breeding, conducted agricultural research, and taught.

Coming to MSU in 1991, he provided leadership for sustainable agriculture and coordinated publications to help farmers manage biological processes on their farms. He created a network to educate farmers, students, and the public about sustainable agriculture.

Achievements

According to J. Ian Gray, MSU vice president for research, "[Harwood] brought instant credibility to the concept of sustainable agriculture."[10]

Ecology for Farm Systems

NSF Research Grant

In 1988, the National Science Foundation (NSF) awarded MSU a grant to establish a Long Term Ecological Research (LTER) program at KBS to study ecological processes in field crop systems.

Sustainable Ag

Richard Harwood defined sustainable agriculture as an agricultural system that would sustain a farm economically and environmentally for generations based on principles of production ecology, using natural soil, plant, and climate systems.

Harwood organized a 7-acre research site at KBS — the Living Field Laboratory (LFL) — designed to measure the key interactions identified on the larger LTER plots. The program focused on building soil organic matter and managing nitrogen.

Publications Result

Since those beginnings, several landmark publications linking this ecosystem science to principles initially generated by LTER and LFL research were released. They all garnered national awards for outstanding content, design, and educational merit, and they became widely used in high school and college classrooms and in Extension and farmer training.[9]

Decisions on Small Farms

Family-Farm Interdependence

In the late 1970s, a group of faculty members proposed studying the interdependence of family life and farming decisions as they relate to sustainable agriculture, energy use, and family resource management.

Three-family Study

With W.K. Kellogg Foundation support, three families were selected to live on small farms (5, 20, and 50 acres) at KBS for three years and begin transition to sustainable farming practices in combination with off-farm work. The goal was to research interrelationships between farm and off-farm work and other environmental systems. Also researched were dynamics of family life as families adapted to a new community and practiced small-scale, sustainable farming.

The families benefited by realizing some of their aspirations and goals. Other farm families benefited from their demonstration of appropriate practices. The research community benefited from the findings and methods used in conducting human ecological research.[11]

Courtesy KBS

Aerial view of Kellogg Dairy at KBS.

New Sprayer Controls Pesticides

"Drifting clouds of pesticides can cause problems. A new sprayer developed by MSU agricultural engineers promises to reduce chemical drift when sprayed on crops."

Uses Air Curtain

"'The machinery is potentially of use anyplace farmers apply chemicals,' says Gary VanEe, who designed the air curtain sprayer with Richard Ledebuhr, a colleague in the Department of Agricultural Engineering. They have field tested the equipment during the past two seasons on orchard and row crops. Rotary atomizer nozzles on the fan units apply a solid curtain of chemicals sandwiched between two high-speed streams of air, traveling between 20 and 60 miles per hour, that keep the chemical on target."

Product Testing

"Ledebuhr and VanEe tested the sprayer's accuracy by placing targets inside plant canopies and measuring the amount of dissolved copper in spray applications that landed on the targets. Tests showed the air curtain sprayer consistently deposited up to twice as much copper throughout the plant canopy as did other sprayers.

"Precision application is the primary selling point for the new sprayer, according to Bill DeWitt Jr., owner of BEI, Inc. His South Haven company has been licensed by MSU to market the air curtain sprayers."[12]

Courtesy VanEe and Ledebuhr collection.

Above: the sprayer at work. Below: the sprayer stands ready for work.

"Michigan has the largest gypsy moth infestation in the country, and is the leading edge as the insect spreads west from the East Coast. Michigan also has the most extensive suppression program — between 250,000 and 300,000 acres were sprayed this year [1993].

"MAES entomologist Deb McCullough is currently researching long-term, large-scale defoliation of trees by the gypsy moth at eight sites in the Manistee National Forest. She is comparing sites with lower numbers of gypsy moths and sites with higher populations to study the diversity and abundance of native insects in defoliated areas."

State is Involved

"In heavily infested regions where local governments are involved in control efforts, *Bacillus thuringiensis* (B.t.) is sprayed in selected wooded residential areas or special-use forests under the MDA Cooperative Suppression Program. Because gypsy moths are most susceptible to this microbal insecticide when they are young, trees are sprayed around Memorial Day weekend, while caterpillars are tiny."[14]

Potato Roots Run Deep at MSU

In 1977, a young crop and soil sciences graduate, Dennis Greenman, was named manager of MCIA (Michigan Crop Improvement Association). When he left that position in 1995, MCIA's Seed Potato Division became an independent entity, the Michigan Seed Potato Association, now based in Gaylord. It is the official certifying agency for Michigan by the Michigan Department of Agriculture.

Industry Council

Despite the distance between Gaylord and East Lansing, ties with MSU remain strong. The Michigan Potato Industry Commission (MPIC) has strongly supported research to improve seed.

Research revealed that crop-damaging virus leaf roll was spread by green peach aphids. Complex control programs enabled growers to keep seed clean of scourges such as ring rot and early and late blight.

Deep Roots Endure

Those long intertwined threads of industry and land-grant institution form an additional cord. The MSPA vice president in 1920 was Melville B. McPherson of Lowell. The next year he was elected to M.A.C.'s governing body. In 1993, one of Hannah's successors began an 11-year tenure as president of MSU. He was M. Peter McPherson, Melville B. McPherson's grandson.[13]

IPM Program: Gypsy Moths

Michigan Pest from Mid-1950s

Though the gypsy moth was present in Michigan in 1954, it remained below detectable levels until the mid-1970s, when pockets of evidence of gypsy moth life stages were found, most notably between Mt. Pleasant and Big Rapids. By the mid-1980s, the northern half of lower Michigan was at risk of large-scale defoliation.

Call for IPM

A call went out for an integrated pest management (IPM) control program. Sought was a cost-effective way to minimize loss of timber resources and nuisance in populated areas, yet protect the environment and human health.

Michigan's land-grant institution was chosen to lead the cooperative effort. Gary Simmons, an MSU forest entomologist, worked with MSUE and state and federal agencies and scientists from other universities to develop an effective IPM plan.

In 1992, more than 700,000 acres were being defoliated. Two years later, that figure bottomed out at just over 3,200 acres.[15]

Entomology and Forensics?

Unless we are devotees of mystery novels, few of us would think to look to "bug experts" for critical evidence in a murder trial. However, crime investigators occasionally turn to entomologists at MSU to seek resolution of an investigation. It is just one more way that MSU faculty members have applied their knowledge to the real world. Two cases illustrate the application of this knowledge.[16]

Case No. One

Courtesy Richard Merritt collection

Suspicious Scene

In June 1989, two scuba divers exploring the waters of the Muskegon River discovered a car. The body of a woman was inside.

Police removed the car and traced it to the woman's husband. Medical examiners found contusions on the women's head that did not appear to result from the plunge into the river. The police thought the husband was lying about the circumstances.

Scientific Findings

Aquatic insects were attached to the windshield and fenders — police sent specimens to Richard Merritt in the MSU Department of Entomology for study.

The insects were identified, and the black fly larvae and cocoons provided a base for establishing the time between death and corpse discovery. From the insects it was determined that the car had gone into the river before June 1989, probably before January.

Sentenced to Life

In April 1990, an autopsy, insect data, and other evidence established that the man lied, his wife had disappeared the previous autumn, and the car had been in the river for nine months as Merritt testified. The man was convicted of murder and sentenced to life in prison, based in part on the life cycle of an aquatic insect.[17]

Case No. Two

Courtesy Richard Merritt collection

When Did She Die?

On July 5, 1997, turtle hunters in a small Michigan lake discovered a partially submerged body of a 19-year-old female. The discovery occurred three days before she was to testify against a man who allegedly sexually assaulted her.

Her eyes and mouth were duct-taped shut and the body weighted down with two cinder blocks. Because of the gaseous buildup of decomposition, the body rose to the surface.

Larval Observations

Police collected insect larvae from the exposed face and sent them to Richard Merritt for identification. Analysis of the fly larvae showed they were mature larvae of the black blowfly.

Diagnostics

Because of the temperature required for larval development of the largest specimens, the floating remains of the body would most likely have been exposed to colonization by this species on July 1 or 2. It was consistent with the estimated time the body had been submerged in the lake.

The suspect was found guilty of murder and sentenced to life in prison, in part because of testimony by an entomologist and a forensic pathologist about the time between death and corpse discovery.[18]

Biotechnology Recognized and Defined

The Second Revolution

"What exactly is biotechnology? A broad definition is 'the management of biological systems for the benefit of humanity.' Biotechnology came of age in late 19th century, with acceptance of genetic principles that led to agricultural practices now referred to as classical breeding."

W.J. Beal Leadership

"Botany professor W.J. Beal tested the idea that more productive crops could be produced by inbreeding promising corn varieties and then cross-breeding the offspring of two inbred varieties.

"Beal's field experiments in 1877 (part of the first biological revolution), were the first recognized attempts to produce high-yielding hybrid corn. Cross-breeding research has doubled crop productivity in the U.S. in the past 50 years, while cultivated acreage has decreased."

Another Revolution

"The second biological revolution was triggered by the discovery of the double helix structure of deoxyribonucleic acid — DNA — the stuff of which genes are made....

"Genetic engineering refers to the ability to transfer genes from one organism to another directly.... The methods of manipulating genetic material ... constitute the new biotechnology."[19]

Biotechnology Program Development

Strong Campus

"'This is one of the strong campuses in plant biology,' says Christopher Somerville, associate professor of botany and plant pathology. Recipient of a Presidential Young Investigator award [1984], he has been offered positions elsewhere but prefers to stay at MSU.

"What attracts capable, creative scientists to a campus? According to Robert Gast, the director of MAES, it's intellectual atmosphere, modern facilities, a financial commitment to research."

Strong State Support

"The university and state government commitment to the plant sciences is evident by:

- "The $30 million Plant and Soil Sciences Building.

- "A $7 million wing for the Department of Energy Plant Research Laboratory.

- "A $17.5 million building for the Michigan Biotechnology Institute.

- "A $300,000 state appropriation in 1984-85 for equipment and research."

Talent Attracted

"Michigan's commitment to biotechnology has not gone unnoticed by scientists looking for career opportunities ... said vice provost James Anderson.

"Jack Preiss, the new chairperson of the Biochemistry Department, left a similar position at the University of California at Davis. Eldor Paul is another recent California transplant. Paul took over MSU's Department of Crop and Soil Sciences in September."

Hannah Seeds Grow

"Hans Kende, new director of the MSU-DOE Plant Research Laboratory (PRL), credits former president John Hannah for convincing the federal government to establish the PRL on campus in 1965. He said,' A very large number of people have studied here and are now [1984] out in all corners of the world. The PRL's impact is enormous.'"[20]

Courtesy MAES

The Michigan Biotechnology Institute building in the University Corporate Research Park.

Michigan Biotechnology Institute

"Construction is underway [1985] for a $17.5 million Michigan Biotechnology Institute, a nonprofit research and business center located adjacent to MSU. Scheduled for completion by September 1986, the facility will house some 200 employees, including senior research scientists.

The MBI, established in 1981, conducts research aimed at developing new processes and products from the state's abundant agricultural crops and forest hardwoods. These renewable resources are expected to become the raw materials for biological factories of the future, which will turn out industrial chemicals, foods, fuels and structural materials."

Dow, WKKF, MEDC

"Grants from the Dow Foundation of Midland and the W.K. Kellogg Foundation contributed to the establishment of MBI research and development programs, along with funds from Michigan's Economic Development Corporation."[21]

Achievements Abound

Harpstead Receives Smuckler Award

"Dale Harpstead, professor of crop and soil sciences, recently received the first Ralph H. Smuckler Award for Leadership in Advancing International Studies and Programs at MSU.

"The award recognizes a sustained contribution to international programs on a university wide level."

Plant Breeding

"Harpstead's area of research is genetics and plant breeding, specifically of maize. From 1961 to 1969, he was a staff member of the Rockefeller Foundation and worked with researchers in Colombia, Venezuela, Ecuador, Peru, and Bolivia on maize breeding and improvement programs.

"From 1969-85, Harpstead served as chairperson of the MSU Department of Crop and Soil Sciences, where he lectured on world food production and nutritional well-being. He also conducted studies on food production and agriculture support systems in Central and South America and in six countries in eastern and southern Africa."

Courtesy Department of Crop and Soil Sciences

Dale D. Harpstead, Professor Emeritus, Department of Crop and Soil Sciences, and first recipient of the Ralph H. Smuckler Award.

USAID Assignment

In 1985, Harpstead joined USAID in Washington, D.C., assisting international program activities at more than 80 U.S. colleges and universities.[22]

Change in Deans

Anderson Shifts

"James H. Anderson, vice provost and dean of the CANR, will step down from this position at the end of summer.

"Anderson was appointed dean of CANR in 1977 and vice provost ... in 1984.

"Anderson has held numerous regional and national responsibilities, including chairperson of the legislative subcommittee of the Experiment Station Committee on Organization and Policy, and chairperson of the National Association of State University and Land Grant Colleges (NASULGC)."

Courtesy UAHC

James H. Anderson, dean, CANR, 1977-1991.

Poston to Fill Position

"Fred L. Poston, the director of the Cooperative Extension Service and associate dean of agriculture and home economics at Washington State University in Pullman, Washington, has been appointed to succeed Anderson as vice provost and dean of the CANR."[23]

Courtesy Office of Finance and Operations

Fred L. Poston, dean, CANR, 1991-1999.

Meat Science Facility Upgraded

The Animal Industry Initiative made possible state-of-the-art animal facilities to serve Michigan for the next 50 years. The funding enabled MSU meat science research and teaching to lead the nation in food science and nutrition practices.

Extensive Processing

The new meat lab contains areas dedicated to red meat and poultry slaughtering and processing, including curing, cooking, and equipment storage. The abattoir is designed to slaughter/dress all major red meat, poultry, and freshwater fish. It also contains refrigeration equipment.

Learning Facilities

The facility houses a sausage kitchen equipped with processing equipment, plus refrigerated curing rooms, smokehouses, and other pertinent cooking equipment. Two classrooms have full access to carcasses, meat cuts, and ready-to-eat foods from the pilot facility.

Three research laboratories are dedicated to advancing knowledge about meat chemistry, muscle growth, meat quality, and meat microbiology.

Students and Public

The new facility has been the site for national meetings, conventions, trade association meetings, industry training and USDA muscle food safety training.[24]

Courtesy MAES

Alden Booren at work in new meat lab.

Ecosystem Management:

Fisheries and Wildlife Department

Students can learn about the biology of fishes, reptiles, birds, and bears in the Department of Zoology, but the MSU Department of Fisheries and Wildlife is the place to learn about managing these animals, their habitats, and the human beings who interact with them.

Conservation Roots

The department began in 1950 as part of the College of Agriculture's new Conservation Division. Peter I. Tack, the first chairperson, led the department through its early development, offering popular undergraduate and graduate classes and field studies.

Niles Kevern became department chair in 1969 and presided over changes in the curriculum, centering it on a holistic, ecosystem approach, including emphasis on limnology. William W. Taylor succeeded him in 1992, creating new partnerships, developing new possibilities, including numerous international study and research efforts, and doubling the number of faculty members.

Program Partners

One of the department's most noteworthy partnerships is PERM (Partnership in Ecosystem Research and Management), developed in cooperation with the MDNR, the U.S. Geological Survey, the Great Lakes Fishery Commission, and the University of Michigan. The partnership enhances the talents of researchers and other stakeholders in identifying significant ecosystem problems in Michigan and conducting research toward their solution.

New Dimensions

The department developed new initiatives such as the MSU Center for Water Sciences and the Center for Systems Integration and Sustainability. New instructional programs included the graduate specialization in fish and wildlife disease ecology and conservation medicine and the cross-college undergraduate specialization in science, technology, environment and public policy (STEPP).[25]

Courtesy Robert Dykeman collection

Young angler proudly displays his GL catch.

The Great Lakes Fishery

Complex Web

From trophy-sized salmon to tiny native emerald shiners, the Great Lakes (GL) fishery is a web of more than 175 species of fish and other organisms.

GL Info Base

Research from the Michigan Sea Grant (MSG) program provides important information for GL fishery managers. MSG Extension provides technical assistance to sport anglers, charter fishing captains, and commercial fishing/fish processing enterprises. Anglers used more than 800,000 images of GL surface water temperatures from MSG's Coast Watch Web site, **coastwatch.msu.edu**.

Staff members such as Charles Pistis have helped achieve consensus on catch limits and stocking rates, and helped lake users avoid commercial trap nets permitted in some areas.

Health Risk Info

Research facilitated by MSG showed a definite correlation between the length and weight of chinook salmon and the concentration of PCBs in their tissues. Michigan state health officials now include this as the rationale for consuming younger, smaller fish in consumption advisories.

MSG Extension educator Ronald Kinnunen trained and technically assisted nearly 300 commercial fish processors in the federally mandated Hazard Analysis and Critical Control Points program to minimize health risks of fish consumers.

Education and Science

MSG led the GL Fishery Leadership Institute, a regional program where Michigan's future fishery leaders learn important concepts. Policy groups tap MSG expertise in their decision making. MSG leaders such as associate director William Taylor have served on the GL Fishery Commission and on MDNR task forces for lakes Michigan, Superior, and Erie.[26]

One of many recreational fishing boats on the Great Lakes.

Courtesy Michigan Sea Grant

More Than Fins, Fur, and Feathers

GEM: Groundwater Ed

A vision for safe groundwater developed into a statewide network of organizations and individuals committed to the Groundwater Education in Michigan (GEM) program.

Human Impacts

Established in 1987 by the Institute of Water Research (IWR) with funding from the W.K. Kellogg Foundation, the GEM program helped people understand the relationship between their actions and groundwater quality.

The "GEM Family"

The 50-some GEM grantees included local nature centers and health departments, regional watershed councils, and councils of government. Six universities served as GEM regional centers providing technical and program support. IWR encouraged networking among the GEM family and other organizations addressing water resource issues.

Diverse Approaches

The GEM program employed a traveling classroom to deliver education to urban schools, workshops to homeowners and small businesses, computerized maps to aid local officials with planning and zoning, and water testing programs to assist community wellhead protection.[27]

Stake in Groundwater Quality

"The realization that groundwater needs protection from pollutants emerged gradually.

'Anything below the [soil] surface has been a big, black box,' says Jon Bartholic, chairperson of the MSU Department of Resource Development and director of the Institute of Water Research (IWR)."

Ag Areas at Risk

"The conventional wisdom that soils can contain chemicals and break them down into harmless substances is being challenged by well tests indicating rising levels of nitrates, particularly in agricultural areas of the nation."

Local Responsibility

"'We don't know what different combinations of organic compounds do and what the breakdown products are,' Bartholic says. 'Groundwater is the major source of drinking water for about half of the U.S. population. Most rural residents rely on groundwater.'

"According to Bartholic, the leadership for groundwater protection and cleanup efforts will have to come from county and township governments. 'The federal government ... sets standards, but it delegates to the states most of the planning and enforcement functions. The state is developing its own

Courtesy MAES

Jon Bartholic, director, Institute of Water Research.

water protection plan, but groundwater protection is a localized problem that needs to be monitored at the county and township levels. Some areas are more vulnerable than others.'"[28]

Pigeon River Council and Professorial Counsel

The Pigeon River Country Advisory Council (PRAC) has the responsibility to advise the MDNR about natural resource management issues. The MDNR established the PRAC in 1974 to help oversee the Pigeon River resources of north central Michigan.

The Big Wild

The "Big Wild" is the only forest in Michigan's 3.8 million acres that has a policy, "The Concept of Management," adopted by the Natural Resources Commission. The advisory council helps the MDNR make management decisions for this special area.

Professor Appointed

The PRAC provided yet another opportunity for the CANR to contribute its expertise to Michigan's well-being. The MDNR director appointed Professor Larry Leefers of the MSU Department of Forestry in 1991 a member of the advisory council. He brought professional expertise in silviculture and forest cover management as well as an abiding appreciation for the natural resources of the Pigeon River Country.

Contributions

Leefers' accomplishments include his initiative in cataloging in electronic format the historical records of the advisory council from its inception. The council and others used this resource to access prior actions of the council.

Leefers often addressed forest management issues, and along with Professor Donald Dickmann, presented an educational program from which the members gained important insight. Leefers was a thoughtful advocate for the big wild character of the forest.[29]

Rural Manpower Center

Agricultural Economics' role in manpower use began in the 1960s with a rural manpower center led by Daniel Sturt. In the 1970s, with grants from the U.S. Labor Department and the Kellogg Foundation, the unit evolved into the Center for Rural Manpower and Public Affairs (CRMPA).

Migrant Labor Aided

The center provided education for migrant laborers and families, assisted growers with housing and human resources, and partnered with the state Migrant Interagency Committee.

New Capabilities

The center fostered a Rural Manpower Policy Research Consortium of national

authorities on labor and employment. James Shaffer, a CRMPA director during the 1970s, developed a program to improve diversity in Extension and expand leadership opportunities for women.

Courtesy Julian Samora Research Institute

Mexican farm workers tending Michigan tomato field.

Off-farm Employment Assistance

Access to government services such as employment and training assistance is an economic development component sometimes lacking in rural areas.

In the mid-1980s, the CANR developed a program to address these needs and to use the Extension Service for program delivery. The pro-

gram trained distressed farmers for off-farm jobs. Before a program could be put in place, farmers had to become legally eligible. Collete Moser, an agricultural economist and program coordinator, worked with the Michigan Department of Labor to expand the definition of employment and Title III disability to

Rich Memories

Over each lifetime, certain contacts suddenly change one's life direction, begin a new chapter, and sometimes a new life. Such were the Ritchie's initial contacts with Michigan State University. Harlan came with a phone call in 1957 inviting him, a graduating senior at Iowa State, to come to MSU for graduate study and teaching in the Department of Animal Science. Leah's came, also in 1957, with trips to 4-H events at MSU. From their initial contacts came a lifelong commitment to MSU and the environment they found.

Creative Environment

For them, MSU was the essence of relationship and place, weaving its way throughout their individual and collective lives. They found throughout their careers at MSU an environment that encouraged and rewarded creativity and an academic freedom to work on the cutting edge of their respective areas of expertise

include farm family members and workers on farms with a high debt-to-asset ratio.

About 1,000 people participated in the program, receiv-

Courtesy Leah Cox Ritchie

Leah Cox Ritchie and Harlan Ritchie

with colleagues who shared their enthusiasm for the university. And, more than at any other land-grant institution—they have worked with most—they found at MSU a desire for excellence in teaching, applied research, and Extension.

Stay the Course

Their hope for MSU is that it remain dedicated to its founding principles of providing a quality and affordable education to the sons and daughters of Michigan and make real, in application, the research of the university.[31]

ing a wide variety of assistance, primarily off-farm skills such as job search, job training, and placement.[30]

Get Skills First

Often careers take shape from a conversation between a counselor and counselee. The following is a brief account of how the career of Extension educator Ann Hinsdale-Knisel came about. This is also a story about a successful counselor.

Mentoring at Its Best

As she explored career opportunities, Hinsdale-Knisel met with Norman Bless, farm management agent in the MSUE southeast region in the early 1970s. Bless counseled her to get a teaching position before coming to MSUE because classroom management/lesson preparation would be invaluable to an Extension agent. She became a teacher at Dundee High School.

You're Ready!

Bless called her in 1976 and urged her to apply for an Extension home economist position in Lenawee County, where he was then CED. He hired her in September.

Building Skills

Hinsdale-Knisel's Extension position included supervising 15 Extension staff members. She had never supervised anyone before, but her mentor began a journey of men-

(Continued on page 241)

...Varied Audiences Benefited

Skills First...

(Continued from page 240)

toring by example and by explaining why he handled an issue in a particular way.

An Inclusive Mentor

Bless was a one-of-a-kind CED — he always looked for ways to involve his team in the office operation. Respecting others and honoring what each person could bring characterized his career. He left his mark!

Cherished Example

Norman Bless will always be a cherished role model/mentor to Hinsdale-Knisel and many others. They appreciate the value lessons he shared with people and the ethical human relations skills he always practiced.[32]

Professor Patricia Norris (standing) observes Citizen Planner class discussion.

Land Use Targets

Risk Survey

The state of Michigan completed a "Relative Risk Survey" in 1992. The study found the absence of land use planning that considers resources, the integrity of ecosystems, and the degradation of urban environments as being among the greatest threats to the state environment.

MSUE Tools Up

MSUE educators formed the Land Use Area of Expertise (AoE) Team in 1995. The team built its capacity, inventoried educational needs, and offered workshops to Extension educators for increased understanding of

Courtesy Land Use AoE Team

land use decision making. Mark Wyckoff, of the Planning and Zoning Center, helped participants understand Michigan's system.

Equipped with this knowledge, MSUE field educators were able to communicate with local officials about land use concerns.

Build Citizen Skills

In 1998, a team from northwestern Michigan joined with the Traverse City Area Chamber of Commerce, Rotary Charities, the Michigan Society of Planning, and MSU North to develop the Citizen Planner Program. Designed for local planning commissions, it provided technical knowledge and leadership skills. MSUE educators developed the curriculum and piloted the program.

Popular Response

By 2001, the Land Use AoE Team was taking the program statewide with financial assistance from the Kellogg Foundation's People and Land Program and the MSU provost, Lou Anna Simon. The Citizen Planner Program has reached nearly 2,100 planning officials and interested citizens in 76 of Michigan's counties.[33]

MSUE Aids Municipalities

ICD Joins the CANR

Several of the CANR programs for Michigan local government were initiated in the Institute for Community Development (ICD). In the 1990s, the ICD programs and services became part of departments in the College of Agriculture and Natural Resources and Extension.

Municipal Clerks Certification

In 1972, Duane Gibson and Robert C. Anderson, of the ICD, helped the newly organized Municipal Clerks Association establish the Michigan Municipal Clerks Institute (MMCI). Conducting a weeklong workshop twice annually, it provided the educational basis for certifying municipal clerks.

Publications

The ICD also published and distributed publications for local governments. Among those that have gone into the third and fourth editions are *Guide to Michigan County Government, Managing the Modern Michigan Township,* and *Laws Related to Planning.*

Local Government AoE

The Local Government Area of Expertise Team conducted surveys and studies for communities around the state. One of the most significant applications of this expertise was applied to five U.P. communities that engaged the services of Lynn Harvey in the late 1990s to assist in the consolidation of three municipalities into a new city in Iron County.

Iron River Area Consolidation

Extension specialists, working in conjunction with community leaders, provided the economic analyses, technical assistance, and education of voters. The effort ultimately led to voters in three of the five municipalities voting in 1999 to form a new city (Iron River). Consolidation of local units has been highly unusual, and the U.P. merger stands as a benchmark in the history of Michigan.[34]

Pursuing Food Safety

"J. Ian Gray [associate director, MAES] has been studying ways to improve food quality and safety — e.g., using natural ingredients — e.g., vitamin E, paprika, tea, rosemary, and sage. These antioxidants slow the spoilage rate in foods.

"'HAAs [heterocyclic aromatic amines] are formed from fried meat because of the creatine content in muscle foods,' Gray explained. 'Most of these compounds are in the charred, dark part on the edges of the meat.

"By manipulating time and temperature combinations, cooks can stop HAAs from forming. Most researchers recommend microwaving hamburgers before frying them and not charring the meat."[35]

What Motivates Customer Shopping?

"How safe do customers think their food is now? How much safety do they want? How much are they willing to pay for it?"

Agricultural economists Eileen VanRavenswaay and John Hoehn are developing a survey using a method called "contingent valuation" to determine what tradeoffs consumers are willing to accept. To address these questions, she said, "We're putting customers through a scenario and having them make choices along the way."

The work may inform agricultural producers on how best to grow and market their crops.[37]

Soybean Tests at KBS

"MAES research on soybean production has a new wrinkle. It is being conducted at KBS on no-till plots. Crop scientist James Kells has a study of three soybean varieties planted in different row spacings on different dates to see how these variables affect maturity dates, height, lodging, yield, and pest problems.

"A smaller, related study involves three varieties planted at the same time in three row spacings under no-till and conventional tillage. 'With no-till you don't cultivate to control weeds so your options are limited to herbicides,' Kells says. 'If farmers can't control the weeds with herbicides, they need to rethink the no-till approach.'"[38]

Keep Wearing the Bean Crown

Michigan is the country's No. 1 producer of cranberry beans, black turtle beans, navy beans, and small white beans, adding more than $110 million to the state economy. Michigan beans are available worldwide and are especially popular in the United Kingdom.

"'Much of the research we do at Saginaw Valley is on variety development and cultural practices,' said Donald Christenson, faculty research coordinator at the station.

"Conducting research at the field station, in an experimental setting, removes growers from having to worry about reduced yield or a higher rate of pest infestations. However, researchers conduct some of their experiments on private farms."[39]

Lifetime of Chestnut Concerns

Earnest Rogers of Jackson grew up in northeast Pennsylvania when the chestnut trees were being hit hard by blight. His concern about chestnut trees in Jackson County in 1990 led to his donating 116 acres to MSU.

Dennis Fulbright, professor of botany and plant pathology, said, "What we will be doing is planting chestnut trees on the land, breeding them, and selecting those resistant to the blight."[36]

Courtesy MAES

Dean Fred Poston, former MSU President Gordon Guyer, and Governor John Engler share a laugh during the 1993 Ag Expo breakfast. Governor Engler used the occasion to announce his plan to award MSU support for the Animal Agriculture Initiative.[41]

MSU, Japanese Collaborate

The United States and Japan approved a contract for collaborative research in 1988. MSU and the Research Development Corporation of Japan formed a $15 million research project with National Science Foundation support.

"The research project focused on the evolution of microbes and their ability to degrade toxic chemicals that persist in the environment — e.g., PCBs and petroleum compounds.

"Scientists anticipate that given sufficient time, microbes that can degrade many environmentally damaging synthetic compounds will evolve."[40]

Exploring Plastic Recycling

What happens to the 650 million pounds of plastic milk jugs discarded each year?

"Some is recycled, but most is buried in landfills ..." says MSU packaging engineer Susan Selke. She is involved in a research program to identify uses for recycled polyethylene and ways to encourage recycling.

"The research ... is funded by the Plastics Recycling Foundation."

Market/Supply Issue

"Researchers face the dilemma that potential users of recycled polyethylene lack a dependable supply. In contrast, suppliers of recycled jugs lack a market. The researchers' goal is to provide the information that will break the deadlock."42

What is a Farm Manager?

"As agribusiness becomes more sophisticated, there is a growing need for individuals who can balance farming, research, and communication abilities.

"'Farm managers facilitate the scientific work being done at the experiment field stations," said Gerald Haarer. 'They perform the production functions that support the field research.'

"'The farm managers play a vital role,' said Maynard Hogberg, chairperson of the Department of Animal Science. 'They have to understand the production system, and we rely on them to carry out the research protocol and methodology. They understand what we are trying to accomplish, and their cooperation is excellent.'"43

Courtesy MAES

Signing the agreement for the Partnership for Ecosystem Research and Management (PERM), May 1993. Front row (l-r) CANR Dean Fred Poston; Mike Moore (deputy director, DNR); Bill Taylor (chair, Department of Fisheries and Wildlife). Back row (l-r) Rick Clark (acting research program manager); John Robertson (chief of DNR Fisheries Division); George Burgoyn (chief, DNR Wildlife Division).

Managing Fish Stocks

In the mid-1980s, Donald Garling (Fisheries and Wildlife Department) worked on changing two fish: salmon and bluegills. He sought to produce sterile fish to achieve similar results but for different reasons.

"With the salmon," Garling said, "our objective was to extend the life of the fish. After they spawn, they die. We want them to grow into bigger fish. With bluegills, we wanted to create sterile fish because this species is very prolific. They overpopulate and stunt their growth for lack of sufficient food for all of them."

The technique employed involved manipulating the maternal chromosomes.44

Trevor Nichols Complex Expands

The Trevor Nichols research site in Fennville was expanded through the purchase of 48 adjacent acres in 1992.

"'It was formerly a commercial orchard, so it already has established acres where we can let bugs eat fruit, which is what we do at Trevor Nichols,' said James Johnson, faculty coordinator.

'Some renovation will be needed, but most of the trees are bearing now, and there is a lot of orchard that is still producing. We'll use it to keep growing bigger and better bugs.'"45

Spartan Ornamental Network

"Is it a dream — accessing a network chock-full of information ... anytime of the day or night?

"Thanks to MSU's Spartan Ornamental Network (SON), 'a greenhouse grower who lives in suburban Detroit ... could quickly find information on insects that attack pansies, and at 2 a.m., if he or she so desired.'

"Sandra Allen, SON manager, said, 'Our subscribers range from greenhouse growers, garden centers, and large and small retailers to ornamental landscapers and vocational technical schools.... Subscribers can get information ranging from growing perennials and choosing ornamental landscape plans to ... treating various plant diseases....'"46

Premier Turfgrass Program Elements

"What does it take to have one of the premier turfgrass management programs in the world?"

MAES turfgrass researcher Paul Rieke's list included the following:

"One: a full staff of researchers and a full curriculum. 'Turfgrass students at MSU have a slate of courses.... The two-year program is a strong technical program. The four-year program includes more science — chemistry, biochemistry, genetics.'

"Two: know the industry's needs. 'We would never be where we are without support of the Michigan Turfgrass Foundation. Their leadership is extremely valuable.'

"Three: know a prime market when you see one."47

The Institute of International Agriculture

The Institute of International Agriculture (IIA) was organized in 1964 under the leadership of Kirk Lawton. It was established to give administrative focus and support to international activities formerly dispersed among the CANR departments. IIA enhanced the ability of the college to provide expanded foreign opportunities for faculty and support personnel.

Varied Agenda

The IIA supports the preparation of proposals for off-campus partnerships with other universities, private sector organizations, and independent individuals; and participation with national organizations representing land-grant and other faculty resources, the USAID, the World Bank, regional development banks, and foundations. Special links with "sister institutions" in Japan, China, Latvia, Nepal, and elsewhere are sustained in the IIA to maintain opportunities for exchange of students and faculty members in both directions.

Other College Links

The IIA reaches beyond the CANR to work with students and faculty members in other colleges. MSUE has strong ties to the IIA, and many Extension staff members have made significant international contributions, ranging from long-term overseas assignments to arranging host families for visiting scholars and international interns. Other MSU colleges participate in joint activities with the IIA.

Midwest Consortium

The institute director (first, Irving Wyeth, then Donald Isleib, Russell Freed, and Daniel Clay) has been a board member of the Midwest Universities Consortium for International Activities (MUCIA). For many years, the IIA has managed important MUCIA projects in which CANR faculty members participated.

USAID Partner

The IIA has been a major factor in sustaining MSU's reputation as the most involved of all the land-grant university participants in rural and agricultural development with USAID.[48]

Michigan Farm Bureau study tour participants at the Great Wall of China.

Courtesy Weijun Zhao

Building China Relations

In the early 1990s, the Institute of International Agriculture (IIA) created the China Rural Development Training Program. The program resulted from the recognition of the need and the opportunity to provide short-term training for Chinese scientists, administrators, and managers in agriculture and rural development.

Understanding U.S.

The program goal is to enable Chinese to gain a better understanding of agricultural education, research, extension, and production systems in the United States under its market-driven economy. The program, highly successful and popular, has had more than 1,500 Chinese participants.

Understanding China

Starting in 1994, the IIA organized study tours of food systems in China. More than 200 MSU faculty members, Extension staff members, and agricultural leaders from Michigan and other states participated in the study tours. Participants gained insights into the growing importance of China to worldwide food production and consumption.

MSU-China Agreement

In March 2003, MSU signed an agreement with four Chinese universities to launch a joint education program on turfgrass management. This agreement provides a pioneering effort in turfgrass education with a foreign country.[49]

International Extension

Twenty-five years and counting! MSUE's commitment to international programming has a quarter of a century of experience. It is continuing to pursue what is best for the world and engaging others in that mission.

Sharing MSUE

Beginning in 1979 with a Title XII proposal to USAID, MSUE began the now widely recognized International Extension Training Program. Over the years, that in-depth professional development experience provided 191 Extension staff members with insights into world development and globalization.

The program provided crucial international exposure through the field training component held for two weeks in a developing country such as the Dominican Republic, Jamaica, Costa Rica, Mexico, Ukraine, India, Thailand, or Bolivia. The program also brought hands-on work experience to more than 100 staff members through post-training externships and assignments abroad.

(Continued on page 245)

...Internationally in Many Ways

Bean/Cowpea Research

The Bean/Cowpea Collaborative Research Program (B/C CRSP) has a multiphase, international mission involving research, institution building, agricultural production, and betterment of human living. The USAID provides funding for the program administered by MSU.

Regional Coordination

Bilateral research projects during the first grant (1980-86) focused on problems of subsistence farmers in their settings. In 1997, the structure was modified to achieve more regional coordination. Currently, the B/C CRSP has regional projects in Latin America, the Caribbean basin, and western, eastern, and southern Africa.

Courtesy B/C CRSP Program

Irvin Widders (director Bean/Cowpea CRSP) and colleagues meet with Bean/Cowpea collaborators in Africa.

Global Plan

MSU's involvement in the B/C CRSP began in 1978. The board of International Agriculture Development (IAD) authorized a new project to address global needs of the bean and cowpea subsectors, and the awarding of a planning grant by USAID. Wayne Adams and Pat Barnes-McConnell, MSU departments of Crop and Soil Sciences and Resource Development, respectively, and Donald Wallace, of Cornell University, identified subsector research constraints, drafted a global plan for the new B/C CRSP, and presented it to the USAID in 1980.

Stable Leadership

Donald Isleib served as director for two years. Barnes-McConnell provided program leadership from 1982 until 2000, when Irvin Widders, Department of Horticulture, took the reins. Russell Freed and Mywish Maredia have served as deputy directors.

As a leading state in dry bean production, MSU provided scientific leadership to the program. It engaged numerous MSU faculty members.[51]

MSUE's International... (Continued from page 244)

Big Payoff at Home

The program has enriched the knowledge and commitment of MSUE staff members to cultural diversity and increased their comfort with international guests. It improved competence with clients about international issues and made MSUE more proactive for international engagement.

Key Effects

Key effects of the international efforts include:

- National leadership within the Extension community.
- Respect for and collaboration with peers.
- Resources and experiences to help MSUE educate partners about international issues.[50]

Introducing Michigan Youth to Chinese Culture

4-H China Project

The Michigan 4-H China Project is a global education program using the arts and social studies for in- and after-school learning. The project focuses on kindergartners through sixth graders but also serves seventh through 12th graders. Since the project began in 1988, more than 300,000 youth from Michigan's counties have been involved.

Folk, Classical Dances

Nine programs resulted from the Michigan 4-H China Project. Most notable is the Chengdu Music and Dance Theatre from Sichuan Province. The troupe of 10 danced their way into the hearts of over 23,000 youth and 4,000 adults, using native folk and classical dances.

Speaking Through Art

A second element of the project is the Children's Art Exchange. Since May 1991, thousands of Michigan children have created artwork or "visual letters" about their lives to share with children their ages in China. Often, they expressed the desire to bring China and the United States together.

A Youth in China

From early 1992, Zhou Hualiang (Warren Joel), a MSU 4-H China Studies graduate assistant from Hangzhou, worked with 5- to 14-year-old Michigan youths in classrooms, assemblies, and other settings. The program, "A Child's Life in China," spoke directly to children about what it is like to be 5, 8, or 13 in China. He presented more than 700 sessions and to more than 35,000 children.

Paint with Treasures

During April and May 1993, Yu-Ping Yung, a Chinese-American raised in Taiwan, taught nearly 5,000 Michigan children the basics of Chinese traditional brush painting. These children painted with the "four treasures" — rice paper, bamboo brushes, ink stick, and ink stone.

Lifetime Experience

The Michigan 4-H China Project is unique among 4-H programs in the United States It is based on the belief that a significant and positive global and cultural experience can last a child's lifetime.[52]

Enhancing an Enjoyable Environment

PRR Department Formation

Early Curriculum

The MSU Board of Trustees approved an academic program in recreation and youth leadership in 1937 within the Department of Health, Physical Education and Recreation (HPER) in the College of Education.

New Organization

The Department of Park and Recreation Resources (PRR), approved by the Board of Trustees in 1969, began in the Forestry and Resource Development departments 20 years earlier. Louis Twardzik chaired the new department.

In 1981, the HPER recreation unit merged into the Department of Park and Recreation Resources. James Bristor, coordinator of the recreation unit, and Twardzik, chair of the new unit, believed the merger was appropriate for students, faculty members, the university, and the profession.

Benefits Abound

Combining these two programs brought cooperation and support from departmental stakeholders and enabled students to acquire broader competencies and a variety of research opportunities.[53]

Contemporary Horticulture Gardens

Carlson and Taylor Lead

Will Carlson, professor of Horticulture, and Jane Taylor, of the 4-H Foundation, began planning and raising funds for a new horticulture garden in 1987. With the help of Naomi Revzin (MSU Development Fund), they raised almost $3 million by the dedication ceremony in August 1993.

Beginning in 1992

Johnson, Johnson, and Roy, an Ann Arbor landscape architectural firm, designed the Horticulture Gardens on

Courtesy Mary L. Andrews

The peacock, made of flowering plants covering a metal frame, greets visitors on their arrival.

Courtesy Mary L. Andrews

Perennial flowers add color to the MSU Horticultural Gardens.

Michigan Tourism Center

The Michigan economy was experiencing difficulties in the early 1980s. A stakeholder forum recommended that MSU create a center to support economic development. State Senator Connie Binsfield led the effort to fund a center, and the Board of Trustees established the Michigan Travel, Tourism, and Recreation Resource Center (MTTRRC) in 1985.

It served as an information clearinghouse for the industry, conducted research, and partnered with the MSUE Tourism AoE Team.

Tourist travel in Michigan doubled.

"We believe that our research and Extension programs have contributed substantially to the growth of Michigan's tourism industry over the past 20 years," notes center director Donald Holecek.[54]

a 5-acre parcel adjacent to the new Plant and Soil Sciences Building.

Planting the gardens began in May 1992. The gardens consist of a large, informal perennial garden, a more formal annual garden that also functions as an All-America Selections Trial Garden, and the 4-H Children's Garden.

Donors Remembered

Some components were dedicated to individuals, including the Judith A. DeLapa Perennial Garden containing flowering perennials and ornamental grasses; the

Florence and Amien Carter Annual Trial Garden, a showcase for more than 1,000 varieties of the best bedding plants; the Franks Nursery and Crafts Rose Garden; and the Idea Garden for new gardening concepts.

Distinctive Visuals

A double row of classical columns and an overhead trellis highlight the entryway. A statue of Liberty Hyde Bailey, Jr., the "dean of American horticulture," stands in the annual trial garden.[55]

Generating Research and Extension

Project GREEEN

Plant Initiative

Funding was insufficient for problem-solving research on plants in the late 1980s and early '90s. The college began working on a plant initiative paralleling the previously funded Animal Initiative.

Project GREEEN

Generating Research and Extension to meet Economic and Environmental Needs, or GREEEN, was designed in 1994 to generate new research and Extension efforts to address challenges facing Michigan growers, commodity groups, and processors. It was a cooperative effort among plant-based commodity groups and busi-nesses to advance Michigan's economy through plant-based agriculture. The mission was to develop research and educational programs, ensure and improve food safety, and protect and preserve environmental quality.

Program Goals

The main program goals are:

- Reduce dependence on chemicals.
- Encourage value-added products such as wine from grapes and juice concentrates from cherries.
- Provide rapid responses to concerns such as plum pox, rose chafer, and European chafer.

A center for integrated plant systems was to be created, with plant diagnostics and IPM as components. Also proposed was an automated weather information system, and college positions in vegetables, fruit, floriculture, woody ornamentals, turf, and field crops with support from commodity groups and processor organizations.

Dean Fred Poston, MAES Director Ian Gray, the Michigan Farm Bureau, and Phillip Korson of the Cherry Marketing Institute, with support from major commodity groups, persuaded the legislature to approve the project, providing $500,000 in 1996 to be increased to $6.5 million over a few years.[56]

Growers go to Europe

What and How?

In the 1980s, Gale Arent, Extension greenhouse agent in southwestern Michigan, became aware of innovative greenhouse practices in Denmark. He also noted that operators in the Netherlands were innovators in greenhouse management. He thought Michigan growers should explore and consider adopting the technology to maintain Michigan's national leadership in floriculture production.

Study Tour Planned

This led to arranging industry study tours in 1988 and 1992. Upon their return, growers adopted innovations such as computerized environmental controls, thermal blankets, high intensity lighting, and rolling plant benches. Such changes reduced labor costs.

Michigan Applications

Timothy Stiles, then manager of a growers cooperative, established the Masterpiece Flower Marketing Company patterned after product distribution systems used in Denmark.

New Methods

Stiles said this enabled the rapid loading of multiple orders for delivery. Growers are able to fine-tune their growing procedures and produce higher quality floriculture products. He is grateful to MSUE for providing this learning experience.[58]

DiBiaggio Departs

"The day he announced his resignation as president of the nation's largest land-grant university, John DiBiaggio lectured to a graduate-level class about MSU's important agricultural-based heritage.

"Six hours earlier, it was announced DiBiaggio would resign effective August 1 to take the helm at Tufts University — a 7,500-student, private liberal-arts college...."

Land-grant to Tufts

"'I feel as if I could bring the land-grant philosophy to a private school,' DiBiaggio said after the 40-minute talk with an educational administration class. But as he walked swiftly through Wells Hall to his car, DiBiaggio denied he was leaving MSU because of controversy the last two years with head football coach George Perles.

"DiBiaggio, 59, said he had to jump at the chance to head Tufts — despite many claims that MSU needs stable direction. 'There'll never be a good time to leave,' he said. 'There'll be problems after I leave.'

"DiBiaggio was approved unanimously by the college's board where he will become the 11th president."[57]

Courtesy Kenneth VerBurg

In the mid-1990s, the Horticulture Department constructed plastic greenhouses at its site on South College Road.

Presidential Changes

Guyer Postpones Retirement

"Gordon Guyer put his retirement on hold to become MSU's interim president. Although he is happy to return to MSU, he said he wants the job for no more than one year. But that does not mean he doesn't want to get down to business.

"In a July 26 interview, after a month at his new job, Guyer used the word 'aggressive' repeatedly to describe his approach to the role of president. He said he is committed to bringing 'significant progress' to the university."

Making Contacts

"Guyer had already met with 800 residence hall staff personnel, with faculty leaders, and college deans. He also had been on the phone almost constantly with various university personnel.

"He was decidedly enthusiastic about breakfast with residence hall students, meeting with potential sponsors for the Sept. 22 presidential debate, and fielding phone calls about the semester switch.

"Guyer had not yet received any complaints, but he said he knew they would eventually come. Even so, he stressed the benefits students receive from the transition, including increased competitiveness in the summer job market.

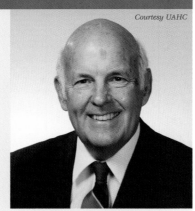

Courtesy UAHC

Gordon Guyer, Interim President.

"'There will be wrinkles to iron out as the transition proceeds,' Guyer said, but he is turning all problems into opportunities. 'I'm going to reestablish my roots with the legislature immediately.'

"He said it is a privilege to fill the shoes of John DiBiaggio, who officially stepped down early this week [at the end of August 1992]."[59]

McPherson's Ready for Day One in Office

"Gordon's gone hunting and the myriad of demands of MSU's varied campus are now falling on the new president, M. Peter McPherson. As Gordon Guyer left the office for the last time, McPherson continued the education he has been receiving since he set up shop a few weeks ago in a room across the hall from Guyer's office.

"Marcellette Williams, executive assistant to the president(s), said McPherson is working overtime. 'He's clearly earnest in all of this....'"

Key Topics

"'Finances, diversity, and faculty rights are hot topics that will demand McPherson's immediate attention. One vital issue is simply making the university affordable to the people who want to attend,' Financial Aids director Tom Scarlett said."

Multiculturalism

"'The debate over multiculturalism and diversity is also at the forefront as McPherson takes office,' said Lee June, assistant provost for student academic support services and racial, ethnic and multicultural issues. June said, 'I'm optimistic he will deal with it.'"

Teaching and Research

"'The relationship between research and teaching also is an important component of an institution like MSU,' said Natural Science Dean Frank Hoppensteadt. 'The creation of knowledge gives people something to teach,' Hoppensteadt said. 'Research has immediate relevancy to undergraduate education.'"

Courtesy UAHC

President M. Peter McPherson scooping ice cream at campus event.

Student Opinions

"Another student leader expressed confidence. 'I'm impressed with his qualifications,' ASMSU Chief of Staff Stacey Flanagan said. 'He knows bureaucracy and can deal with it, which is probably pretty important.'"[60]

Period in Review

The 14th decade of the college, in addition to being a time of transition, was also a time of maturation. Many of the programs became more complex and advanced. The Animal Initiative and Project GREEEN gave several college programs new platforms for advancing the sciences and expanding their knowledge.

The growing sophistication of the sciences had significant implications for on-campus instruction as well as the off-campus Extension programs.

The ongoing transition of farming to larger farms and fewer farmers called for more technology and biotechnology and counseling for those leaving the agricultural business.

The changes also raised demands for the college to assist local and county governments guide the changing uses of land. In addition, the CANR's reaching out to nations around the world was but one more mark of the maturing international institution.

The acorn planted in 1855 was growing into a giant oak.

Courtesy Anne Ottoway

"*Traditionally, coffee has been Rwanda's largest export crop. With the global decline in coffee prices and the economic effects of the genocide, however, growers had little incentive to grow coffee. Together with its partners, PEARL identified the potential for Rwanda to enter the 'specialty coffee' market that would pay higher prices to growers.*"

Courtesy Institute of
International Agriculture

"*As never before, advances in agricultural science and technology present opportunities to make major gains in overcoming constraints to improving human nutrition, alleviating poverty, increasing agriculture production and promoting sustainable use of natural resources.*"

Courtesy
MSU Bean/Cowpea CRSP

Chapter Overview

The activities of the college have been broadening over the decades, and this chapter gives some perspective on the great diversity of service and its impacts.

International Focus

The interest of the college and university in international programming has been expanding vigorously. This chapter describes the ways the college has been working to improve the lives of people across the seas while improving our own understanding.

Community Interests

Other CANR programs target the improvement of Michigan communities. Programs relating to land use planning and management, to improved development, community economic development, and natural resource management have enriched the meaning of teaching, research, and service. New beneficial collaborations were forged with stakeholders throughout the state.

Periods of Stress

Stress has not been uncommon during the preceding periods. The 15th decade did not escape such experiences either. A series of state budget challenges threatened the future of MSUE and MAES. Fortunately, the efforts to communicate the significance of the programs to people on the farms and in the suburbs and central cities were successful.

A second event occurred just hours prior to the close of the 20th century. The widely discussed Y2K problem was not the concern. Rather it was the work of a terrorist group that ignited the offices of the Institute of International Agriculture in Agriculture Hall.

New Leaders

The period also experienced changes in college leadership. Dean Fred Poston left to become the vice president for university finance. Jeffrey D. Armstrong was recruited to become the new dean. At the close of the period, President M. Peter McPherson left to take up new duties in Washington. Lou Anna K. Simon became the first woman president of the university.

PEARL—Part of "Global Grant"

Agriculture Partners in Rwanda

MSU's Institute of International Agriculture (IIA) began the PEARL Project — Partnership for Enhancing Agriculture in Rwanda through Linkages — in 2000. Daniel Clay, IIA director, and Emile Rwanasirabo, rector of the National University of Rwanda, initiated the USAID project.

Coffee beans being sorted.

Courtesy Anne Ottaway

Rebuilding Communities

The purpose was to assist Rwandan agricultural institutions and communities in working together after the war and genocide of 1994.

Traditionally, coffee has been Rwanda's largest export crop. With the global decline in coffee prices and the economic effects of the genocide, however, growers had little incentive to grow coffee.

Courtesy Anne Ottaway

Rwanda's first specialty coffee washing station built in 2001 by the Maraba growers' cooperative and PEARL.

PEARL identified the potential for Rwanda to enter the specialty coffee market, which would pay higher prices to growers.

In 2001, PEARL began working with a growers' cooperative of 250 members. After three years, nine others organized across Rwanda.

Specialty Coffee

By 2005, Clay said the price had risen from 46 cents to about $1.50, which is a big deal for people who earn $1 a day. "What we're looking at, is completely transforming the coffee industry in Rwanda."

"On campus, Sparty's Convenience Stores will soon be selling the Rwandan coffee, manager Joe Garza said. Sparty's has been selling fair trade coffee since last spring. 'Fair trade guarantees family farmers receive a fair price and ensures they have food and their kids can go to school.'"[1]

...Becomes Worldwide

Idea Born in Africa Becomes Global

One evening near the Victoria Falls in Zimbabwe, an animated discussion took place on food and nutrition issues in southern Africa. The discussants included academicians from Africa and Europe, plus U.S. food producers and processors, and officials of government and international agencies. The vision and the ideas were global.

IFLR Seeded and Born

The World Trade Organization (WTO) was established in 1995; the Internet was in its infancy. The factors of education and global participation led to discussions of the need for universities to provide up-to-date information on food regulations of countries around the world.

Vincent Hegarty came home confident that MSU could address this need. The informal discussions in Africa became reality in Michigan when the Institute for Food Laws and Regulations (IFLR) was created under Hegarty's long-term leadership.

MSU supported the examination of issues in food and agriculture and became the leader in world food regulatory education. In 2003, the IFLR was given an award for distance education.

From Farm to Fork

Governments establish food regulations. The food industry must implement the regulations. Consumers are affected by the successes and failures of governments and industry to protect the safety of our food. IFLR food regulatory distance education courses help producers meet food standards by having lead instructors and guest lecturers from many parts of the world.[2]

The Seti River Program in Nepal

Needs in Nepal

In 1999, Extension specialist Murari Suvedi, assisted by MSU Study Abroad students, surveyed teachers in the Kaski district of Nepal, in the foothills of the Himalayas. The surveyors concluded that educational programs could alert students to their changing environment.

Suvedi contacted Patrick Livingston, the Macomb County MSUE 4-H agent and former Peace Corps volunteer in Nepal. He had recently implemented a water quality monitoring program for schools in Macomb County that became the model for Nepal.

Planting a Few Seeds

In January 2000, Livingston, Suvedi, and MSU students went to Nepal to train a district education officer and four teachers to implement the program at two schools. Livingston returned to Nepal a year later to organize his first-year teachers into a training team. They trained 11 additional teachers at five schools.

Lessons at Home

Livingston returned to work with local teachers involved in monitoring Clinton River and Lake St. Clair waters. He linked those teachers with teachers in the Kaski schools. They began sharing information about their watershed experiences. Livingston hosted the Kaski education officer at two Macomb schools to observe students' monitoring of the Clinton River.

In October 2003, Livingston and Suvedi led a Fulbright-Hays Group Project Abroad for 14 Michigan school teachers to Nepal to meet with teachers from the Nepalese schools. It strengthened the information sharing among schools in the two countries and also resulted in a study guide, *Nepal: The Rivers, Environments and Cultures.*[3]

Courtesy Jay A. Rodman

Nepali students and Michigan educators at river shore.

Broadening in Scope...

Internationalizing Extension

Courtesy Mary L. Andrews

Mary L. Andrews receives the Ralph H. Smuckler International Award from John K. Hudzik, Dean of International Studies and Programs.

The following brief accounts illustrate MSUE's notable international involvements.

Poland, Russia, Ukraine

Philip A. Seitz, an agriculture specialist, worked in Poland (1991-92) to establish an agricultural extension service; in St. Petersburg, Russia (1994-96) supporting privatized farms; and in the Ukraine (1996-98) with a USDA team to support newly privatized Ukrainian farms.

"Save the Children"

Larry Stebbins, county Extension horticultural agent, was the first agent assigned to the "Save the Children"

program to backstop its food-production and home gardening initiatives.

China

The Michigan 4-H Program coordinated a children's art exchange with Sichuan Province, China, and managed an integrated social studies enrichment program for Michigan elementary schools, "A Child's Life in China."

Ireland

MSUE collaborated with the extension services of Northern Ireland and the Republic of Ireland to host a series of rural development exchanges as a student internship program for Bailey scholars.

India

MSUE provided in-depth assistance to the National Agricultural Technology Project in India during the late 1990s to help bring a participatory approach to extension work. Assisted by the World Bank, Mary Andrews, Arlen Leholm, Murari Suvedi, and Raymond Vlasin provided training workshops and training materials, and participated in leadership forums.[4]

Pursuing Food-based Solutions

Young girl at the roadside market near bean/cowpea experimental area.

Courtesy IIA

MSU played a key role in establishing the Beans for Health Alliance (BHA), promoting sustainable food-based solutions to world health problems. MSU's Bean/Cowpea Collaborative Research Program (B/C CRSP) helps manage the health research program.

USAID-funded Project

The BHA has more than 45 members including major companies and American universities partnering in the B/C CRSP effort.

Targeted Diseases

Malnutrition is widespread in the developing world, and chronic diseases such as type 2 diabetes, nutrition-related cancers, and heart disease are global health concerns. The HIV/AIDS pandemic is also a

major problem. The BHA believes that beans, cowpeas, and chickpeas — nutrient-dense foods high in protein — can improve health and alleviate child malnutrition.

BHA Strategic Goals

- Educate about the health benefits of eating beans.

- Generate scientific knowledge regarding bean consumption and chronic disease prevention.

- Advance recognition of the role that beans play in diets.

One project deals with HIV/AIDS and involves scientists Maurice Bennink and Lorraine Weatherspoon of Food Science and Human Nutrition plus scientists in Tanzania and Botswana.[5]

Daily World Contact

Distance Ed Course

MSU's Mary Anne Verleger talks daily to people around the world. She is the manager for the distance education courses in international food law. She interacts with lead instructors and guest lecturers in 30 countries. Many are lawyers, retired government officials, and faculty members in overseas universities. Her work is one result of the "idea born in Africa."

International Food Regs

Participants come from 80 countries. All information is delivered through the Internet. Courses include an overview course entitled "International Food Laws," courses on food laws and regulations of the U.S., the E.U., Canada, and Latin America, and courses by the World Animal Health Organization and the International Plant Protection Convention. MSU courses literally cover the regulatory world, all from the East Lansing campus.

Verleger coordinates all these contacts from her computer in a small office on the campus.[6]

...and Enhancing People's Lives

Building Human Resources Worldwide

Terrorists Firebomb Agriculture Hall

MSU's history of building international human resources by sharing knowledge and experience with the global community goes back many years. The Institute of International Agriculture (IIA) in the CANR is the coordinating unit for international agricultural development activities.

Training Programs

The IIA assists countries in building their human and institutional capacity. One of IIA's strengths is its ability to design programs tailored to international agricultural and rural development needs. It employs several innovative approaches in short-term capacity building: short courses, individual training, workshops, symposia, internships, and seminars on campus and in international settings.

Human Development

During the past 10 years, IIA has designed annual training programs in integrated pest management, intellectual property rights, and technology transfer, food safety, biosafety, and agricultural biotechnology — all cutting-edge areas of international development. More than 500 participants, representing every region of the world, have attended these courses. Many participants, upon returning home, developed similar programs to build capacity in their countries and regions.

Mutual Benefit

The programs greatly help the global community gain new knowledge and upgrade research, policy, networking, extension, and management skills. The programs also build new linkages for the CANR in bringing new knowledge and ideas to benefit Michigan and U.S. agriculture.[7]

Courtesy Russell D. Freed.

The E.L.F.-initiated fire left the Institute of International Agriculture offices in chaos.

Fire illuminated the sky above Ag Hall on New Year's Eve, December 31, 1999. Fortunately, the fire was discovered before Ag Hall was destroyed. Finding accelerants at the scene, investigators identified arson as the cause of the fire that caused over $500,000 in damage.

International Ag is Target

The fire started in the third floor offices of the Institute of International Agriculture (IIA) that housed the USAID Agricultural Biotechnology Support Project (ABSP). Smoke and water caused damage on all floors. Paper files in the ABSP offices were destroyed. The computers incurred extensive heat and water damage, but the hard drive data were recovered.

E.L.F. Claims Credit

Three weeks later, the Earth Liberation Front (E.L.F.) claimed responsibility. The communiqué sent to Fox News by the E.L.F. read:

"On the eve of the new millennium, the E.L.F. struck back at one of the many threats to the natural world as we know it. On December 31, 1999, at approximately 9:00 p.m., the E.L.F. entered the Agricultural Hall at MSU in Lansing, Michigan. Our destination was the room 324 offices. The project being conducted through this office is funded by Monsanto and USAID ... designed to pursue research concerning genetically engineered sweet potatoes, corn, and other crop vegetables.... Local newspapers have put the damage done to the building at $400,000, with documents and equipment totally destroyed."

Courtesy Russell D. Freed.

The fire was intense and destructive.

Perpetrators Sought

The IIA and ABSP staff members moved to Olds Hall for several months. The FBI, the U.S. Bureau of Alcohol, Tobacco and Firearms, and the MSU police investigated the case but never found the individuals who started the fire.[8]

Treasuring the Water Resource

The Great Lakes Education Program

The Great Lakes surround most of Michigan. Actions and decisions of today will affect this ecosystem for generations. To educate young people about natural resources, Michigan Sea Grant Extension agent Steve Stewart and Macomb County agents Terry Gibb and Patrick Livingston developed the Great Lakes Education Program (GLEP), with natural resources agent Gary Williams joining the crew as the program expanded to the Detroit River.

Linked to Public Schooling

The GLEP supplements Michigan's fourth grade introduction to the Great Lakes as an important part of the students' environment and as a significant element in the state's history and culture. The GLEP curriculum's themes are land, water, life, and people.

A GLEP highlight is cruising on the Clinton River-Lake St. Clair or the Detroit River. Measuring water temperature and collecting and analyzing benthic (bottom) samples help teach scientific concepts and processes. Charting a navigational course encourages collaboration while students learn about hydrology and geography.

Before and after the cruise, teachers use lessons from the GLEP Educators Handbook to help their students meet the science, mathematics, social studies, and English benchmarks of the Michigan curriculum framework. Each class receives a video of its activities for classroom use.

50,000 Participants by 2004

The GLEP began with 151 Macomb County students in 1991. As of 2004, more than 50,000 Macomb and Wayne county students and accompanying adults had participated. Selected middle school and college classes, youth organizations, and adult groups also have experienced the GLEP. Sea Grant-sponsored research has shown that GLEP students significantly increase their knowledge of Great Lakes resources.[9]

A Strait Story

American Heritage River Initiative

Strictly speaking, the Detroit River is not a river — it is a strait, a 32-mile channel connecting lakes St. Clair and Erie. That fact did not stop Michigan Sea Grant leaders from nominating the waterway as an American Heritage River (AHR). They seized the opportunity to accomplish a dream — the river's renaissance.

The AHR program began in 1997 to assist riverfront communities to coordinate the search for funding for environmental protection, economic revitalization, and historic/cultural preservation. A 1998 presidential executive order designated the river one of 14 AHRs.

A diverse group of stakeholders seeking to enhance their strongest connection — the river — submitted the application. Officials sought federal funds to enhance their cities and townships. Business owners found opportunities to improve the quality of life and the business climate through river enhancements. Environmental organizations saw the prospect of reducing pollution and reclaiming brownfields.

Canadian Heritage River

In 2001, the Canadian government designated the Detroit River as a Canadian Heritage River. It is the first to be designated by two sovereign nations.

Sea Grant Extension educator Mark Breederland chaired the steering committee, which defined the AHR goals and helped develop specific objectives for a five-year plan. "River navigator" John Hartig, a federal employee, facilitated access to critical federal funds to support river improvement.

In its first five years, the Greater Detroit American Heritage River Initiative helped leverage more than $40 million in projects — from developing riverfront greenways and engineering shorelines to remediating contaminated sites.[10]

Courtesy USEPA Great Lakes Image Collection

The Ambassador Bridge crossing the Detroit River between Detroit and Windsor.

Fighting Lake and Plant Enemies

Battling Aquatic Invasive Species

As of 2002, 160 non-native species had been brought into the Great Lakes from faraway places. Some of these introduced organisms — such as sea lamprey, gobies, zebra mussels, purple loosestrife, and water fleas — are highly invasive and are multiplying and permanently altering the ecosystem permanently.

Zebra Mussels

Zebra mussels became infamous in the late 1980s. Sea Grant research and conferences, led by Extension agent Charles Pistis, sought out industries, municipalities, and marinas seeking to cope with the zebra mussel invasion. Michigan Sea Grant has attacked the problem with research and outreach.

Purple Loosestrife

By the 1990s, invasive purple loosestrife was disrupting many Michigan wetlands. Sea Grant specialist Michael Klepinger and entomologist Douglas Landis initiated a project to stop the spread. Their weapon was a tiny beetle, *Galerucella calmariensis.* University researchers and project cooperators inoculated more than 200 wetland sites with this biological control agent. By 2003, the plant had lost its dominance in dozens of Michigan wetlands, and native plants were reemerging.

Promote Awareness

Another way of battling biological pollution is to work with the organizations and individuals who could play a role in introducing or spreading invasive species. Staff members Ronald Kinnunen and Klepinger persuaded baitfish industry leaders that it would be easier to prevent an invasion than to control one once it had started.

The war against invasive species is far from over. Strategies developed and used by Sea Grant in Michigan are helping people across the nation to fight such battles.[11]

Plant and Insect Warfare

Strategic Option

Stroll across the campus and you may see hole-ridden leaves that testify to some bug's voracious appetite. Pests can devastate crops the same way. Every year, crop losses resulting from insects are a problem, despite the use of chemical pesticides. Strategies that use the built-in defense systems found in many plants are attractive alternatives to the use of pesticides.

Enemy of My Enemy

Plants and herbivorous insects have been engaged in a battle to eat or not be eaten for centuries. To counteract predators, plants produce an arsenal of defensive chemicals that exert toxic or anti-nutritive effects on herbivores. Some plants also release volatile compounds that travel through the air to summon friendly insects that prey upon the attacking herbivores. This phenomenon is a good example of the old adage "the enemy of my enemy is my friend."

Solution at Hand?

Ongoing research by MAES scientists at the MSU Plant Research Laboratory uses the tomato as a model system to understand how induced chemical defense systems are switched on and off. Researchers discovered that insect damage activates the production of the plant hormone jasmonic acid (JA), which in turn switches on the expression of hundreds of plant genes needed to produce defensive chemical barriers. This was demonstrated by the use of genetic mutations that block JA biosynthesis and, consequently, interfere with the plant's ability to mount defense responses (see figures above). Scientists hope that a greater understanding of JA will contribute to environmentally friendly approaches to crop protection and reduce reliance on manufactured pesticides.[12]

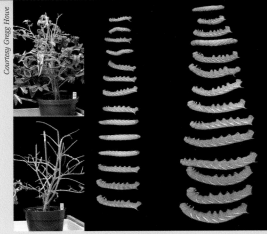

Courtesy Gregg Howe

A normal (top) and a JA-deficient (bottom) tomato plant after attack by tobacco hornworm larvae. Larvae recovered from normal plants (center) are smaller, a finding that demonstrates the effectiveness of JA as a natural regulator of plant resistance to insect pests.

Courtesy Michigan Sea Grant Archives

Courtesy Michigan Sea Grant Archives

Zebra mussels.

Purple loosestrife.

The Citizen Planner Program

Traffic congestion, sprawl, urban decay, and the loss of open space and farmland challenge many communities. Elected members of local governing bodies and appointed planning commissioners are called upon to guide development of their communities while administering complex planning regulations.

Program for Planners

The Citizen Planner Program (CPP) addresses the needs of people serving on land use planning commissions. Beginning as a pilot program in northwestern Michigan in 2000, it was launched statewide in 2002 with funding from MSU and the W.K. Kellogg Foundation. In four years, the eight-week short course trained 2,500 planning officials across Michigan.

"The CPP was created because research in northwest Michigan revealed a general lack of training and access to planning resources," said James Wiesing, Grand Traverse County Extension director and key initiator of the program.

"The CPP is a shortcut to the college of hard knocks," said Mark Pitzer, program participant and planning commission chairman for Brooks Township in Newaygo County. "Instead of learning things over a slow, long learning curve, this really gives you access to experts and ... an opportunity to see what others have been working on." Pitzer and six other Brooks Township Planning Commission members completed the CPP in 2004.

Web-based Access

The CPP, coordinated by Extension specialist Wayne Beyea, provides additional resources and access statewide. Participants can progress to Master Citizen Planner status by completing the course, a Web-based

(L-R) Steve Steinhauser, Gayle Miller and Mike Anschuetz are recognized for their Citizen Planner Program adapted for school children.

exam, and a capstone project benefiting their community. Graduates are encouraged to share their knowledge by teaching Junior Citizen Planner lesson plans developed for elementary school-aged children and 4-H clubs.[13]

Mainstreet in downtown Howell.

Land Policy Programs Supported

A three-year, $5.9 million grant provided by the W.K. Kellogg Foundation will support land use policy research, education and innovation in the MSU Land Policy Program in partnership with Public Sector Consultants, a Lansing–based public policy research firm.

State Partnership

The grant builds upon People and Land (PAL), a statewide partnership. PAL has played a major role in initiating change in Michigan land use policy. The approach focuses on educating citizens and policy-makers about land use issues.

Land Use Relations

"Everything we care about— quality of life, income levels, obesity, school funding, the environment, zoning—are all related to land use," said Soji Adelaja, John A. Hannah Distinguished professor in land use policy and head of MSU's Land Policy Program.

Increase Impact

The grant will allow MSU to deepen its research and expand its outreach in land policy. Bill Rustem, president of Public Sector, and Soji Adelaja will co-direct implementing the grant.

Wise Use Approaches

This research and outreach follows prior support for the Victor Institute formed in 2000 with funding from David V. Johnson, chairperson of Victor International Corporation and Bay Harbor, L.L.C. Its focus is on creative use of brownfields and the wise use of greenfields.

The institute was formed to assist communities facing land use challenges while balancing competing interests. It was housed in MSUE to capitalize on its history of excellence in outreach education. Phillip Davis, MSUE, served as its first director.[14]

...and Community Development

Helping Voters Make Informed Decisions

Michigan is one of the 15 states where citizens may vote to change the state constitution, initiate new laws, or change existing state laws. Since 1980, MSUE has explained 56 state ballot proposals.

Ballot Bulletins

Ballot issue bulletins reflect MSUE's commitment to assist Michiganians to obtain information on public policy issues. Elizabeth Moore, Extension public policy specialist, said that the challenge — and satisfaction — comes

from taking a politically charged issue and writing an analysis that helps people sort through the associated rhetoric. Moore has served as the primary author, working closely with other Extension educators, including the MSUE State and Local Government AoE Team.

Multiple Circulation

Each ballot bulletin describes the proposal, provides background information, and reviews policy implications. The bulletins are available electronically and in print.

One county Extension office manager commented: "Libraries, clubs, radio stations ... everybody wants the ballot issue bulletins." Legislators and other elected officials often distribute them with their campaign literature. Local newspapers frequently publish complete bulletins.

County officials and others have praised Extension for providing balanced information on ballot questions and have drawn upon that expertise when publishing information about local issues.[15]

Courtesy State News

MSU sophomores Dan Tingstad, left, and Tyler Pearsall cast their votes at All Saints Episcopal Church polling place.

Community Leadership Development

Courtesy MSUE

Lela Vandenberg

In the early 1990s, academic literature on leadership heralded a new paradigm. MSU Extension applied it to leadership development—collaborative, empowering, experiential and focused on mutual issues.

CLIMB

Community Leadership Initiative, Michigan's Best— CLIMB—was a five-year statewide leadership development effort funded by the W.K. Kellogg Foundation. Sixty participants developed a mission, vision, and processes to create positive change in communities from the U.P. to Detroit to Benton Harbor.

U.P. Lead

One CLIMB outcome was U.P. Lead, involving 13 U.P. coun-

ties. People came together to discuss issues facing their communities, design action plans, and report on progress. Extension educators Rita Hodgins and Steve Nelson provided leadership for this effort. Many wonderful community projects were created.

LeadNet

CLIMB also influenced Lela Vandenberg, Elizabeth Moore, Thomas Schneider, and Joan Witter to design in 1995 a network for Extension educators to create facilitative lead-

ership for community action. LeadNet supported leadership processes and programs across the state. In 2005, LeadNet and the Community Development AoE team published a comprehensive leadership curriculum, "Developing Community Leadership" that is used throughout Michigan.

Leadership Academy

Earlier efforts led to other initiatives including a new program for leaders in government, business and industry.

In 2004, the CANR, MSUE and MAES brought together a diverse group of stakeholders to address need for broadened perspectives among current leaders about sustainability issues.

With funding from the W.K. Kellogg Foundation, the Great Lakes Leadership Academy was created and will begin operations in fall 2006 under MSUE's Michael Kovacic, academy director. [16]

Economic Development Assistance...

Rural Betterment

In early 1998, the USDA funded a proposal for "enhancing rural economies through comprehensive extension, research, and partnering approaches using multi-county clusters." Under the Fund for Rural America, Professors Collette Moser and Ray Vlasin, project co-directors, received a $450,000 grant used to support 131 educational programs to enhance cluster economies.

The four multicounty clusters consisted of 18 counties located across Michigan. They represented a group of counties adjacent to a metro area; a value-added agricultural group; a retirement/tourism-based Interstate 75 corridor group; and a low population density and extractive industry-based group in the western U.P.

Some program offerings were single events. Many encompassed multiple events and continued beyond the end of the project. Extension educators Sally Carpenter, Don Smucker, Roy Spangler, and Jerry Murphy were coordinators for the clusters. Campus-based Extension specialists and researchers were members of the Economic Development AoE team.[17]

Communication for Communities, Agriculture, and Natural Resources

Media Avenues for Extension

Communications within the college has its roots in the Cooperative Extension Service of the early 1900s. Broadcast media were hungry for content and Extension agents became fixtures on local radio. They found the mass media an efficient means for reaching an expanding audience. Extension bulletins, local newspapers, and farm journals also provided effective means for disseminating knowledge.

Campus Structure

The increasing use of mass media required a professional communications staff. In 1943, a new Extension information division, the Department of Publications, was established. In 1948, MSC organized the Department of Information Services, combining information divisions from across campus and encompassing Extension and Experiment Station communications and other dimensions of MSC. Since then, the pendulum returned to a less centralized approach.

In close collaboration with MSU University Relations, the ANR Communications office brings together public relations, marketing, and information management to serve the CANR, MSUE, and the MAES. Staff members provide strategic counsel, communication, graphic design, and broadcast services to advance knowledge and transform lives in communities, agriculture, and natural resources.[18]

Product Center for Ag and Natural Resources

Courtesy Product Center

Michael Score (L) meets with rabbit grower in Chene Street neighborhood.

The Product Center for Agriculture and Natural Resources (PCANR) is helping create business opportunities through product and market innovation. CANR, MAES, and MSUE administrators created the MSU PCANR in early 2003 and appointed H. Christopher Peterson and Arlen Leholm — professors in Agricultural Economics — co-directors of the center.

Peterson, holder of the Nowlin chair for consumer-responsive agriculture, and Leholm, former director of MSU Extension (1997-2000), together crafted the center and garnered support for it.

The PCANR has an initial term of five years (2003-08), an annual operating budget of $250,000 (MAES and MSUE GREEEN funds), and commitment of the co-directors' time. In 2003, a $1 million USDA Agriculture Innovation Center grant was awarded.

Threefold Action

The PCANR has a threefold responsibility — education, research, and engagement. Its innovation academy, led by Barbara Fails, inspires entrepreneurs to achieve business success through product and market innovations. Its strategic marketing institute, led by Peterson, analyzes market factors vital to new product and market ventures. Tom Kalchik counsels new business ventures in providing business and professional services.[19]

...at the Community Level

Family and Consumer Sciences Programs

Consumers make decisions every day — about health, nutrition, safety, relationships, parenting, caregiving, and financial security. The goal of Extension's Family and Consumer Sciences (FCS) program is to provide people with practical, research-based, objective information so they can make decisions that have desired outcomes.

All Counties Served

FCS educators serve every Michigan county. They share information through home visits, classes, workshops, presentations, and training, and through the media and the Internet. Educators are skilled at building partnerships and leveraging funds to enhance their capacity to deliver education that families need.

State, Federal, Extension

FCS coordinates a wide variety of programs directed to improving the lives of people. Many programs are funded by state agencies such as Michigan's Department of Human Services, Department of Community Health, and Office of Services to the Aging, as well as by federal human service agencies. The programs focus on providing education to adults and children on a range of topics relating to health and nutrition, disease management, child training, financial management, and many related topics.

Paraprofessionals play a key role in delivering FCS programs through home visits. They are trained and supervised by professional staff members and often have a special ability to work with targeted families because they are part of the community.

As a result of the work of Extension's FCS educators, children enter school healthy

Courtesy Trent Wakenight

Paul McConaughy encouraging the use of meat thermometers.

and ready to learn, parents positively nurture their children, people make more nutritious food choices and prepare food safely. Those with chronic diseases manage them more effectively, families manage their resources better, and more seniors age in place.[20]

Courtesy Product Center

Members of the Chene Ferry Market Cooperative working with Michael Score.

Forming a Neighborhood Cooperative

As Michigan's landscape and population change, MSUE educators continue innovative workings with clients to apply research-based information to community needs. In 2003, the Michigan Coalition of Black Farmers and Peacemakers Ministry invited Extension educators to help develop a plan for a new food system business to strengthen farm profitability and address food needs of low-income residents of Detroit's Chene Street neighborhood.

Reviving Neighborhoods

The business plan included a food cooperative to give residents leverage in purchasing fresh food from farm sources. It also included urban gardening and small livestock

Extension educators coached residents to develop a business plan that accounted for food preferences, limited transportation, and use of food stamps as the primary currency for food purchases.

enterprises that supply the cooperative. MSU educators persuaded the Michigan Farm Bureau to provide seed money for the cooperative.

Extension educators work closely with urban residents to address the interests of urban and rural clients. The food purchasing cooperative, combined with new ethanol production facilities and food processing ventures in southeast Michigan, has led to new urban/rural partnerships.[21]

Perfect Vegetable Packaging

"Each vegetable has an individual minimum level of oxygen tolerance [and] if it drops below this level, the produce can start to ferment."

Arthur Cameron, a horticultural scientist at MSU, has been studying modified-atmosphere packaging to provide consumers with fresher fruits and vegetables.

"In his quest for a strategy to halt the fermentation process [of packaged vegetables], Cameron must consider the respiration rate of the produce, the permeability of the film packaging, and temperature.

"Higher temperatures can affect the oxygen level tolerance of produce — in fact, a change in any one of the variables affects all the others.

"Cameron believes that some type of sense-and-respond packaging would be the ideal way to wrap produce....

"'That's a futuristic dream, though,' he said. 'Now we're looking at something that will respond to physiological characteristics of the produce.'"[22]

Uses for Sprouted Wheat

"My first preference is to use wheat and wheat flour as food for people, but if ... it is sprouted and not suitable for producing quality products, this is a good alternative use."

So said Perry Ng, Food Science and Human Nutrition researcher. In the mid-1990s, his interest was finding an alternate use for wheat that has sprouted before being harvested. Sprouted wheat is otherwise useable only as animal feed.

Protective Film

Ng began developing a film from white wheat flour protein, film that could be used to make cereal box liners, wrapping for meat or other foods, or perhaps as coatings for pills or gel caps. The liner or wrapping would serve as an oxygen barrier and thus keep the products fresh.

The university received two patents on his film product. Ng's next project was working with colleagues in the School of Packaging to develop a similar product from soybean protein.[24]

Cancer Drug from Yew Clippings

During the 1990s, Taxol* was a go-to drug for ovarian and breast cancer. The compound was extracted from the bark of Pacific yew trees growing in the northwestern United States and British Columbia. The availability of Taxol was limited because 1,500 trees could produce only 2.2 pounds, enough to treat only 500 people.

MAES scientists Muraleedharan Nair (bioactive natural products chemist) and Robert Schutzki (MAES horticulturist) began exploring whether ornamental yews could be a renewable source for Taxol. Michigan is the largest producer of yews in the United States.

MSU received a patent for Nair's process of extracting and purifying Taxol from ornamental yew clippings.

"We should be able to get about 1.1 million pounds of yew clippings from nurseries in Michigan and Ohio, enough to make about 132 pounds of Taxol per year," Nair said. "That will treat 30,000 people...."[23]

Courtesy Kenneth VerBurg

Tomato research plot under harvest.

---

*Taxol is a registered trademark of Bristol Myers-Squib Company.

Lung Disease in Horses

"Heaves is an asthma-like equine disease that is chronic in older horses. Horses develop it when they inhale dust that contains mold and other allergens," says N. Edward Robinson, MAES large animal clinical sciences researcher. "What we don't understand is why some horses are susceptible and some horses aren't. It's similar to people with asthma."

The Robinson team sampled the mucus of 260 horses and looked at cell types to see if lungs were inflamed. The studies revealed some correlation between lung diseases and horses that feed from large round bales. The healthiest horses seem to be those kept inside and feeding from square bales in the wintertime. Horses eating from round bales appeared to inhale dust as they bury their noses in the round bales seeking good hay.

Researchers in Australia and Britain attribute the lung inflammation of race horses to bacteria, but Robinson and colleagues are considering how the horses' environment may affect the disease in horses.[25]

Organic Apple Study

Increase Understanding

"Though wild apple trees can be found practically everywhere, managing them to produce the unblemished fruit consumers expect is a complicated."

Suppress Pest Populations

"The principal goal is to understand organic agriculture better and to develop a protocol that suppresses pest populations and problems related to growing apples organically and profitably.

"The project focuses on soil quality, pest management, and marketing.

"Deepa Ramsinghani coordinates work of researchers, producers, and cooperators committed to its success."[26]

Courtesy Deborah Williams

Pheromone trap is used to attract insect pests in the organic orchard and reduce insect pest populations.

"This is why Mark Whalon and George W. Bird (professors, Department of Entomology) and Ronald L. Perry (professor, Department of Horticulture) study the dynamics of producing organic apples, in the first organic plot ... at MSU...."

Michigan's Wine Industry — Near World-class

Courtesy Jamie DePolo

G. Stanley Howell is a long-time leader in grape and wine research in the Department of Horticulture.

"'Making wine is an interesting mix of agriculture, science and art,' said G. Stanley Howell, MAES horticultural scientist and renowned wine researcher. During his 35 years at MSU, Howell has been a catalyst for a revolution in the Michigan wine industry. Other scientists also are adding to the industry's body of knowledge.

"Quality has improved dramatically—several wineries have been recognized with international awards... Wine production and winery tourism contribute 75 million to Michigan's economy each year."

Grape and Wine Council

"Linda Jones, executive Director of the Michigan Grape and Wine Industry Council, is excited about the future of wine in Michigan.

"'We need more wine grape growers in Michigan,' she said. 'Wineries help preserve farmland and business opportunities for investors. As the industry grows, we need new information and we look to MSU for that.'"[28]

Linda Jones of the Michigan Grape and Wine Industry Council.

National Center Hosts Diverse Disciplines

The National Food Safety and Toxicology Center at MSU can undertake key issues because of its diversity of disciplines and the willingness of faculty members to participate in collaborative efforts.

One distinctive element of the center is the presence of both toxicological and microbiological perspectives. Traditionally, toxins and bacteria have been studied in separate realms, but center scientists are discovering ways in which they interact to produce disease conditions. One example concerns endotoxins, toxic cell wall structures found in gram-negative bacteria such as *E.coli, Salmonella, and Shigella.* High levels of endotoxin have been reported in environments such as farms.

Center scientists have identified factors that lead to injury to the liver and other organs through inflammation. They found that small, normally harmless doses of endotoxin markedly increased the toxic effects of some food-borne contaminants. Without collaboration, this potentially serious condition might not have been discovered.[27]

Courtesy Jamie DePolo

Questions and Issues of Importance

What it Means to be a Bailey Scholar

Liberty Hyde Bailey, the scholars' namesake, honored in MSU's horticulture gardens.

Courtesy Bailey Scholars

Faculty members and students design learning experiences collaboratively in this 21-credit undergraduate specialization named in honor of Liberty Hyde Bailey, the legendary horticulturist who emphasized active learning.

Origins of Bailey

In the mid-1990s, CANR leaders decided to offer a world-class undergraduate experience. The goal was to broaden the undergraduate experience through a program enabling students to take greater control of their learning.

A group of administrators and faculty members led by Frank Fear (then chairperson of the Department of Resource Development) began designing the program. To season their thinking, Dean Fred Poston invited Richard Bawden, of the Hawkesbury School at the University of Western Sydney in Australia, to work with the design team. The initial class (January 1998) had 15 students.

The Five Bailey Questions

Four members of the Bailey inaugural class — Kristie McElhaney, Andrea Fox, Hunter Freeman, and Melinda Dailey — connected their academic journeys with their personal lives through Bailey by asking: "What if we connect what we are studying in college to what is happening in our lives?" Learning experiences are guided by "The Bailey Five Questions": *Who am I? What do I value? What is my worldview? How do I learn? How do my answers connect, personally and professionally?*

Award-winning Program

The Bailey Scholars program has received several national awards, and the Bailey scholars are frequently recognized for their academic and service accomplishments.

But this is not a program reserved for the academic elite. Bailey scholars come from diverse backgrounds, have varying academic achievement levels, and work side by side, respectfully and collegially.[29]

MSUE Focuses on Michigan Issues

MSUE systematically gathers public comments to determine priorities for programming. Gail L. Imig, director of MSUE (1991-96), provided leadership for one such major public input process.

Future Focus

She launched a process in 1992 to determine current and emerging local, regional, and statewide issues of greatest interest to corresponding residents. The document summarizing the process, *Focus on Michigan's Future* (April 1997), stated that the results were to help formulate policy and link MSU knowledge resources to issues of greatest concern.

Faculty Sets Stage

More than 80 campus-based faculty members and staff members initiated the process by writing *Michigan's Future: Trends and Perspectives.* The publication identified, clarified, and prioritized concerns in their communities.

Multicounty and regional teams reviewed county and regional reports. A statewide group used the regional results to designate three statewide issue areas for major outreach efforts during the next few years:

Courtesy MSU Extension

Gail L. Imig, Extension Director, 1991-96.

- Children, youth, and family.
- Agriculture and natural resources.
- Community and economic development.

Response Teams

Three statewide issue response teams (SIRTs) analyzed and developed a response strategy for the priority areas. The SIRTs were made up of multidisciplinary faculty members, county Extension staff members, and agency and organization representatives. The SIRT findings were instrumental in shaping future Extension programs.[30]

Extending Perspectives and Careers

Students Visit Land-scarce Environments

The university has a strong interest in having students and faculty members be involved in overseas study. Participants experience different cultures, socioeconomic conditions, and environmental practices. The programs vary from semesterlong courses at colleges abroad to courses involving on-campus classes with 3- to 4-week international field experiences.

Natural Resource Management

Gerhardus Schultink, of the Department of Community, Agriculture, Recreation, and Resource Studies, directed a 3-week study in The Netherlands. The course examined policies in managing land and water resources of this small and densely populated European nation.

With the land area less than one-third that of Michigan and a 60 percent greater population, The Netherlands ranks third in agricultural export revenues after the United States and France.

Presentations

The course involves lectures by instructors from institutions such as Wageningen University and presentations by national or regional officials outlining policies, incentives, and enforcement practices. These give students a sense of the cultural differences and the policies for comparison to those of the United States.

Site Visits

Topics of field visits include agricultural practices related to water contamination risks;

solid waste programs that promote source reduction, recycling, and composting, combined with environmentally controlled landfilling and incineration; and flood control and water treatment practices.

Students also learn about practices to revitalize and preserve urban areas, historical preservation, and related enforcement policies.

Lowland Management

Much of The Netherlands is below sea level, and the unique opportunity exists to examine creative approaches to drainage management and flood protection while addressing environmental impacts. Class participants had the opportunity to explore creative solutions to periodic storm surge protection.[31]

Students inspect Ijsselmeer shoreline for zebra mussels in The Netherlands.

Courtesy Gerhardus Schultink

IAT Offers Careers for a Changing World

Courtesy ANR Communications

Eunice F. Foster, Associate Dean and Director of IAT.

The Institute of Agricultural Technology (IAT) has retained a steadfast commitment to the land-grant mission to meet the needs of Michiganians. IAT's educational programs continue to prepare career-ready graduates through intensive, practical learning and skill enhancement in agricultural, environmental, and applied technologies.

Mission: ANR and Beyond

Staying true to its mission, the IAT continues to develop new programs addressing Michigan needs. Possibilities are unlimited. Areas for future exploration and investigation include working with Native American tribes to develop timberland forestry programs at tribal sites; and developing a landscape and nursery program in southeastern Michigan, an urban forestry program, and programs for retraining, reeducating, and retooling Michigan's workers for new careers and job skill enhancement.

Other potential programs include abbreviated noncredit courses to assist in training and developing industrial employees and continuing

education programs in agricultural and natural resource sciences for teachers to help them teach scientific principles in K-12 classrooms.

Partnerships Ensure Success

IAT's programming responds to changing societal needs by building long-lasting relationships with industrial and academic partners to enhance current programs, develop new ones, and increase program accessibility for people unable to take courses on the campus. The IAT anticipates a closer working relationship with MSUE by including field educators among those who teach IAT courses. In addition, the IAT continues to build collaborative relationships with community colleges so students can complete IAT certificate programs and earn associate degrees in the convenience of their own communities.[32]

Approaches: New and Trusted

Organic Agriculture Before It Was Cool

Organic food and agriculture was not always on the front page. Some MSU folks supported organic farmers long before organic became popular.

Early Studies

During the 1960s, Dean Haynes, professor of entomology, conducted research on the ecological management of cereal leaf beetles. It led to systems-based pest management principles that enabled MSU to host a federally funded pilot integrated pest management (IPM) project in 1972.

During the late 1970s, Thomas Edens, professor of entomology and resource development, and Donald Christianson, professor of crop and soil sciences, presented a "Biological Agriculture" program during ANR Week. Over the next couple of years, they developed programs featuring farm-level demonstrations.

Early Meetings at MSU

Organic leaders, especially Joseph Scrimger, an organic farmer from Marlette, played key organizing roles. The programs provided a statewide focus on this new approach to farming, and for many years Organic Growers of Michigan (OGM) held its annual meetings at MSU.

Reorganization

As OGM chapters lagged during the 1980s, members organized a tax-exempt and charitable organization qualified to receive grant funding. The Michigan Organic Growers Advancement Project was incorporated in 1992. Early strategic planning clarified the leaders' vision and resulted in a name change to Michigan Organic Food and Farm Alliance (MOFFA), with a mission to promote food systems that rely on organic methods and revitalize and sustain local communities. Laura DeLind, a MOFFA leader, organized programs from 1993 through 1997.[33]

MFB Honors "Jake" Ferris

The Michigan Farm Bureau (MFB) honored John "Jake" Ferris, MAES agricultural economics researcher, with its Distinguished Service to Agriculture Award at its annual meeting in Traverse City in December [1997].

"Ferris was honored for his 40 years of service to Michigan agriculture, especially his extensive economic analyses of Michigan agriculture and natural resources. He has provided information to state and national legislators that was critical to policy development, and he was instrumental in developing supporting research for the $70 million Animal Industry Initiative at MSU.

Courtesy MAES

John "Jake" Ferris, Professor Emeritus, Agricultural Economics.

"MFB cited Ferris for his presentation of many workshops across the state to help farmers hone their marketing skills. He was also responsible for a biweekly crop and market outlook report, which helped farmers make pricing decisions. The author of more than 1,000 publications, he is frequently called upon to provide accurate economic data analysis and interpretation for legislators, local community economic development agencies, agribusiness firms, and commodity groups.

"In addition, Jake always found time to be a patient, supportive mentor to young faculty members, and, most importantly, to students. He pioneered teaching methods for commodity futures courses and commodity market analysis...."[35]

4-H Children's Horticulture Gardens

Courtesy Claire Vlasin

Beside the Horticulture Demonstration Garden is the fulfilled dream of Jane L. Taylor of the 4-H Youth Development program. She wanted a garden where children could interact with plants, rather than being put off by "Keep Out!" and "Don't Touch!" signs.

Fifty Mini-Gardens

Fifty mini-gardens were built on themes that children know best. They include herbs described in Peter Rabbit stories, topiary bears, a dinosaur, a tree house, dance chimes activated by little feet, and a replica of the bridge in Claude Monet's Garden in France. Others include a kitchen garden, a life-size bronze and epoxy stone sheep, and a rainbow garden representing cultural groups that introduced various foods into America.

The purposes, Taylor says, were "to help children understand the importance of plants, to promote healthy environmental attitudes ... with a hands-on approach."

Destination Site

Many schools schedule tours and 250,000 persons visit the gardens annually. Currently, Barbara Fails is the director and curator of the facility. Norman Lownds is the horticultural curator of the Children's Garden. Douglas Badgero is the garden manager.[34]

Enjoying the 4-H Children's Garden and statue of Mary Turner — a character from the book *The Secret Garden*, by Frances Hodgson Burnett.

Departmental Reorganizations

Building a Department

Making One of Several

In November 2003, the MSU Board of Trustees established the Department of Community, Agriculture, Recreation, and Resource Studies (CARRS) in the CANR. The new department resulted from the unification of four units as a new interdisciplinary department.

- Agriculture and Natural Resources Education and Communication Systems.
- Resource Development.
- Park, Recreation, and Tourism Resources.
- Travel, Tourism, and Recreation Resources Center.

Mission

The mission of CARRS is to assist the development of sustainable communities by conducting scholarly research, teaching, and outreach in leadership, education, and communication; community, food, and agriculture; natural resources, land use, and the environment; and recreation and tourism.

The four units are experienced in interdisciplinary studies, although on a less extensive scale than that envisioned for the restructured unit. "Interdisciplinary research can ... provide a format for conversations and connections that lead to new knowledge."[36]

Role of CARRS in CANR

A major role of CARRS is to function as an interdisciplinary department. The overall goal of the department is to develop teaching, outreach, and research programs to address human and social issues of agriculture, natural resources, recreation, and communities.[37]

Log Cabins to Skyscrapers

The construction management (CM) program, now part of the School of Planning, Design, and Construction, has been a national leader in preparing managers for construction of everything from individual dwellings made of logs to skyscrapers.

Begun in Forestry

The beginning at MSU was in 1948, when the housing and lumber management major was established in the Forestry Department. In 2005, after undergoing several changes in emphases, it became part of the new School of Planning, Design, and Construction.

Management Skills

Early discipline focused on wood use; today the emphasis is on processes and methods. Scheduling and management are key elements, as are methods based on "just-in-time" principles, financial reporting and controls, and contractual arrangements.

Grad Achievements

The 3,000 graduates of the CM program hold positions ranging from estimators to CEOs. A 1951 graduate, Al Ratner, co-chair of Forest City Enterprises, Inc., was key in reconstructing a mixed-use complex, a project regarded as the catalyst for downtown Cleveland's rebirth.

A 1986 graduate, Tom Gores, founded Platinum Equity in 1995, ranked No. 32 on Forbes' Largest Private Companies list for 2004.[38]

Engineering Transforms Agricultural Way of Life

Transforming Agriculture

Two-thirds of Americans lived on farms 100 years ago. The main source of power was manual labor or animals. Engineers have helped transform agriculture into a modern industry, mechanizing agricultural operations, building roads, irrigation and drainage systems, connecting farms to electrical systems, and designing crop storage and processing systems.

"The increase did not come without a price. Excessive

"Michigan Agricultural College was founded not to teach a boy to plow straight furrows, nor to milk reluctant cows; but to teach him to apply science to the practice of agriculture.... It was to render agriculture not only useful but a learned and liberal profession."[39]

tillage created erosion problems. The increased use of chemicals created environmental and food safety concerns. Large animal feeding operations created issues of animal waste disposal, air quality, and odor. Agriculture found itself in the middle of everybody's backyard," says Ajit Srivastava, chairperson of the Department of Biosystems and Agricultural Engineering.

Engineering and Biosystems Linkage

The response from the agricultural community was to consider these broader societal issues and move toward applying engineering principles and combining them with biological innovations and discoveries to address the issues. "When you're dealing with a system, anything you do will have a domino effect. So you must take a systems approach to solving these problems," Srivastava said.

To prepare graduates to meet changing societal needs, the department reconfigured its agricultural engineering degree program in 1995, integrating biology and engineering and addressing problems in a systems context.[40]

Challenges and Progress

Gray Named MAES Director

Ian Gray, Director of MAES.

J. Ian Gray, professor of food science and human nutrition, was named director of the Michigan Agricultural Experiment Station in July 1996.

Gray came to MSU in 1978 as associate professor of food science and human nutrition. In 1984, he was also named

professor of packaging, and later (1988), associate director of the MAES.

Gray developed strong ties between research and commodity groups, worked with USDA and MAES researchers, and promoted multidisciplinary research.

While an administrator, Gray continued to advise and guide graduate students and pursue his own research on the formation of toxic compounds in food. He received numerous awards and honors, including the MSU Distinguished Faculty Award in 1994.

In 2004, Gray became vice president for research at the university.[41]

Livestock Education Pavilion Dedicated

The college dedicated its 200,000-square-foot Pavilion for Agriculture and Livestock Education on March 15, 1997.

The ceremonies, which included Governor John Engler, agricultural industry leaders, and university officials, were a focal point of the Michigan Horse Council's International Stallion Exposition and Trade Show being conducted at the $14.5 million facility.

Benchmark Facility

The pavilion is one of the largest facilities of its kind in the region. Events held in the facility have included the

Courtesy MSU Land Office

The Agriculture and Livestock Pavilion.

MSU Winter Beef Show, an elk auction, draft and quarter horse shows, and many other regional and national events.

The pavilion is "dedicated to the advancement of Michigan's livestock industry through education, exhibition and livestock distribution." The Animal Agriculture Initiative enabled the university to "undertake a campus-wide modernization of research, teaching, and demonstration facilities to serve Michigan's livestock industry."[42]

C. Gerald "Jerry" Haarer, the first Land Management Director, was a key advocate for building the pavilion.

Guiding MSUE Through Financial Crisis

Courtesy MSUE

Arlen Leholm, MSUE Director, 1997-2000.

Bethel Named Director

Margaret (Maggie) Bethel succeeded Arlen Leholm as Extension director in 2001. She planned to serve for only six months, but President McPherson asked her to extend her term as director during the time of economic downturn and grim budget outlook.

The first step, belt tightening and operating reductions, was

insufficient. Reduction of the work force was necessary. A series of early retirement buyouts was followed by a consolidation of positions.

Fiscal Impact

Over three years, the downsizing cost 120 positions. Bethel's focus was to protect the budget, preserve the assets, and tend to the mission: "Helping people improve their lives

through an educational process that applies knowledge to critical needs, issues, and opportunities."

Extension is a decentralized, dynamic, complex, and uniquely funded organization. The identifiable components of Extension and the synergy created among these parts kept MSUE strong during this fiscal turmoil.[43]

Courtesy MSUE

Margaret Bethel, MSUE Director, 2001-2005.

Living Through Fiscal Challenge

A Textbook Case of Citizen Involvement

As Governor Jennifer Granholm struggled with the state budget deficit, she presented a list of options for reducing state expenditures including eliminating state funding for MSUE and the MAES. She held forums around the state as part of a process to obtain citizen feedback.

Public Supports CANR

The public response to possible elimination of funding for these two organizations was swift and intense. The public showed how research and education affect people's lives.

- *Media published* supportive editorials throughout Michigan.
- *County* commissioners passed resolutions supporting Extension funding.
- *MSU faculty and staff members and students* wrote letters and met with legislators.
- *State administrators* explained that MSUE educates people on how to utilize state services.
- *Local libraries* showed citizens how to support MSUE and MAES.

Eliminating state funding for MSUE and the MAES portended another serious threat. The programs receive federal appropriations that require state matching funds. Eliminating state funds could cause a loss of federal funds.

A Challenging Time

It was a challenging time for MSUE and MAES leaders, people such as the CANR dean Jeffrey Armstrong; MSUE director Margaret Bethel; MAES director J. Ian Gray, MSUE associate director Lynn Harvey; Extension specialist Elizabeth Moore; the CANR director of stakeholder relations, Gale Arent; and others. All worked intensively to assure the governor and legislators that if they approved the budget reductions, they would do so with full knowledge of some of the effects of the action.

Gratifying Outcome

Governor Granholm eventually put these programs on

MSU Extension Specialist Elizabeth "Beth" Moore.

Courtesy MSUE

her "do not touch" list. "Critical programs are protected. We are not cutting the Cooperative Extension Service or the Agricultural Experiment Station," she said in her executive order to reduce the state budget by $380 million on December 10, 2003. These words culminated a monthlong campaign. One lobbyist termed it a "'textbook' case of citizen involvement."[44]

County, State and National Population

2000		
	Number	Percent change, 1990-2000
Ingham County	279,320	- 0.9
Michigan	9,938,444	4.3
USA	281,421,906	13.1

U.S. Bureau of Census

One Grower's Defense of MSUE Funding

The Detroit News published the following report regarding the possible reductions in state support for the MSUE and MAES annual budgets for 2004. The comments reflect the concern of the consumers of MSUE and MAES services.

"Marvin Wiegand normally pays far more attention to his Macomb County nursery and hundreds of acres of trees and shrubs than to budget negotiations in Lansing.

"But when $26.8 million in statewide funding for the MSU Extension Service was jeopardized by a shortfall in the state budget, Wiegand and other Metro Detroiters who depend on Extension offices for agricultural information got a wake-up call and took notice.

"'The professors [at MSU] can do all the experimentation, but if they can't get it to the users, what good is it?' said Wiegand, co-owner of Wiegand's Nursery in Macomb Township. 'Their function is quite important to growers in Macomb County.'"[45]

Courtesy Mary L. Andrews

Group XII of the International Extension Training Program at its debriefing session at MacMillan Center after their return from India and Thailand. Mary Andrews, International Extension leader, is at the right end of the front row.

Two CANR Long-term Models

Willard R. Sparks, An Example to Observe

A Life of Giving

Outstanding Ag Econ Grad

Willard R. Sparks was an outstanding graduate of MSU's Department of Agricultural Economics, which awarded him a doctorate in 1961. In 1963 Sparks became "director of research and trading at Cook Industries, a major grain and cotton exporter in Memphis, Tennessee. He began 'Sparks Commodities. Inc.' in 1975. It was the precursor to the world-renowned Sparks Companies, one of the first in the world to help agribusinesses manage risk. Its customers were multinationals such as Cargill, General Mills, Quaker, and Ralston Purina."[46]

Les Manderscheid, a professor of ag economics when Sparks was a Ph.D. candidate, served as chair of Sparks' guidance committee during the final months of Sparks' program.

Brilliant Student

Sparks' dissertation was the first application of a new and highly efficient technique for analyzing consumer food demand when weekly family purchase data were available over a period of years. The most significant challenge,

Manderscheid said, was helping Sparks present the brilliant work in language that economists and agricultural economists less sophisticated in mathematics and statistics could understand. Sparks achieved that goal. The American Agricultural Economics Association awarded him an Outstanding Dissertation Award. Sparks received earlier degrees at Oklahoma State University.

Skilled in Applying Theory

Sparks was known for his skill in applying his knowledge to benefit the agricultural community. "He developed practical, systematic, and analytical approaches to the fundamental analyses now in use by the USDA to understand the volatile commodity market."[47]

The CANR planned to give to Sparks its 2005 Outstanding Alumnus Award for his "record of achievement in many areas of agriculture and commodity marketing, analysis, and consulting." Sadly, Sparks passed away shortly before the award was to be presented. The college presented the award posthumously to his wife and son.[48]

From Dairy to Beef

David Morris was born in Eagle Township in 1927. Over the years, David and his wife, Betty, expanded the farm to nearly 1,800 acres. The farm is now a centennial farm.

The farm was a dairy farm until 1956, when the Morrises switched to growing pigs and beef cattle, and eventually, only beef cattle. "I've sold choice or prime cattle every month for 46 years," Morris said.

Leadership

"I was born of good parents who taught me to work, to save, and to appreciate the finer things of life," Morris said. "I truly believe that each one of us can help others and this is our mission, be it a handshake, a smile, or words of encouragement."

Over the years, those who knew him recognized his leadership capabilities. In 1963, he was elected to the board of the Farm Bureau Insurance Co. and was president from 1964 to 1973. In 1982, the Eagle Township board appointed him township supervisor. He and Betty then became certified property tax assessors.

MSU Friends

The Morrises had a long-time affiliation with MSU. David Morris completed a two-year Ag Tech program in 1948. Betty Morris graduated from the College of Business in 1949.

Morris expressed his gratitude to MSU in 2005 by making a planned gift of approximately $7.5 million. His gift is dedicated to endowments for livestock research, MAES and MSUE programming, state and local government finance programs, and discretionary funds for the CANR.

In remarks at a gathering to honor Morris, state Senator Diane Byrum (an MSU alumna) quoted Winston Churchill saying, "'We make a living by what we get, we make a life by what we give.'"

David and Betty Morris not only made a life by what they have given but also by lives that will grow from their generous gifts and support to MSU.[49]

Courtesy David Morris

David Morris on his centennial farm.

Sharing Expertise in New Ways

MSUE Pioneers AoE Teams

Unmet Needs

In the early 1990s, some agricultural interests indicated they were not receiving the assistance they needed for timely decisions and business profitability. Some also complained of a perceived disconnect on campus among colleges and departments relevant to their needs. At the time, educational program leaders and faculty specialists were located on campus and generalist agricultural educators at the county level.

Responsive Action

The complaints greeted Arlen Leholm when he joined MSUE as associate director. Under his leadership, MSUE in partnership with the MAES implemented self-directed AoE (area of expertise) teams as its major educational delivery model. The AoE teams were an outgrowth of experiences with previous temporary research/Extension teams and quick response professional groups that operated within traditional line responsibilities for research and Extension.

AoE Teams Created

"The AoE teams differ from the teams and group efforts of the past. These AoE teams are more permanent, self-directed in their operation, tightly linked with public leaders and groups. All support systems — including staff development, personnel, budgets, communications, technology, and evaluation — were redesigned to serve the educational programming needs of the AoE teams."[50]

Crops, Livestock, Dairy First

The field crops, livestock and dairy AoE teams were launched in early 1994. The AoE approach was expanded in 1995 to include teams for children, youth and families, communities, natural resources, and economic development. Twenty-nine AoE teams were operating in 2005 and have received widespread positive responses from those served.[51]

Area of Expertise Teams

Beef
Christmas Trees
Community Development
Dairy
Economic Development
Equine
Family Resource Management
Farm Management (FIRM)
Field Crops
Fisheries and Wildlife
Food, Nutrition & Health
Food Safety
Forage/Pasture/Grazing
Forestry
Fruit
Human Development
Land Use
Leadership (LeadNet)
Manure
Ornamentals
Poultry
Sheep
State and Local Government
Swine
Tourism
Vegetables
Volunteerism
Water Quality
Youth Development[52]

MSUE and AgrAbility

Have you ever known a farmer who took a leave of absence because of back trouble or an injury? Farmers just keep going even though they are limited by injury or illness and are unable to work.

Present to Assist

Injured farmers can receive assistance from the Michigan AgrAbility Project. The program assists farm family members and workers to continue working in agriculture by providing work-site and work-style adjustments. MSUE directs this USDA-funded special project.

MSUE AgrAbility responds to requests with an on-farm assessment by an agricultural engineer. The program works with Michigan Rehabilitation Services (MRS) to connect the farmers with a plan to enable them to perform their tasks more easily and safely.

One Example

Numerous successful stories could be told. One such case involves Joe, an Ingham County farmer who, for the first time since a construction injury in 1962, is able to plant his 700 acres of corn and soybeans. Michigan AgrAbility recommended installing a lightbar integrated with GPS (global positioning system) technology on his tractor. The resulting guide enables him to plant a straight and evenly planted row. Through the Farmer Rehabilitation Fund and matching funds from MRS, the program was able to purchase and install this equipment.[53]

Courtesy Vicki Morrone

Mechanical elevator enables user to access tractor seat.

Achievements Far and Near

Crews laying out the sod for the Olympic Games.

Courtesy Timothy Vanloo

Turfgrass for 2004 Olympics

Multiple-use Stadium Floor

Athens, Greece, home of the original Olympic Games, was the site of the 2004 Summer Olympics. The opening ceremonies, held near the first Olympic stadium, included laser lights, fireworks, and a stadium floor full of water. Because of the aquatic theme and the need for a perfect field only 72 hours later, modular turf was deemed the only option. The organizers turned to turf scientists at MSU.

Experienced Crew

They contacted MSU to construct the modular field for the 2004 Olympics because of its experiences with the 1994 Soccer World Cup at the Pontiac Silverdome and its conversion of Spartan Stadium to grass in 2001.

MSU staff members visited Athens in 2003 and selected the medium for the root zone and type of turfgrass. They chose a sand-based Bermudagrass field to provide the playing surface. In early 2004, John N. "Trey" Rogers and James R. Crum (professors of crop and soil sciences), Matthew Anderson (CSS master's graduate), and Timothy Vanloo (CSS master's student) went to Athens to construct, establish, and maintain the field from April though August.

Modules Placed

After the opening ceremony, they transported the grass modules with semitrucks and unloaded them on a 100-yard conveyer belt. The modules were then placed in the same order in which they were grown. About 6,000 modules were placed in a 72-hour marathon. The experience and hard work of many people made for a world-class athletic surface that could be moved anywhere![54]

Courtesy Timothy Vanloo

The field is ready for the 2004 Olympic Games.

4-H Foundation's 50th Year

The Michigan 4-H Foundation was regarded as the nation's most successful state 4-H support organization as it celebrated its 50th anniversary in 2002. A group of Michigan business leaders established the foundation with assistant director of Extension for 4-H Arne G. Kettunen as its key initiator. Kettunen was concluding 29 years as state 4-H leader in the mid-1950s.

The foundation achieved unparalleled accomplishments in 1975 when the foundation took key leadership while working in close coordination with MSUE leaders. The foundation's assets grew to $8.5 million by 1995; more than $36 million of foundation revenues had been used to support Michigan's 4-H Youth Programs.

4-H Garden

The idea for the 4-H Children's Garden, all its construction and operating costs, and its program support were the work of the Michigan 4-H Foundation and its donors. This garden quickly became an internationally renowned public garden area devoted to children.

Kettunen Center

The foundation's largest fundraising campaign provided $4.3 million in the 1990s to expand Kettunen Center into a full-service conference site.

International Support

Foundation staff members and trustees served as key advisers to the Poland 4-H Foundation, organized to bring 4-H to that nation's children and families. It also created partnerships in China and Belize to put their kids in touch with Michigan 4-H'ers.

All 4-H alumni in Michigan have benefited from the 4-H Foundation's leadership to train and sustain 4-H educational programs.[55]

4-H program participants.

Courtesy 4-H Foundation

College and University Leadership Changes

New CANR Leadership Team

Poston Becomes VP

Fred L. Poston's role as dean of the CANR ended in 1999 as he became university vice president and treasurer. William Taylor, chair of the Department of Fisheries and Wildlife, became interim CANR dean.

Jeffrey D. Armstrong, dean, CANR (L), Thomas G. Coon, MSUE director (C), and Steven G. Pueppke, MAES director.
Courtesy ANR Communications

Dean Armstrong

After a national search, the board of trustees appointed Jeffrey D. Armstrong dean of the CANR and professor of animal science. He assumed the position on July 1, 2001.

Armstrong grew up on a beef cattle, swine, and tobacco farm in western Kentucky and was active in Future Farmers of America. He received his bachelor's degree at Murray State University and his master's and Ph.D. (1986) degrees in physiology from North Carolina State University.

At NC State, he served in several capacities in the animal science department and in 1995-96 was the interim assistant director of research and academic programs. The following year he was director of the Agricultural Institute in the College of Agriculture and Life Sciences.

In 1997, he moved to Purdue University to be professor and chairperson of the Department of Animal Sciences. He served in that capacity until coming to MSU.

Extension Directorship

Another change as the period closed involved Maggie Bethel. She stepped aside as Extension director in early 2005 and was replaced by Thomas G. Coon, who had been working as associate CANR dean. Previously, Coon had been professor and acting chairperson in the Department of Fisheries and Wildlife.

MAES Director

Near the end of the period, J. Ian Gray, who had been director of the MAES, was appointed vice president for research and graduate studies. John C. Baker, associate dean in the College of Veterinary Medicine, filled the MAES position until Steven G. Pueppke became MAES director on January 1, 2006. Pueppke is an MSU alumnus and had been an associate dean at the University of Illinois since 1998.

Academic Coordinator

One of the more senior CANR administrators in length of service is Richard  Brandenburg. He came to the dean's office as assistant director in 1984 from the School of Packaging, where he specialized in packaging dynamics. He became assistant dean in 1990 and, three years later, director of academic and student affairs. He is currently also acting associate dean for graduate programs.

President McPherson Career Change

With the closing of the period covered by this chapter came also the closing of M. Peter McPherson's presidency at Michigan State University. He served in that position for 11 years and left his imprint in many places and programs associated with the institution.

During his tenure, the university experienced the largest expansion of facilities in several decades. Among the facilities added were the Biomed and Physical Sciences Building, the Agriculture Hall annex, the MSU Law School building, the Smith Student Athletic Academic Support Center, the Henry Center for Executive Development, and the McPhail Equine Performance Center.

His imprint, though, went well beyond the buildings and grounds. McPherson was instrumental in relocating the Detroit College of Law to MSU. He initiated a $1.2 billion capital campaign fund drive that had reached more than two-thirds of its goal at his departure. He also worked ceaselessly to enhance the university research capacity with the placement of the rare isotope accelerator facility.

Courtesy University Relations

M. Peter McPherson, President Emeritus.

McPherson was a strong advocate on behalf of students. He worked diligently to hold tuition increases to the rate of inflation, strongly urged students to participate in the overseas study programs, and called upon students "to dream and act globally — to think beyond yourselves in lives of public service."

McPherson moved to work on his goals in Washington, D.C. He retained his role as chairperson of the Board of International Food and Agriculture Development (BIFAD). In January 2006, he became the president of the National Association of State Universities and Land-Grant Colleges (NASULGC).

MSU Welcomes First Woman President

MSU Veteran Becomes 20th President

Period in Review

The MSU Board of Trustees wasted little time in selecting a successor to President McPherson. McPherson announced in midspring 2004 that he would be stepping down as president on January 1, 2005. On June 18, the board announced that it had made its decision and that its choice would be Lou Anna K. Simon, the first woman to hold that position at MSU.

Highly Experienced at MSU

Simon had been serving as university provost for the past 11 years, and in the prior summer season she had also served as interim president while McPherson was in Iraq at the request of President George W. Bush. Simon and McPherson worked as university administrative leaders longer than any other president-provost team in the Big Ten.

Simon received her Ph.D. in administration and higher education in 1974 and filled many administrative roles on the campus. One of her first assignments was assistant director of the Office of Institutional Research, which is now known as the Office of Planning and Budgets. Later

Courtesy University Relations

Lou Anna Simon, President, Michigan State University.

she became assistant provost for general academic administration and, in the early 1990s, associate provost.

McPherson Pleased

"McPherson said he was pleased the board had chosen a 'confident, experienced person who can do the job. There is a great momentum here,' he said. 'So many people on this campus have worked hard to achieve so many things. With Lou Anna Simon as the next president, we can ensure that this momentum not only continues, but grows.'"[56]

The period 1995-2004 brought to a close the college's first 150 years of teaching, research, and outreach. The time was one of continuing development for the college, a time of addressing new conditions and circumstances, and a time of meeting continually evolving needs. At the same time, the college remained true to its mission — teaching, research, and serving the people who came into its ever widening purview.

In the latest decade, the departments and other program units continued to address the needs of people, whether they were farmers, agribusinesses, urbanites, adults, or children in Michigan, America, or elsewhere. The CANR units continued in their pursuit of what is best for the world.

The decade past can be viewed in several ways. One perspective is to consider the numerous individual programs, whether they be carried out in classrooms, research laboratories and stations, or in various locales around the state and world.

Another perspective is to view the numerous programs designed to enhance economic development and the quality of life through improved agriculture, community, and natural resources.

A third perspective requires somewhat more intense contemplation. This view grows through an appreciation of the combined totality and the richness of the programs as they link not only to the departments and programs of the CANR but to the sciences of many of the other colleges and departments of the university and beyond.

The editors of this publication trust that the collection of the various accounts and photographs in this chapter and all those preceding have provided a meaningful foundation for understanding what has gone on before to produce the institution we respect and love. The editors also trust that the accounts will convey a sense of meaning and commitment to those who follow and pioneer in the coming decades.

Building on the best of the past

The university acquired the H.D. Box farm in 1977. The barn, carrying the date 1884, is one of the few remaining traditional barns on the campus grounds.

"We have an important role to serve in the world. Because of our land-grant tradition, those of us in the land-grant university need to look upon this as an obligation. Also, as our Extension educators become more mature and more experienced, they need to be challenged at the edge to keep them growing and learning."

Mary L. Andrews,
Associate Professor Emeritus,
Director of International Extension

"Agricultural and environmental sectors need to be closely interrelated. The big problem in future agriculture in most parts of this country and in the world will be water. We must have these fields of concern working closely together."

Russell G. Mawby, MSU Trustee Emeritus

"Future studies on plant cell wall (biomass), plant genomes, plant physiology, and cellulose conversion ... will help transition a major segment of the nation's transportation fuels sector away from imported gasoline, to domestically grown, cleaner burning fuels."

Michael Thomashow, University Distinguished Professor, Department of Crop and Soil Sciences, and President of the American Society of Plant Biologists

M.A.C. banner.

Courtesy of Lynn and Millie Brumm.

Fostering a New Breadth

Chapter Overview

What will the CANR celebrate on February 12, 2055, the time of its bicentennial?

That question, of course, cannot be answered with certainty. One thing is certain: during the next 50 years, many changes in society, the environment, and technology will take place. Widespread change, of course, makes difficult the generation of a definitive plan of action for that period. But uncertainty occurred during the previous 150 years, too. Those of the past could not know what lay ahead. Those of the future, like those in the past, will respond to issues, needs, and opportunities of their time.

Those of the past and present have been dedicated to the land-grant mission. Those who follow will build on that mission as it expands to the "global grant."

The institution will be devoted to preparing young people to serve society, to uncover the complexities of nature, and to carry those discoveries to people of the state, nation, and world.

This closing chapter offers statements relating to future responsibilities, challenges, and opportunities such as the development of the bioeconomy and the reduced dependence of the economy on petroleum. The statements reflect perspectives of the responsibilities, problems, and goals that lie ahead for the college, the Michigan Agricultural Experiment Station, and the MSU Extension.

Contemporary view of Agriculture Hall, which continues to house many CANR functions, including the MAES, MSUE, the Department of Agricultural Economics and numerous other administrative and program functions.

Courtesy Kenneth VerBurg

Broader Perspectives to be Advanced

How the Career Began

Russell Mawby's affiliation with MSU began as a student in horticulture. While a student, he worked as a reporter for *The State News* and became the founding editor of *The Homesteader*, a student magazine. Professor Harold Tukey, head of horticulture, urged him to sample this great university, and he took courses ranging from anthropology to the great religions. He said another great experience was the International Farm Youth Exchange in Europe. Mawby came to believe that breadth in educational experiences is vital.

MSUE Background

He received a master's degree in agricultural economics at Purdue University and returned to MSU to be an Extension specialist. After military service (1956) he became assistant director of Extension in charge of 4-H programs. He completed his Ph.D. in 1959 and in 1964 became director of the Division of Agriculture at the W.K. Kellogg Foundation. Three years later, he became vice president, and in 1970, he began his 25-year term as CEO of the Kellogg Foundation.

Courtesy W.K. Kellogg Foundation

As a 4-H leader, Russell Mawby had a continuing love for giving children new experiences.

Fostering a New Breadth

Mawby said he was intrigued that the early leaders took a broad view of their college. It was the colleges of agriculture that started the professions of home economics because they were concerned with the farm family and of rural sociology because of their interest in community issues.

Over time, he thought the colleges of agriculture across the nation were narrowing their vision and needed to link with such areas as human medicine, nutrition, and communications. When he was a member of the MSU Board of Trustees and the board explored having the Detroit College of Law join MSU, he argued that a law college at MSU could advance some of the university's strengths, such as agriculture, natural resources, family issues and child development — fostering new breadth.

As CEO of the Kellogg Foundation, he helped MSU extend its breadth through his involvement with the Kellogg Biological Station and a grant to MSU in the amount of $10.3 million.[1]

The Power of the Land-Grant

Proud, Grateful, and Dedicated

Courtesy Lynn Vecziedins

Dave Guikema

Passion for Educating

David Guikema expresses his gratitude for having had "a wonderful career working for Michigan State University Extension." He said he was able to combine his passion for educating and helping people to improve their lives and communities.

He was able to work across a spectrum of positions in Extension — from being a small-county agricultural county Extension director (CED) to an economic development educator, a large-county CED, and now the director of the MSU Extension Central Region.

Supportive Public

In every position, the public has been highly supportive of Extension efforts to work in the community to improve people's lives and the environment in which they live and work. Over the years it was very rewarding and interesting to watch Extension evolve to meet the changing needs of society.

Given the investment of his working career and life in MSU Extension, Guikema, like other lifetime devotees to CANR and its programs, expects that the institution's commitment to the land-grant mission will continue to drive efforts and programs of the future. The commitment and dedication to advance the well-being of individuals and communities of our state, the nation, and, indeed, the world will continue as an ongoing goal for MSUE, CANR, and MSU.[2]

Hannah's Legacy

Mirroring Guikema's gratefulness are Diane (1972) and Tom (1973) Emling. They are indebted to John Hannah's legacy of making a positive difference in the lives of people throughout Michigan. Hannah established the university's first regional continuing education center in partnership with Northwestern Michigan College, a community college in Traverse City, shortly after its founding in 1951.

In 1990, MSU expanded its outreach framework by integrating the university's community-based Extension and Lifelong Education programs into six readily accessible, comprehensive regional centers. MSU combined the best of both land-grant worlds by retaining CANR's broad scope and East Lansing's cross-campus academic links and bringing together a cadre of committed professional Extension educators. They provide "close to home and work" agriculture and natural resources, family and consumer science, youth development, and community and leadership development teaching, research, and service plus cross-campus opportunities.

Treasured Covenant

This MSU land-grant and democratic model is indeed a covenant to be treasured by all Michiganians in communities from the foot of Woodward Avenue in Detroit to the shores of Lake Superior at Copper Harbor.[3]

Lasting Relationship with Land-Grant

The following story is one of many that could be told about the way 4-H programs shape the lives of rural and urban youth. The loyalties established in the past and coming years are key to the continuation of the land-grant mission.

Roots in Indiana

Joining 4-H in Indiana at age 9 was exciting for Sandra (Clarkson) and Noel Stuckman. It was the beginning of a long-term relationship with the land-grant philosophy. They are both grateful for the role 4-H played in shaping their values and skills.

Transplanted to Michigan

Graduate programs in agricultural economics (Noel) and family and child ecology (Sandy) drew them to MSU. What they learned and the people they connected with at MSU enabled them to launch the next phases of their careers.

Noel joined the Michigan Farm Bureau (MFB) and provided leadership for the Michigan Agricultural Marketing Cooperative Association. He partnered with MSU on various initiatives during his career at MFB. Sandy worked with MSUE as program leader for family living education, regional supervisor, and diversity specialist.

Loyalty Runs Deep

In their lives after MFB and MSUE, they continue their commitment to MSU as Master Gardener volunteers; investors in the Michigan 4-H Foundation, the CANR, the Ralph Young Fund, and the Wharton Center. They are active members of the Lansing Farmers' Club, and Sandy continues as an MSUE diversity facilitator. They see these actions as providing future students with opportunities similar to those they enjoyed.

The Stuckmans strongly believe in the land-grant tradition of educating people from all walks of life. MSU must remain steadfast in enabling people to apply knowledge and transform their lives. And MSU must maintain its commitment to people. To paraphrase John Hannah's eloquent statement, "People are our most important product."[4]

Extension Mission: Serve Communities...

Challenging Extension Leaders

Extension educators have always been hired and respected for their subject matter expertise. Increasingly, however, the desired skill sets include the ability to assist groups in producing sustainable change by applying knowledge. Such skill, commonly called "process expertise," is essential for community-based educators.

Sharing Leadership

Today's Extension educators work to identify a group's knowledge needs. But they must also increase a group's capacity to create movement and sustainable change through shared leadership and power, and to create energy in a community to stimulate change. Group leaders learn about themselves as they carry out transformational education.

Emergent Wisdom

Tomorrow's Extension educators must be ready to help challenge the status quo.

They can draw on the intellectual capacity and energy of community members who share a vision for a new future. Cultivating the convergence of ideas and creating context for emergent wisdom to grow within the group is the role of the Extension educator. Our community partners and their capacity to create potential futures are among our greatest resources and hope as we address great societal challenges.[5]

Emergency Management: People First

Each disaster, whether an act of God or humans, will be a challenge for MSUE in the years ahead. Emergency managers agree that "all disasters are local," as each one affects a community. MSUE must be ready to serve and assist.

Emergency managers are learning that Extension is a credible source for information that can provide sound counsel throughout the disaster process. After emergency response crews have performed their jobs, Extension will still be part of the community. Extension must be knowledgeable about potential threats, know the players in the emergency management, and inform communities about precautionary actions.

Storms, exotic pests, hazardous material spills, financial downturns, and terrorist acts will continue to be part of life in Michigan. When one occurs, MSUE will assist and bring safety, security, and peace of mind through education.[6]

Courtesy Juan Marinez

Rosa Morales of the MSU School of Journalism interviewing Hector Lierena, who began as a farm worker and now, with his brothers, owns a 380-acre blueberry farm.

Hola, Extension

Juan Marinez was recently watching, "for the 22nd time," *Butch Cassidy and the Sundance Kid.* He says he is always amused by the scene in which the Pinkerton detectives are chasing Butch and Sundance. Throughout the chase, Butch and Sundance keep asking, "Who are these guys?"

The question can well be asked about the many immigrants from Mexico and just what their presence means for MSU's land-grant future.

Mexican immigrants, whether welcome or unwelcome, legal or illegal, will be a significant component of Michigan farm and non-farm economics, and the social, cultural, linguistic, and political landscape from here on. Some of the challenges before us include:

- The continued development of these people so that they may be assets rather than liabilities to Michigan.

- Their inclusion by those in MSUE with roles in community development to ensure their acceptance once they are here.

- Fostering the means to protect and ensure the civil rights of people with a Mexican heritage.

- Identifying and achieving a balance in the ongoing debate about immigrants and homeland security.[7]

...Families and Children

Ozzie and Harriet Don't Live Here Anymore

CANR Tradition

Throughout much of American history, large farm families were predominant. The hands of multiple children were needed to till fields, harvest crops, haul water, tend livestock, and perform other tasks for the family's survival. Families consisted of Mom, Dad, and children all residing under the same roof.

Today's Complexity

Today's families are far more complex. Images of families are reshaped by single parenthood, unmarried couples, childlessness, urban and suburban lifestyles, and high rates of divorce. Despite the changing faces, many Michigan residents live as some sort of a family.

True to Mission

Through all this change, MSUE remains true to its mission of helping people improve their lives through an educational process that applies knowledge to critical issues, needs, and opportunities. Tomorrow's families want to learn to be good parents, to raise physically healthy children, make their communities strong, and prepare for retirement.

While the issues, needs, and opportunities evolve, MSUE will continue to help families make decisions that will improve their lives.[8]

Courtesy Christine M. Flood

Young student enjoying a healthy lunch.

Healthy Children Are Our Future

Obesity Hurdle

Obesity in children has reached epidemic proportions and will likely remain an issue. Being overweight as a child can lead to chronic health problems. The consequences include economic costs for both medical care and lost wages.

The land-grant system will continue to play a key role in health-related research and providing research and education to foster healthy behaviors.

MSUE will work to increase access to health foods and provide opportunities for children and families to be physically active.

FACT Assistance

These programs will be research-based in part because of MSUE and MAES support for the FACT (Families and Communities Together) coalition that assists university personnel in gaining access to resources for research.

These strategies are embedded in the belief that children must feel accepted and valued. Our children are our future, and having healthy children — in mind, body, and spirit — is vital to our world.[10]

Enhancing Our Future: Youth and Adult Connection

The 4-H program in Michigan will celebrate its 100th birthday in 2008. 4-H is a community of young people across America learning leadership, citizenship, and life skills. Its early efforts focused on Michigan farm children, and it will continue to adapt to meet the needs of today's and tomorrow's youth.

Connect Youth

Apathy toward government is one important challenge that today's communities face. Neighborhoods, schools, and parents wrestle with issues related to services, education, and policy development. Our youth are our future — they must feel connected to government and policy-making and have the skills to be active participants and make their voices heard.

They need experiences through which they can learn about decision making and citizenship, and about how their actions can contribute to the common good.

Youth Poised

Our youth are poised to take on tomorrow. 4-H will continue to help them to be sound stewards of their relationships with their communities, peers, and partners to build a compassionate and just society for those who will come after us.[9]

Biotechnology: Opportunities and Challenges

Biotechnology offers many opportunities for agriculture and will affect the future in many significant ways. These new technologies currently involve production traits such as insect and herbicide resistance. In the future, traits affecting the quality of the crop will likely become commercially available.

Agricultural scientists and educators will play a major role in adopting these new technologies.

Benefits and Risks

As with all technologies, biotechnology offers opportunities but also has risks. Agricultural educators will have a significant role in helping growers and advisers understand both the benefits and risks of any new biotechnology trait. This will require a high level of scientific expertise and effective teamwork. Connection with policy-makers, agricultural leaders, the public, and the media through educational programs will also be necessary.[11]

Face of Animal Agriculture Changing

Food Challenge

The U.S. Bureau of Census predicts that the world population will grow to 9.2 billion by 2050. If so, food production must increase by 300 percent in Africa, 80 percent in Latin America, 70 percent in Asia, and 30 percent in North America. These are substantial challenges as the Department of Animal Science marks it 100th anniversary in 2006.

Is the World Ready?

The future is about *choice.* Some farms will become larger; others will depend on organic practices. Some may capitalize on using manure and/or methane for electricity generation, make and sell compost for gardens, or capitalize on agritourism. Among these different ways of farming are many commonalities. How can MSU help?

Research and Extension

MAES scientists will conduct research that enhances environmental stewardship and strengthens animal welfare. It will include technologies such as robotic applications, improved pasture-based systems, and decreasing feed nutrients to lessen the animal waste impact on land, water, and air quality. MSUE will continue its work with farmers and the public.

Teaching

Young people must learn to think critically. Communicating with the public about environmental stewardship and animal welfare will be fundamental to the success of animal agriculture. Through classwork, internships, and study abroad, students will be prepared to contribute to a global agricultural system that will be sustainable for years to come.[12]

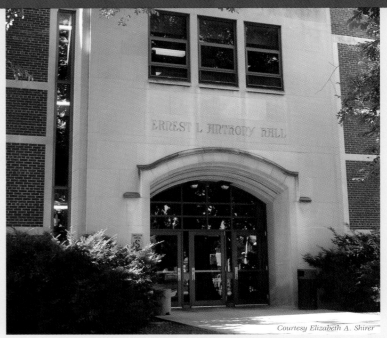
Courtesy Elizabeth A. Shirer

Ernest L. Anthony Hall houses the Department of Animal Science.

Packaging Changes for the Future

Packaging has gone from containers that simply hold products to packages that preserve products and extend shelf life. Modern packaging allows us to have many products, especially agricultural products, year round.

Digitized Info

New packaging developments will take us to materials that interact with products and with the world around them. New materials will have the capacity to release fresh flavors or aromas when a package is opened. Electronic chips will be applied to track packages and also imbed information such as pricing, shelf-life dates, and consumer instructions that can be read automatically by appliances at home.

Customizing

Packages will be designed so they are easy for the consumer to use and still provide protection against theft and counterfeiting. Future opportunities will include design and print packages customized to individuals and their needs.

The opportunities are limitless for us to continue to make products better simply by making packaging better.[13]

...Anticipate Changing Needs

Water Science: The Future

The U.S. Environmental Protection Agency and the Department of Homeland Security awarded $10 million to MSU and Drexel University in Philadelphia in October 2005. The grant will fund a Center for Advancing Microbial Risk Assessment (CAMRA). The center will be a first responder national resource for understanding of infectious disease and bioterrorism outbreaks.

Joan B. Rose, the Homer Nowlin Chair for Water Research at MSU, will co-direct the CAMRA along with Charles Hass of Drexel University. Regarding the future of water science, she

Courtesy Kenneth VerBurg

offered the following comments.

Value of Water

Is safe water important in our lives? Imagine the need to walk more than a mile each day just to access water from a polluted river and bring it to your family in a jug. Imagine learning your ulcer or stomach cancer was caused by a bacterium in

your well water. Such things are happening.

Our water environment and the connection to our quality of life in Michigan are unusual. The water agreement among the Great Lakes states and provinces of Canada is one of the best international agreements protecting the world's greatest freshwater resource.

New Questions

New questions about water quantity and quality, water management, and water monitoring are coming into play. Others concern the need for a widely understood ethical paradigm for community, industry, and government leaders, and society in general.

Tools and Ethics

New technology for monitoring water quantity and quality is accessible and should be applied to address the hydrologic cycle holistically.[14]

Courtesy of Joan Rose

Water research team sampling water off beach area.

Planning, Design, Construction

Courtesy Robert von Bernuth

Challenges

The next 50 years will bring many challenges and opportunities. The world's population may double; global warming may cause oceans to rise, affecting coastal areas; land use will change and require economic and social adaptations. Technological tools and materials will be invented to help manage the built and natural environments.

New Directions

Planning, design, construction, and management will require the integration of science-based solutions. Not only will the challenges change — the approach to solutions will also change. Innovations in environmental planning, design, construction, and management will foster cooperation across programs, departments, and colleges on campus and beyond.

One of several options for a proposed new facility for the School of Planning, Design, and Construction would encompass the old power plant and operate within the shadow of Spartan Stadium.

The faculty will need to be multifaceted, capable of engaging social science, engineering, and natural resource issues in an integrated holistic manner, and adapting their skills to ever-changing problems and opportunities.

Future faculty members and students will not be limited by the traditions, institutional organizations, and intellectual structures founded in the century just past. It will be a new age of scholarship and intellectual activity.[15]

Food Safety, A Goal Pursued...

Engineering and Biosystems Challenges

The Department of Biosystems and Agricultural Engineering celebrated its 100-year anniversary in March 2006. The joyful time also had some somber moments as the celebrants addressed questions about the future such as:

- Can the world feed as many as 11 billion people?
- Can producers ensure high quality and safe food?
- Can the agriculture industry protect the environment?
- Will land and water resources be sufficient to produce the needed food?
- Can colleges prepare students for such issues?

Applied Science

During the next 50 years the biosystems curriculum will become a discipline firmly grounded in biology, with applications in food, agriculture, the environment, and human health. Biosystems engineers will also be called upon to detect and isolate pathogens in the fight against bioterrorism.

A new biosafety level II food safety research laboratory, will enable work that can be done only in an isolated lab. This facility will benefit the food processing industry in an immediate way. MAES research helps to chart the course to new solutions.[16]

Courtesy Elizabeth A. Shirer

"Agricultural engineering ... involves specifically biological and environmental factors, since it deals with engineering applied to biological matter — food, feed, natural fiber, animals and humans.... The ability to combine the knowledge of biology and engineering ... offers the greatest opportunity ... to our profession in years."

ASAE President A.W. Farrall, in an address at the 1962 annual meeting.

A.W. Farrall Agricultural Engineering Hall.

Food Science and Nutrition

The Food Challenge

During recent history, human beings have been concerned with access to a food supply that is safe, nutritious, and sufficient to meet daily needs. The safety of food has continually improved but will continue to be an issue as new pathogens pose new threats.

Drive for Safety

The food industry may never be able to assure a completely risk-free food supply. But research will eventually lead to rapid, non-invasive testing methods that will report within seconds whether a product contains a microorganism that may cause illness.

Designer Foods

Enormous strides in public health were made by fortifying foods with vitamins and minerals. Most recently, flour was fortified with folate to reduce the incidence of neural tube defect in newborn infants. Scientists are increasingly emphasizing discovery of "nutraceuticals," non-nutrient compounds from natural products — plants, algae, microbes, etc.— that hold the potential to reduce risk for chronic disease.

Personal Nutrition

Advances in genetics that have linked specific genes to metabolism and risk for chronic disease provide the foundation for personalizing nutritional recommendations. It is increasingly evident that a dietary recommendation for one individual, such as increasing consumption of fish oils, may reduce that person's risk for cardiovascular disease while increasing another's risk, depending on gender and genotype.

Genetic Weight Factors

Nutritionists are focusing on obesity and its consequent diseases. Success with the

Courtesy Kenneth VerBurg

G. Malcolm Trout Food Science and Human Nutrition Building.

obesity crisis requires nutritional scientists, the food industry, educators and health care professionals to modify the food supply and regulations.[17]

Food Safety Research, Education, and Outreach

One of the top university food safety centers in the country, the National Food Safety and Toxicology Center (NFSTC), has made significant strides in food safety research, education, and outreach. As the NFSTC continues to contribute to the safety of the food supply, its goals include:

- Address the issues facing society today — resolve deadly pathogen issues, improve public health, provide consumer education tools, and help businesses think proactively about safety.

- Anticipate future issues — deadlier pathogens, vaccine development, and home and policy recommendations.

(continued on page 281)

...with Biological Sciences

Sustainable Food Systems in Biobased Economy

Future Scenario

The early part of the 21st century will be known as the peak oil period. Major new agriculture and engineering initiatives are developing to substitute agricultural products for energy and manufacturing chemicals from petroleum. An era of intense competition for agricultural crops is emerging.

As world population grows, we will experience food trade deficits and get increasing percentages of our fruits and vegetables from non-domestic sources. Michigan needs the equivalent of half of its current farmland to feed the present population; matching the current oil equivalent through ag-based production will require a tremendous amount of agricultural production.

Foods and Biofuels

We have an opportunity to develop a sustainable approach to balancing our need for food, energy, and products in a biobased economy while reducing resource utilization. The Michigan Agricultural Experiment Station has both a challenge and opportunity to lead as it seeks new solutions for the coming decades.

Don't Forget

- Gains in our knowledge of sustainable agricultural practices must not be abandoned in our drive for energy sources.

- Losing our food production capacity is as dire a threat as losing our energy sources.

- Linking healthy diet and local agriculture can be a key to managing health care costs.

- Rural communities with a diversified farming base are key to continued development as a nation.

MSU can help lead our research in systemic, sustainable approaches; the education of the next generation leaders; and our outreach to communities and families across Michigan. Developing a sustainable agricultural production that balances need in these areas and maintains opportunity for our children's children is the goal.[18]

Sugar, Brine, and Road Salt

Looking to the future can be intimidating. Responders to the question of what the future will bring unanimously acknowledge that tomorrow will be different from today.

Hope and Fear

The previous story carries an element of hope — the expectation that biofuels will offset the impending shortage of oil. It also stimulates an element of fear — that incentives to generate biofuels could lessen production of an adequate food supply. The following current example illustrates the point.

Good News

As the winter snowfall began, the *Lansing State Journal*[20] reported that, for the first time, road service agencies are using a mixture of sugar beets and brine to improve the ice-melting effectiveness of salt on roadways.

Jurisdictions are still experimenting with the product, and some may see it as a positive example of value-added agricultural products. Reportedly, the product is environmentally friendly as it reduces the need for road salt and, if effective, will reduce fuel costs of service vehicles and labor by 40 percent.

Other News

Sugar beet growers may rejoice at the new use of their products, but others may fear that the increased demand for sugar beets will lead traditional growers of corn, beans, or other food products to shift to growing sugar beets and cause price increases in the food products.

Also, commentators on the story feared that the solution might attract deer and increase automobile and deer collisions.

Innovations are still coming. Many will have both positive and negative effects.[21]

Food Safety Research... *(continued from page 280)*

- Transmit the expertise of faculty members to the stewards of tomorrow — the students. Growing scientists, entrepreneurs, and leaders in food safety is a key NFSTC goal.

- Develop an international focus in collaboration with universities in Europe, the Middle East, and Asia on joint programs.

- Continue transdisciplinary collaboration for societal improvement. The mission includes disciplines in and outside the university and partnerships with government, industry, and other stakeholders.

- Attract, develop, and maintain a diverse and high quality faculty within the

NFSTC. The NFSTC's faculty members represent more than 15 departments in seven colleges. A recent joint appointment in risk communication underlines the continuing commitment to combine the life sciences with the social sciences.[19]

Courtesy Kenneth VerBurg

The Plant Pathology Research Center on College Road.

Community Services to Continue

Community and Economic Development Challenge

Michigan's position in terms of per capita income has trended downward since the 1960s. The basic reason is the state's reliance on high-wage, low-skill manufacturing jobs. Mechanization and outsourcing are displacing the state's traditional economic base.

Key Resources

The main drivers of economic growth have changed. Assets such as clean air, water, recreational opportunities, a skilled work force, and cultural amenities are much more important today than they were in the 20th century. In the future, the quality of the environment will be a major determinant of growth and development.

Communities must develop strategies to carry them to success in the revised economy.

MSU's Role

Michigan has abundant assets: natural beauty, coasts, a friendly international border, well developed transportation systems, high quality universities, and a hardworking, creative work force. To build on these assets, communities need MSU Extension to help grow leaders and infuse innovation into local businesses, educational systems, and community infrastructure.[22]

The Natural Resources Building is the home of natural resource and community-based studies.

Creating Sustainable Cities

Central City Future

Sir Isaac Newton proved that what goes up comes down. Statisticians teach us that populations regress to a mean. For many years, urban planning and community development specialists have focused on strengthening the central city and its business district. The automobile and improved road system, however, facilitated "wealth flight" from the central cities, leaving a much different population in many central cities. Reinventing central cities to encourage the population to return will not likely be successful. City planners should create sustainable "cool" cities for those who live there.

Population Mixture

The U.S. Bureau of Census projects that the U.S. population mix in 2050 will be about 50 percent Caucasian and 50 percent other races. Now is the time for universities and industry, commerce, and government representatives to invest in recruiting and training the next generation of diverse community leaders to build sustainable communities.

Next Generation Leaders

To defy gravity and stay on the positive limb of a normal distribution, we need to train a new cadre of diverse leaders who understand planning, zoning, economics, laws, and policy, and are committed to serve their communities. They need to enhance the cultural base in ways that make housing, utilities, jobs, health care, food, etc., available to all who live there.[23]

Future of Land-Grant Mission and Local Government

50-year Tradition

MSU has provided education and technical assistance outreach to local governments in Michigan since the late 1950s. Helping to build the governing skills of local officials as well as assisting communities and residents to participate in the democratic process is consistent with the land-grant mission.

The role that the university can play to foster good governance, assist distressed local units, and link university resources to elected and appointed officials in fulfillment of their duties will remain an important contributor to the quality of life in local communities.

Endowed Obligation

Extension's state and local government program, through the recent endowment of a faculty position in the Department of Agricultural Economics, will continue the legacy and the commitment of the land-grant university to train local officials, conduct research for state policy-makers, and educate Michigan residents on public issues.[24]

Challenges and Opportunities for MAES

New Fronts for Research

The greatest challenge of the MAES in the coming years is to respond effectively to an expanding and changing clientele as the land-grant mission is redefined and reinvigorated for the 21st century. The MAES is being challenged on many new fronts, many of which are highly controversial.

Address Problems

Indeed, the world has changed immensely during the past 150 years, but one thing remains clear: MSU still has an indisputable responsibility to address the problems that the residents of Michigan and the world face. The people and their problems have changed, but the fundamental responsibility of a great land-grant university has not.

Define Opportunities

In research, this means conducting fundamental work that defines new scientific and economic opportunities while applying the best science to the day-to-day issues facing people and industries. The ability of the CANR to respond effectively to these challenges will determine our future relevance. The college must respond wisely.[25]

CANR Stakeholders and the Future

The CANR, together with the MAES and MSUE, have had strong, long-term relationships with those whom it serves—its stakeholders. The relationships have continued over the decades because of their mutual benefit. CANR research expertise and outreach services have contributed to the profitability and sustainability of Michigan's agricultural and natural resource sectors and the continued vital work of building successful Michigan communities.

One lesson from the early history is that stakeholders created M.A.C. and strongly supported the formation and continued support of the Michigan Agricultural Experiment Station and the Cooperative Extension Service. The stakeholder actions were driven by their avid desire for educated children, science-based problem solving, newly applied knowledge for living, and meaningful interaction with their land-grant university.

Over the years, these stakeholders were strong supporters of governmental support for these institutions and have articulated the importance of the land-grant institution not only to the quality of their lives but to the economy of Michigan.

As Gale Arent, former director of stakeholder relations, stated, "Continued affirmative recognition for these mutual benefits will assure a continued synergy between the people and the people's university. Current supporters believe that the CANR will continue to engage Michigan residents with relevant programs that advance knowledge and transform lives to pioneer in the 21st century."[26]

Systemic development in action in India.

Courtesy Richard Bawden

Sustainability for the Future

A century and a half ago, the basic challenge to the college was straightforward: harness science and technology to increase the production of farm commodities in Michigan. Over the intervening years, through its teaching, research, and extension activities, the college has been undeniably successful in this mission.

Complex Challenges

Agriculture has become much more multifunctional and global, and the challenges have become much more complex in both context and content. The new context is "sustainability," and it dictates that the content must now include ethical and ecological dimensions as well as the more conventional technical, social, and economic ones.

Holistic and Systemic

To maintain its commitment to serve the people in this new dynamic era, the college must develop new ways of engaging with them in a much more holistic manner. This, in turn, will demand new ways of thinking and new ways of doing things that are much more systemic than in the past.[27]

283

Broadened Responsibilities Ahead

John C. Baker, Associate Director, Michigan Agricultural Experiment Station.

John C. Baker served in the College of Veterinary Medicine as associate dean for research and graduate studies. In 2005 he served as interim director of MAES. Baker calls his experience with the MAES "an education, to say the least." The comment that follows reflects perspectives he gained about the MAES, the breadth of its interests and linkages to other units of the university, and its importance to private and public sectors. He is now an Associate Director of MAES.

Society's Needs

The challenge before the MAES is to address society's needs within the context of its mission by developing solutions to problems its stakeholders face. The MAES serves the residents of Michigan — all of them. For example, the land policy program in which we are investing addresses the issues of farmland preservation and urban revitalization.

Environmental Policy

Environmental policy is another area in which we need to be active. The issues range from pollutants to global warming and the effects on agriculture. Farmers face increasing environmental regulations, particularly those applying to concentrated animal feeding operations. Needed are answers about how best to protect the environment while offering cost-effective solutions for agricultural producers.

Ag Operations

There is room for every type of agriculture — small, medium, and large. As small farms make a comeback, mid-sized farms are probably the stress point now. Our goal is to foster economic development in Michigan. The state can benefit from all sizes of farms. So the MAES focuses on the issues facing both small farming and large production operations.

Value-added Actions

Another challenge is to facilitate value-added agricultural production. Researchers, producers, and others in the agricultural community must continue to explore the possibilities. Creativity from these relationships is essential for economic development. The MSU Product Center for the CANR is leading this effort.

Michigan cannot ignore any economic development opportunity. For example, the Eastern Market in Detroit is a pilot project for the MAES to broaden its urban research programs. The project addresses issues such as food distribution through local food cooperatives and even matters of obesity and diabetes. Some people in Detroit simply do not have access to fresh produce or food stores that are not convenience shops.

Biocomposites/Fuels

Biofuels and biocomposites are agriculturally based renewable resources for manufacturing. The new mechanical engineering facility for automotive research, now under construction, may provide another opportunity for joint relationships as engineers explore developing biofuels and plant scientists seek to modify plants to increase their biofuel contributions.

Biofuels and biocomposites are research areas we need to examine. They are areas in which MSU can contribute real expertise to help build Michigan's future economy. We already have a project with Green Meadows Farm using a methane digester to convert waste materials and plant products into fuels.

Cooperation Essential

The CANR cannot address all research issues by itself. Currently the MAES has linkages with five colleges: Agriculture and Natural Resources, Veterinary Medicine, Social Science, Natural Science, and Engineering. The MAES has developed linkages with other colleges on the campus and will need to expand these partnerships to meet our mission obligations. For example, partnering with the medical community will be important in addressing nutrition and health issues. In addition, linkages need to be formed with other universities and the private sector.

Who Will Be Farmers?

Another aspect of change is the in-migration of farm workers. These workers begin as laborers, but over time they gather resources and become farm owners. A visit to the graduation of persons receiving certificates for blueberry production was an eye-opener. This is a key entry point for Hispanic farmers. Michigan is No.1 in blueberry production and growing blueberries is popular among Hispanic farmers.

The Horticulture Teaching and Research Center on south College Road focuses on fruit, ornamentals, vegetables, organic farming, and vineyard and grape production.

...and Thoughtful Analysis

Forward-looking Solutions

Courtesy Susan Smalley

The student organic farm at MSU tests organic crop production in two growing seasons — a summer season using the open fields, and a winter season using the unheated "high tunnels" (temporary greenhouses) shown in the picture. The Kellogg Foundation has been an important initiator and supporter of the student farm.

Equipment Innovations

Will large agricultural operations need new machinery or new mechanisms to deal with their operations, animal waste, aroma, and other environmental issues? The demand for new machines and mechanisms will continue, and new ideas will continue to emerge. Equipment advances may include robotic equipment that replaces much of the human labor, especially in large-scale farming.

Future devices are likely to rely heavily on electronic technology. One can already see a range of field equipment that uses global positioning equipment, which measures the harvest from different parts of a field and may generate a printout indicating the need to fertilize one part of the field more than others. Other advances involving sensors and Internet applications have changed farming.

At one time, fruit growers applied chemicals every 2 weeks following a strict schedule. Now they remotely monitor temperature, humidity, and other variables to forecast possible increases of certain pest populations or a damaging fungal infection. Growers can apply what is needed when it is needed.

Sustainability

Many issues relate to questions of sustainable agriculture in the context of ecosystem, social, and economic health. That is an area in which the MAES needs to continue and expand its research portfolio.

Applied and Basic

Applied research is related to specific problems of today. Basic research provides the tools to address the problems of tomorrow. In fundamental research, one can never predict the findings that creative minds will generate. For example, pasteurization was developed for a problem in the wine industry, but its application to milk processing has had an enormous impact on public health.

Consider the Australians who just received the Nobel Prize in medicine. For years, the accepted cause of gastric ulcers was stress, but the Australian scientists found a bacterial organism associated with gastric ulcers. To prove the relationship of the bacterium to gastric ulcers, one of the investigators inoculated himself, induced the ulcers, and then cured himself through antibiotic therapy. Sometimes you need people who think outside the box, and sometimes people in universities need to challenge dogma.[28]

Courtesy Kenneth VerBurg

Odor control is one area of study at the new Swine Teaching and Research Center east of College Road.

Key Insights and Implications

As incomes rise and people move into suburban environments, they tend to value rural conditions such as rural landscapes, open space, clean water, clean air, wildlife habitat, and more. Their concerns may include treatment of farm animals and small-farm viability. Also, the public increasingly recognizes the existence of tradeoffs.

"Scientific Progress?"

A decline in the overall faith in scientific progress tends to accompany these value shifts. The premise that science leads to resulting progress comes under greater scrutiny, and concern that the products of science can have unintended but negative consequences grows.

Integrated Approaches Addressing Tradeoffs

If the public is to embrace science more, researchers must understand the role of the public in validating science and the social choices. In this climate, researchers will be more effective if they attempt to identify the tradeoffs embedded in various social choices, and if they use this information to inform debates.

Also, research will be more beneficial if it is designed and conducted with colleagues in other disciplines and includes stakeholders in meaningful ways. Such approaches will aid farmers, businesses, citizens and their representatives to make informed choices.[29]

Confidence and Energetic Work...

Complex Learning

Opportunity

Online courses offer the possibility of reaching students anywhere and anytime. The rapidly advancing Web technology is allowing the university to extend the campus across the entire globe. Students in China, Antarctica, and East Lansing will interact and learn with one another and the professor through the virtual classroom in ways unprecedented in human history.

Subtleties Valued

The challenge in realizing this new opportunity, however, is that faculty members and students not lose or dilute our one valued privilege — the person-to-person interaction that occurs in the real classroom, where all of the subtleties and nuances of true learning interplay and promote real understanding. The face-to-face dialogue between students and teachers, a quintessential human action dating back well before

Socrates and responsible for the creation of the first universities, is impossible to replicate through electronic intermediaries.

Face to Face

The challenge is to balance the reach, effectiveness, and efficiencies of the expanding technologies with the need for students and teachers to talk and learn, as one human to another, together in the classrooms and laboratories and beyond.[30]

MSUE Benefits to Persevere

County Extension offices have been trusted, go-to places to find up-to-date information regarding agriculture and natural resources, family and consumer sciences, community development, and 4-H Youth Development. County Extension professionals have contributed greatly to society by connecting local issues to university research and creating opportunities for people to apply this new knowledge to meet their needs.

The type of knowledge and its delivery will evolve to meet future demands for information. Daniel Pink in *A Whole New Mind* asserts that society is transitioning from an informational economy to a conceptual age in which creative right-brain thinkers will reap society's richest rewards and share its greatest joys.[32]

Extension educators will continue to build human capital and encourage conceptual thinking within the context of a global society.[33]

Now It's Our Obligation, Our Responsibility

Land-granter

"Access, opportunity, and applications" are his values and the reasons he joined the land-grant ranks more than 30 years ago. The connections between past and present are too compelling to ignore. Frank Fear grew up in a small New York town, four doors away from a county Extension office, with absolutely no idea that he would have a lifelong connection to the land-grant tradition.

People's College

Higher education in the mid-1800s was reserved for those from society's upper strata. M.A.C. was a radical idea — a "people's college" — that in focus, subject matter, and constitution was unique in the higher education landscape. Is he honoring that heritage?

Frank Fear was thinking about that question while reading a *New York Times* editorial about standards for organic agriculture and the

circumstances facing small to medium-sized farms. How he and you answer those and other challenges will define land-grant in contemporary terms.

Keep Flame Bright

What better place than MSU — the first land-grant college — to show the world how to live the founders' values? It's our obligation, our responsibility, to keep the flames of land-grant burning brightly.[31]

Jane Bush of Eaton County follows practices of sustainable agriculture in producing swine, eggs, apples, and apple products, which she sells in the region.

Courtesy Marty Heller

Forestry Opportunities

Daniel E. Keathley, Chairperson, Forestry Department.

The Best is Coming

As one looks at the evolving Department of Forestry, it appears the finest years are yet to come. The science appears to be heading into the golden age of forest management. As has been true since 1902, the Department of Forestry is positioned to lead in that new era.

Demand Growing

The resource base of Michigan is expanding. Demands for wood products and related goods and services are rising. Forests as biological systems are intimately linked with watersheds and wildlife populations. Forestry has shifted to an ecosystem perspective vital for prudent utilization of forest resources.

Best Use of Products

Maintaining undisturbed forest ecosystems places increased pressure to harvest timber from non-industrial, privately held forests, and the need to rework timber supply models. These pressures also necessitate research to increase efficiency, promote recycling of wood products, develop environmentally benign wood preservatives, and expand the use of wood composites.

Public Involvement

Public outrage over past practices has encouraged planning processes that involve public participation and recognize the importance of the full integration of social, economic, and biological principles. Recent wildfires and damage by invasive insects have focused public attention on the need for forest management research and policy development.

Department Will Succeed

The department's responsibility in the future, then, is to advance the science and educational programs and provide the foundation for a management system that balances these forces and leads to improved forest resources for future generations. This daunting task will require the best science and finest thinking.[34]

Tree research center on Jolly Road is used by the Department of Forestry to test new tree varieties, evaluate new forest management practices, and help assure sustainable management of Michigan forests.

Courtesy Kenneth VerBurg

Guyer-Seevers Endowed Chair

The future of the CANR will focus increasingly on the sustainability of agriculture and natural resources. Leadership in natural resource conservation will be assured, in part, through the Gordon and Norma Guyer and Gary L. Seevers Endowed Chair in Natural Resource Conservation.

Gordon Guyer and Gary Seevers are both three-degree alumni of the college. Guyer's degrees in entomology led to a lifetime interest in conservation. His career within nonprofit organizations, state government and MSU culminated in Guyer's service as the 18th president of MSU.

Long-term CANR Loyalist

Seevers was the first CANR student within the Honors College. He followed his B.S. degree in animal science with an M.S. and a Ph.D. in agricultural economics. His expertise led to a career in Washington and on Wall Street, where he served on councils under Presidents Nixon and Ford and later became vice president and partner of Goldman Sachs.

Gary L. Seevers and Gordon Guyer

Seevers' interest in agriculture began in his childhood on a farm when involved in 4-H and FFA programs.

In addition to other generous gifts to the Michigan 4-H Foundation, college scholarship funds, Seevers served as co-chair of the President's Cabinet in the MSU capital campaign and a member of the CANR Stakeholders' Advisory Committee. In 2004, he was awarded an honorary doctor of business degree from MSU for his lifetime contributions to his profession and MSU.

At the kick-off for the Campaign for MSU, Seevers said this will be "an opportunity to ... be part of the future direction of this college for generations to come."[35]

Biofuels Benefit Communities...

Growing Demand for Biofuels

Ready to Lead a Developing Economy

Oil Addiction

In his 2006 State of the Union address, President George W. Bush said, "America is addicted to oil." Underlying the comment were elevated oil prices, world environmental concerns, and new technologies for alternative fuels.

Deb Price, a *Detroit News* Washington columnist, reported, "The potential of ethanol biofuels has huge implications for Michigan, home of ... rich farmland that is already the second-biggest income generator in the state."[36]

Oil Alternatives

"'I've believed for a long time that this day would come,' says Bruce Dale, the director of the Biomass Conversion Laboratory at Michigan State University. For a decade, the lab has researched how to produce ethanol cheaply from fast-growing crops like switchgrass or plant debris, as is done with corn. Switchgrass, sawdust, and corn stalks are examples of abundant, renewable organic matter — known as cellulosic biomass — that scientists want to turn into fuel because corn requires large areas of land and is used for human and animal food.

"'We're not quite there yet, but that is completely realistic.'"[37]

MSU Role

MSU's commitment to bio-based technologies was strengthened with the formation of the Office of Bio-Based Technologies in March 2006. Steven Pueppke, director of MAES and assistant vice president for research and graduate studies, will direct the new office.

Ian Gray, vice president for research and graduate studies, said the new office "will ensure that MSU's expertise in plant sciences, chemistry, agricultural sciences, and engineering is fully ... engaged in transforming Michigan's economy.

Similarly, Pueppke stated, "The development of new bio-based materials, chemicals, and fuels will require partnerships that reach across research, industry, labor, and state and federal governments. One of the main goals of the new office will be to further strengthen existing partnerships and forging new ones...."

The terms "biomass" and "bioeconomy" have been used around MSU for some time. They have come to the forefront statewide and nationally in discussions of alternative energy.

Funding Support

"Governor Jennifer Granholm announced plans to invest in alternative energy research through the 21st Century Jobs Fund during her 2006 State of the State address. She singled out Lou Anna Simon,

In her 2006 State of the State address, Governor Granholm said, "President Lou Anna Simon and her 'Spartans' are positioning our state to lead the world in the new 'bio-economy' developing energy and other products from our agricultural sector."[38]

a special guest on the House floor, as a university president who would be leading the way."

Biobased Economic Sector

"For Michigan and MSU researchers, the possibilities expand far beyond alternative energy. The state ... is positioned to build a new, biobased economic sector on the foundation of its agricultural, forestry, and natural resources sector and its industrial and manufacturing sectors, according to Simon. The result would be the advancement of a new, sustainable biobased sector that will provide a competitive advantage in meeting the growing global market demand for renewable sources of materials, chemicals, and energy in their products, processes, and packaging."

Cellulose-based Packaging

"Most plastics contain petroleum products, as do common building and furniture materials such as fiberglass, and demand is rising for non-petroleum replacements.

"Michigan can take the lead in developing the products and the processes needed for creating them by connecting our industries with research and entrepreneurial activities in the basic sciences, engineering, plant science, and agriculture at MSU and state institutions, according to Mike Thomashow, University distinguished professor in crop and soil sciences.

"Collaboration can provide our state with a foundation for vigorous development of a biobased economic sector. It will produce not only non-petroleum, plant-based products for industry but new businesses, new jobs, and new intellectual property in Michigan—literally, to grow a new economy. As a world leader in plant science research, MSU has a strong patent portfolio for leading Michigan in developing the bioeconomy.

"The thousands of jobs that can arise from the new biobased economy span many sectors of the workforce, including research, agriculture, forestry, equipment and product manufacturing, education, business management, and marketing."[39]

Economic Impact Study

"The Economic Impact and Potential of the Michigan Agri-Food System" highlights how the agri-food system has the potential to add nearly $1 billion annually to the Michigan economy if current investment trends continue over the next three to five years.

"The paper, released by the MSU Product Center for Agriculture and Natural Resources in January [2006], examines economic contributions from agriculture and related industries, including leather, nursery, turfgrass, ornamental plants, and food processing. This total food and fiber system has a $60.1 billion impact each year for the state economy.

"'This is the first time a study of the economic impact, including investment and future potential of the agri-food system, has been completed,'" says Bill Knudson, product marketing economist with the product center. 'The idea was to look at areas that show potential for growth....'"

Strong Employment

The paper highlights how the state agri-food system also employs nearly one quarter of all employed Michiganians.

More than 725,000 are directly employed in the industry; others are employed in related sectors. Agri-food is the state's second largest production sector, behind the automotive industry.

"'These findings underscore that Michigan's dynamic agricultural industry — with its robust capital investment in new technology — is growing and diversifying our state's economic base,' said Mitch Irwin, director of the Michigan Department of Agriculture, who requested the study. 'MSU's conclusions bode well for Michigan's future.'"[41]

Bioenergy Industry Potential

The paper includes two scenarios for potential expansion across the agri-food system; one based on knowledge of current investments in the system and a second based on a more general pattern of investment. Both show the potential for considerable economic growth — nearly $1 billion per year over the next three to five years. The result would be an increase in jobs of more than 23,000 annually from direct and indirect sources.

Courtesy David Bransby

Switchgrass can be a source of biomass in Michigan and adjacent states.

Basics of Biomass Conversion [40]

Feedstock	Conversion	Bioproducts
Biomass resources Waste materials Energy crops • Herbaceous • Woody crops **Biomass** Starch Lipid Lignocellulose	**Biochemical** Enzymatic Chemical **Thermochemical** Combustion Liquefaction Gasification **Biological** Fermentation Digestion	**Bioenergy/biofuels** Electricity Heat **Gaseous Fuels** Biogas Syngas Hydrogen **Liquid Fuels** Ethanol Biodiesel Dimethyl ether Biocatalysis **Biochemicals/biomaterials** Industrial chemicals Biodegradable plastics Biofibers Biocomposites **Food and Pharmaceuticals** Nutraceuticals Functional foods Plant-based antibiotics

Courtesy Kris Berglund

Questions and Answers about Bioeconomy

What does bioeconomy or biobased economy mean?
A bioeconomy means ... connecting the strengths in agriculture, forestry, and natural resources to strengths in manufacturing and industry.

What is biomass?
Biomass, biosolids, and feedstock refer to the plant-based raw materials refined into replacements for petroleum and other fossil fuels in chemicals, energy, and materials such as plastics.

What kinds of jobs can be created in a bioeconomy?
The many jobs ... include research, agriculture, forestry, equipment and product manufacturing, education and training, business management, marketing, sales, and distribution.

Why is MSU central to building a bioeconomy?
MSU has historic strengths in plant science and chemistry and deep connections with manufacturing and agricultural industries. In cooperation with other institutions, MSU has a wealth of collected assets to achieve this goal.

What could this mean for a Michigan farmer?
A farmer would think of crops not purely as a food product but would consider all potential uses of the plant....and realize a much higher price per acre than from a food commodity.[42]

The IIA Looks Forward

Today, U.S. agrifood industries and supply chains, running "from farm to fork," are boldly shaped by international interests and global markets. Traditional food systems have been transformed — increasingly interconnected, dominated by multinational corporations, and stretching to all corners of the globe.

Access to new technologies and markets and understanding of international regulatory systems for food safety and quality will determine which nations and producer groups will succeed in this new environment. The land-grant universities of today stand at a threshold where even local problems are often rooted in seemingly distant trends.

Guiding Principles

The importance of internationalizing MSU's faculty and departments will be greater than ever. To meet this escalating need, the Institute of International Agriculture (IIA) must be prepared and make the investments today that will yield the greatest positive impact tomorrow. Three overarching principles will guide these investments:

- *Be forward-looking and strategic in program development.* The IIA must be adept at identifying and proactive in shaping future priority demands for international research, education, and outreach. The first step is coalescing interdisciplinary faculty teams committed to meet priority challenges, including partnerships with other institutions.

- *Be committed to intellectual leadership.* The IIA must support departments and faculty members in ways that help MSU build "centers of excellence." Selected priority areas will allow MSU to be proactive in defining the issues and working with funding agencies to develop new opportunities.

- *Live what it means to be a land-grant university in the 21st century.* MSU's commitment to "advancing knowledge and transforming lives" can be no more profound than in service to people less fortunate than ourselves. Commitment by the IIA and the CANR is more than just a great challenge — it is a moral responsibility.[43]

International Service

A world with nearly 3 billion people earning less than $2 per day is not sustainable. Environmental degradation, communicable disease proliferation, and increased terrorism are only a few of the tragic outcomes of this global income gap. Therefore, global poverty is a local Michigan problem, and MSU is uniquely qualified to help address the global poverty issue.

Mutual Benefits

Globally competent students and professionals result from our participation in international collaborative research and development programs. The agriculture of the state and nation has benefited significantly from MSU's international participation — e.g., germ plasm* collected from the developing world that was used as the foundation of increased crop yields. Our international development involvement has also increased the number of markets for our food and industrial products.

Challenges

- Current academic emphasis on peer-reviewed publications in prestigious journals as opposed to applied

Courtesy Raymond D. Vlasin

Ashok Seth of the World Bank (L), Arlen Leholm, Director of Extension (C), and Raymond Vlasin, University Distinguished Professor (R) of MSU Extension, conducted a workshop in Hyderabad, India, in 1998.

research and problem-solving activities.

- Diminished funding for applied research and the shift of competitive grants to basic research.

- Intellectual property rights holdings that threaten access to important crop germ plasm needed for plant breeding programs.

Opportunities

- MSU faculty members have developed knowledge that can help reduce global poverty.

- Faculty member participation in international development will improve recruitment of quality faculty members and students.

International service has long been an important component of the CANR's globalization strategy. MSU's mission is and must continue to be the use of knowledge to enhance the quality of life for the masses.[44]

---

*Hereditary material of germ cells.

...Mutually Beneficial

Pioneering International Extension

Begun in Okinawa

MSU Extension's international programs began with the work of Margaret Harris in the 1950s. The Okinawa project was the very first international project in "institution building" by land-grant universities. Harris interviewed Okinawan families, determined what skills they needed, and built those skills into a curriculum so bachelor's degree students could teach them.

Mutual Building

Since then, Extension has involved personnel abroad in many ways and shared those experiences at home. Many students from other countries have come here to be educated. MSUE needs to continue building the capacity of Extension educators so they can translate what they experience to American communities.

Guest Scholar Model

Also, we need to assist Extension services abroad, as was done in India when we helped their Extension apply tools and techniques that were found workable elsewhere. MSUE should assist more guest scholars such as the Indian Fulbright Fellow, V.V. Sadamate, whose findings on public-private partnerships have been adopted by the government for use in Extension throughout India.[45]

> *Extension educators in the field are a best kept secret. They have talent, skills, and experiences that offer us a wonderful opportunity for global development.*
>
> Mary L. Andrews

Internationalizing CANR Students

The CANR is committed to providing study abroad opportunities for every academic major. The experience helps students gain perspectives of the world and their own country. Employers view it as a distinctive benefit.

Program Choices

The college offers 43 programs in North America, Europe, Latin America, Asia, Africa, Australia/New Zealand, and Antarctica.

The short-term programs — five weeks or less — are especially popular. Some are sub-ject specific — for example, food laws, packaging, and building construction. Others, such as environmental conditions and agricultural issues, are more general.

Benefits

The departments' development and support of international experiences, integration of offerings into department curricula, and stronger ties with specific educational institutions in other countries, are excellent opportunities for internationalizing the CANR majors.[46]

Courtesy Mary L. Andrews

Mark Longstroth (R), MSUE Educator, hosts Dr. V.V. Sadamate, Fulbright Research Fellow from India, on a tour of southwestern Michigan orchards.

College of the Future

Contributing colleagues have shared their collective vision. Their college of the future:

- Believes in its land-grant heritage and its broad mission, is dedicated to serving society, and views changes and challenges as opportunities for creative action.

- Provides high quality education embodying strong international experiences; extension education and technical assistance that is capacity building and directly beneficial; and research that targets today's issues and develops capabilities for challenges of tomorrow.

- Addresses the immediate and future issues of CANR rural and urban stakeholders.

- Selects issues responsively and proactively, defines issues comprehensively and systemically, and addresses productivity and sustainability and the public good.

- Employs multidisciplinary approaches throughout the college, the university, and beyond; seeks divergent views for enhanced outcomes; and prizes objectivity.

- Utilizes creative team approaches, encompassing research, extension, and stakeholder expertise in active, ongoing relationships to produce timely and beneficial outcomes.

- Seeks to enhance the state economy and the well-being of its farms, businesses, youths, families, communities, and natural resources.

- Carries the respect and support of its many stakeholders and the high regard of its academic peers nationally and internationally.

These and related attributes will ensure strong, beneficial contributions to the state, the nation, and the world.[47]

At the opening of Michigan Agricultural College in 1857, President J.R. Williams said,
"The acorn we bury today, will not branch into a majestic oak tomorrow."
One hundred fifty years after its founding, that MAC acorn has grown into Michigan State University,
a world-class university with worldwide impact — a mighty oak indeed!

Enhancing the quality of life for people in Michigan and around the globe is the mission of this "Giant Oak." Mission—success relies on **Learning** that imbues stakeholders with intellectual curiosity, knowledge, and skills; **Discovery** that advances knowledge, productivity, and sustainability; **Engagement** that achieves social, economic, and environmental equity.

Endnotes

Prologue

1 Richard W. Welch, *County Evolution in Michigan, 1790-1897*, State Library Services, Occasional Paper No. 2 (Lansing, Mich.: State Department of Education, 1972), p. 24.

2 Willis F. Dunbar, *Michigan: A History of the Wolverine State* (Grand Rapids, Mich.: William B. Eerdmans Publishing Co., 1965), p. 317.

3 *Michigan Farmer*, March 17, 1845, p. 6.

4 *Michigan Farmer*, January 1845, pp. 77-78; from Henry Colman's *European Agriculture* (1785-1849).

5 Gang plow. *Michigan Farmer.*

6 *Michigan Farmer*, September 1851, pp. 76-77.

7 *Michigan Farmer*, February 1847, p. 175.

8 Henry Colman (1785-1849) in *Michigan Farmer*, Jan. 1, 1845.

9 *Michigan Farmer*, January 1850, pp. 18-19.

10 C.A. Kenaston, *Annual Report of the Board of Agriculture*, 1863, p. 5.

11 *Ibid.*

12 *Michigan Farmer*, July 1851, p. 236.

13 *Michigan Farmer*, September 1853, pp. 262-264.

14 Kenaston, 1863, p. 5 ff.

15 *Michigan Farmer*, June 1, 1852, pp. 185-186.

16 *Michigan Farmer*, May 1853, pp. 90-93.

17 *Michigan Farmer*, November 1853, p. 351.

18 *Michigan Farmer*, January 1853, p. 18.

19 Kenaston, p. 5.

20 *Michigan Farmer*, March 1855, p. 88.

21 George Weeks, *Stewards of the State, The Governors of Michigan* (Ann Arbor: The Detroit News and Historical Society of Michigan, 1987), pp. 40-41.

22 *Michigan Farmer*, January 1845, pp. 77-78; from Henry Colman's *European Agriculture* (1785-1849).

Chapter 1

1 *Michigan Farmer*, August 1855, pp. 232-233.

2 *Michigan Farmer*, No. 7, 1856, pp. 208-209.

3 Madison Kuhn, *Michigan State, The First Hundred Years* (East Lansing: MSU Press, 1955), pp. 8-14.

4 Kenaston, p. 25.

5 Kuhn, p. 15.

6 Kuhn, p. 15.

7 *Michigan Farmer*, No. 1, 1857, p. 27.

8 *Michigan Farmer*, No. 2, 1857, p. 58.

9 *Michigan Farmer*, May 1857, p. 152.

10 Annual Report, Department of Public Instruction, October 1857, p. 279 ff.

11 *Michigan Farmer*, No. 1, 1858, p. 28.

12 *Michigan Farmer*, No. 6, 1857, p. 161.

13 *Michigan Farmer*, No. 45, 1859, p. 345.

14 *Michigan Farmer*, No. 45, 1859, p. 215.

15 *Michigan Farmer*, May 1860, p. 405.

16 *Michigan Farmer*, No. 6, June 1857.

17 Kuhn, pp. 49-51.

18 *Michigan Farmer*, No. 10, 1859, p. 77.

19 *Michigan Farmer*, No. 12, 1859, p. 89.

20 *Michigan Farmer*, No. 14, 1859, p. 10.

21 *Report of the State Board of Education 1858.*

22 *Michigan Farmer*, No. 12, 1859.

23 *Michigan Farmer*, No. 51, 1858, p. 381.

24 *Ibid.;* Kenaston, p. 381.

25 *Michigan Farmer*, No. 51, 1860, p. 402.

26 *Michigan Farmer*, February 23, 1861; Kenaston, p. 28.

27 *Michigan Farmer*, January 12, 1861, p. 19.

28 *Ibid.*

29 *Michigan Farmer*, April 20, 1861.

30 *Lansing Republican* in *Michigan Farmer*, March 22, 1862.

31 Kuhn, p. 32.

32 *Michigan Farmer*, No. 51, 1860, p. 402.

33 Kuhn, p. 76.

Chapter 2

1 Kuhn, p. 78.

2 *Report of the State Board of Agriculture 1866*, pp. 47-48.

3 *Report of the State Board of Agriculture 1868*, pp. 7-8.

4 *Ibid.*

5 *Report of the State Board of Agriculture 1868*, p. 48.

6 *Report of the State Board of Agriculture 1870*, pp. 9-10.

7 *Report of the State Board of Agriculture 1867*, pp. 265-267.

8 *Ibid.*, pp. 287-288.

9 *Report of the State Board of Agriculture 1897*, pp. 265-267.

10 *Report of the State Board of Agriculture 1870*, p. 50.

11 *Report of the State Board of Agriculture 1871*, pp. 8-9.

12 Beal, W.J., *History of the Michigan Agricultural College and Biographical Sketches of Trustees and Professors* (East Lansing: the Agricultural College, 1915), p. 70.

13 Joseph Harris, editor of the *Genesee Farmer*, in *Report of the State Board of Agriculture 1870*, pp. 8-9.

14 *Report of the State Board of Agriculture 1870*, pp. 8-9.

15 www.nationalgrange.org (2004).

16 *Report of the State Board of Agriculture 1873*, p. 8.

17 *Report of the State Board of Agriculture 1870*, p. 9.

18 *Report of the State Board of Agriculture 1868*, pp. 12-13.

19 *Report of the State Board of Agriculture 1871*, pp. 8-9.

20 Beal, p. 302.

21 Beal, p. 73.

22 *Report of the State Board of Agriculture 1871*, pp. 20-21.

23 Beal, p. 67.

24 Kuhn, pp. 132-133.

25 Kuhn, p. 12.

26 Beal, pp. 306-307.

27 Don J. Gemmel, "Efforts at Constitutional Reform in Michigan," MSU Political Science 550, Seminar in State Government. Unpublished, circa 1950.

28 Allen Gulley, a member of the class of 1868, in Beal, pp. 63-64.

29 *Report of the State Board of Agriculture 1873*, p. 8.

30 *Ibid.*, p. 12.

31 *Report of the State Board of Agriculture 1868*, pp. 14-15.

32 *Report of the State Board of Agriculture 1867*, p. 11.

33 *Ibid.*

34 Beal, p. 59.

35 *Report of the State Board of Agriculture 1871*, pp. 291-295.

Endnotes

Chapter 3

1 *Report of the State Board of Agriculture 1874,* pp. 64-84. [Ed. note: President Abbot delivered the speech in March 1875. It was reported in the 1874 edition of the annual report as a result of an error by Abbot, who was preparing the 1874 report. See Abbot's explanation in the 1875 annual report, p. 20.]

2 *Report of the State Board of Agriculture 1875,* p. 20.

3 Lowell Eklund, *Colleges for our Land and Time,* dissertation, Syracuse University, 1956, p. 58.

4 *Report of the State Board of Agriculture 1875,* pp. 55-56.

5 *Ibid.,* p. 23.

6 *Report of the State Board of Agriculture 1877,* p. 21.

7 *Report of the State Board of Agriculture 1875,* pp. 75-76.

8 *Ibid.*

9 Eklund, pp. 278-279. "Experiments" appended to address by President Abbot entitled "Agricultural Education," March 4, 1875, New Education, V. 1, MSU Library, p. 23.

10 *Report of the State Board of Agriculture 1875,* p. 61.

11 *Ibid.*

12 *Report of the State Board of Agriculture 1874,* pp. 64-84.

13 *Report of the State Board of Agriculture 1876,* p. 79.

14 *Report of the State Board of Agriculture 1877,* p. 31.

15 *Journal of the Michigan Legislature,* March 23, 1879.

16 *Report of the State Board of Agriculture 1879,* pp. 16-17.

17 *Report of the State Board of Agriculture, September 1877,* p. 21.

18 *Report of the State Board of Agriculture 1876,* p. 71.

19 *Report of the State Board of Agriculture 1875,* pp. 21 and 26.

20 *Report of the State Board of Agriculture 1879,* pp. 17-18.

21 *Report of the State Board of Agriculture 1880-81,* p. 17.

22 Beal, pp. 77-78.

23 *Report of the State Board of Agriculture 1881-82,* pp. 187-188.

24 *Report of the State Board of Agriculture 1880,* p. 18; 1881-82, p. 23.

25 *Report of the State Board of Agriculture 1880,* pp. 17-18.

26 *Report of the State Board of Agriculture 1884,* p. 30.

27 *Report of the State Board of Agriculture 1878,* pp. 20-21.

28 *Report of the State Board of Agriculture 1880,* pp. 54-55.

29 Beal, p. 75.

30 *Report of the State Board of Agriculture 1871,* pp. 291-295.

31 *Report of the State Board of Agriculture 1879,* pp. 413-415.

32 *Ibid.,* pp. 25-26.

33 *Ibid.,* pp. 24-25.

34 *College Speculum,* October 15, 1884, cited in Beal, pp. 77-78.

35 *College Speculum,* August 1, 1881, V. 1, No. 1, p. 1.

36 *Report of the State Board of Agriculture 1879,* pp. 23-24.

37 *College Speculum,* April 1, 1882, V. 1, No. 3.

38 *Report of the State Board of Agriculture 1880,* pp. 29-30.

39 *Ibid.,* pp. 20-21.

40 Beal, p. 84.

41 *Ibid.,* p. 78.

42 *Ibid.,* pp. 79-80.

Chapter 4

1 Beal, p. 84.

2 *Ibid.,* pp. 391-392.

3 *Report of the State Board of Agriculture 1885,* pp. 31-32.

4 *Ibid.,* p. 18.

5 Willits in *Report of the State Board of Agriculture 1885,* p. 58.

6 *Report of the State Board of Agriculture 1887,* pp. 215-221.

7 *Report of the State Board of Agriculture 1884,* pp. 88-99.

8 *Report of the State Board of Agriculture 1887,* p. 220.

9 *Ibid.,* p. xvii.

10 *Ibid.,* p. 27.

11 *Ibid.,* pp. 25-26.

12 *Ibid.,* p. xxiii.

13 *Ibid.,* pp. 28-29.

14 *Report of the State Board of Agriculture 1886-87,* pp. 27-28.

15 *Report of the State Board of Agriculture 1888,* pp. 32-33.

16 *Ibid.,* p. 70; Beal, p. 144.

17 Beal in *Report of the State Board of Agriculture 1888,* p. 72.

18 *Report of the State Board of Agriculture 1887,* p. 27.

19 *Report of the State Board of Agriculture 1889,* pp. 28-29.

20 *Report of the State Board of Agriculture 1887,* p. xx.

21 *Report of the State Board of Agriculture 1885,* pp. 57-58.

22 Beal, p. 392.

23 Beal, p. 93.

24 Beal, pp. 91-92, 393-394.

25 *Report of the State Board of Agriculture 1889,* pp. 27-28.

26 Beal, p. 92.

27 *Report of the State Board of Agriculture 1889,* p. 29.

28 *Report of the State Board of Agriculture 1890,* pp. 87-88.

29 *Ibid.,* pp. 281-294.

30 *Report of the State Board of Agriculture 1893,* p. 29.

31 *Report of the State Board of Agriculture 1890,* pp. 47-48.

32 *Report of the State Board of Agriculture 1892,* p. 155.

33 *Ibid.,* p. 28.

34 *Ibid.,* pp. 44-46.

35 *Report of the State Board of Agriculture 1891,* pp. 153-154.

36 *Report of the State Board of Agriculture 1892,* p. 38.

37 Kuhn, p. 194.

38 Beal, p. 101.

39 *Report of the State Board of Agriculture 1892,* pp. 149-150.

40 Kuhn, p. 161.

41 *Report of the State Board of Agriculture 1891,* pp. 74-75.

42 *Report of the State Board of Agriculture 1894,* pp. 30-31.

43 *Ibid.,* pp. 40-41.

44 *Ibid.,* p. 37.

Chapter 5

1 *Report of the State Board of Agriculture 1896,* pp. 439-455.

2 Kuhn, p. 191.

3 *Report of the State Board of Agriculture 1895,* p. 31.

4 *Report of the State Board of Agriculture 1898,* p. 39.

5 *Report of the State Board of Agriculture 1895,* p. 29.

6 Whitney Miller, *Images of America, East Lansing, Collegeville Revisited* (Chicago: Arcadia Publishing, 2002), p. 18.

7 *Ibid.,* p. 21.

8 *Ibid.,* p. 34.

9 *Report of the State Board of Agriculture 1896,* pp. 55-68.

10 *Ibid.*

11 *Report of the State Board of Agriculture 1896,* pp. 77-79.

Endnotes

[12] Clark L. Brody, *In the Service of the Farmer, My Life in the Michigan Farm Bureau* (East Lansing: Michigan State University Press, 1959), pp. 12-13.

[13] *Report of the State Board of Agriculture 1898*, p. 41.

[14] *Ibid.*, p. 42.

[15] *Ibid.*, p. 40.

[16] Kuhn, p. 199.

[17] *Ibid.*, p. 201.

[18] *Report of the State Board of Agriculture 1896*, p. 27.

[19] Beal, p. 439.

[20] *Report of the State Board of Agriculture 1898*, pp. 28-29.

[21] *The M.A.C. RECORD*, October 10, 1899, p. 1.

[22] *The M.A.C. RECORD*, December 20, 1899, p. 1.

[23] *The M.A.C. RECORD*, October 10, 1899, p. 1.

[24] *Report of the State Board of Agriculture 1898*, p. 652.

[25] *Report of the State Board of Agriculture 1895*, pp. 35-37; Beal, p. 144.

[26] *Report of the State Board of Agriculture 1898*, pp. 98-99.

[27] *MAES Field Research Stations* (East Lansing: Michigan State University Land Management Office).

[28] MSU's Upper Peninsula Experiment Station, Einer Olstrom collection.

[29] *Report of the State Board of Agriculture 1903*, p. 20.

[30] MSU's Upper Peninsula Experiment Station, Einer Olstrom collection.

[31] *Ibid.*

[32] *Ibid.*

[33] Kuhn, p. 164.

[34] *Report of the State Board of Agriculture 1899*, p. 59.

[35] *The M.A.C. RECORD*, February 13, 1900, p. 1.

[36] *The M.A.C. RECORD*, October 24, 1899, p. 1.

[37] *Report of the State Board of Agriculture 1900*, pp. 451-454.

[38] *Report of the State Board of Agriculture 1901*, pp. 23-24.

[39] Beal, pp. 59-60; S.M. Millard speech in Chicago.

[40] *The M.A.C. RECORD*, October 2, 1900, p. 2.

[41] Beal, pp. 406-408.

[42] *Report of the State Board of Agriculture 1903*, p. 22.

[43] Kuhn, pp. 106-108.

[44] Linda O. Stanford and C. Kurt Dewhurst, *MSU Campus: Buildings, Places, Spaces* (East Lansing: Michigan State University Press, 2002), pp. 79-80.

[45] Beal, pp. 302-304; *Report of the State Board of Agriculture 1901*, p. 24.

[46] *Report of the State Board of Agriculture 1902*, p. 20.

[47] *Report of the State Board of Agriculture 1901*, pp. 25-26.

[48] *Report of the State Board of Agriculture 1900*, p. 32; Miller, p. 22.

[49] *Report of the State Board of Agriculture 1901*, p. 22.

[50] *Report of the State Board of Agriculture 1898*, pp. 35-36.

[51] Brody, pp. 14-15.

[52] *Report of the State Board of Agriculture 1904*, pp. 25, 27.

[53] *Report of the State Board of Agriculture 1896*, p. 53.

Chapter 6

[1] *Report of the State Board of Agriculture 1905*, p. 22.

[2] *Report of the State Board of Agriculture 1906*, pp. 37-38.

[3] *Ibid.*, p. 33.

[4] *Report of the State Board of Agriculture 1907*, p. 26.

[5] *Report of the State Board of Agriculture 1905*, pp. 21-22.

[6] *Ibid.*, p. 22.

[7] *Report of the State Board of Agriculture 1908*, pp. 33-34.

[8] *Report of the State Board of Agriculture 1906*, p. 32.

[9] *Report of the State Board of Agriculture 1908*, p. 31.

[10] *Report of the State Board of Agriculture 1910*, p. 37.

[11] *Report of the State Board of Agriculture 1911*, p. 38.

[12] *Report of the State Board of Agriculture 1906*, p. 39.

[13] *Report of the State Board of Agriculture 1907*, p. 28.

[14] *Ibid.*, pp. 31-32.

[15] *Ibid.*, pp. 34-35.

[16] *Ibid.*, p. 31.

[17] *Ibid.*, pp. 35-37.

[18] *Ibid.*, pp. 35-36.

[19] Miller, p. 26.

[20] *Report of the State Board of Agriculture 1908*, p. 29.

[21] Beal, p. 214.

[22] *Report of the State Board of Agriculture 1908*, pp. 34-35.

[23] *The M.A.C. RECORD*, November 30, 1909, p. 1.

[24] Beal, pp. 303-304; *Report of the State Board of Agriculture 1912-13*, Section 7.

[25] *Report of the State Board of Agriculture, 1910*, p. 33.

[26] *The M.A.C. RECORD*, December 7, 1909, p. 2.

[27] Stanford and Dewhurst, p. 56.

[28] Beal, p. 285.

[29] *Ibid.*

[30] L.S. Robertson, E.P. Whiteside, R.E. Lucas, R.L. Cook, *The Michigan State University Soil Science Department 1909-1969, A Historical Narrative* (East Lansing: Department of Crop and Soil Sciences, 1988), pp. 8-9.

[31] *Report of the State Board of Agriculture 1908*, pp. 29, 32.

[32] *Report of the State Board of Agriculture 1909*, pp. 24-25.

[33] *Report of the State Board of Agriculture 1909*, pp. 44-45.

[34] Contributed by Lynn F. Brumm, Professor Emeritus, MSU Department of Osteopathic Medicine. The photograph is from the L.S. Brumm collection.

[35] Eklund, p. 314.

[36] *Ibid.*, p. 298; Beal, p. 158.

[37] *Ibid.*, p. 301.

[38] *Ibid.*, p. 307.

[39] Eklund, pp. 307-309, and Kuhn, p. 241.

[40] *Report of the State Board of Agriculture 1909*, p. 40.

[41] Edward Danforth Eddy, Jr., *Colleges for Our Land and Time, The Land-Grant Idea in American Education* (New York: Harper & Brothers, 1956), pp. 140-142.

[42] R.S. Shaw, *Report of the State Board of Agriculture 1913*, pp. 44-45.

[43] Summarized by Eklund, p. 329.

[44] F. Clever Bald, *Michigan in Four Centuries* (New York: Harper and Row Publishers, 1954), p. 335.

[45] *Ibid.*, p. 12.

[46] *The M.A.C. RECORD*, November 16, 1909, No. 3, p. 1.

[47] Beal, pp. 303-304. The information is also available in *Report of the State Board of Agriculture 1912-13*.

[48] *The Holcad*, April 23, 1914, p. 2.

[49] *Report of the State Board of Agriculture 1914*, pp. 38-44.

Endnotes

50 *The M.A.C. RECORD,* November 13, 1912, p. 1.

51 *Report of the State Board of Agriculture 1913,* p. 37.

Chapter 7

1 Kuhn, p. 197.

2 Kuhn, pp. 260-262.

3 *Report of the State Board of Agriculture 1915,* p. 327.

4 *The M.A.C. RECORD,* May 16, 1918, p. 4; April 25, 1918, p. 4.

5 Kuhn, p. 236.

6 *Report of the State Board of Agriculture 1915,* pp. 37-38.

7 Brody, pp. 22-24.

8 *Report of the State Board of Agriculture 1915,* p. 64.

9 Kuhn, p. 315.

10 *Report of the State Board of Agriculture 1915,* pp. 62-63.

11 *Ibid.,* p. 62.

12 *Ibid.,* pp. 76-77.

13 *Ibid.,* p. 7.

14 *Ibid.,* p. 68.

15 *Report of the State Board of Agriculture 1917,* pp. 71-72.

16 *Report of the State Board of Agriculture 1915,* pp. 57-61.

17 *Report of the State Board of Agriculture 1917,* p. 73.

18 *Report of the State Board of Agriculture 1916,* pp. 44-45.

19 *The M.A.C. RECORD,* May 9, 1919, p. 3.

20 *The M.A.C. RECORD,* January 10, 1919, p. 5.

21 *Report of the State Board of Agriculture 1917,* pp. 45-46.

22 *The M.A.C. RECORD,* September 30, 1918, p. 4.

23 *The M.A.C. RECORD,* November 15, 1918, p. 4.

24 *The M.A.C. RECORD,* January 14, 1919, p. 3.

25 *The M.A.C. RECORD,* May 9, 1919, p. 3.

26 *The M.A.C. RECORD,* October 11, 1918, p. 4.

27 *Report of the State Board of Agriculture 1917,* p. 51.

28 *The M.A.C. RECORD,* May 2, 1918, p. 4.

29 *The M.A.C. RECORD,* April 18, 1918, p. 4.

30 *The Holcad,* November 16, 1923, pp. 1-4.

31 *The Holcad,* April 16, 1923, p. 2.

32 *The M.A.C. RECORD,* May 14, 1920, p. 8.

33 *The M.A.C. RECORD,* October 25, 1918, p. 3.

34 *Report of the State Board of Agriculture 1915,* p. 56.

35 *Ibid.*

36 *The M.A.C. RECORD,* November 8, 1918, p. 1.

37 *The M.A.C. RECORD,* November 1, 1918, p. 1.

38 *The M.A.C. RECORD,* December 6, 1918, p. 1.

39 John A. Hannah, *A Memoir* (East Lansing: Michigan State University Press, 1980), pp. 16-17.

40 Brody, p. 32.

41 *The M.A.C. RECORD,* January 24, 1919, p. 1.

42 Records of the Michigan State Farm Bureau Organized at East Lansing, Michigan, February 4, 1919, No. 485, pp. 3-6.

43 Brody, pp. 33-34.

44 Records of the Michigan State Farm Bureau, No. 485, p. 3.

45 *The M.A.C. RECORD,* January 24, 1919, p. 4.

46 Kuhn, pp. 278-285.

47 *Ibid.,* p. 279.

48 *Ibid.,* pp. 276-277.

49 Brody, p. 66.

50 Friday left for a position at the new School for Social Research in New York.

51 Kuhn, p. 286.

52 *Ibid.,* p. 260.

53 *Ibid.,* p. 186.

Chapter 8

1 *The State Journal,* January 8, 1925.

2 *The M.A.C. RECORD,* May 18, 1925, p. 467.

3 *Ibid.,* p. 472.

4 *The State Journal,* January 1, 1925, p. 10.

5 *The M.S.C. RECORD,* October 1926, p. 12.

6 George Alderton, *The M.S.C. RECORD,* July 1945.

7 *The M.S.C. RECORD,* October 1927.

8 *Ibid.,* July 1926, pp. 551-552.

9 *Ibid.,* January 1928.

10 *Ibid.,* February 1925, p. 276.

11 *Ibid.,* September 1926, p. 11.

12 *The M.A.C. RECORD,* February 9, 1925.

13 *The State Journal,* May 23, 1928.

14 *Ibid.*

15 *Ibid.,* January 14, 1925.

16 *Ibid.,* May 2, 1928, p. 1.

17 *Ibid.,* May 23, 1928.

18 *Ibid.,* May 22, 1928.

19 *Ibid.,* May 23, 1928.

20 *Ibid.*

21 *Ibid.*

22 Contributed by Harlan Ritchie, Professor Emeritus, Department of Animal Science.

23 *The M.S.C. RECORD,* July 1929, pp. 7-8.

24 *Ibid.,* January 1942.

25 The KBS website, www.kbs.edu.

26 *The M.S.C. RECORD,* August 1930.

27 *Ibid.,* November 1926, p. 9.

28 *Ibid.,* May 1930.

29 *Ibid.,* March 1929, p. 8.

30 *Ibid.,* September 1929, p. 7.

31 *Ibid.,* March-April 1932, p. 3.

32 *Ibid.,* June-July 1932.

33 *Ibid.,* May 1929, p. 7.

34 *Report of the Board of Agriculture 1933,* p. 219.

35 Dunbar, p. 675.

36 L.S. Robertson et al., p. 12.

37 *Michigan State News,* May 11, 1934.

38 *Ibid.,* May 8, 1934.

39 *Ibid.,* February 29, 1934.

40 *Ibid.,* April 6, 1934.

41 *Ibid.,* May 4, 1934.

42 *The M.S.C. RECORD,* March-April 1932, p. 13.

43 Hannah, pp. 20-21.

44 *The State News,* April 3, 1934.

45 *Ibid.,* December 7, 1933.

46 *Ibid.,* May 8, 1934.

47 Contributed by Peter O. Cookingham, librarian for Turfgrass Information Center, and James B. Beard, initiator of turfgrass program.

48 *History of Cooperative Extension Work in Michigan, 1914-1939* (East Lansing: Michigan State College, Extension Division), p. 14.

Chapter 9

1 *Michigan State News,* January 22, 1935, p. 1.

2 *Michigan State News,* April 23, 1935, p. 4.

3 *The M.S.C. RECORD,* March 1935.

4 *The M.S.C. RECORD,* January 1935, p. 7.

5 *Michigan State News,* April 19, 1935, p. 1.

6 *Michigan State News,* April 28, 1936, p. 1.

Endnotes

[7] *Michigan State News,* January 25, 1935, p. 1.

[8] *Michigan State News,* January 22, 1935, p. 1.

[9] *Michigan State News,* April 12, 1935, p. 1.

[10] *Michigan State News,* April 30, 1935, p. 1.

[11] Contributed by Eckhart Dersch and Raleigh Barlowe, Professors Emeriti, Department of Resource Development.

[12] Contributed by Eckhart Dersch, Professor Emeritus, Department of Resource Development.

[13] Contributed by Raleigh Barlowe, Professor Emeritus, Department of Resource Development.

[14] *Michigan State News,* December 7, 1937, p. 1.

[15] *Michigan State News,* December 18, 1936, p. 1.

[16] *Michigan State News,* October 17, 1939, p. 1.

[17] *Michigan State News,* September, 1938, p. 1.

[18] John A. Hannah, "Some Facts About State," *The Michigan State College Record,* April 1940, p. 1.

[19] *The M.S.C. RECORD,* May 1938.

[20] *Michigan State News,* December 5, 1942, p. 1.

[21] *Michigan State News,* February 1, 1935, p. 1.

[22] *Michigan State News,* June 5, 1934, p. 2.

[23] *Michigan State News,* November 6, 1936, p. 1.

[24] *The M.S.C. RECORD,* March 1935, p. 6.

[25] *Michigan State News,* December 14, 1935, p. 1.

[26] *Michigan State News,* May 14, 1935, p. 3.

[27] *The M.S.C. RECORD,* February 1938, p 2.

[28] *Michigan State News,* May 28, 1937, p. 1.

[29] *Michigan State News,* November 2, 1937, p. 1.

[30] *Michigan State News,* November 4, 1939, p. 1.

[31] *Michigan State News,* October 7, 1939, p. 1.

[32] *The M.S.C. RECORD,* January 1941.

[33] *The M.S.C. RECORD,* January 1942.

[34] *Michigan State News,* October 15, 1942, p. 1.

[35] *Michigan State News,* March 31, 1943, p. 1.

[36] *The M.S.C. RECORD,* December 1943.

[37] *Michigan State News,* July 7, 1943, p. 1.

[38] *Michigan State News,* March 12, 1943, p. 1.

[39] *Michigan State News,* December 9, 1942, p. 1.

[40] *The M.S.C. RECORD,* February 1938.

Chapter 10

[1] *The M.S.C. RECORD,* July 1945.

[2] *The M.S.C. RECORD,* January 1945, pp. 3-4.

[3] *Ibid.*

[4] Einer Olstrom and Howard Miller, *Plus Two Score, The Cooperative Extension Service in Michigan 1940 to 1980* (East Lansing: Cooperative Extension Service, 1984), pp. 25-26.

[5] *The State News,* January 17, 1946.

[6] *Ibid.*

[7] Kuhn, pp. 408-444.

[8] *Michigan State News,* October 25, 1945.

[9] *Michigan State News,* April 17, 1946.

[10] *The M.S.C. RECORD,* April 1944, p. 3.

[11] *Michigan State News,* January 31, 1946.

[12] Olstrom and Miller, pp. 16-17.

[13] *Ibid.,* p. 10.

[14] *Ibid.,* pp. 40-41.

[15] Contributed by Donald R. Isleib, Director Emeritus, Institute of International Agriculture, and Patricia K. Riley, retired, International Studies and Program.

[16] Olstrom and Miller, pp. 34-35.

[17] *Ibid.,* p. 35.

[18] Sources: James Cooke Mills, *History of Saginaw County,* Michigan (Seemann and Peters, 1918). See pp. 466-487 for a description and history of the Saginaw sugar beet industry, Saginaw.

E. Wilson Cressey, "A Brief History of the Beet Sugar Industry in Michigan," *Sugar Beet Journal,* December 1935, Vol. 1, No. 3. A publication of the Farmers and Manufacturers Beet Sugar Association, Saginaw, Michigan. Also, *Facts About the Farmers and Manufacturers Beet Sugar Association.* Issues of the *Sugar Beet Journal* are out of circulation but are available at the Bay County Historical Society, Bay City, Michigan.

[19] Contributed by Thomas Mahar, retired Executive Vice President, Monitor Sugar Company.

[20] R.L. Henley and C.F. Ojala, *Michigan's Changing Beet Sugar Industry* (Boyne City, Mich.: Prestige Press, 1977).

[21] *The M.S.C. RECORD,* April 1, 1945. The article was first published in the *Detroit Free Press* on March 18, 1945, and was written by Norman Kenyon.

[22] *Ibid.*

[23] Contributed by Clarence M. Hansen, Professor Emeritus, Department of Biosystems and Agricultural Engineering.

[24] Olstrom and Miller, p. 20.

[25] *Ibid.,* p. 33.

[26] Contributed by Alden M. Booren, Professor, Department of Animal Science and Department of Food Science and Human Nutrition, and Robert A. Merkel, Professor Emeritus, Animal Science.

[27] Contributed by George W. Bird, Professor, Plant Pathology and Entomology.

[28] Contributed by Eckhart Dersch, Professor Emeritus, Department of Resource Development.

[29] Olstrom and Miller, pp. 18-19.

[30] Contributed by Diana Twede, Associate Professor, School of Packaging.

[31] Olstrom and Miller, pp. 10, 11, and 15.

[32] *Ibid.,* pp. 5, 23, 29, and 30.

[33] *Ibid.,* pp. 29-30.

[34] *Ibid.,* pp. 20-21.

[35] *Ibid.,* p. 28.

[36] *The M.S.C. RECORD,* January 1945, p. 3.

[37] Olstrom and Miller, p. 24.

[38] A memoir written by the late Einer Olstrom, then Missaukee County agricultural agent (February 1953). Vivian Olstrom provided the memoir.

[39] Olstrom and Miller, pp. 22-23.

[40] *MSU Alumni Magazine,* Winter 2004, pp. 30-34.

Endnotes

[41] Kuhn, pp. 461-462.

[42] Tom Lambert, *Lansing State Journal*, September 18, 2004.

[43] Kuhn, p. 461.

Chapter 11

[1] *The Michigan State University Centennial...Its Planning and Execution* (East Lansing: Michigan State University, 1955), p. 15.

[2] *Ibid.*, pp. 22-23.

[3] *Ibid.*, pp. 27-30; Olstrom and Miller, pp. 55-56.

[4] Olstrom and Miller, p. 54.

[5] *Ibid.*, p. 15.

[6] *Ibid.*, p. 18.

[7] *The 1956 Wolverine*, p. 62.

[8] Olstrom and Miller, p. 49.

[9] *Ibid.*, p. 47.

[10] *Ibid.*, pp. 46-47.

[11] Contributed by M. John Bukovac, University Distinguished Professor Emeritus, and Frank Dennis, Professor Emeritus, Department of Horticulture.

[12] Olstrom and Miller, p. 100.

[13] *Ibid.*, pp. 56-57.

[14] *The 1956 Wolverine*, p. 61.

[15] *Ibid.*, p. 62.

[16] *Ibid.*, pp. 60-61.

[17] *Ibid.*, p. 47.

[18] *Ibid.*, pp. 49-50.

[19] *Ibid.*, p. 49.

[20] Contributed by Alden M. Booren, Professor, Department of Animal Science, Department of Food Science and Human Nutrition, and Robert A. Merkel, Professor Emeritus, Animal Science.

[21] Contributed by Harlan Ritchie, Professor Emeritus, Department of Animal Science.

[22] Olstrom and Miller, p. 45.

[23] Contributed by Bukovac and Dennis.

[24] Contributed by Daniel Hager, Michigan Potato Industry Commission.

[25] Contributed by Stanley K. Ries, Professor Emeritus, Department of Horticulture.

[26] *Ibid.*

[27] Contributed by William W. Shane, District Extension Fruit and Marketing Educator and Academic Specialist, Southwest Michigan Research and Extension Center, with assistance of Frank Dennis, Professor Emeritus, Department of Horticulture.

[28] William W. Shane; and W.R. Okie, *Handbook of Peach and Nectarine Varieties* (Washington, D.C.: U.S. Department of Agriculture, Handbook No. 714, May 1998).

[29] The fifth edition was re-titled *The Sensory Evaluation of Dairy Products*.

[30] Contributed by John A. Partridge, Professor, Department of Animal Science.

[31] *Michigan State News*, January 28, 1963.

[32] *The State Journal*, January 16, 1960.

[33] Olstrom and Miller, p. 94.

[34] *Ibid.*, p. 61.

[35] Contributed by Alvin E. House, Professor Emeritus, Agricultural Economics.

[36] Contributed by Eckhart Dersch, Professor Emeritus, Department of Resource Development.

[37] Contributed by Raleigh Barlowe, Professor Emeritus, Department of Resource Development.

[38] Contributed by William Kimball, Professor Emeritus, Department of Resource Development.

[39] *Michigan State News*, October 31, 1962.

[40] *Michigan State News*, September 28, 1962, p. 10.

[41] *Michigan State News*, January 7, 1963.

Chapter 12

[1] Contributed by Hans Kende, University Distinguished Professor of Plant Biology, and Kenneth G. Keestra, Director, Plant Research Laboratory.

[2] Contributed by Daniel E. Keathley, Professor and Chairperson, Department of Forestry.

[3] Olstrom and Miller, pp. 160-161.

[4] Mark Allen, *Futures*, Vol. 1, No. 3, pp. 11-13.

[5] Contributed by Raymond O. Miller, Manager, U.P. Tree Improvement Center.

[6] Contributed by Paul Horny, Farm Manager, Saginaw Valley Bean and Beet Research Farm.

[7] Contributed by Frank Dennis, Professor Emeritus, Department of Horticulture.

[8] This account is taken from a paper presented by Daniel Bouk (Princeton University) at Cornell University during the opening plenary session of the Agricultural History Symposium of the Agricultural History Society. Contributed by Frank Dennis, Professor Emeritus, Department of Horticulture.

[9] *Michigan State News*, February 12, 1965.

[10] J. Bruce McCristal, *The Spirit of Michigan State* (Bloomfield Hills, Mich.: J. Bruce McCristal, 2004), p. 142.

[11] Olstrom and Miller, p. 91.

[12] *Michigan State News*, October 17, 1969.

[13] *Michigan State News*, January 31, 1966.

[14] Contributed by Thomas Jewett, former Iron-Dickinson counties 4-H agent. He is now a practicing attorney in East Lansing.

[15] Olstrom and Miller, p. 96.

[16] *Ibid.*, pp. 121-123.

[17] *Ibid.*, pp. 124-125.

[18] *Ibid.*, pp. 90-91.

[19] McCristal, p. 141.

[20] *Ibid.*

[21] The stories on irrigation are drawn from Sara A. Stuby's interview of Fred Henningsen, retired MSU CED and Extension Irrigation Specialist, and Laura Trombley's preparation of the account. Stuby is the Regional Director of the Southwest Region of MSU Extension; Trombly is an Extension agent in the region.

[22] Contributed by Donald R. Isleib, Director Emeritus, Institute of International Agriculture, and Patricia Riley, retired Administrative Assistant.

[23] Olstrom and Miller, p. 133.

[24] Contributed by Clarence Hansen, Professor Emeritus, Department of Biosystems and Agricultural Engineering.

[25] Olstrom and Miller, p. 185.

[26] Contributed by Philip J. Korson II, President, and Jane DePriest, Marketing Director, of the Cherry Marketing Institute.

Endnotes

27 *Ibid.*

28 Contributed by M. John Bukovac, University Distinguished Professor Emeritus, Department of Horticulture, and Frank Dennis, Professor Emeritus, Department of Horticulture.

29 Contributed by Alvin E. House, Professor Emeritus, Department of Agricultural Economics.

30 Contributed by Daniel Bronstein, Professor, Department of Community, Agriculture, Recreation, and Resource Studies (CARRS).

31 *Michigan State News,* January 31, 1966.

32 Olstrom and Miller, p. 99.

33 Contributed by George M. Kessler, Frank Dennis, and Harold Davidson, Associate Professor Emeritus, Professor Emeritus and Professor Emeritus, respectively, Department of Horticulture.

34 Contributed by William Kimball, Professor Emeritus, Department of Resource Development.

35 *Ibid.*

36 Michigan Farm Economics, No. 323 (MSU Department of Agricultural Economics), December 1969, in Olstrom and Miller, p. 99.

Chapter 13

1 Contributed by A. Allan Schmid, University Distinguished Professor, Department of Agricultural Economics.

2 Contributed by Lois Wolfson, Specialist, Institute of Water Research and Department of Fisheries and Wildlife; Thomas Burton, Professor, departments of Zoology and Fisheries and Wildlife; and Frank D'Itri, Professor Emeritus, Institute of Water Research.

3 *Futures,* Vol. 1, No. 4, p. 4.

4 Contributed by Lois Wolfson, Specialist, Institute of Water Research and Department of Fisheries and Wildlife; Thomas Burton, Professor, departments of Zoology and Fisheries and Wildlife; and Frank D'Itri, Professor Emeritus, Institute of Water Research.

5 Contributed by Carol Y. Swinehart, Communications Manager, Department of Fisheries and Wildlife.

6 *Ibid.*

7 *Ibid.*

8 *Ibid.*

9 Contributed by Raymond D. Vlasin, University Distinguished Professor Emeritus; Chairperson of the Department of Resource Development, 1971-79.

10 Contributed by Larry G. Olsen, Associate Professor, Department of Entomology.

11 *Ibid.*

12 Contributed by Mark F. Hansen, Extension Specialist and former Clinton County Agricultural Extension Agent.

13 Olstrom and Miller, pp. 160-161.

14 Contributed by Peter Kakela, Professor, CARRS.

15 *Ibid.*

16 Contributed by Lynn R. Harvey, Professor of Agricultural Economics and MSUE Associate Director Emeritus.

17 Contributed by David J. Ivan, Clinton County Extension Director.

18 Contributed by Lynn R. Harvey, Professor of Agricultural Economics and MSUE Associate Director Emeritus.

19 Contributed by William L. Bortel, Tuscola County Extension Director Emeritus and chairman/coordinator of the Tuscola exhibitions.

20 Contributed by William Kimball, Professor Emeritus, Department of Resource Development.

21 Contributed by Mark F. Hansen, Extension Specialist.

22 Contributed by Richard W. Merritt, Chairperson, Department of Entomology.

23 Contributed by Richard Ledebuhr, Specialist, and Clarence M. Hansen, Professor Emeritus, Department of Biosystems and Agricultural Engineering.

24 Olstrom and Miller, p. 161.

25 Contributed by Gerald A. Huizenga, resident of Walker, Michigan.

26 *The State News,* October 27, 1977.

27 *The State News,* January 5, 1978.

28 *Lansing State Journal,* June 6, 1979.

29 Contributed by William G. Bickert, Professor, Department of Biosystems and Agricultural Engineering.

30 *Futures,* Vol. 1, No. 3, Winter 1983.

31 *Futures,* Vol. 1, No. 1, Winter 1982.

32 *Futures,* Vol. 3, No. 3, March 1985.

33 *Futures,* Vol. 1, No. 2, Fall 1982.

34 Contributed by Paul Horny, Farm Manager, Saginaw Valley Bean and Beet Research Farm.

35 *Red Cedar Log,* 1976, p. 181.

36 Contributed by William Enslin, Senior Research Specialist, Center for Remote Sensing and Geographic Information Systems.

Chapter 14

1 *The State News* summer orientation issue, 1985.

2 *Futures,* Vol. 5, No. 1, Fall 1986.

3 Contributed by Harlan Ritchie, Professor Emeritus, Department of Animal Science.

4 *Futures,* Vol. 9, No. 3, Fall 1991.

5 Contributed by Alden M. Booren, Professor, Department of Food Science and Human Nutrition.

6 Contributed by Bernard Knezek, Professor Emeritus, Department of Crop and Soil Sciences.

7 Contributed by Dean R. Solomon, MSUE Coordinator, Southwest Region.

8 Contributed by Bernard Knezek, Professor Emeritus, Department of Crop and Soil Sciences.

9 Contributed by Richard R. Harwood, Professor, Department of Crop and Soil Sciences.

10 Contributed by Susan B. Smalley, Extension Specialist, MSUE Director's Office.

Endnotes

11 Contributed by Bernard Knezek, Professor Emeritus, Department of Crop and Soil Sciences.

12 *Futures,* Vol. 4, No. 2, Spring 1986.

13 Contributed by Daniel Hager, Michigan Potato Industry Commission.

14 *Futures,* Vol. 11, No. 2, Summer 1993.

15 Contributed by Thomas Ellis, Specialist Emeritus, Department of Entomology.

16 Contributed by Richard Merritt, Chairperson and Professor, Department of Entomology.

17 *Ibid.*

18 *Ibid.*

19 *Futures,* Vol. 4, No. 1, Fall 1985.

20 *Ibid.*

21 *Ibid.*

22 *Futures,* Vol. 9, No. 2, Summer 1991.

23 *Ibid.*

24 Contributed by Alden M. Booren, Professor, Department of Food Science and Human Nutrition.

25 Contributed by Carol Y. Swinehart, Communications Manager, Department of Fisheries and Wildlife.

26 *Ibid.*

27 Contributed by Ruth Kline-Robach, Specialist, Institute of Water Research.

28 *Futures,* Vol. 5, No. 1, Fall 1986.

29 Contributed by Peter L. Gustafson, Pigeon River Council member.

30 Rural manpower and off-farm employment articles by Collette Moser, Professor, Department of Agricultural Economics.

31 Contributed by Leah Cox Ritchie and Harlan D. Ritchie.

32 Contributed by Ann Hinsdale-Knisel, Extension Educator, Lenawee County.

33 Contributed by Patricia E. Norris, Professor, departments of Agricultural Economics and CARRS.

34 Contributed by Kenneth VerBurg, Extension Specialist and Professor Emeritus, Department of Resource Development.

35 *Futures,* Vol. 9, No. 4, Winter 1992.

36 *Futures,* Vol. 12, Nos. 3 & 4, Fall 1994/Winter 1995.

37 *Futures,* Vol. 8, No. 1, Spring 1990.

38 *Futures,* Vol. 10, No. 1, Spring 1992.

39 *Futures,* Vol. 2, No. 1, Summer 1983.

40 *Futures,* Vol. 9, No. 1, Spring 1991.

41 *Futures,* Vol. 10, No. 2, Summer 1993.

42 *Futures,* Vol. 4, No. 4, Summer 1986.

43 *Futures,* Vol. 10, No. 1, Spring 1992.

44 *Futures,* Vol. 9, No. 2, Summer 1991.

45 *Futures,* Vol. 10, No. 3, Fall 1992.

46 *Futures,* Vol. 9, No. 3, Fall 1991.

47 *Futures,* Vol. 10, No. 3, Fall 1992.

48 Contributed by Donald R. Isleib, Director Emeritus, Institute of International Agriculture.

49 Contributed by Weijun Zhao, Associate Professor of International Agriculture and coordinator of the China Program of IIA.

50 Contributed by Mary L. Andrews, Associate Professor Emeritus, MSUE Director's Office.

51 Contributed by Irvin E. Widders, Director of Bean/Cowpea CRSP.

52 Contributed by Betsy McPherson Knox, 4-H Youth Development Program Leader in Global, Cultural, and Arts Education.

53 Contributed by James Bristor, Professor Emeritus, CARRS.

54 Contributed by Donald Holecek, Director, Michigan Travel, Tourism, and Recreation Resource Center, and Professor, CARRS.

55 Contributed by Frank Dennis, Professor Emeritus, Department of Horticulture; Norman Lownds, Associate Professor and Curator of the Michigan 4-H Children's Garden; and Jane L. Taylor, first Curator, Michigan 4-H Children's Garden.

56 2004 Industry Impacts (East Lansing: Project GREEEN, Michigan State University, 2004).

57 *The State News,* May 20, 1992.

58 Contributed by Gale Arent, Director of Stakeholder Relations, CANR.

59 *The State News,* September 2, 1992.

60 *The State News,* October 1, 1993.

Chapter 15

1 Contributed by Anne Ottaway. The 2005 statements were reported in *The State News,* March 23, 3005.

2 Contributed by P. Vincent Hegarty, Director, Institute for Food Laws and Regulations.

3 Contributed by Mary L. Andrews, Professor Emeritus, MSUE Director's Office.

4 *Ibid.*

5 Contributed by Irvin E. Widders, Director of Bean/Cowpea CRSP at the Institute of International Agriculture and Professor of Horticulture.

6 Contributed by P. Vincent Hegarty, Director, Institute for Food Laws and Regulations.

7 Contributed by Karim M. Maredia, Physical Scientist, Institute of International Agriculture and Department of Entomology.

8 Contributed by Russell Freed, Professor, Department of Crop and Soil Sciences.

9 Contributed by Carol Y. Swinehart, Communications Coordinator, Department of Fisheries and Wildlife.

10 *Ibid.*

11 *Ibid.*

12 Contributed by Gregg A. Howe, Associate Professor, Department of Biochemistry and Molecular Biology, and Plant Research Lab.

13 Contributed by Wayne Beyea, Coordinator, Citizen Planner Program.

14 Contributed by Raymond D. Vlasin, Professor Emeritus, Department of Resource Development.

15 Contributed by Elizabeth Moore, Extension Public Policy Specialist.

16 Contributed by Lela VandenBerg, Extension Specialist, Leadership Development; and Michael Kovacic, Director, Great Lakes Leadership Academy.

17 Contributed by Gatachew Abatekassa, Project Manager, with assistance from Collette Moser and Ray Vlasin, early Co-directors.

18 Contributed by Francie Todd, Communications Manager, ANR Communications.

Endnotes

19 The Product Center for Agriculture and Natural Resources, Hatching Innovation: First Annual Report 2004-2005 (East Lansing: Michigan State University, October 2005). Contributed by H.C. Peterson, Director, PCANR.

20 Contributed by Paul McConaughy, Program Leader, MSUE Family and Consumer Sciences.

21 Contributed by Michael Score, Extension Educator, Southeast Michigan.

22 *Futures,* Vol. 13, No. 1, Spring 1995.

23 *Futures,* Vol. 12, Nos. 3 and 4, Fall 1994/Winter 1995.

24 *Ibid.*

25 *Futures,* Vol. 23, No. 2, Summer 2005.

26 *Futures,* Vol. 18, No. 3; Vol. 19, Nos. 1, 2 and 3, 2001.

27 Contributed by Ewen Todd, Director, NFSTC.

28 *Futures,* Vol. 22, No. 3, Fall 2004.

29 Contributed by Frank A. Fear, Carole F. Robinson, and Bailey Scholars Cortney A. Peissig, Blong K. Yang, and Lindsay R. Bodner. Fear is a professor of CARRS; Robinson is a doctoral graduate in resource development; Peissig is majoring in ANR communications, Yang in biosystems engineering, and Bodner in fisheries and wildlife.

30 Contributed by Elizabeth C. Moore, Extension Specialist.

31 Contributed by Gerhardus Schultink, Professor of International Development, CARRS.

32 Contributed by Eunice Foster, Associate Dean, CANR.

33 Contributed by Susan B. Smalley, Extension Specialist, Office of the Extension Director.

34 Contributed by Frank Dennis, Professor Emeritus, Department of Horticulture; Norman Lownds, Associate Professor and Curator of Children's 4-H Garden; and Jane L. Taylor, former Curator, Michigan 4-H Children's Garden.

35 *Futures,* Vol. 14, No. 4, Winter 1997.

36 "Facilitating Interdisciplinary Research" Executive Summary (National Academies Press, 2004), p. 1.

37 Contributed by Scott G. Witter, Professor and Chairperson, CARRS.

38 Contributed by Robert von Bernuth, Director, School of Planning, Design, and Construction.

39 N.S. Meador, *History of the Agricultural Engineering Department, Michigan State University, 1906-1964* (East Lansing: Department of Agricultural Engineering, Michigan State University, 1964).

40 Contributed by Ajit K. Srivastava, Chairperson, Department of Biosystems and Agricultural Engineering.

41 *Futures,* Vol. 14, Nos. 1 and 2, Spring/Summer 1996, p. 22.

42 *Futures,* Vol. 14, No. 4, 1997.

43 Contributed by Margaret Bethel, former Director, MSUE.

44 Contributed by Elizabeth C. Moore, Extension Specialist.

45 Edward L. Cardenas, *The Detroit News,* December 31, 2003, p. 1B.

46 ANR Week Luncheon Program, March 8, 2005, Michigan State University, East Lansing.

47 *Ibid.*

48 Developed with the assistance of Lester Manderscheid, Professor Emeritus, Agricultural Economics, and John Whims, Sparks Companies.

49 Interview with David Morris; Futures, Vol. 12, No. 3, 1996, and Francie Todd, Communications Manager, CANR, July 26, 2005.

50 Arlen Leholm et al., "Area of Expertise Teams: The Michigan Approach to Applied Research and Extension." Paper presented to the American Agricultural Economics Association, August 1998, pp. 1-13.

51 Contributed by Raymond D. Vlasin, Professor Emeritus, Department of Resource Development.

52 Michigan State University Extension (http://msue.msu.edu. portal/), October 20, 2005.

53 Contributed by Vicki Morrone, Extension Agricultural and Natural Resources Educator, East Central Region.

54 Contributed by Darlene Johnson, Administrative Assistant, Department of Crop and Soil Sciences.

55 Contributed by Donald R. Jost, Program Leader Emeritus, 4-H Program.

56 *MSU Alumni Magazine,* Vol. 21, No. 4, Summer 2004.

Postlogue

1 Contributed by Raymond D. Vlasin from an interview with Russell Mawby.

2 Contributed by David J. Guikema, Director, MSU Extension Central Region.

3 Contributed by Thomas and Diane Emling. Thomas is Extension Specialist for Outreach; Diane a faculty member of Northwest Michigan Community College.

4 Contributed by Sandy (Clarkson) and Noel Stuckman. Sandy is an Extension Specialist Emeritus; Noel is retired from the Michigan Farm Bureau.

5 Contributed by Margaret Bethel, former MSUE Director.

6 Contributed by Mark F. Hansen, Extension Specialist.

7 Contributed by Juan Marinez, Program Director, MSUE Director's Office.

8 Contributed by Kathryn S. Foerster, Coordinator, CYF Family and Consumer Sciences.

9 Contributed by Cheryl Booth, State Leader, Extension 4-H Youth Development.

10 Contributed by Patricia Hammerschmidt, Program Leader, CYF Family and Consumer Sciences.

11 Contributed by James J. Kells, Chairperson, Crop and Soil Sciences.

12 Contributed by Karen I. Plaut, Chairperson, Department of Animal Science.

13 Contributed by Sara Risch, Director, School of Packaging.

14 Contributed by Joan B. Rose, Homer Nowlin Chair for Water Research.

15 Contributed by Jon Bryan Burley, Associate Professor and Director, Landscape Architecture Program, and Robert D. von Bernuth, Director, School of Planning, Design, and Construction.

Endnotes

[16] Contributed by Ajit K. Srivastava, Chairperson, Department of Biosystems and Agricultural Engineering.

[17] Contributed by Gale Strasburg, Chairperson, Department of Food Science and Human Nutrition.

[18] Contributed by Ewen Todd, Director, National Food Safety and Technology Center.

[19] Contributed by Michael W. Hamm, Mott Professor, CARRS.

[20] *Lansing State Journal*, December 3, 2005, pp. 1B-2B.

[21] Contributed by Kenneth VerBurg, Professor Emeritus, Department of Resource Development.

[22] Contributed by Scott Loveridge, MSUE State Leader, Community and Economic Development.

[23] Contributed by Scott G. Witter, Chairperson, CARRS.

[24] Contributed by Lynn R. Harvey, Professor Emeritus, Agricultural Economics.

[25] Contributed by Douglas D. Buhler, Associate Director, Michigan Agricultural Experiment Station, and Associate Dean for Research, CANR.

[26] Contributed by Gale L. Arent, CANR Stakeholder Relations Director Emeritus.

[27] Contributed by Richard Bawden, Visiting Distinguished University Professor, CARRS.

[28] Contributed by John C. Baker, former Assistant Dean, College of Veterinary Medicine, and now Associate Director, MAES.

[29] Contributed by Sandra Batie, Agricultural Economist and Elton R. Smith Professor of Food and Agricultural Policy.

[30] Contributed by Richard Brandenburg, Assistant Dean, CANR.

[31] Contributed by Frank A. Fear, Professor, CARRS.

[32] Daniel Pink, *A Whole New Mind: Moving from the Information Age to the Conceptual Age* (New York: Penguin Group, 2005).

[33] Contributed by Mona J. Ellard, county Extension Director, Eaton County.

[34] Contributed by Daniel E. Keathley, Chairperson, Department of Forestry.

[35] Contributed by ANR Communications.

[36] Deb Price, *The Detroit News*, February 13, 2006, p. 1A.

[37] Contributed by ANR Communications.

[38] Governor Jennifer Granholm, State of the State 2006: "Working Our Plan, Securing Our Future," address to the Michigan Legislature, January 25, 2006.

[39] *MSU News Bulletin*, February 9, 2006, p. 3.

[40] *Ibid.*

[41] Laura Probyn, ANR Communications (*MSU News Bulletin*, February 8, 2006), p. 3.

[42] http://special.newsroom.msu.edu/biobased_economy/

[43] Contributed by Daniel C. Clay, Director, Institute of International Agriculture.

[44] Contributed by Russell D. Freed, Professor, Department of Crop and Soil Sciences.

[45] Interview with Mary L. Andrews, Associate Professor Emerita, Director of International Extension. Contributed by Raymond D. Vlasin, Professor Emeritus.

[46] Interview with Paul Roberts, Director, Office of Study Abroad, November 17, 2005. Contributed by Raymond D. Vlasin, Professor Emeritus, Department of Resource Development.

[47] Summarized by Raymond D. Vlasin and Kenneth VerBurg from the insights of other contributors.

Index

Index

Index

Index

Index

Index

Index

Index

Index

Index